W9-AOH-759

WITHDRAWN

Gramley Library
Salem College
Winston-Salem, NC 27108

Straight Lick

J. RONALD GREEN

Straight Lick: The Cinema of Oscar Micheaux

INDIANA UNIVERSITY PRESS

Bloomington and Indianapolis

Gramley Library
Salem College
Winston-Salem, NC 27108

This book is a publication of

Indiana University Press
601 North Morton Street
Bloomington, IN 47404-3797 USA

http://www.indiana.edu/~iupress

Telephone orders   800-842-6796
Fax orders   812-855-7931
Orders by e-mail   iuporder@indiana.edu

© 2000 by J. Ronald Green

All rights reserved

No part of this book may be reproduced or utilized in any form or by any means, electronic or mechanical, including photocopying and recording, or by any information storage and retrieval system, without permission in writing from the publisher. The Association of American University Presses' Resolution on Permissions constitutes the only exception to this prohibition.

The paper used in this publication meets the minimum requirements of American National Standard for Information Sciences—Permanence of Paper for Printed Library Materials, ANSI Z39.48-1984.

Manufactured in the United States of America

Library of Congress Cataloging-in-Publication Data

Green, J. Ronald, date
    Straight lick : the cinema of Oscar Micheaux / J. Ronald Green
        p.   cm
    Includes bibliographical references and index.
    ISBN 0-253-33753-4 (cl : alk. paper)
        1. Micheaux, Oscar, 1884–1951—Criticism and interpretation.   I. Title.

    PN1998.3.M494 G74 2000
    791.43′0233′092—dc21

                                                                    99-087110

1   2   3   4   5   05   04   03   02   01   00

To My Parents

E. L. Green and Ann Jones Green

With Love, Admiration, and Gratitude

Rather than going straight at a possibly somnolent white southern audience in Atlanta—and at lovers of minstrelsy throughout the nation—[Booker T.] Washington strikes a "straight lick with a crooked stick." He turns minstrel nonsense into what he believes is the only available good sense, or, sense intended for a common black good. . . . He demonstrates in his manipulations of form that there *are* rhetorical possibilities for crafting a voice out of tight places.

—Houston A. Baker, Jr., *Modernism and the Harlem Renaissance* (1987)

They *is* help if you knows how tuh git it. Some folks kin hit uh straight lick wid uh crooked stick.

—Zora Neal Hurston, *Jonah's Gourd Vine* (1934)

A stick is, in turn, a deterritorialized branch.

—Gilles Deleuze and Félix Guattari, *What Is Philosophy?*
(1991, translation 1994)

No matter if we're from Asia, or Europe, or Africa like Mr. Micheaux, we are all branches on one tree.

—Kevin Locke, Hoop Dancer and Attorney, Lakota Sioux
Third Annual Micheaux Film Festival, August 7, 1998

Contents

Acknowledgments

My wife, Louisa Bertch Green, an active scholar and professional writer and editor, has been the most important advisor and supporter of my work on this project.

Jane Gaines has given constant encouragement and generous discussion from the very beginning; she has read more drafts than any other reader and has made numerous critical interventions and suggestions. I don't know how she finds the energy, since her projects are numerous. Charles Musser was also an early and constant supporter.

Others who have made important editorial suggestions include Khalfon Ben-Horus (Horace Neal, Jr.), Alan Williams, Mary Murrell at Princeton University Press, Peter Lehman, Pearl Bowser, Louise Spence, Charlene Regester, Thomas Cripps, Edward Luna Brough, Cinda Becker, Joe Wlodarz, Dan Fader, Manthia Diawara, and unknown outside readers for several presses.

People who have helped in other ways include Mable Haddock, Thom Andersen, James Wheeler, Ihsan Kabil, Bill Gaskins, Mark Hansen, John Hess, Carlos Gutiérrez, Phyllis Klotman, Ann Morra (Museum of Modern Art), Brian Taves (Library of Congress), Charles Silver (Museum of Modern Art), Donald Harris (former Dean, College of the Arts, Ohio State University), Judith Koroscik (Dean, College of the Arts, Ohio State University), Christine Verzar (former Chair, Department of History of Art, Ohio State University), Mark Fullerton (Chair, Department of History of Art, Ohio State University), Gloria Gibson, Ed Dimendberg, Ken Wissoker, Richard Papousek, Francie Johnson, David Strain, Klaus and Inge Rifbjerg, Bibi and Ulrich Petersen, John Taormina, Oliver Hill, Traci Temple, Mark Pompelia, Mildred Micheaux Lewis, Alfreda Micheaux, Harley Robinson, Lee Barry, Stephanie Pochop, Pamela Thomas, Jack Broome, Mario De Sapio, Lynette O'Neil at Sunny Spirits, Martin J. Keenan, Piera Patat, Mark Reid, Richard Grupenhoff, Paul Sandro, Frank Gabrenya, Judith Mayne, Linda Williams, Ann Martin, Bill Horrigan, John R. Alley, John Kisch, and Eric Smoodin.

Important institutional support was provided by the College of the Arts, the Department of History of Art, the Wexner Center for the Arts, and the Academic Computing Center for Art and Design (all at the Ohio State University); the Ohio Arts Council; the Rockefeller Foundation's Bellagio Study Center; the Fundación Valparaíso of Mojacar, Spain; the Film Department and the Film Study Center at the Museum of Modern Art in New York; the Motion Picture Division at the Library of Congress; the National Black Programming Consortium in Columbus; the Pordenone Silent Film Festival in Italy; the Virginia Film Festival; the Annual Oscar Micheaux Film Festival and study center in Gregory,

South Dakota (including the Naper's Store and the Gregory Public Library); the Society for Cinema Studies; and the Yale and Duke University Conference on Oscar Micheaux (including the catalog project, "Oscar Micheaux and His Circle").

For all of this support, which comprises the living tissue of research, I am very grateful.

Introduction

One of the most original and successful filmmakers of all time, Oscar Micheaux was born into a rural, working-class, African-American family in mid-America in 1884. He was not formally educated beyond the most modest and basic public schooling; he was subjected all his life to race and class prejudice; and yet he created an impressive legacy in one of the most sophisticated, expensive, and fragile cultural endeavors of the twentieth century—commercial cinema. In the process of making himself into the first African-American film *auteur,* without the slightest aid of the huge film industries on either coast of the United States, Micheaux lived in two of the most sophisticated, competitive cities in the world, Chicago and New York; he (probably) traveled to Latin America and Europe to establish his own business connections; and he circulated continuously through the great black communities of America's northern cities and throughout the American South. During that time (1913 to 1951), he wrote, published, and distributed his seven novels, and he wrote, produced, directed, and distributed some forty-three feature films—more than any other black filmmaker in the world, a record of production that is likely to stand for a very long time.

In African-American circles, the legend of Oscar Micheaux has persisted since the 1930s. Now stories of Micheaux's life and work are spreading into the rest of American culture through museums, universities, publications, and broadcasting—word of Micheaux has even spread to the Phil Donahue Show.[1] This book, however, is not a study of that legend, nor a biography of Micheaux, nor even a history of his films. It is a thematic, textual, and contextual analysis and critical assessment of his accomplishment in the art of cinema. Some new historical and biographical facts appear here, but their discovery, though exciting for the author, was not the main purpose of this work. Nevertheless, knowledge of who this man was, what he did, and why people are excited about him is relevant to an assessment of his work. His is a story worth telling.[2]

Micheaux's first novel, published in 1913, is a good guide to his first three decades, because it is a thinly disguised biography. Though critics have been careful—and rightly so—to call *The Conquest* a fictionalized account of Micheaux's first twenty-nine years, the biographical and historical accuracy of the book should not be underemphasized.[3] Enough historical documentation exists to suggest that *The Conquest* is fundamentally trustworthy as autobiography and as history. Micheaux's subsequent novels are also rich in autobiographical material.

The Conquest describes Micheaux's early fortune seeking in and around Chicago, which finally, and most significantly, resulted in his employment as a porter on a Pullman railroad car. It was through Pullman portering that Micheaux began to see the country; to meet a successful class of people, especially western landowners and eastern businessmen; and to expand his vision of opportunity and "empire." His career on the railroad, along with his assiduous personal and financial management, allowed Micheaux to save enough money to take advantage of one of the business opportunities that he learned about on his regular runs from Chicago to the Pacific Northwest—the purchase of a "relinquishment" homestead on the newly opened Rosebud Indian Reservation in southern South Dakota.[4]

This was a happy time in Micheaux's life. In his second novel, *The Forged Note*, Micheaux refers to the Rosebud country as his favorite because of the relative lack of racial prejudice and because of the respect he earned as a successful large-scale farmer on the prairie. In *The Conquest*, Micheaux describes in great detail, with humor and occasional anger, the life of a black homesteader on the Great Plains. Some of the homesteading stories from *The Conquest* recur later in his films. A version of the chapter entitled "The Oklahoma Grafter," for example—in which Micheaux's surrogate, Devereaux, is bilked by a crooked horse trader—appears in the film *The Symbol of the Unconquered* (1920). The town in which this "graft" occurs, in both the book and the film, is "Oristown" (in reality, Bonesteel, South Dakota).

More significant to an understanding of Micheaux's films is the second half of *The Conquest*, which deals with Micheaux's problems in love and marriage. Aspects of this story also form the main action in three of Micheaux's seven novels and several of his films, including his first and last films, *The Homesteader* and *The Betrayal* (1919 and 1948; both now lost), and his first full-length sound film, *The Exile* (1931; extant). As told in *The Conquest*, Oscar Devereaux, the character who represents Micheaux in the novel, fell in love with a young white woman, whom he refers to as "the Scotch girl," the daughter of a neighboring widower farmer in South Dakota. Their mutual respect and need, their loneliness and isolated proximity, led to attraction, affection, and probably to mature love, and, more or less against their better judgment, it led to some degree of physical lovemaking. Devereaux eventually reluctantly rejects the relationship with this white woman as impractical for the couple and for any future children.

The upshot is that Devereaux (Micheaux) breaks off definitively with the white woman and begins to actively seek an African-American spouse. After several abortive courtings, he marries the daughter of a ranking elder of the African Methodist Episcopal Church, a well-known figure in the black community in Chicago. Devereaux is immediately and continuously at loggerheads with the black minister, and he refuses to flatter the old man, who is physically vain, ignorant, hypocritical, and egotistical. Devereaux perennially argues with his father-in-law, which contributes to the deterioration of the marriage. After Devereaux has struggled heroically to help his wife acquire a homestead of her own some fifty miles from his original claim and after he has mortgaged his land and tried to work both farms (while also helping his sister and his grandmother to acquire and make good on similar homesteads), the marriage falls apart. Reverend McCraline (in real life, McCracken) travels to South Dakota and takes his daughter, who has been weakened by unusual hardships and by an unsuccessful breach birth, back to Chicago.

Though Micheaux was desperately struggling with debt, drought, and farming on four (or five) different homesteads (his "empire"),[5] he made several trips to Chicago to attempt to convince his wife to return to him. Micheaux implies that it was his interfering father-in-law who caused Micheaux's farming venture to fail, a charge that is probably partly true, since Micheaux had to spend on his troubled marriage much time, money, and energy that he could not spare from his farms. He might have failed anyway, owing to the onset of a major drought that drove most of the new settlers off the land. As Micheaux described and analyzed those conditions, he revealed his own fortitude and his talent for entrepreneurship and crisis management. That fortitude and talent would later allow him to become a successful independent writer and publisher and to become the first African American to successfully write, produce, direct, and distribute films from the era of D. W. Griffith's *The Birth of a Nation* up to the eve of integration.

When Micheaux's farms failed, some of his white neighbors suggested that his story was unique and that he should write and publish it. So he wrote *The Conquest* while still living somewhere near the Rosebud country that he loved. He then published the novel himself. His second novel, *The Forged Note,* was probably also written near the Rosebud country in Sioux City, Iowa, after an eighteen-month trip through the American Midwest and South. That intervening trip, which included significant stops in Dayton, Columbus, Cincinnati, Atlanta, Memphis, and New Orleans, was for the purpose of selling his first book, *The Conquest,* which in *The Forged Note* he calls *The Tempest.* The trip was also explicitly designed to allow Micheaux to gather information and impressions for the second novel. The distribution and sales operation he organized during the course of the trip was important to his later success in marketing his films, and the second novel is worth reading for that information alone. Because *The Forged Note* is consciously a story of research about "the race," it is also a rich source of information regarding the development of the racial and political attitudes that would make Micheaux such a controversial filmmaker. It is also another powerful story of love and suppressed sexuality.[6] As such, it is a key to certain subtexts of Micheaux's films and would be interesting to consider in a comparison with the stories of repressed sexuality that are more common in white American culture.

If Micheaux's career as a novelist can be understood as a result of the failure of his farming, Micheaux's film career was a result of the success of his writing. By the time his third novel, *The Homesteader* (1917), was circulating, D. W. Griffith's *The Birth of a Nation* (1915), a film version of Thomas Dixon's white-supremacist propaganda, had become the first American blockbuster. Leaders of the national African-American community were fighting Griffith's film on all fronts, a fight that included numerous calls for the formation of a black film industry that could answer the "charges" and insults of *The Birth*. Numerous black film companies were formed, most of which never produced a film; some produced one film, and a rare few produced several films.

One of the companies that produced more than one film was the Lincoln Motion Picture Company, run by the Johnson brothers of Nebraska and Los Angeles. At the time Micheaux's third novel was published, Noble Johnson was a successful black actor working in Hollywood, and George P. Johnson worked for the post office in Omaha. They approached Micheaux with an offer to buy the rights to *The Homesteader* for their film company. The record of the negotiation between the Johnson brothers and Micheaux, which includes several letters, telegrams, and other documents, is preserved in the George P. Johnson collection at the University of California at Los Angeles.[7] Micheaux was interested in their proposition, but he had several substantive objections: the Lincoln Company was producing films only in the Johnson brothers' spare time; the Lincoln Company proposed to make the film in three reels, while Micheaux wanted at least six; Micheaux did not want to produce in Los Angeles, because it was too expensive and too far from sources of black talent; and Micheaux wanted to participate in the production. In the end, Micheaux decided to form his own company to make the film himself. From that point, in mid-summer of 1918, Micheaux never looked back.

Micheaux's Straight Lick with a Crooked Stick: Toward a "Middle-Class" Cinema

Micheaux's overarching goal was the attainment and maintenance of a middle-class social and economic life through "racial uplift," a philosophy fraught with internal and external contradictions, such as is the case in W. E. B. DuBois's famous "twoness," or double-consciousness dilemma, and the dilemma of "race" in relation to class, which placed the "black middle class" in a position "irretrievably mired in racial and class inequalities, with [race and class] fused together in a manner that grants neither one primacy."[8] Micheaux's cinema seems an almost literal manifestation of Kevin Gaines's historical observation that "many blacks, or whites, for that matter, were not middle-class in any truly material or economic sense, but rather, represented themselves as such, in a complex variety of ways. . . . [M]any of these 'representative' blacks lived out the very contradictions of uplift ideology."[9] But there is an overriding progressive aspect to Micheaux's cinematic manifestation of uplift.

In relentlessly pursuing a goal of upward mobility for himself and other African Americans, Oscar Micheaux created a mode of cinema that was significantly different from the Hollywood mode in both its content and style. Micheaux's mode, shaped as all race movies were by relative poverty and overt racism, has long been considered inferior to the Hollywood mode developed by D. W. Griffith and adopted by most of the world's film cultures. However, given the goal of a cinema that is oriented toward the middle class—a culturally and historically important goal and a goal common to both Micheaux and Griffith—Micheaux's films (and some other race movies and independent films) are in this important way superior to Griffith's. Micheaux's failure to raise large amounts of capital necessitated that he adopt values, such as moderation, that were actually more consistent with historically middle-class values than were the values of mainstream cinema. Ironically, Griffith's very success in mass-marketing in the new consumer society led him to adopt upper-class cinematic values, such as expensiveness, that were incongruous and inappropriate to the lower- and middle-class audience he aimed at and reached. Griffith's personal values were pseudo-aristocratically bourgeois; when Griffith's film style was adopted by Hollywood, those values became purely bourgeois in the Marxian sense (i.e., ownership class and not middle class).[10]

In pursuing a goal of uplift under conditions of racist obstruction—of two-ness (ethnic double consciousness) as opposed to Hollywood's oneness (mass-culture single consciousness)—Micheaux produced a cinema that is distinguished by a unique combination of authorial and discursive qualities; he developed values and artistic forms that were appropriate not only to his conditions of film production but that were also appropriate to the general condition of political deconstruction. Micheaux, much more than Hollywood, was a contributor to what Virginia Wright Wexman has called "heteroglossic voices that could speak of America's diverse cultures."[11] He developed the idea of a middle path in his films by confronting controversial dialectical phenomena, such as blackness vs. whiteness; poverty vs. wealth; blues culture vs. Broadway; rural vs. urban; traditionalist jubilee spiritual vs. modernist city-symphony montage; and "darktown" vs. Harlem Renaissance. In addressing such issues, Micheaux mounted some unusual critiques of mainstream cinematic production values, of bourgeois patriarchal views of women, of positive- and negative-image aesthetics, of the material conditions—such as white financing—of anti-racist filmmaking, of racial stereotyping in entertainment, of passing for white in relation to film style, and of the material conditions of independent filmmaking.

Micheaux's pursuit of moderation and the middle path and his application of those principles to a wide variety of circumstances amounts to a thoroughly middle-class cinema with an integrity that was forged from some three decades' and forty films' worth of rigorously middle-class producing experience. Micheaux's is a cinema that occupies a class position from which both oppressedness and oppressiveness can be criticized with integrity, something Hollywood cannot do. His is a style that is not classical, owing to the continuing relation of classical values to the upper classes. And, very significantly, in his pursuit, Micheaux demonstrated that middle-class cinema can, in the right hands, resist racism and sexism, even in the face of market economies and majority politics. Thus, his is a demonstration that has much to teach about the conditions of filmmaking in the early twenty-first century.

A Note on Auteurism

This book assumes that, for the reasons suggested above, auteur studies are still valid. Though authorship is complex and theoretically vexed, it remains vital to the politics of representation, including discussions of canon and the margins of canon. As Clyde Taylor has said,

> The deconstruction of "authenticity" is both valid and productive. But the use of these insights is what matters. Authenticity, closely interrogated, turns out to be a myth, woven around each cultural object. Yet because that myth functions as part of the object, as . . . one of its co-authors, we must learn to read the narrative and its myth of origin simultaneously, and politically.[12]

To say, as this study will, that Micheaux accomplished "greatness" in relation to certain cultural and political forces is to recognize that any artistic event, whatever its mythic origin or historic facticity and authenticity, is judged always in relation to certain significant discourses. "Greatness" is our critical appreciation of impressive and meaningful artistic negotiations—textual, intertextual, meta-textual, contextual—with discourses that shape the possibilities of life. One of those greatnesses bears the name of Oscar Micheaux.

Straight Lick

1   Micheaux vs. Griffith

An epigraph introducing D. W. Griffith's film *The Romance of Happy Valley* (1919) reads

> Harm not the stranger
> *Within your gates,*
> Lest you yourself be hurt. [Emphasis added]

Micheaux chose the title *Within Our Gates* for a film he made a few months after Griffith's film and a few weeks after living through the Chicago race riots of 1919; by choosing this title, Micheaux was throwing Griffith's sentimentality back in his face.[1] For Griffith to have recorded such generous sentiments toward strangers after having recommended the deportation of all African Americans in the coda of *The Birth of a Nation* (1915) was intolerable—so intolerable that Micheaux dared to threaten that unless the harm against African Americans ceased, white Americans themselves would "be hurt."

Micheaux and the leadership of the black community were involved in a pitched battle with D. W. Griffith and his audience. Micheaux's *The Symbol of the Unconquered*[2] (December 1920) includes a vision of the white-on-black terrorism that is a response to D. W. Griffith's invocation of the Ku Klux Klan in *The Birth of a Nation.* And, consciously or unconsciously, Micheaux commented on Griffith's style of narrative in other ways: for example, through the use of the replication in *Within Our Gates* of melodramatic narrative dynamics and Griffith-like scenes, such as the daring rescue of a child from the path of the automobile of a rich woman and the consequent reward for the heroine. Micheaux's white characters in *Within Our Gates,* such as the owners of the southern plantation and the two philanthropic women (especially, and perhaps consciously, the hilariously ironic Lillian Gish lookalike, Mrs. Stratton), *and* his middle-class African Americans, such as the hero and heroine, are without a doubt casted, dressed, and photographed to approximate Griffith's aesthetic.

Micheaux was poaching and "signifying" on Griffith's estate. A letter from Micheaux to the Virginia State Board of Censors shows that Micheaux was measuring himself against Griffith in order to counter the damage done by *The Birth of a Nation:* "I must also add that you are unduly alarmed as to how my race is likely to take even the discussion in the second reel [of *The House Behind the Cedars*]. There has been but one picture that incited the colored people to riot, and that still does, that picture is the 'BIRTH OF A NATION.'"[3]

African-American Responses to *The Birth*

It would be extraordinary if Micheaux were not thinking often of the damage done by *The Birth of a Nation* during the first part of his film career, given the success of Griffith's film, its effect on the revitalization of the Klan, and the extensive and intense negative reaction to the film by the black press, which Micheaux read avidly. Examples (among many) of coverage by the black press include a lead article in the Baltimore *Afro-American Ledger* (March 6, 1915), entitled "Censors Bar 'The Birth of a Nation': National Association For The Advancement Of Colored People Wins Notable Victory," and another in the Chicago *Defender* (December 1, 1915), entitled "Supreme Court Rules Out 'Birth of a Nation': Mayor Nye, Minneapolis' Fearless Executive Upheld by Court of Last Resort—Revoked Licenses Granted by City Council and State's Highest Tribunal Sustains Him . . . Farreaching Decision Will Benefit Race Wherever Attempt Is Made to Show Film." One of the treatments of the Griffith film, rendered by the Chicago *Defender* (May 22, 1915), is fully indicative of the staying power that would characterize African-American anger toward and resistance to *The Birth of a Nation,* Griffith, and Hollywood. That article is worth quoting at some length because of its illumination of Micheaux's mission with respect to Hollywood and because of the forceful character of its writing:

> MAYOR THOMPSON BARS "BIRTH OF A NATION" FROM CHICAGO
> Courageous Executive Refuses Promoters Permit to Exhibit Films Based on "The Clansman" in City—Takes High Ground in Defense of Many Nationalities That Make Up His Constituents.
> WILL ALLOW NO RACE TO SUFFER RIDICULE
> Declares That Whatever Power There Is in the Mayor's Office Will Be Used to Stop Film Tabooed or Any Other Films That Reflect on the Citizens of Any Race or Nationality.

After this unusually discursive sequence of headlines, there follows a story of about 200 words that describes Chicago mayor Thompson's approach to the censorship issue; this is followed in turn by an excellent description of the plot of the film (about 1200 words) that would be worth reprinting for its clarity, restraint, and contextual irony but which is too lengthy a digression for the point under consideration here. The following, however, is an unabridged quotation of the last section of the long feature announced by the headlines above—the tone of this last section is so angry that clarity suffers under the demands of strong feeling; it is the only portion of the feature that has its own byline:

> THE BIRTH OF A NATION RUNS UP AGAINST A SUBMARINE—IN HON. WM. HALE THOMPSON, THE MAYOR OF CHICAGO.
> (By Jull [Juli] Jones, Jr.[)][4]
> The no-end to trouble film, the Birth of a Nation, at last found one man, Hon. Wm. Hale Thompson, that believes in keeping down race trouble. This moving picture has caused more trouble than all the moving pictures made in ten years. Every

scene is made up with subjects of race hatred. The Birth of a Nation is nothing more than "The Clansman" the book and play that the Rev. Thos. Dixon wrote for revenue, regardless of the cost of race trouble. If it is a good thing for the public to see such rotten films as the Birth of a Nation, why not let the Negro show some spicey [sic] scenes of mixed plays, institute the ruination of the Negro race in a moving picture [for which the] age limit would not be [under] forty years. True facts would be shown, that would make the Ku Klux Klans look like scenes from the fairy story—Mid Summer Night's Dream—beginning some ten years ago and not ended yet, such scenes as [white] half-brothers forcing the[ir] love on the[ir] sister [born of] Negroes. Mistresses [and] men shot down in their own homes just for things they were being wronged [for through] the forced attention of some cracker.

The best name for such movies would be "250 years in murder, force and adultery." Such films would make the public forget such a book or show as "Uncle Tom's Cabin," was ever written on the same basis that it would show the first Negro landing at Jamestown by the Dutch. Then such scenes of a cracker sitting on a horse under the shade of a palmetto tree with big bull whips, whipping old and young, sick and well, until they were red with blood.

Then there is another scene showing this same brute at night, sending a Negro runner going to the old slave's cabin calling out his wife or daughter, and telling them that their master wanted them. If the father or husband would not keep out of his cabin he would be taken out and flogged half to death. Let's call this scene "the Birth of a Mixed Race." The next scene will be after Abraham Lincoln had declared that all Negroes were free showing that kind-hearted Southerner, showing some real Southern hospitality, driving from the cabin poor Negroes in the dead of the winter. Children without shoes on and in pain had to travel the muddy, frozen roads. No place to go after 250 years free labor, such scenes would make the cruelty [toward] the Jews in Russia look like a musical comedy. Another scene, that of a mob trying to find Fred Douglas[s] and lynch him because he had learned to read and write. Another scene in Georgia's daily burning a Negro at a stake until four or five exclusive trains could reach the scene before the big production was staged[.] [T]he Tribune special writer had the nerve to say that the film cost so much money and trouble, it would show how the Southern white man had been wronged by the Northern man and also said in part, so many moving picture lovers were crazy to see the great Dixon-Griffith film. Why not take it down South? Big field, no kicks. The American negro will put one proposition up to the owners of the Birth of a Nation. The colored race will produce at their own expense [a] film [based] on facts to run at the same time as the Birth of a Nation, run on the same screen with the Birth of a Nation free of charge. The Negro is trying to forget the days of lash and cruelty and to appreciate his white friend, but if the truth must be told nothing can beat a moving picture to tell it. We can show that beautiful scene, slave marke[t], Negro women, girls, children of all ages, stripped naked in pens for marke[t,] men buying and selling their own blood. The heathen in the dance in the jungle of Africa has more soul than the degenerate white Southern cracker. If the people of the north [want] to see the Birth of a Nation so bad, let's deal fair: let's see the Negro side of it. They will present to the world a moving picture that would make the whole American nation feel ashamed of themselves. The American Negro has stood more humiliation from the grafting trouble[-]breeders like Thos. Dixon in the last twenty-five years than any race under the sun.

Let us all thank Mayor Wm. Hale Thompson for his real courageous stand against this outrageous moving picture.[5]

The style, content, and even the production mistakes in the article by Juli Jones communicate the intense feeling behind the response in the black community to *The Birth of a Nation*. Micheaux was certainly aware of this type of response to *The Birth* and of the repeated calls in the black press for a champion to counter the slander of Griffith and Hollywood. Several African-American organizations, including the Booker T. Washington organization at Tuskegee, tried to respond literally to the suggestion to produce a film and a film industry of their own.[6]

Micheaux may have seen his own films as preeminent among those attempts. The arguments in Micheaux's only existing early films, *Within Our Gates* and *Symbol of the Unconquered,* are similar to the arguments in the article by Jones. First, white crackers *are* crackers—they are not the sturdy, clean-living yeomen of Griffith's world but are cruel and degenerate in their treatment of and attitudes toward both whites and blacks. Second, a factual portrait of the Klan would make Griffith's Klan look like the fairy tale it is. Third, a factual portrait of the cruel effects of Lincoln's emancipation proclamation would more closely resemble the melodramatic persecution scenes of Griffith's own *Way Down East*—innocents driven from their homes into the snow—than would the idealized history Griffith constructs in *The Birth of a Nation*. Juli Jones's ironical reference to southern hospitality is analogous to Micheaux's ironic reference to Griffith's "Harm not the stranger / Within your gates." Fourth, since Griffith, in *The Birth*, wanted to make a fanatical case about sexual mixing of the races, it would have been fairer and more scientific to have portrayed the 300 years of systematic sexual abuse of black women and their ever-lighter-complexioned children by southern white men, as Micheaux did in *Within Our Gates,* instead of what Griffith chose to portray in *The Birth:* the attempted "rape" and suicide of little Flora Cameron; the attempted forced marriage of Elsie Stoneman; the sexual Machiavellianism of the racially mixed carpetbagger, Lynch; the licentiousness of Austin Stoneman's black mistress; and the readiness of the brave white men to smash in the skulls of their wives, daughters, and other southern ladies at the prospect of their defeat by African-American militiamen.

A Bipolarity

In *The Birth,* Micheaux was confronted, as a black filmmaker, not only with a virtually phobic white supremacism but also with a Manichean historicism, in which forces of nobility and degradation competed with each other for enormous emotional and material stakes. The grandness of Griffith's conflict is supported by an analogously grand style. Micheaux's content is less Manichean and his style less grand than Griffith's. Certain qualitative differences between Griffith's and Micheaux's films can be arranged in a table:

GRIFFITH	MICHEAUX
spectacle	documentation
rescue	redemption; retribution
criminality	citizenship
vengefulness	justice
impunity	responsibility
aggrandizement	uplift
possessiveness	mutuality
purity	hybridity
exposé	interrogation
illusionism	exposition
convergence of action	woven interaction
narrative centering	narrative decentering
heteronomy	autonomy
oneness	twoness

Many of the terms in Griffith's column, such as "spectacle," "vengefulness," and "impunity," suggest giganticism and immoderation; others, such as "possessiveness," "purity," "narrative centering," and "heteronomy," suggest control. Many of the terms in Micheaux's column, such as "citizenship," "responsibility," and "investigation," suggest moderation rather than giganticism; others, such as "mutuality," "hybidity," and "autonomy," suggest negotiation rather than control. These dialectical terms refer, in some cases, to content and themes and in other cases, to form and style. Griffith's famous narrative trope of the last-minute rescue, in fact, functions as both content and form—the rescues are recurring plot events that occasion other recurring and concomitant stylistic events. Griffith returned often to the theme of the threatened virgin; the resolution of that theme often takes the form of shots and reverse-shots, alternating shots that gradually decline in duration. Theme and style are wedded in the figure of the accelerating shot/reverse-shot—the violence that approaches the victim seems to create, in the character and in the viewer, an ever-faster racing heart, replicated by the accelerating shot/reverse-shot editing rhythm; the decreasing opportunity to effect a solution to the victim's predicament seems to create, in the character and the viewer, a racing mind, which is also suggested by the accelerating rhythm of editing. And, famously, the shots that alternate between hurrying rescuer and anxious victim spatially converge to center the narrative on a single precious point in time and space—the longed-for rescue itself. That point is an analog in classical narrative film to the perspectival system in Renaissance and pre-Modernist painting.

Oscar Micheaux's style and themes, however, reflect damage already done, a condition in which rescue is already too late. In Micheaux's narrative tropes, virginity is not threatened, it is already lost; manhood is not to be proven by rescue, it is to be constructed in some other way or simply recognized for what it already is. Since Micheaux attacked lynching and since lynching was an apotheosis of the impunity exemplified by Griffith's narrative excesses, then Micheaux, in order to avoid the contradiction—as well as the harsh, reactionary consequences—of indulging in counter-excesses, sought a cooler narrative solution.[7]

A Cooler Style

Since, in *The Birth of a Nation*, cinematic spectacle and provocatively expressionistic editing were being experienced as an attack on the black community, it made some sense for a black filmmaker to favor a less spectacular, more expository style. Since the defining qualities of Hollywood professionalism (larger-than-life spectacle; seamless, illusionistic continuity; broad aesthetic and ideological assimilation), as developed and exemplified by Griffith, seemed to be Micheaux's thematic target, such professionalism could not, without contradiction, have served as Micheaux's stylistic goal. Many of these points need considerable argument. A starting place for such arguments can be found readily at hand in the personal priorities of Griffith and Micheaux, as reflected in their respective representations of coupling, of that point where the personal is driven to become social, where the "one" of individuality reaches out to form the "two" of sociality.

Within Our Gates and the Bourgeois Marriage Icon

Within Our Gates ends with a shot of a happy bourgeois couple standing centered in the frame before a window that looks out on broadleaf trees and on what appears to be a suburban landscape; the couple are facing the camera while affectionately entwining themselves together, having reached the intimate mutual understanding that will lead to marriage. This could also be the final shot of a D. W. Griffith film. The couple is dressed just as a Griffith couple would be dressed, standing in a Griffith-like setting, much like the final shot of *The Lonely Villa* or like any number of shots of courting whites in *The Birth of a Nation*. All the politics of North against South, agrarian aristocracy against urban capitalism, all the rhetoric promoting racism and patriarchy that make up the content of a Griffith story could be subsumed under the core concern for the integrity of the couple. Griffith's icon of the desirable female marriage partner is informed by all the qualities listed under Griffith's column in the table above. Particularly relevant are "spectacle" (the woman is primarily on display), "rescue" (the woman must be saved), "vengefulness" (the woman's violation must be avenged), "impunity" (the violation of the woman motivates illegal vigilantism), "possession" (the primary characteristic of women under patriarchy is to be solely owned and "closely held"), "purity" (an absolute requirement in a woman, more than in any other figure of value and desire), "convergence of action" (the woman is the target of the converging actions of threat and rescue), and "narrative centering" (the woman, object of desire, centers the storytelling).

Micheaux's films and novels, however, recognize that for African Americans

Fig. 1. A period version of the ideal bourgeois couple of D. W.
Griffith—the southern Little Colonel and the northern Elsie Stoneman
(Lillian Gish)—at the conclusion of *The Birth of a Nation.*

to gain access to the marriage icon and to the middle-class life it represents
would be a contradiction if the icon were to continue to represent grandiose and
exclusive privilege in any arbitrary form. Ed Guerrero has made the point that,
on the one hand, the African-American cinema that has recently emerged from
Hollywood has often attacked racism and has seldom attacked other systems of
domination, such as patriarchy, sexual preference, or class, and that, on the other
hand, recent independent African-American filmmakers working outside of
Hollywood, such as Julie Dash, Charles Burnett, Haile Gerima, and Marlon
Riggs, have attacked many forms of systematic privilege, not just racism.[8] The
import of Guerrero's call for African Americans not to forget the general idea of
exploitation as they address its most egregious form, racism, seems to have been
understood decades earlier by Micheaux. If any radical redefinition of the bourgeois icon of marriage was to have integrity for Micheaux, it had to be stripped
not only of the racial "purity" Griffith and his audience gave it but also, at the
same time, of its less explicit implications of patriarchal and class privilege.[9]

Two Versions of the Ideal Woman

In the shot of the triumphal march at the end of *The Birth of a Nation,*
after the Klan's successful rescue effort, the two previously threatened, most-

marriageable women, Margaret Cameron and Elsie Stoneman, ride into the camera, toward the viewer, at the head of the Klan's victory parade. Margaret, the southern belle, is the prize for the northern abolitionist who has been converted to racism; his sister, Elsie (Lillian Gish), also converted to southern racist values, is especially prized; she, severely shaken by her close call in a forced marriage with "the mulatto" race leader, reaches gently and frailly to touch the belt of her rescuer's Klan costume as these reconciled lovers ride into their ethnically sanitized future together. The two virgin white women—one from the South and one from the North—*are* the object and prize of the new white nation that is being born.

In Micheaux's responding film, *Within Our Gates*, Sylvia (played by Evelyn Preer) is a comparable prize. The final shot of Sylvia and Dr. Vivian is so like the Griffith images of the bourgeois couple that critics have been tempted to equate Micheaux's goals and values with those of Griffith and Hollywood. Such an equation will not stand up to any but the most superficial examination, however. Sylvia is not dependent on men, she is not a virgin, she is not "racially pure," and she does not spring from a privileged class. She is not helpless and does not need to be saved by her lover. She is, in fact, the agent rather than the object of much of the dramatic action in the film. Through her successful efforts to obtain an education in order to help her tenant-farming foster family and through her act of encouraging her foster father to confront the abuses of the tenant system, she directly motivates her foster father's progressive confrontation with the white aristocracy (and indirectly causes his ultimate lynching); through her rescue of a little white child from the wheels of a rich woman's automobile and through her persistence in arguing with that northern philanthropist against the racist urging of the rich southern woman, she provides a temporary, but essential, resolution to a dilemma of institutional racism; through her willingness to brave the sophisticated mores of the North in order to raise money for the poor black school in the South, she gains significant philanthropical aid and, incidentally, makes possible the love relationship with Dr. Vivian that will unite the *African*-American North and South after the northward migrations and that will yield a new narrative understanding of the black middle-class couple.

Micheaux and Feminism

Though Micheaux has often been called conservative, he seems to have had an ideological affinity for important liberal causes, especially for feminism; in that regard, he found himself in the same tradition as Frederick Douglass, who worked all his life on an equal, and often officially subordinate, basis with great feminist leaders. And Douglass was considered not just liberal but radical. Women in Micheaux's work, as distinct from Griffith's, are characterized by agency, activity, and subjecthood. The crucial action of *Within Our Gates* occurs in a narrative triangle of women. Sylvia (the black heroine of uplift) is

Fig. 2. The sweet, vulnerable Elsie Stoneman (Gish), the converted northern liberal recently rescued from sexual and racial catastrophe, reaching for the belt of her hero, the leader of the Ku Klux Klan.

pitted specifically against Mrs. Stratton (the reactionary white supremacist who also specifically reviles suffragists) in a debate that is adjudicated by Mrs. Warwick (a northern feminist). Such a triangle of strong (including feminist) women at the very center of a narrative action could not happen in a Griffith film. Though Dr. Vivian does win Sylvia in the end, as would happen in a Griffith movie, Dr. Vivian has been virtually extraneous, playing a supporting role.[10]

Critiquing the Lillian Gish Construction

Within that central triangle, Micheaux's thoroughly benighted southern woman, Mrs. Stratton, is explicitly contrasted with Mrs. Warwick, Micheaux's modern feminist; Mrs. Stratton, an anti-feminist as well as a racist, looks so much like the Lillian Gish character might have looked five years after *The Birth of a Nation* (*Within Our Gates* was, in fact, released five years after *The Birth*) that it appears as if Micheaux's heroine, Sylvia, has entered a liminal, intertextual world to struggle against the characters from Griffith's movie. Many African Americans must have wanted to do something like that, as the angry personal tone of the Juli Jones article indicates.

Micheaux gave voice to such an urge by causing the southern woman who looks like Gish to express the sordid implications of Griffith's racism, previously romanticized in *The Birth of a Nation*. Micheaux seems to say that if the character that Lillian Gish plays in *The Birth of a Nation*—the loyal daughter of a northern arch-abolitionist modeled on Thaddeus Stevens—can be converted to white supremacism and can wind up betrothed to the leader of the Ku Klux Klan at the end of the film, then let her speak aloud the hateful sentiments that underlie that conversion. Micheaux gave considerable analytical attention to the specific arguments of this Gish surrogate, Mrs. Stratton, who directly and financially supports a black preacher, old Ned, who is tricking his people and is himself, according to his own cynical assessment, bound for hellfire. Mrs. Stratton's idea of African-American distaste for education had already been proven wrong by Micheaux early in the film through the portrayal of the strong educational values of Sylvia's family and of the impoverished but determined patrons of the rural black school. As soon as racist and anti-feminist sentiments are uttered in Micheaux's film by Mrs. Stratton, in her conversation with Mrs. Warwick, any intertextual vestige of divine womanliness in Lillian Gish's and D. W. Griffith's character collapses. In Mrs. Stratton, Micheaux discomposed the southern Gish.

Micheaux's exposition of southern racism and patriarchy (and by implication, of aristocracy) through Mrs. Stratton functions whether or not Micheaux or the viewer makes an explicit connection between Mrs. Stratton and Lillian Gish herself; Micheaux exploited a general idea of southern womanhood that was, by the time of the shooting of *Within Our Gates,* both Griffith-like and Griffith-influenced. In any case, because a response to *The Birth of a Nation* was high on the African-American agenda, *Within Our Gates* may reasonably be accepted as a direct rebuttal to Griffith's politics and sensibility.

Micheaux continued that rebuttal by constructing images of women that were more autonomous, diverse, and realistic than Griffith's ideal woman. The woman who represents the best of African-American womanhood in Micheaux's film does not need to be rescued in the same way as Griffith's women do. Unlike Griffith's heroines, Sylvia is an adult figure who is actively working out her own salvation and that of her people; she is also experienced in ways of the world that would have been disturbing to Griffith and that would have frightened most of Griffith's heroes away from her.[11] Micheaux's Sylvia represents the flower of a "race" of people—as well as a sex and class of people—who have passed through hell, are struggling in purgatory, and are truly scathed but not martyred. Griffith's Gish, by contrast, represents the flower of aristocratic, bourgeois, and middle-class women who have been martyred (Flora in *Birth*), who might require martyrdom (the young women trapped in the cabin surrounded by black militiamen in *Birth*), or who (preferably) remain racially and sexually unscathed through the agency and intervention of white men and loyal black servants. Gish is the ideal bourgeois marriage partner under the system raised up by Griffith from the ruins of southern aristocracy. Thus, Griffith's and Gish's reconstructed "southern" woman is an avatar of a previous aristocratic ideal; Micheaux's and Evelyn Preer's Sylvia is no such thing.

Fig. 3a. The Lillian Gish look-alike, the southern racist Mrs. Stratton (*right*), giving Mrs. Warwick, the northern liberal philanthropist, "advice" about how to keep the Negroes in their place.

Fig. 3b. Mrs. Stratton, the intertextual "Lillian Gish/Elsie Stoneman," reacts with dismay upon learning that Mrs. Warwick has rejected her advice and decided to give the African-American school $50,000, ten times the $5,000 requested.

Micheaux vs. Griffith 11

Gramley Library
Salem College
Winston-Salem, NC 27108

Bourgeois Love and Marriage

Proto-feminist and anti-aristocrat though Micheaux may have been, he was, however, not above the influence of the bourgeois ideals of love and marriage. Quite the contrary, since Sylvia is partly, if illegitimately and unwillingly, both white and aristocratic in origin, she is the outcome of the rape of her light-skinned mother by her mother's white owner. And Micheaux obviously loved the light skin, straight hair, and elegant dress codes of the white bourgeoisie,[12] since he constructed many of his favorite and most desirable characters in those modes. And he, like Griffith, was patriarchal in many ways; he was terrified of the implications of the "impure" woman. Nevertheless, Micheaux, unlike Griffith and his audience, faced that fear by dealing with hybridity of race and class as a discourse and by dealing with female characters as agents in that discourse. Micheaux's first heroine is "the Scotch girl," his neighbor in the South Dakota venue of his first novel, *The Conquest*.[13] She is pure and white and girl-like, a heroine worthy of Griffith. When Micheaux's strong, competent, and very black hero kisses her for the first time, it is his response to their reading *Othello* together.[14] In *The Homesteader*, Micheaux's third novel, the Scotch-girl character, now called Agnes Stewart, is still the lover of the black hero, but there are significant changes from the previous novel.[15] Both hero and heroine are older, they are both successful writers, she of songs (one called "O, My Homesteader") and he of novels; the hero goes through a farming failure, losing his homestead and entering into a disastrous marriage that results in parricide and suicide by his wife and in false criminal charges and incarceration for the hero. Not only does the Scotch-girl heroine not require rescue in this version of their love story, she becomes, in fact, a spectator to the hero's near conviction—in other words, she is submitted to a narrative that seems to call for *his* rescue. (In a later novel, *The Wind from Nowhere*, 1941, this heroine's character will have evolved to the point where she rescues him through extraordinary courage and intelligence, a situation that will culminate in a long, Griffith-like chase.) And though the heroine of *The Homesteader* is still a virgin, she must endure a failed engagement before she and the hero finally come together.

The most important of the distinctions between the first two versions of the Scotch girl is that in the second version—and all later versions, whether they appear in novels or films—she turns out to be black. By virtue of a small African-American contribution to her genealogical origins, she becomes undesirable—according to the fascistic criteria of racial purity and the patriarchal criteria of sexual purity of D. W. Griffith's system—and is abandoned by her white fiancé. Because she is racially a hybrid, however, she becomes partially suitable as a lover and marriage partner for Micheaux's hero.

That the leading man in some of Micheaux's early novels and films is in trouble instead of the woman and that the leading man must be rescued by the woman are facts that are not inconsistent with some of Griffith's narratives—the modern story in *Intolerance* (1916), for example—but Micheaux extended his exploration of the "new woman" beyond a threshold that Griffith only approached. In between those two novels that feature the evolving Scotch girl, Micheaux created a significantly different heroine. Mildred Latham in *The Forged Note* is from the outset an African American, though she has some of the physical and mental characteristics of the white Scotch-girl paragon:

> He had been struck at once by her appearance, and something about her expression—her obvious intelligence. She seemed possibly twenty-one or two. "And such features," he breathed unheard. She also had, he quickly observed, a wonderful skin—smooth, velvety olive, with round checks [*sic*]; where, notwithstanding the slight darkness a faint flush came and went. As to size, she was not tall; and still not short; nor was she stout or slender; but of that indefinite type called medium. Serenely perched, her head leaned slightly back. She had a frank face and rounded forehead, from under which large, lustrous, soft dark eyes—somewhat sad—gazed out at him. And as he continued in his subtle observation, he was pleased to note that her nose was not large or flat, but stood up beautifully. Her lips were red as cherries. The chin was handsomely molded and firm, but slightly thin, and protruding. Her hair was the most captivating of all. Done in the fashion, it was coal black and wavy. It was of a fine, silken texture, and apparently long, from the size of the knot at the back of her head. All this he observed with favor. He had never seen a figure so clear cut. The girl was, furthermore, dressed in a plain, dark silk dress, with small feet, the toes of which at the moment, peeped like mice from beneath the trimly hanging skirt. Now, before he had gotten far in his dynamic spiel, the sun, all red and glorious, as its rays slanted in the west, came suddenly from beneath a cloud, and played hide and seek upon her face. And, in that moment, he saw that she was exquisitely beautiful.[16]

Mildred, wonderful and beautiful as she is, is still not a perfect fit. It is not that there can be no perfect fit for Micheaux; it is certainly not the "taint" of race, the "slight darkness," that makes Mildred unfit; his fascination with white bourgeois ideals does not extend to "racial" disloyalty. In fact, none of Micheaux's heroes wish to marry a white woman; there is no evidence in the full reach of Micheaux's available work and biographical information to suggest the desire for white women per se, and there is considerable evidence of a sincere desire for racial loyalty in marriage. Mildred Latham is an imperfect fit not because she is not white but because she is not a virgin. Her sexual history does not match her rhapsodically described image.

The Ideal of Sexual Purity

In a Griffith film, and in any mainstream film for several years after Griffith's and Micheaux's era, such a heroine could not be a love or marriage partner for most American heroes. A study of exceptions to this general rule would be interesting and would include *Stagecoach* (1939) and *River of No Return* (1954), stories of a sexual redemption that can recuperate the bourgeois ideal, a redemption that requires a superstrong male redeemer, certainly. Those stories also seem to be accompanied by a move to the American West, and in fact, a move to the West will be part of the solution in Micheaux's work, including *The Forged Note*. Exceptions to the criterion of virginity also occur in Griffith's work, including *Way Down East* (1920) and *The White Rose* (1923); those two films of sexual redemption are, more than Micheaux's films, structured around strong masculine intervention, and Griffith's equivalent to Micheaux's "safe place" in the American West appears to be the merely rural America, including the agrarian South. Griffith's rural ideal is one of nostalgia for a previous regime, whereas Micheaux's western ideal is one of destiny and enterprise.

The formula of sexual transgression by the female and her redemption by a male is an inversion of the Griffith formula of the last-minute rescue of the sexually threatened woman. Again, Griffith's basic rescue formula is not Griffith's only version of rescue, as William Rothman has pointed out in his analysis of *Judith of Bethulia* (1914; Judith rescues her city state by killing the aggressor) and as can be seen in the famous rescue at the end of the modern story in *Intolerance* (1916; a woman rescues a man about to be unjustly hanged). However, the formula of male rescue of the female is the narrative backbone of *The Birth of a Nation* and is sufficiently common in his other films to serve as a fundamental aspect of Griffith's narrative style. To repeat, for the sake of clarity, Griffith's master formula called for the rescue of the woman from sexual violation or imposition by others, not her redemption from her own sexual transgression.

William Rothman's sympathetic study of Griffith's struggle with mainstream Victorian sexual beliefs is a correction of any tendency to anachronistically oversimplify Griffith's "old-fashioned" approach to sexual politics. Rothman's sympathy for Griffith does, however, produce some incredible readings—such as the statement that the Little Colonel in *The Birth of a Nation* is aware that he should not blame Gus, the sexually interested black militiaman, for the death of Flora and that he should not seek revenge through the violence of the Klan; Rothman would find few other critics to support his claim that the Little Colonel is consciously struggling with his darker self.[17] Some of Rothman's sympathetic reading of Griffith's sexual complexity is more convincing; the fact remains, however, that in the realm of love and marriage, there were many artists for whom the adequacy of the rescue formula was tested more realistically than it was tested by Griffith. Neither Griffith nor Micheaux was sympathetic to the tough approach of the naturalistic and realistic movements represented by Zola, Dreiser, and Stephen Crane, for example. When Dreiser published *Sister Carrie* in 1900, Micheaux was sixteen years old, and Griffith was twenty-five. It is improbable that either Griffith or Micheaux was directly affected by the book, but for many complex reasons, besides the relatively unimportant dates of their births—reasons such as race, regional affiliation, and class—Micheaux was to come the closer of the two to negotiating the sensibility represented by the following passage from *Sister Carrie:*

In the light of the world's attitude toward woman and her duties, the nature of Carrie's mental state deserves consideration. Actions such as hers are measured by an arbitrary scale. Society possesses a conventional standard whereby it judges all things. All men should be good, all women virtuous. Wherefore, villain, hast thou failed?

For all the liberal analysis of [Herbert] Spencer and our modern naturalistic philosophers, we have but an infantile perception of morals. There is more in the subject than mere conformity to a law of evolution.

. . .

"Oh," thought Drouet, "how delicious is my conquest."

"Ah," thought Carrie, with mournful misgivings, "what is it I have lost?"

Before this world-old proposition we stand, serious, interested, confused; endeavoring to evolve the true theory of morals—the true answer to what is right.[18]

Whether or not Micheaux drew upon Dreiser, he certainly was influenced by the equally hard-headed but cruder and more popular form of Herbert-Spencerian fiction represented by Jack London's *Martin Eden,* the nastier elements of which would have been incommensurate with Griffith's worldview. Micheaux, however, named his hero Martin Eden in his extraordinary fourth novel about the Scotch girl, *The Wind from Nowhere,* which was published in 1941.

Griffith's need to have his heroines rescued from sexual violation was probably a need to rescue his heroes from their own proclivity to sexual perpetration. As Michael Rogin has shown, Griffith's rescues were reflexive—they were rescues of both partner and self, subject and object. In his personal life, Griffith failed to overcome the contradiction of his ideal woman—who was both sexually innocent and sexually attractive; in real life, he was a failure in marriage and thus, perhaps, had failed to rescue himself from his dilemma.

Rescue Fantasy

To envision oneself as being in need of rescue is to have externalized one's problems. The heterosexual-male narrative fantasy of "rescuing the girl" is a scenario of oedipal conflict in which the main threat is the father, the exemplary external source of sexual denial. Griffith apparently never got beyond the oedipal stage of development in his problem solving, never successfully internalized the dialectics and politics of love and desire. Rogin has concentrated on the biographical scenes of Griffith's fearful father wielding the sword in "fun" against the faithful black retainer and on the early death of that father in order to explain Griffith's sexual and ideological confusion. Miriam Hansen has examined Griffith's fond relationship with his much older sister, who raised and "educated" him and who died sexually unattached, an "old maid." Hansen has suggested that Griffith's films with "missing mothers" are more likely about his dead sister, and as such, they comprise a complex triangle of father–daughter incest and father–son "oedipal" jealousy. Hansen relates Griffith's attachment to his dead sister to "*Intolerance*'s concern with the fate of the single mother" and to "the host of abandoned, unadjusted, excessive women that populate the film, its major source of fascination and anxiety."[19] Griffith chose the twin externalities of the "race problem" and the "woman problem" to represent unresolved psychological antagonisms. His artistic resolution to those problems was brutal—the final solution in his rescue stories in *The Birth of a Nation* was graphically violent both for the threatening black man, who was caught and castrated by repeated sword thrusts until he died (in scenes that were censored from the original version of *The Birth of a Nation*), and for the threatened white women, who either leaped from cliffs so that they died bleeding from the mouth or kneeled to have their skulls crushed by their well-wishers.

And, as Marian Hansen shows, those threatened women who did not die in *The Birth,* who were rescued, were figures in a rescue fantasy that was, if less brutal, equally regressive. Hansen very usefully relates the theme-and-variation of rescue in Griffith's films to Freud's treatments of rescue fantasy:

> Freud observes a "most startling" tendency: the urge, on the part of the infatuated man, to "rescue" the woman he loves, to keep her on the path of "virtue." . . .
>
> The "rescue-motif" as such has a more archaic history, which Freud traces through the child's wish to return the gift of life to the mother. . . .
>
> Both strands of this fantasy are easily detected in Griffith's favorite narrative paradigm: the last-minute rescue plot of victimized womanhood, rehearsed in so many Biograph films and consummated in *Birth*—a psychic drama of threat, hysteria, and penetration enacted through crosscutting and accelerated editing. . . . By projecting repressed incestuous desire onto a social or racial other and preventing the violation in the nick of time, Griffith's rescue scenario permits the narrator to pursue an "essentially . . . chivalrous project," which ennobles both object and subject of the rescue fantasy.[20]

In contrast, Micheaux had far greater external threats to deal with in his life and art than Griffith did. Not only was Micheaux thus better equipped by experience to handle themes of political and social conflict, he also internalized problems and solutions in a different way from that of Griffith, working them out within himself without blaming everyone but himself and his own group. Micheaux, nevertheless, certainly had his own oedipal struggles. All his life he obsessively blamed black ministers for absorbing the attention of his mother while he was growing up, for holding back the economic and cultural uplifting of his ethnic group with their preaching (Micheaux favored his own entrepreneurialist "preaching," which he, however, backed up with exemplary action), and for breaking up his first marriage (his first wife was the daughter of a prominent Southside-Chicago minister). In spite of a very long, rocky, and only partially resolved oedipal passage and in spite of a real, rather than imagined, racial oppression (in contrast to Griffith's paranoid vision of postbellum Reconstruction), Micheaux accepted many of his problems and assumed responsibility for solving them. He also projected that philosophy onto the black community; the successes and failures of his ethnic group Micheaux treated ultimately as an

African-American responsibility, though that did not mean that white racism had to be left out of account.

The Forged Note

Micheaux's aesthetics of moderation and his philosophy of internal responsibility was less dramatic than Griffith's extremism, but it nonetheless held out the possibility of dynamic personal change. An impressive example of Micheaux's ability to oppose and supersede paradigms, rather than to fight Manichean monsters, occurs at the end of his second novel, *The Forged Note: A Romance of the Darker Races* (1915), in which the male protagonist (always a surrogate for Micheaux himself), Sidney Wyeth, undergoes an emotional collapse, or epiphany. Epiphanies are rare in Micheaux's work; his style usually shows less dynamic range and less subjective dramatic conflict, in spite of his internalization of responsibility. Throughout his novels and films, his protagonists, both male and female, are seldom placed in serious jeopardy or in need of rescue or of redemption of any kind. Often they rescue or redeem a third party.

The Forged Note is different, however; at the end, the physical, mental, and spiritual stress for *both* the male and female protagonists is intense. Both characters badly need rescue and redemption. For the hero, Wyeth, the intense need for rescue comes after he has solved the external problems of selling his first book, researching his next book, and setting up his publishing and book-distribution business as a going concern in the South as well as the Midwest. In other words, Wyeth's self-definition would seem, in the logic of the story, to be healthy, thorough, and confident, based as it is on a notebook full of ethnic and racial distinctions he has drawn on his "research" trip to the South. Wyeth believes he will be successful as an author and publisher, "since he has learned, by contact, the art of reaching his people" (p. 456).[21] He has, in his "pilgrimage" and his "critical observations" (p. 456), created a strong positive identity for himself by distinguishing his own personal qualities from some of the negative qualities he feels characterize African-American and other socially oppressed groups. His "findings" have demonstrated, to his satisfaction, that his people need to "improve," that black people are separated in public theaters in the South because they genuinely disturb white (and presumably middle-class black) patrons with their boisterous behavior, the "unruly" blacks making no effort to understand their effect on contemptuous whites (p. 356). Wyeth has found that the majority of the members of his race do not "think deeply." He has expressed admiration for Theodore Roosevelt for his personal fortitude, as demonstrated by the storming of San Juan Hill in the Spanish–American War, implying that African Americans could learn not only from Roosevelt but also from Wyeth's (and Micheaux's) interest in and identification with such leaders, an identification that crosses ethnic boundaries for its models. Wyeth (and Micheaux) has also, on the positive side of his ethnic identity, distinguished the accomplishments and qualities of African Americans in comparison with those of other oppressed groups, stating that Navajos are being treated better than African Americans in America, even though the Navajos have never done anything to make the country better. Such "irrational" American preferences, Wyeth finds, demonstrate that prejudice still prevails. In the face of such findings, Wyeth again distances himself from what he considers the ineffectual "bemoaning and the boasting" of many African Americans by asking whether African Americans should continue to grieve or should rather face up to reality and make men of themselves (pp. 372–73). In addition to these "research findings," Wyeth has also measured himself against a petty Jim-Crow ticket taker at a southern train station, who has willfully caused Wyeth to miss his train. Wyeth's complaints against the Jim-Crower take a form that might be called the bemoaning and boasting that Wyeth had previously rejected; in fact, however, this particular bemoaning and boasting has a historical and biographical referent within the story—Wyeth wishes he had the man in Rosebud Country, where previously Wyeth (and Micheaux) had built his homestead, written his first novel, and begun his fortune. The Rosebud Country of South Dakota represents a relatively level playing field, which Wyeth has already found to be historically and personally viable for African Americans. It is the place in the American West that Wyeth has already "conquered"; Micheaux's own first, autobiographical novel about his experience in the former Rosebud Indian reservation was, in fact, called *The Conquest*. Wyeth's wish to get the Jim-Crower there, where Wyeth could deal with his racist insult man to man, is not a despairing bemoaning or a fantastic boasting—it is just within the realm of possibility.

Wyeth (and Micheaux) has even come to the point in his meditations and observations where he can compare himself favorably to some of the most accomplished African-American writers of fiction. Wyeth is self-confident enough to chastise "the most successful fiction writer our race has known" (in 1915; in real life, probably Charles Chesnutt, whose fiction Micheaux later adapted for the screen) for discussing white hatred of blacks without mentioning the "traits" of blacks that "cause" that hatred. He criticizes the great black intellectual Derwin (in real life, probably W. E. B. DuBois) for writing a novel (probably *The Quest of the Silver Fleece*, 1911, DuBois's second book and first novel) about prejudice that is "void of humor."[22]

This listing of the "findings" and attitudes of Wyeth and Micheaux is not presented here uncritically; those attitudes represent complexities in Micheaux's attitude that this study will treat but not resolve. Much more research and discussion are needed.

Identity Crisis and Psychic Collapse

Precisely at the point of Wyeth's satisfactory completion of these "research" observations and at the point of his formation of a distinctive identity for himself, he suffers a debilitating reversal. As he walks around the city that stands for the real-life New Orleans, pulling his thoughts together and getting ready to return to the North, he develops a mysterious illness that is accompanied by a "dark vision." As he absorbs the radically conflicted ambience of "Bienville" (in real life, the Storyville section of New Orleans), the 'redlight' district with its contiguous Catholic cemeteries that seem to force the conjunction of sex, religion, and death, "something in him burst[s]." He suffers a complete collapse and is unable to leave Bienville/Storyville.

The extremes represented by the crisis at the end of *The Forged Note* are sex and death, prostitution and religion, red lights and church bells, id and superego, body and soul. *Body and Soul* (1925), starring Paul Robeson in a dual role—good and evil brothers—is Micheaux's most famous film. The suspension of protagonists between extremes of high and low status or valuation is consistent with Micheaux's other work and was generally constructed to support Micheaux's tendency to look for a middle way between extremes. Micheaux consciously negotiated paths of moderation between the extreme polarities of Griffith's Manichean system, between DuBois's aspects of "twoness," between high and low production values, and between upper and lower classes. Micheaux's path, though it be called one of moderation, was also clearly exposed to the considerable strain of all these active bipolarities. Just such a strain causes the collapse in Wyeth that requires his rescue. Wyeth's ego disintegrates under the pressure, and he passes into unconsciousness and ennui. The identity that he had so carefully constructed from distinctions drawn from his research of the South (the observations of "his people") is completely helpless among the whores and priests of Bienville. Such a collapse as Wyeth's, in the face of bipolar extremes, could be a motive for choosing a middle path through the force fields of such extremes throughout the rest of Micheaux's own career.

None of the distinctions of identity that Wyeth has drawn is objectionable or problematic from Micheaux's point of view. The reason for Wyeth's collapse is not that he has isolated himself from his people or taken a false path in his meditations about "racial" and personal progress. All of Wyeth's work so far has been necessary for uplift, but it has not been sufficient. Wyeth seems to have done everything he can do by himself. He now needs help. Micheaux had himself always been an individualist but not a separatist.[23] He got along well with his neighbors in South Dakota and was well liked. He was quick to enter into the commercial networks of the new territories, borrowing money, hiring neighbors' sons to work his land, trading animals, contracting for his meals with neighboring families, and attending festivals. He was forever encouraging and offering to help other black families to move into the new territories; he was fond of taking trips to Chicago to keep up his acquaintances and social life. And he particularly sought out a wife in Chicago, because he was intensely lonely and sexually frustrated in his home life in Dakota. Since that marriage had failed dramatically and mortifyingly by the time he wrote *The Forged Note*, one can assume that Micheaux was not just continuing to wish for a supersession of his "individuality"—his individuality must have been a painful disability, not unlike Wyeth's mysterious disability.

Rescuing the Hero

While Micheaux's surrogate, Wyeth, lies helpless in Bienville/Storyville, Mildred Latham, the female protagonist of *The Forged Note*, takes over his business for him. The relationship between Mildred and Wyeth's art and career strikingly parallels and foreshadows the relationship between Alice B. Russell and Micheaux's own career. Russell was Micheaux's second wife and lifelong companion; she was one of his most constant, dependable, and accomplished actresses; and, as "A. Burton Russell," she was the credited producer of his later films. She was, like Mildred Latham in *The Forged Note*, a business partner as well as a "vision" of the ideal middle-class spouse. When Wyeth recovers enough to return to his office, he discovers that Mildred has kept it running and has even built it up into a going concern, having made her own decisions for improvements that are in Wyeth's interest. Wyeth is thunderstruck and perplexed. He is not inclined to feel defensive about the intervention of a woman; on the contrary, he is impressed and delighted that a woman should be so sensible and practical. He is, however, still unhappy about it because there is an insurmountable barrier blocking their partnership, a perception of a flaw in her past that he cannot fully understand because of the altogether fine qualities of her character, which he has witnessed for himself.

Forging the Couple as Partnership in Uplift

One reason for this long description of Micheaux's hero's need for rescue is to establish the nature of the barrier that hinders the formation of a relationship between the couple; the barrier is that Mildred has an unsavory past. When Wyeth had been interested in her several years before, near the time during which she had become involved in his distribution business (a relationship she had secretly continued by serving, without Wyeth's knowledge, as a door-to-door salesperson for his books), he had discovered her "with another man." It is almost certainly the contradictory feelings of wanting and admiring her, on the one hand, and of moral repulsion, on the other hand, that have caused Wyeth's debilitating malaise in Bienville/Storyville.

It is crucial to understand that, contrary to the accusations that Micheaux constructed a white, patriarchal, bourgeois ideal of marriage, his construction of the couple is entirely different from Griffith's. Micheaux's couple is specifically black, non-patriarchal, and middle-class. Wyeth and Mildred's potential relationship is not a frustrated romance of male possession (as Griffith's is), but rather a partnership of work and mission. What occurs for the remainder of the denouement of *The Forged Note* is a "forging" of an African-American partnership that supersedes the injuries and conventions of the past, including those inflicted by the Griffith of *The Birth of a Nation* and by his audience. Several points of difference between Micheaux and Griffith suggest the directions that Micheaux was taking in order to correct past injuries to African-American sexual partnership and to revise the conventions of marriage. First, the woman is again rescuing the man, a rarity in Griffith; second, the rescue takes the form of work, not romance—she saves his business; third, the woman is making headway in the man's game of modern entrepreneurial business, headway that the leading man could not have accomplished by himself. In Griffith's films, leading women often work hard, but only at women's work, and usually the condition of work is temporary (though it may be long), while the woman waits to be rescued *from work* by a man.[24] Lillian Gish works dutifully for her farming family in *Way Down East* and for her cruel father in *Broken Blossoms,* until Richard Barthelmess claims her and redeems her; she does drudge work at home in *True Heart Susie,* until she is saved by Bobby Harron. Bobby Harron saves Mae Marsh from working womanhood, and from potential prostitution, in *Intolerance,* even though in the end, he must be saved himself and restored to his jeopardized role as savior and provider by Mae Marsh and a reformed prostitute, Miriam Cooper.

Lillian Gish, however, performs no work in *The Birth of a Nation.* In *Broken Blossoms,* after being rescued by the Chinese man, Gish again represents the antithesis of work; she is set up like a priceless jewel in an exotic coffer. Micheaux's Mildred, in contrast, though she is "exquisitely beautiful," performs for Wyeth like a promising junior partner in the firm, like a rising young man in a William Dean Howells novel. If there is to be progress or uplift in Wyeth's (or Micheaux's) world, such a marriage partner is necessary; but she is denied him by the bourgeois ideals inherent in Griffith's (and, at this stage, Wyeth's own) received view of marriage.

Rescue as Redemption

Micheaux's denouement for *The Forged Note* is not, however, the sort of rescue that would serve to save the old absolutes of racial, sexual, and class purity. Rather, it is a mutually negotiated redemption founded in self-consciousness of the sort that facilitates a cascading insight and crescendo of spirit, as imagined by Hegel in *The Phenomenology of Mind*; Micheaux's denouement portrays enlargement of mind as compared to Griffith's enlargement of ego. Micheaux's resolutions of extreme conflict typically involve education, whereas Griffith's involve force, an entirely different notion of "overcoming."

Micheaux's denouement calls for Wyeth to discover, through an old acquaintance of Mildred's, her trials and tribulations (including her total blamelessness in the so-called loss of her virtue) and her selfless, uplifting accomplishments (including her funding of a YMCA for African Americans) during the period of her "shame." Mildred had decided, in the midst of her adversity at the hands of an upper-class white man, that although she had "never known kindness," she can still be "an example for others" (p. 494). It is an existentialist moral position, and Wyeth is deeply impressed; he reflects that though "virtue in woman had been his highest regard," and though "he was still revolted" (p. 496) by the idea of her impurity because of his "ideal of womanhood" (p. 497), nevertheless, Mildred was "more than his ideal" [p. 498]. Griffith, in contrast, was, in his class, sexual, and racial politics, calling for restoration of the threatened but still unsullied absolutes, not for a new beginning for the "sullied."

Once Wyeth has seen the way to superseding some of his deepest, received bourgeois values through a new idea of the African-American couple, a new set of rationales emerges in him—he recalls that he really never had respected conformity or conventionality for itself (p. 499) and that there was no conventionality at all that he and Mildred (and other African Americans) were under any obligation to honor (p. 502). He has visions that yield a new sense of citizenship—when he sees the slave market in New Orleans he has a fantasy of a slave auction (p. 508); this image is connected, in his reverie, by way of the Mississippi and Missouri Rivers to the Rosebud Country in South Dakota, which he here calls "the great Northwest" (pp. 508–509). It has occurred to him that, as long as they have conquered their own phobias and accepted each other for who they are, he and Mildred have a new kind of freedom and can start their lives over in the Rosebud Country, out west (p. 499).

In Micheaux's vision, deep heterosexual union is the foundation for spiritual happiness, for material wealth, and for social standing. Micheaux suggests that such a union can occur, for African Americans, only through the supersession of certain self-images created through identification with social ideals that contradict historical and political realities. Once the two African Americans recognize each other—across the barriers of sex, gender, class, region, racial and ethnic prejudice, and personal history—a new, if perhaps frighteningly inconclusive, freedom results, which is both personal and social. That freedom, for Micheaux, depends not just on passing through fear and trembling (Wyeth's collapse; Micheaux's catastrophic first marriage), but on practical matters, such as his future spouse's business ability and the availability of lands in the West that are open to them economically, socially, and politically. As this couple suggests, African Americans were not simply rejecting the old dialectics of the South and the North; rather, they were migrating for reasons similar to those that brought European immigrants to America. Micheaux, however, was proud that his race had not been late-coming immigrants but rather had been part of the force that originally conquered America—Dr. Vivian says something like that to Sylvia at the end of *Within Our Gates* in order to convince Sylvia that she needs to think differently about her racial background. Dr. Vivian's and Micheaux's distinction, however, is a kind of political misprision (a willful misreading of the historical record) and a kind of invention of tradition (a recent claiming of the distant past). Such misreadings and inventions, according to Harold Bloom (in his discussion of poets) and Eric Hobsbawm (in his discussion of public ritual), are entirely justified or, at the very least, inevitable among "the strong."[25] Therefore, in Bloom's terms, if Wyeth and Mildred, Dr. Vivian and Sylvia, or Micheaux and Alice B. Russell have the strength of will to overcome, one should not be surprised or dismayed by misprision.[26] That is why it seems inappropriate to complain, as some critics have, that Micheaux did not draw a politically realistic picture of the racial problems of his time. Rather,

Micheaux staked a counterclaim; he constructed his own reality in the face of historical and political "realities," a claim that he intended to be strong enough to defend *as* a reality in the face of everything. He, as a strong human body, mind, and spirit, was implying that he could prove the new reading of reality by practicing it.

DuBois's *Silver Fleece*

Micheaux's vision was shared by DuBois, whose extraordinary novel, *The Quest of the Silver Fleece* (1911), serves as a prior, confirming example of the significance of reforging the African-American couple as an economic, sexual, spiritual, and social foundation for uplift. *The Quest of the Silver Fleece* ends, as do Micheaux's *The Forged Note* and *Within Our Gates*, with an epiphany and a mutual heterosexual rescue and redemption. The last chapter of *Silver Fleece*, called "Atonement," refers to female purity of body and soul. The book ends with the central female protagonist, Zora, experiencing an epiphany in the revelatory presence of her lover:

> His voice came slow and firm:
> "Emma? But I don't love Emma. I love—some one else."
> Her heart bounded and again was still. It was that Washington girl then. She answered dully, groping for words, for she was tired:
> "Who is it?"
> "The best woman in all the world, Zora."
> "And is"—she struggled at the word madly—"is she pure?"
> "She is more than pure."
> "Then you must marry her, Bles."
> "I am not worthy of her," he answered, sinking before her.
> Then at last illumination dawned upon her blindness. She stood very still and lifted up her eyes. The swamp was living, vibrant, tremulous. There where the first long note of night lay shot with burning crimson, burst in sudden radiance the wide beauty of the moon. There pulsed a glory in the air. Her little hands groped and wandered over his close-curled hair, and she sobbed, deep voiced:
> "Will you—marry me, Bles?"

Zora's proposal of marriage to Bles is, of course, a conspicuous reversal of the normal male proposal to the woman, but it is also not just a proposal, it is a real question, posed in the light of their mutual concern, up to this point in the story, for Zora's own sexual "impurity." Bles's response to her question, that she is "more than pure," replicates Wyeth's statement in Micheaux's novel—that Mildred is "more than his ideal" of sexual purity in women. DuBois's story, like Micheaux's, ends with this apotheosis of mutual self-redemption in marriage, a heterosexual couple reborn for themselves in each other. The story also shows, as does Micheaux's, that the economic and political future of African Americans is also regenerated in this couple, since Zora and Bles have been raising a cotton crop together as a business venture; other than the sexual politics between Bles and Zora, the main conflict in the novel, before the marriage proposal, has been the struggle of their cotton business against a cotton monopoly attempted by white supremacists.

DuBois amplified the import of his apotheosis by attaching a nondiegetic authorial political threat addressed directly to white readers, very much like the threat issued by Micheaux when he titled his post-Chicago-riot film *Within Our Gates*, thereby intimating that white terrorists themselves might "be hurt." Addressing the white reader as a kind of god, DuBois assumed a god-like role himself by proclaiming Bles and Zora's marriage to be a declaration of African-American independence. This couple's independent future and DuBois's declaration of it were to be granted by white America upon pain of retributive holocaust:

L'ENVOI

Lend me thine ears, O God the Reader, whose Fathers aforetime sent mine down into the land of Egypt, into this House of Bondage. Lay not these words aside for a moment's phantasy, but lift up thine eyes upon the Horror in this land;—the maiming and mocking and murdering of my people, and the prisonment of their souls. Let my people go, O Infinite One, lest the world shudder at
THE END[27]

This "L'Envoi" follows Zora's proposal of marriage. This passage, like the similarly threatening but transformative message of Micheaux's treatment of marriage, suggests that, for the young DuBois (and the young Micheaux), the construction of the African-American couple—as a narrative of sexual and moral revision, as a base of economic and social progress, and as a base for political action—was at the core of the African-American struggle. The threat of national holocaust by DuBois and by other black leaders was not unheard of, as the following pre-Wilsonian letter from black ministers to President Taft shows: "Our Nation is already the laughing stock of civilized peoples throughout the world, and unless something is done to make human life more valuable and law more universally respected, we feel that our beloved country is doomed to destruction at no distant date."[28] What DuBois did artistically in his novel and what Micheaux did in his novels and films was to connect this powerful political sentiment and threat with the volcanic emotions of sexual frustration and release. And since Bles and Zora also comprise a business partnership that is competing with the white cotton monopoly, and since Micheaux's couples comprise business partnerships, their construction of the couple represents a political and economic unit as well. The power for uplift in such a foundation, in the face of the oppression caused by Griffith's model, justifies DuBois's threat at "the end" of his novel and Micheaux's threat at the beginning of *Within Our Gates*.

Restitution vs. Retribution

At the crisis of Wyeth's epiphanic collapse in *The Forged Note*, Wyeth and Mildred make eye contact, Wyeth's soul cries "Restitution!," and their union is finally born. Though "restitution" seems an odd way of expressing the union of sexual soul mates, it is, upon reflection, the right word, since it refers to the return of stolen values. Wyeth and Mildred had already fallen in love long ago, but they had been stolen from each other by the combination of the white-imposed values of absolute sexual purity and the (contradictory) violation of those same values by white slave breeders and *droit-du-seigneur* rapists and concubinists under white supremacism.

Interestingly enough, D. W. Griffith also calls for restitution as the foundation for union. In *The Birth of a Nation*, Griffith founded his vision of American union, both sexual (the Little Colonel and Elsie Stoneman) and political (South and North) on the violent retributions that comprise his last-minute rescues. Griffith's restitution takes the form of revenge; it is founded on repayment, Shylock-like, of blood, at exaggerated rates of interest. DuBois, too, hints at the end of *Silver Fleece* that a God-like, apocalyptic revenge might be justly visited on white supremacists, but he does not ask for that; he only really asks for the rights of citizenship. Micheaux's Wyeth more completely internalizes his apocalyptic rage, passing his soul through a kind of love-death. Neither DuBois nor Micheaux expressed the kind of violent revenge fantasy of Griffith's that swept white America in 1915 (though other African Americans did call for violence; Martin Delaney intimated such revenge in his 1859 novel *Blake*, and Sutton Griggs portrayed it in his powerful novels around the turn of the twentieth century). And neither DuBois nor Micheaux artistically conceived individual egos so large as to produce the kind of monumental and bloody visions of nationhood that Griffith did. Griffith demanded sacrificial slaughter of the (historically, largely imagined) black sexual imposers on white women; DuBois and Micheaux, in contrast, demanded merely the restored capacity to love the black women, who were more often and more systematically abused ("ruined," in Victorian terms) by white sexual transgressors than Griffith cared to imagine. There could hardly be a clearer picture of how a people can be psychologically damaged by their *own* transgressions than the picture of the Little Colonel, the white hero in *The Birth of a Nation*, repeatedly hacking the dying black "transgressor" in the name of an ancient ethnic religion. This picture of inadequately displaced white self-loathing had to be censored from the film by more sophisticated white supremacists than Griffith. The ways in which Griffith and Micheaux handled the idea of restitution reflect oneness and twoness, respectively.

Within Our Gates

Micheaux's film *Within Our Gates* articulates the bipolarity of restitution and retribution in a way similar to that found in DuBois's novel *The Silver Fleece* and in Micheaux's novel *The Forged Note*. After a denouement in the middle of the film, in which Sylvia succeeds in raising (restitutional) funds from white philanthropists, another sort of restitution remains to be accomplished.

Sylvia celebrates her fundraising victory with Dr. Vivian, but she does not consummate that moment with him through marriage. She returns to the South and immediately becomes the victim of benignant sexual imposition and then malignant sexual harassment. Immediately upon her return to the South, Rev. Jacobs, the director of the black school, quite legitimately proposes marriage, but he is rejected politely by Sylvia because she is in love with Dr. Vivian. Then the criminal stepbrother of her cousin Alma, Larry, who has come south to escape police investigation of his murder of Rosario, tries to blackmail Sylvia into a sexual relationship. The knowledge that he possesses of her past becomes the crucial problem of the rest of the film for the protagonists. It is that knowledge, which is of a violent and sexual nature, that keeps the leading man and woman apart, owing to Sylvia's feeling that she is unworthy of Dr. Vivian's love and partnership.

Sylvia's feeling of unworthiness places the main couple in the same dilemma as that of Zora and Bles in DuBois's novel and of Sidney Wyeth and Mildred Latham in Micheaux's novel. Dr. Vivian, however, is placed in a position to resolve this problem, the second and main problem of the film, after he hears the story of Sylvia's origins from Alma. That story is the context in which Micheaux introduces the lynching story, the most famous aspect of the film's plot. The story of the lynching reveals, among many things, that Sylvia is the daughter of a white man and a black woman. The Spanish-intertitled version of the film indicates that this union is one of marriage, but given the historical unlikelihood of interracial marriage in the South in 1900, when the story is set, or in 1919, when the film was made, and given the shame that Sylvia feels for her origins, it is probable that in Micheaux's original version of the film, Sylvia was the *illegitimate* offspring of white-on-black rape, concubinage, or *droit du seigneur*. That is the "terrible" core fact of the background that separates her from middle-class legitimacy, the fact that seems to devalue her in relation to Dr. Vivian, the fact that makes her a mark for Larry's blackmail.[29]

If *Within Our Gates* had been made in the style of *The Birth of a Nation,* much of the action described above would have been presented in the present tense and would have comprised a scene of rescue. The saving of Sylvia's virtue by the leading man would have resolved the fears and confirmed the manhood of Dr. Vivian and of the male spectator. The person threatening that manhood would have been killed or captured to assuage the anger and to reconfirm the manhood of the hero through an excess of retribution. The action would have emphasized the freedom, omnipotence, perfect timing, resolution, and spectacular monumentality of the hero's, the filmmaker's, and the intended spectator's manhood. That is basically the way *The Birth of a Nation* works.

Micheaux's version of Sylvia's rescue, by comparison, is modest. Dr. Vivian, compared to the Little Colonel of *The Birth of a Nation,* might be characterized as a "wimp," and some of Micheaux's later heroes could be said to be stunning in their "wimpiness."[30] Dr. Vivian, however, is disadvantaged in that he arrives on the scene several decades too late to rescue Sylvia from her provenance and several years too late to save Sylvia from disgrace. He represents an African-American manhood that has been placed in that position in perpetuity.[31] Dr. Vivian is given the unenviable task of seeking redemption after the fact of injury, of delivering retribution for injury, and of constructing legitimacy in the face of continuing, but ever more diffuse, racist injury.

After Dr. Vivian hears the story of the lynching and the ancient rapes, he understands Sylvia's struggle with personal and social legitimacy, but he does not agree with her assessment of that legitimacy and begins to try to talk her out of it. He begins by asking her to think of her own problem in the context of racism. This is implied by a series of observations not of oppression *of* blacks (which the whole lynching story and Sylvia's background have adequately demonstrated) but of heroic Americanisms *by* blacks (which are presumably not demonstrated or thought of often enough). He tells her that they "will never forget what we [black soldiers] did in Cuba under the command of Roosevelt," "in Mexico and Carrizal," "and later in France, from Bruges to Chateau Thiery, from Saint Mihiel to the Alps!" He points out that African Americans "were never immigrants" and thus were "[a]lways proud of [their] country, always!"[32] He wants her not to think so much of her misfortunes but rather to think of her priority of place, as an African American, with the conquerors, founders, and builders of the country. He says: "And you, Sylvia, have been thinking deeply about this, I know, but unfortunately in the wrong way. . . . And in spite of your misfortunes, you always will be a good citizen and a tender wife . . . and I love you!"[33] Dr. Vivian not only accepts her along with her past, which solves part of the problem as presented in the novels of DuBois and Micheaux (discussed above), but Dr. Vivian also talks to her about thinking of herself in a positive light, through pride in her racial background and its implications for American citizenship. Contrary to the common critical perception that Micheaux was racially negative, this positive approach was Micheaux's own ultimate priority in racial uplift.

The last intertitle of the film reads thus: "And a little while later we see that Sylvia understood that perhaps Dr. Vivian was right"; this intertitle is followed by the last shot of the film, in which the couple looks out a window, with backs to the camera, and then slowly turns toward the camera, forming a perfect icon of the happy, heterosexual, middle-class couple, an image that had been presented in the middle of the film but not yet consecrated by marriage or the possibility of marriage. This is the image that looks so much like a Griffith image of a bourgeois couple.

Each filmmaker intended the images of the heterosexual couple that ended their two films to be emblematic of the basic social unit, since Griffith's occurs in the context of restored nationhood and Micheaux's occurs as a result of Dr. Vivian's argument for African-American citizenship. The narrative routes to and the construction and the implications of those two versions of a precious and familiar image of heterosexual union are, however, as different as the "unum" and "pluribus" in "E pluribus unum."

Fig. 4a. The sweet, vulnerable, but experienced and competent heroine, Sylvia Landry (Evelyn Preer), at the conclusion of *Within Our Gates.*

Fig. 4b. The sweet, vulnerable, but pioneering and rescuing heroine, Evon Mason (Iris Hall), at the conclusion of *The Symbol of the Unconquered.*

Conclusion

Micheaux and DuBois had to revise the fictional couple prescribed by Griffith and by western culture. Micheaux's films and novels and DuBois's novels are about black men and black women who are trying to overcome a complex set of hindrances, including the visual and narrative treatment of romantic love and the devaluing of all forms of hybridity, including stylistic hybridity. Griffith, Micheaux, and DuBois were all struggling for a new middle-class society for Americans, and for each of these artists, an idea of marriage served as a proto-society and even a proto-economy and proto-polity. In general, for Griffith, marriage was a conservative act, because it was a reaffirmation of classical liberalism (the [male] individual as free agent) and of patriarchy and because he emphasized an old vision of racial purity and white supremacism. For DuBois and Micheaux, however, marriage was a progressive act, an affirmation of the social self, of mutuality rather than radical individuality, of the right of women to free agency, and of racial hybridity and equality.

These fundamental differences result from divergent readings of the same icon: the bourgeois-looking, ideal couple that one sees at the end of such Griffith movies as *The Lonely Villa* and that virtually all Griffith romances strive for, in spite of a contradictory (in Griffith's confused state) aspiration for sexual joy. Griffith's couple looks like the same ideal couple one sees at the end of such Micheaux movies as *Within Our Gates* and that all Micheaux's films also seem to strive for. Griffith, however, was trying to hold on to the exclusive privilege that the icon had represented, whereas Micheaux was trying to force access to the middle-class life that the same icon had denied him. Both Griffith and Micheaux were hurt by the convention represented by the icon. Griffith was a victim of psychological repression and he responded, in kind, by victimizing imagined culprits. The "darker races" he ostracized and brutalized were, according to Rogin's analysis, his darker self externalized. Micheaux victimized no one; instances of meanness in his films and novels are rare (though not nonexistent). Micheaux instead worked to revise his attitudes toward the bourgeois conventions, including those of cinema, that were hurting him and his ostracized group.

These divergent readings of a similar icon derive from the implications of the radically different personal and social histories of blacks and whites in America, including the centuries of sexual violation of black women by white men and the resulting racial hybridity imposed on the black community in America. Divergent readings of the common icon also derive from the differing conditions of production and reception of Griffith's and Micheaux's films. In addition to breaching the formidable, racially defined, closely held icon of the bourgeois couple, Micheaux also had to confront, like David before Goliath, the Manichean giganticism, dynamism, and polish of Griffith's style, a style vitally linked to Griffith's overwrought content. Micheaux's aesthetics of moderation had the unenviable task of constructing an appropriately and necessarily small but effectively refutational film style.

Micheaux's and Griffith's styles and concerns represented two radically different approaches to class uplift, approaches based on entirely different conditions of production. Griffith's approach implied that the middle-class American Dream would be defined from the top down; the already successful upper class, big capital, would be the self-appointed producers of expensive visions of the Dream. That is what the modifier "bourgeois" means when applied to the middle class, that the middle class, while not financially capitalized enough to be bourgeois (i.e., owners of the means of production) itself, is nonetheless bourgeois-constructed and bourgeois-identified. Micheaux's approach implied that the expensive visions and their conventional content had to be revised if the Dream was to be defined by the "Dreamers"—the poorer citizens who were still seeking middle-class status. His vision of the middle class was not bourgeois. Micheaux's career and aesthetics exemplify the entrepreneurial independent filmmaker as the producer of inexpensive visions of the American Dream for the upwardly mobile. In both Griffith's and Micheaux's cases, groups of spectators were created. In the case of Griffith's approach, which became Hollywood's approach, the spectators became a class with little access to production. In the case of Micheaux, the spectators had greater proximity and reasonable access to the institutions of production, because those institutions were less capitalized.

The common complaint by critics of Micheaux's class orientation—that his ideal couple and his film style are bourgeois—should be revised. His couple and his style are "middle-class," a category that includes the majority of Americans today. That class has a material interest in films such as Micheaux's, films that could deliver "a straight lick with a crooked stick."

2 Micheaux's Class Position

Since Micheaux's artistic vision was driven by the goal of racial uplift, or class advancement under a racist regime, class was always as important an issue as race; ideas of class underlay many of the most distinctive and controversial aspects of his subject matter and style.

Micheaux's Idea of Class

Though Micheaux always had something to say about class, he did not formulate his ideas within a consciously theoretic discourse. Micheaux's ideas took shape in the context of fictional and autobiographical narrative, not theory, so any definition of Micheaux's idea of class must be inferred from his narratives. Analysis of his films shows that "middle-class" qualities for Micheaux consisted of upright carriage; articulate, grammatical English speech; broad literacy; clean, well-tailored clothes in the British and Northern European tradition or clean, homespun clothes for individuals living in rural environments; urban sophistication; thoughtfulness, even intellectuality; culture; education; sexual morality; self-reliance; entrepreneurial ambition; economic conservatism; political liberalism; patriotism; racial and ethnic loyalty; ethnic tolerance; broad travel and perspective; respect for privacy; the work ethic; fair play; collegial confidence and trust; candor; and romantic love.

Micheaux's characterization of the middle class was consistent with his tendency to take the middle path through most vertical hazards, such as those of "twoness" (double consciousness based on "racial" or ethnic stratification and assimilation) and of expensiveness (economic class). Thus, there is a kind of bipolar dialectic that can be abstracted from Micheaux's works that places the middle class, which is represented by the qualities listed above, in a vertical bracket of grave dangers that threaten that class from below and above. Below lies the class condition represented by the disdainful qualities of weak, stooped, shrinking, or shuffling carriage; dialect and ungrammatical English; illiteracy and narrow interests; unclean or disheveled clothing or eccentric ostentation of dress; rural spiritualism; careless mental simplicity; cultural ignorance and philistinism; sexual promiscuity; social dependency; lack of initiative; economic profligacy; ethnic nationalisms and ethnic reaction; racial and ethnic betrayal and jealousy; African-American bigotry toward whites, Jews, and others; narrow travel perspective; loud and public exercising of private matters; fear of or disdain for work; unfair play through rackets and tricks; cynicism and distrust; furtiveness; and exploitative sexual love.

From above, the middle class is threatened by the class whose characteristic behaviors include passing for white; racial, sexual, legal, social, religious, and economic exploitation and abuse of power; cooperation and collaboration with white supremacism; insouciance; alienation; hubris; patronization; ignorance; foolishness; and overt racial betrayal.

Class and Race

The three lists above represent, in one positive (middle-class) and two negative (lower- and upper-class) groupings, a picture of the American class situation according to Micheaux's work. Those lists and the pictures they offer of class life for African Americans are similar to the lists produced, almost off-handedly, by Shelby Steele in his recent essays on race and class:

> The middle-class values by which we [middle-class blacks] were raised [are] . . . the work ethic, the importance of education, the value of private ownership, of respectability, of "getting ahead," of stable family life, of initiative, of self-reliance, et cetera. . . .
>
> . . .
>
> Though my father was born poor, he achieved middle-class standing through much hard work and sacrifice (one of his favorite words) and by identifying fully with solid middle-class values—mainly hard work, family life, property ownership, and education for his children.

Steele has clearly portrayed the African-American middle class as being in conflict with a lower class, drawing pictures of that class that could be perceived as representing the kind of complicity in stereotype and the racial self-hatred that Micheaux has been accused of:

> No one in my family remembers how it happened, but as time went on, the negative images congealed into an imaginary character named Sam who, from the extensive service we put him to, quickly grew to mythic proportions. In our family lore he was sometimes a trickster, sometimes a boob, but always possessed of a catalogue of sly faults that gave up graphic images of everything we should not be. On sacrifice: "Sam never thinks about tomorrow. He wants it now or he doesn't care about it." On work: "Sam doesn't favor it too much." On children: "Sam likes to have them but not to raise them." On money: "Sam drinks it up and pisses it out." On fidelity: "Sam has to have two or three women." On clothes: "Sam features loud clothes. He likes to see and be seen." And so on. Sam's persona amounted to a negative instruction manual in class identity.[1]

Steele has addressed the perception of racial self-hatred:

> I don't think that any of us believed Sam's faults were accurate representations of lower-class black life. He was an instrument of [our own] self-definition, not of sociological accuracy. It never occurred to us that he looked very much like the white racist stereotype of blacks, or that he might have been a manifestation of our own racial self-hatred. He simply gave us a counterpoint against which to ex-

press our aspirations. If self-hatred was a factor, it was not, for us, a matter of hating lower-class blacks but of hating what we did not want to be.[2]

Steele does not draw up a list of the qualities of a class higher than the middle class; his essays are missing precisely such a group. In his concern to explore the increasing significance of class for African Americans—specifically in relation to racial identity—Steele has focused more on the opening horizons of uplift—specifically in contrast to past, lower-class conditions. Especially in his insistence on the debilitating effects of overemphasizing African-American victimization, Steele has not emphasized the classes that have represented (and will continue to represent) oppression. In that respect, too, Steele's picture of African-American middle-class concerns is remarkably, but not exactly, similar to Micheaux's.

Questions arise from these lists of Micheaux and Steele. How do they relate to classic, social-science definitions of class, including the middle class? How do they relate to Micheaux's alleged bourgeois values and to related, socialist critiques of Micheaux? How do they relate to the false degradation and false uplift Micheaux represented in his own narratives? How do they relate to race or ethnicity in general and in Micheaux's own value system?

Micheaux refused to see any character traits, on either the positive or the negative list, as *essentially* connected with race or ethnicity, though he has been accused of doing so (see chapter 13). On the one hand, he presented black people who conformed to the values and qualities of the first list, the middle-class traits, as good; such good characters included all of his heroes and heroines. On the other hand, he presented black people who conform to the values of the second and third lists as bad, including all of his major and minor antagonists. He presented relatively few white people in his films, but of those he did present, there are very few who are middle-class in his terms. There are some whites who are lower-class, who conform to the debasing negative values listed above; these include the white crackers and lynchers in *Within Our Gates* (1919) and the white bank teller, the sheriff, and some townsfolk in *Birthright* (1939). On the whole, however, the lower-class threat in Micheaux's films comes from prodigal African Americans. The inverse is true of the upper class. White people who conform to the qualities in the second list (upper-class) are relatively plentiful, including the white planters who cheat and rape their black tenants in *Within Our Gates,* the white plant manager who is a rapist and who believes himself also to be a murderer in *Murder in Harlem,* the white boxing managers who rig the fight in *Underworld,* the white club owners who prostitute their black chorus girls in *Lying Lips,* and the white southern philanthropist with fantasies of Aryan purity in *Birthright.*

There are also some upper-class whites who play a positive role, such as the northern philanthropist who contributes to the southern black school in *Within Our Gates;* the white school-board chairman who defends the slandered black schoolteacher in *God's Stepchildren;* the white theater owner who, though something of a fool, nonetheless benevolently invests in the black musical production in *Swing!;* and the white southern aristocrat in *Birthright,* who, though even more of a fool than the theater owner in *Swing!,* still hires and protects the black hero, finally leaving his entire white-aristocratic fortune to him, allowing the hero to establish two institutions of African-American uplift.

Most of Micheaux's lower classes are black, but some are white, and most of his upper classes are white, but some are black. Also, not all the lower classes, black or white, are bad, and not all the upper class, white or black, are bad. Micheaux's portrayal of light and dark skin reflects a complex value system that cannot easily be simplified to accommodate charges of racism or self-hatred. It is true that there may have been a tendency to favor light-skinned characters in Micheaux's work—in other words, to correlate light skin with the character traits of the first list above and to correlate dark skin with the second list. That tendency was anything but consistent, however, and its contradictions are often significant and telling. Also, the favoring of light skin can be partially explained, though perhaps not excused, by the broadly accepted convention in race movies (and in the minds of their audiences) of light-skinned heroes and heroines and dark-skinned antagonists. Micheaux's work may have been affected by that convention, but it also worked to counter it. Micheaux was himself dark, though his own dark color would not necessarily have prevented racial self-hatred from affecting his work as a project of denial (issues of skin tone are discussed in chapter 4).

Micheaux's work is not racial or ethnic in its basic values and rhetoric. Rather, it is "middle-class." The goodness and badness of characters in Micheaux's films and novels are not primarily defined by the characters' skin tones—white or black, light or dark. An example of a black film whose rhetoric is racial and ethnic would be Melvin Van Peebles's *Sweet Sweetback's Baadasssss Song* (1970), which focuses on specifically white oppression of blacks. The dedication of Van Peebles's book about the film reads: "This book—like the film—is dedicated to all the Brothers and Sisters who had enough of the Man."[3] "The Man" is white; the "Brothers and Sisters" are black. Van Peebles's position has an integrity that is based on the militant black movements of the 1960s and the underlying refusal by blacks to be patient with white racism. It has continuing relevance today, for similar reasons. The blaxploitation films that were inspired by *Sweetback*'s commercial success reflect the same racial rhetoric, the same militancy and refusal of patience, though their integrity was undermined by the corporate nature of their commercialism; for example, their production values were not true to life nor consistent with any realistic or thoughtful political philosophy.

Micheaux did not make films that could bear a dedication such as that of Van Peebles. Micheaux's rhetoric is more like Spike Lee's. Lee makes films with virtually all-black casts that deal with black issues such as gender relations, sexual relations, economic success, class, artistic integrity, fair play, and ethnic self-criticism. He does not shirk treating the issue of white culpability, but neither did Micheaux. Lee has dedicated films to militancy in the sense that his concluding two epigraphs in *Do the Right Thing* (1989) end with a militant quotation from Malcolm X. W. J. T. Mitchell has pointed out, however, that the narrative action of that film works to protect the white people threatened by black militancy; the film advocates violence to (white) property as a response to violence to a (black) person.[4] Paula J. Masood argues brilliantly that Lee connects money, property, and institutions directly to violence by having Mookie, at the end of *Do the Right Thing* (1988), redirect the black violence to white property—to the pizza "institution"—as the true source of Sal's (the pizza shop owner's) power; Masood sees Mookie's insistence on being paid by Sal after the shop is destroyed as a further insistence on the centrality of money in the equation of race and class.[5] And Mark Reid has argued further that Lee's use of the quotation from Malcolm X is inappropriate, because Lee's underlying middle-class values are inconsistent with the militancy that Malcolm X demonstrated at the direct risk of his person.[6]

Micheaux's films, like Spike Lee's, are more middle-class than militant. Like Lee's, they are directed at black problems and issues, though Micheaux was never able to interest white audiences in those problems. Lee's ability to reach white audiences with black issues is an important breakthrough in American popular culture.

The Idea of the Middle Class

Micheaux's critics have often denigrated Micheaux's relation to the middle class, as will be seen in later chapters. Blacks seeking advancement to middle-class rank have been accused of emulating whiteness. Fatuousness has been seen to be a common result of such emulations. Micheaux has been seen as having been thrust into the bourgeois economic class merely by virtue of the fact that he was a film producer. For some critics, the middle class has represented implicitly the unflattering traits associated with middling lives of reduced expectation, of endlessly delayed gratification that devalues pleasure, and of conformity that produces alienation, self-diminishment, quietism, and joylessness.

The middle class, however, was and is also the vast repository of most citizens in the developed world. Virtually 100 percent of all critics and scholars who have made judgments about Micheaux's middle-class values are themselves of the middle class—so is the writer of this study and, most likely, the reader. Thus, the term "middle class," though clearly appropriate in many ways to Micheaux's values, seems too inclusive to help in differentiating among the critical responses that have employed the term and thus too vague to assist in assigning a significant class position to Micheaux's films and their style. Kevin Gaines's use of the term "middle class" is useful, because he roots this term in detailed discussion of the specific historical problems of racial uplift, but Gaines's use of the term remains problematic in the sense that it is insufficiently distinguished from the bourgeois class, which, in the context of Micheaux's case, is misleading. Critical confusion surrounding Micheaux is thus partly a semantic problem. In order to search for relevant specificity within the idea of the middle class, a perspective needs to be constructed within the basic definitions of class.

An appropriate beginning point is provided by William Julius Wilson:

> Since "class" is a slippery concept that has been defined in a variety of ways in the social science literature, I should like to indicate that in this study the concept means any group of people who have more or less similar goods, services, or skills to offer for income in a given economic order and who therefore receive similar financial remuneration in the marketplace. One's economic class position determines in major measure one's life chances, including the chances for external living conditions and personal life experiences.[7]

Wilson's definition is appropriate in that it appears in a work that attempts to redirect attention from race to class, as Micheaux's work did. As Wilson warns above, however, "class" is a term that in common usage confuses several realms of ideas, and for the purposes of sorting out related confusions surrounding Micheaux, it is useful to explore some of the complexities in the idea of class (see Appendix 1).

Class and Evaluation

Aside from the relevance of class to Micheaux's overriding goal of uplift, class—because of its association with *artistic evaluation*—is of theoretic interest in any attempt to reassess the accomplishment of Micheaux. Underlying Thomas Cripps's negative evaluation of Micheaux's films in *Slow Fade to Black* was his uncritical acceptance of artistic criteria developed by Hollywood *classicism* (an evaluation Cripps revised in *Black Film as Genre;* see chapter 3, below, for a discussion of Cripps's work on Micheaux). The classic films of the 1930s "had class" in the sense meant by Gellius in the second century A.D. (see Appendix 1 for a discussion of the relation of class to the classicisms defined by Tullius, Gellius, and Amiri Baraka). The Hollywood films by Lubitsch, Cukor, and Hawks were, artistically, not only thoroughly elegant, beautiful, literary, witty, and well made, they were also expensive, and they were parables and icons of first-class citizenship, as defined by Tullius in the sixth century B.C. Compared to such standards of beauty, much of Micheaux's work has been found wanting.

The criticisms surrounding Micheaux's middle-class and bourgeois values reflect a confusion about Micheaux's own relation to the middle class. Discussions about Micheaux that consider the class positions from which films are made—whether Micheaux was automatically thrust into the bourgeois class; the validity of an analogy between jazz and race movies; and the confusions about class in the literature of Third Cinema—beg a more analytical model of class, a version of which is sketched in Appendix 1.

Micheaux's Class Position

Despite the confusion, it is clear that Micheaux's work is *not* a critique of capitalism. Nevertheless, the tendency for criticism of Micheaux to bifurcate into admiration or disdain for his entrepreneurship or for his production values is symptomatic of a polarity of normative values behind such criticisms and is indicative of the need to discuss Micheaux's relation, on the one hand, to capital and, on the other hand, to the proletariat and the "truly disadvantaged" (cf. Wilson, *The Truly Disadvantaged*). According to Marx, class is always defined by conflict, so any vertically situated class in the "middle" would be fighting two enemies, the one just above it and the one just below it. This idea suggests a model that is simpler than a mere listing of all the categories that make up the middle class, categories that are applicable also to most intellectuals, white or black, who are likely to write and publish about Micheaux. Also, Marx's simpler analytical model is more useful in explaining complex situations, since middle-class characters can be seen in any given act as engaging in either struggle or identification with a bourgeois or with a proletarian class interest or with a more or less analyzable mix of struggle and identification with both or either of Marx's opposing classes.

The question of the extent of Micheaux's association with bourgeois values needs to be treated in the light of a historical perspective that suggests that bourgeois values were—the goals of the 1920s and 1930s Old Left notwithstanding—a crucial practical necessity for African Americans after the collapse of Reconstruction and the beginning of the major black migrations. Fisk University, for example, could not have proceeded in the 1870s on any other basis than the raising of funds from established groups in America, groups whose own principles were thoroughly bourgeois. The enormity of the material problem of "racial" uplift—in the short term, the education of thousands of teachers for millions of children; in the middle term, the education of thousands of leaders for hundreds of black institutions; and in the long term, the education of millions of white Americans so that black Americans could be accepted as full citizens—might have demanded, ideally, some other system besides that of the bourgeoisie, but no other system was at hand. The very enormity of the problem in 1871 made any call for help from any other system simply irrelevant. Any argument claiming that African Americans in 1871 would have been better off aligning themselves with more radical political ideals has no practical basis in history, since the potential for success of any such ideals or associated movements could not have been assessed by the parties most affected. Most African Americans, many of them recently freed and many others profoundly rural, equivalent to agrarian peasants, did not have the experiential basis for the sophisticated judgment that, because of American "exceptionalism" (resistance to socialism), any successful negotiation of radical politics in America would certainly have required. Even if they had had such sophistication, they might well have judged radical measures to be inappropriate, since, in fact, America has never been close to considering a non-bourgeois regime. There has never been an opposition party significant enough to challenge the fundamentals of economic liberalism. (The issues of Micheaux's and African Americans' relation to the American "Left" will be addressed further in *Visions of Uplift*, forthcoming.)

The extent of Micheaux's alignment with the bourgeois class is the issue in Jane Gaines's questioning of any analogy between Micheaux's films and African-American music of the 1920s and 1930s; Gaines says that in any attempt to theorize film in terms of music, one should "be wary of the tendency to idealize an African-American cinema that might have seen a Golden Age analogous to the Golden Age of jazz," because "analogies between film and other forms . . . have a built-in tendency to gloss over economic realities." Her warning suggests that the elevated expense of film production in relation to music production may "thrust filmmakers (no matter what their class origins) into the bourgeois class."[8]

Gaines's emphasis on Micheaux's class position, defined, as she has implied, as fundamentally economic in the Marxist sense, is appropriate (as long as one keeps in mind the historical perspective of American exceptionalism and its rejection of socialism). In spite of the appropriateness of the question, however, the jazz-music/race-movie analogy that she challenges may still be useful if one does not idealize the golden age of, not just African-American cinema, but jazz itself. Jazz, as Baraka has pointed out, and even blues, are already partially assimilated forms. Baraka has speculated that the prototype of the black middle class was probably formed about ten seconds after the first slave ship arrived in America.[9] Jazz, in particular, would never have had a golden age if it had not modified its style so as to be acceptable to wider audiences. Often that meant bending to pressures to become acceptable to the middle class, to white people, and to the bourgeoisie. Often such revision required various kinds of fatuousness—consider the case of Louis Armstrong: he was arguably the greatest jazz innovator and improviser ever, but he was also arguably made fatuous through his participation in classicizing jazz. In other words, jazz of the golden age can be accused of the same critical failures of bourgeoisness and fatuousness that have been applied to Micheaux.

It is true that the analogy of music to film does not always hold at the level of primary production itself, but in significant ways, it holds more than one might imagine. Admittedly, the production of solo music only needs a single individual and the basic means to support that individual—any economic class position, even poverty, will do. Classic blues and jazz of the golden age were, however, relatively well-capitalized art forms. It probably took as much money in a given year to maintain a big band as it took for Micheaux to produce whatever films he produced in one year, maybe more. The difference in economic class between a primitive jazz solo and the typical big band of the golden age becomes staggering if the expenses and capitalization of broadcast and recording are considered, and clearly these technologies are elements of classic jazz. While it might have taken considerably more for Micheaux to produce a film with the production values and distribution apparatus of a Hollywood classic film, that is precisely the break point in the scale of capital that this study has tried to emphasize—*that* is the break point that would have thrust Micheaux into the bourgeois class; but Micheaux avoided it. And though it is probably true that it took substantially more to support a classic white swing band, such as those of Paul Whiteman and Benny Goodman, than it did to support even the greatest black swing bands, the truly exponential leap in capital accumulation in the ontogeny of large ensemble music is the *classical* symphony orchestra. It costs roughly the same amount to support a symphony orchestra for one year as it costs to produce a Hollywood movie. An analogous leap in capital accumulation in the film world can be found in the hundred-fold difference in capitalization between race movies and Hollywood movies. The very fact of that difference (the 1% capitalization or 99% undercapitalization of race movies, compared with Hollywood movies) is what kept race movie producers from being thrust into the bourgeois class, since, on the contrary, they were held below it (depending on where the borderline of the bourgeois class is drawn). In Marx's terms, the exponential disparity of capitalization—what Martha Rosler calls "factors of ten"[10]—placed producers like Micheaux in class conflict, not alignment, with the bourgeoisie. It was a conflict that played out in the fabric of daily life of Micheaux as producer, since he had to keep Hollywood in his sights at all times. Hollywood threatened Micheaux's existence at every moment for more than two decades, and it eventually defeated him, though not before he had substantially succeeded in creating a middle-class career and in modeling a middle-class cinema that stands as a historical legacy and, as such, a challenge and a torch for succeeding generations.

Live and Dead Labor

The value of life and culture on a human-to-human scale before the infusion of capital is analogous to what Marx called the value of direct labor, and direct labor is, under capitalism, structurally in conflict with dead labor or accumulated capital. There is no question that the infusion of African-American values into the mainstream has enriched the dominant culture and that the infusion should continue. There is also, however, no question that the most important aspects—the human-scale aspects—of those African-American values were already there in pre-classic black music and in race movies. There is no inherent improvement in the artistic and cultural value of Spike Lee's or Charles Burnett's films over that associated with Oscar Micheaux's films, and with increased (accumulated) capital, there has developed a softening of the stylistic expression of structural class conflict (this softening comes with the improved class position of African-American middle-class filmmakers in American life). For example, Spike Lee's and Charles Burnett's early films, such as (respectively) *She's Gotta Have It* (1986) and *Killer of Sheep* (1977), look more like Micheaux's films than do their later films; the styles of those early films, when compared with mainstream film styles, reflected class difference and struggle. In no sense are Lee's and Burnett's early films less artistically valuable than their later films, such as (respectively) *Mo' Better Blues* (1990) and *To Sleep with Anger* (1990); the major difference between the earlier and later films of each of these superb filmmakers, other than the possible evidence (or lack of it) of individual artistic growth in one or the other case, is the infusion of capital that raised the production values of the later films. That manifold increase perhaps in fact does thrust those filmmakers into the bourgeois class, because it tends to remove the evidence of class struggle from the films' *styles* (though not from their subject matter, in either case). Spike Lee's expensive production values in *Malcolm X* (1992), for example, have been defended as an appropriate way to represent the global scale and amplified social import of Malcolm X's later thinking;[11] but that defense begs the question of whether a message couched in such production values contradicts the message of Malcolm X's own life of principled avoidance of the temptations of money, class, and privilege.[12] There may be good reasons why Charles Burnett and Spike Lee should make their later films in styles that are increasingly bourgeois, but those reasons have nothing to do with any inherent increase in artistic quality; artistic quality may in fact be damaged by such "improvement," since capital has the effect of erasing the history of labor, abstractly and materially mediating in an alienating way the human-to-human—including artist-to-audience—channels of expression and communication.

Conclusion

The concern in this study for proposing an analogy between the histories of black music and black film will be to emphasize the value of the poorer forms, not the classical eras, of each. The original analysis of Micheaux's inexpensive style, to which Jane Gaines has referred, stated that the so-called amateurishness of Micheaux would be a saving grace in replacing the glib slickness provided by the dead labor in Hollywood classicism.[13] Implicit in that judgment is the equating of race movies not with classic jazz but with pre-classic black music. Nevertheless, Gaines's implied point—that pre-classic film (e.g., Micheaux's *Body and Soul* or Spencer Williams's *Blood of Jesus*) is more expensive than pre-classic music (e.g., a Ma Rainey or a Robert Johnson tour)—is well taken. Whether that significant fact thrusts pre-classic film producers into the bourgeois class remains, however, an unanswered question.

In answering that question, it is important to suggest where or how the line is to be drawn in determining class position or what level of capital accumulation comprises membership in the bourgeois class. That is not easy to do. This study makes a case for Micheaux's work as middle-class, and as demonstrably in conflict with the bourgeois class.[14]

3 Twoness and Micheaux's Style

The implied nemesis of African-American uplift has always been racism. One of the force fields through which Micheaux had to negotiate a path toward his goal of middle-class status was that characterized by the polarized extremes of African-ness and American-ness. W. E. B. DuBois presented the now-familiar, paradigmatic notion of "twoness" in the first few pages of *The Souls of Black Folk:*

> It is a peculiar sensation, this double-consciousness, this sense of always looking at one's soul by the tape of a world that looks on in amused contempt and pity. One ever feels his twoness,—an American, a Negro; two souls, two thoughts, two unreconciled strivings; two warring ideals in one dark body, whose dogged strength alone keeps it from being torn asunder.[1]

African Americans, that is, individually have faced the simultaneous possibilities of two identities whose relations to each other are bipolar and strained, creating a dilemma that each African-American individual must somehow resolve. The horns of the dilemma are to be found (1) in the dominant white culture that cannot be ignored and that has itself tended to demand and at the same time to reject the assimilation of people of color and (2) in the ethnic black culture of the African-American community. The concept of twoness has recognized a resistance by blacks to their assimilation by white culture, a will to retain a black ethnic identity. Whereas assimilation seemed necessary for survival by blacks in America, it also threatened black self-esteem and the integrity of their African identity.

Thomas Cripps has identified a debilitating dilemma for African-American film that he has associated with DuBois's concept of twoness. Cripps's book *Slow Fade to Black* was the groundbreaking work on the history of race movies, early films made by blacks for black audiences.[2] Cripps's monumental effort, under difficult research conditions, to locate and interpret the primary and secondary source materials of black cinema—alongside the prior pioneering efforts by Donald Bogle and Daniel J. Leab[3]—adumbrates an ethnic cinema that was previously invisible. Cripps's thesis is founded on the historical myth of the American melting pot and the phenomenon of assimilation, addressing black cinema as a problem of non-assimilation.

Cripps has proposed that the future of black cinema and of black criticism and spectatorship lies properly with assimilation and, thus, with Hollywood. Though he attempts, in *Slow Fade to Black,* to find works of artistic value that were created by the "black underground" outside Hollywood, which included Micheaux and the Colored Players, Cripps nevertheless concludes that no black producer was sufficiently capitalized to produce good films (Cripps revised this opinion in his next book, *Black Film as Genre*). Cripps also concludes that Hollywood was sufficiently capitalized to co-opt any successful idea produced by black producers of race movies—hence, the double meaning of Cripps's title *Slow Fade to Black*—the slow fade-*out* of the *independent* black producer (the "blackout" of blackness) and the slow fade-*in* of the *Hollywood* black producer (the slowness of the emergence of assimilated blackness).

The *Slow Fade* thesis, however, undervalues the loss represented by the fade-out of the independent race movie, blaming that loss on the inadequacies of independent films. *Slow Fade* also overvalues the gain, both realized and potential, in the African-American fade-in to mainstream film.

After posing the dilemma of twoness, and after considerable detailed criticism of particular films and filmmakers, including Micheaux, Cripps indeed ends his study by celebrating reforms in Hollywood as the best hope for black cinema. Of the written agreement reached by "delegates of the National Association for the Advancement of Colored People [NAACP] and the heads of several Hollywood studios," who "met and codified some social changes and procedures" in 1942, Cripps says: "The studios agreed to abandon pejorative racial roles, to place Negroes in positions as extras they could reasonably be expected to occupy in society, and to begin the slow task of integrating blacks into the ranks of studio technicians."[4] Cripps capped the initial statement of his thesis by observing that "[t]he 1942 agreement accomplished far more than allowing a few blacks to appear in roles that were not overtly racist. It changed the whole tune and nature of Hollywood's response to the Afro-American's role in film and, by extension, in American life as well."[5] The optimism of this denouement seems inappropriate, however, since the agreement of 1942 addressed only the problem of assimilation—only, that is, one horn of the dilemma. The assimilation of blacks might have been expected to ethnicize Hollywood to some extent, but there was little historical evidence on Hollywood screens—in relation to black or any other ethnic groups—that the expectation was realized. The recent successes of black cinema on Hollywood screens are the result of Spike Lee's successful assault on Hollywood as an *independent*—he forced his way in by making money on the outside first. Any success derived from the agreement of 1942 to integrate blacks into the Hollywood culture industry would appear to be a gain primarily for assimilation, for one side of the twoness dilemma but not for the other. While it is the case today that more positive black characters appear on American film and television screens, their African-American characteristics are very often either reduced (Bill Cosby) or caricatured (Eddie Murphy). And when African-American characteristics are delivered in a fully rounded fashion, as in *Frank's Place*, Charles Burnett's *To Sleep with Anger* (1990), and Julie Dash's *Daughters of the Dust* (1991), they are often poorly handled by the industry. Still, Cripps is certainly right in emphasizing that Hollywood should be held responsible for its extreme and peculiar misrepresentation of blacks. Nevertheless, even though the efforts of DuBois and the NAACP that resulted in the 1942 agreements were necessary and laudable, they were not and are not sufficient. In response to an earlier published version of this chapter, Cripps has pointed to facts and figures that are signs of progress in black representation in Hollywood; Jesse Rhines has recently argued, however, that similar facts and figures represent a society still racked by fundamental racial, gender, and class injustices and imbalances, thus indicating a continuing need for independent film.[6]

The predictable effects of the 1942 agreements are analogous to the effects of the 1947 decision to sign Jackie Robinson to the roster of the Brooklyn Dodgers, a decision that opened major-league baseball to the assimilation of black players. As Nelson George points out in *The Death of Rhythm & Blues,* that was "a major event in the integration of America" and "now lies at the heart of this nation's popular culture." He also points out, however, that

> Unfortunately, not too many people cared that it meant the end of Negro baseball and the demise of a "naturally integrated" black institution. Ask an older black man about it and you'll be told sagely, "That is the price you have to pay for entry into the game. Look at the number of black players who dominate Major League Baseball, making millions and becoming role models for the nation." Yet if, following the advice of Bob Woodward and Carl Bernstein's Deep Throat, we follow the money, we see that this trade-off, while on the surface great for blacks, was in reality an economic steal for baseball's owners.

George was drawing on the analogy of black baseball to support his thesis that black music had been co-opted by the white owners of larger institutions, but the same analogy applies even more faithfully to the co-opting of black film talent by the 1942 agreements between the NAACP and Hollywood film companies. Hollywood, like baseball, had been lobbied hard by blacks who wished to open it up, whereas black musicians did not have to lobby the music industry to have their talents co-opted (and they were co-opted in a more underhanded way). As George makes clear, the sort of institutional co-opting that unifies the three historical examples of this triple analogy has consequences in two related dimensions—representational imagination and economic class:

> Since Robinson's debut, blacks have done the same thing in Major League Baseball that they have done in popular music: entertain, make large salaries, and generate money for businesses that funnel precious little of it back into black communities. They feed the dream machine that tells black youths that entertaining—on a stage or a ball field [or a movie screen-JRG]—is the surest way to leap racial barriers. But without access to power, blacks lost more than they gained economically from integrating Major League Baseball.[7]

Perhaps Micheaux's greatest contribution, the one that all critics have recognized, was his establishment and successful operation of a black film institution over an extended period, a going concern analogous to pre-integration black baseball. And no matter what one thinks of Micheaux's actual films, what is not debatable is that they could not have been made any other way—certainly not through any arrangements approximating the NAACP–studio agreements of 1942. Micheaux's institutional accomplishment—his ability to turn out film after film, addressing directly the needs of an all-black audience—has not been replicated since, though it is more than half a century after the 1942 agreements.[8]

A Knowledge Worth Having

The issue of twoness is important for understanding Micheaux, race movies, and Cripps's thesis about them. As DuBois noted, twoness is not an enviable state, and the value of the knowledge of twoness in no way *justifies* the color line. The knowledge, however, may still be valuable, and its probable value justifies not only the study of Micheaux but also the place of race movies in any canon that claims to represent American cinema, or a cinema of American society. Cultural theorist bell hooks makes a related point in discussing whiteness in the black imagination, and Carol Clover makes an analogous point about gender ambiguity in spectators of modern horror films.[9] A canon of such a cinema would need to include representation of the dialectical aspects of American hegemony, including not only Hollywood's role in that hegemony but also the effect of Hollywood hegemony on African-American identity. Robert Stam considers this sort of "twoness," or what he calls "relational vision," as an advantageous aspect of a Bakhtinian approach to ethnic studies:

> A Bakhtinian approach thinks "from the margins," seeing Native Americans, African Americans and Hispanics, for example, not as interest groups to be added on to a preexisting pluralism, but rather as being at the very core of the American experience from the beginning, each offering an invaluable "dialogical angle" on the national experience. . . . [A] Bakhtinian approach recognizes *an epistemological advantage on the part of those who are oppressed and therefore bicultural.* The oppressed, because they are obliged by circumstances and the imperatives of survival to know both the dominant and the marginal culture, are *ideally placed* to deconstruct the mystifications of the dominant group.[10] [Emphasis added]

Cripps has, in *Slow Fade to Black,* resolved the dilemma of twoness solely by reference to Hollywood, thus opting for assimilation. There is no evidence so far, however, that Hollywood can handle controversial differences of identity as significant as the color line, economic class, patriarchal sexism, or sexual taboo. Robin Wood's and Carol Clover's studies of sexuality and gender ambiguity and repression in the horror film might seem to suggest that Hollywood can and does deal in a healthy way with difference and denial; but, in fact, their theses ultimately reveal that Hollywood's treatments of gender "bending" leave the prevailing gender relations intact and that independent, inexpensive, non-Hollywood films treat repressed material more directly.[11] Hollywood has certainly not taken the lead in broaching, much less celebrating, significant differences in society. That sort of leadership in cinema must come from undercapitalized and unassimilated independent and alternative cinemas, such as race movies, documentary, and the avant garde. Cripps's answer to the dilemma—to turn away from "underground" films—seems, therefore, inadequate.[12]

If Cripps could, in *Slow Fade to Black* (and again in *Making Movies Black*), write off independent race movies by saying that black-produced cinema acquiesced in segregation, placed white cupidity off limits as a theme, rehashed the stereotypes for which Hollywood had been blamed, set black against black, and imitated white movies, it is because he has accepted the rhetoric and aesthetics of assimilation in Hollywood.[13] All of Cripps's specific criticisms of independent race movies (listed above) are answerable. For example, it is not fair to say that black-produced cinema "acquiesced" in segregation when the necessity to avoid topics of integration was imposed by white censorship and when black audiences were themselves divided on the benefits of integration—one could be "for" separation without being "acquiescent" to segregation. Race movies did not "place white cupidity off-limits"; white cupidity was placed off-limits by white boards of censorship. Micheaux fought such censor boards for years and still managed to treat white oppression both directly and indirectly in films such as *Within Our Gates, Symbol of the Unconquered, The Girl from Chicago, Birthright,* and others. Some race movies may have "rehashed" Hollywood stereotypes of blacks, but some did not, and some race movies, such as Micheaux's, developed a complex critique of those stereotypes. If race movies sometimes "set black against black," then those movies reflected the reality of all-black-cast narratives as well as the realities of the larger black community, which, like any community, was unanimous on virtually no issue. If some race movies "imitated white movies," they did so only to a greater or lesser degree. White movies were the only movies that existed; to the extent that there was a community standard of cinema, it was a white standard. Even those filmmakers working against that standard had to work with a legacy that was both unavoidable and basically—because historically—white. To reject on the basis of white imitation all non-Hollywood cinemas that used or referred to some aspects of the Hollywood contributions to film style would be to ignore the issue of hegemony and to misunderstand some basic processes of culture, such as those discussed by Harold Bloom in *The Anxiety of Influence.*[14]

Twoness and Style

No existing Micheaux film looks much like a well-made Hollywood film, and Cripps's initial intolerance, in *Slow Fade to Black,* of the deviation from Hollywood style in Micheaux's films even in the 1970s, 1980s, and 1990s represents a generally negative or uncertain attitude about Micheaux's accomplishment.

Cripps has described the pervasive, typical mistakes in Micheaux's style and has shown that Micheaux's production company was aware of them but unable to correct them because of the prohibitive expense of higher shooting ratios, retakes, master shots, and professional editing. The apparatus of Cripps's own critical assessment, however, ignores the contradiction inherent in twoness. At the beginning of his discussion of Micheaux, Cripps has described the central dilemma for Micheaux (and black-produced race movies) as the "temptation to make mirror images of white movies [in which case] . . . success itself might be a false god for Negroes."[15] Throughout the discussions on Micheaux, Cripps uses the term "mirror images" to signify this dilemma.

One Horn of a Dilemma

The no-win, mirror-image dilemma in race movies and in Micheaux's work remains unresolved in Cripps's treatment. Instead of holding up this dilemma as a structural contradiction (black success at imitating white movies comprises failure; success equals failure) that illuminates the struggles of black filmmakers and critics, Cripps has alternated in his loyalties toward each pole of the dilemma. It remains difficult to discuss Micheaux or the phenomenon of race movies at all until something is said about the possible cinematic outcomes of the dilemma of twoness.

Cripps's critical stance urges assimilation rather than confrontation of the dilemma of black production, a dilemma in which assimilation was half the problem. He regrets the lost opportunity for successful black movie making in Hollywood without positing what that success might mean and how it might accommodate the dilemma of twoness that was previously introduced. Furthermore, in his argument, Cripps castigated criticisms of Matthews and Ottley in the black press that seem now to have suggested the most responsible approach to the dilemma:

> Roi Ottley, a major figure among black newspapermen, called forth even less precise objections and settled for a rhetorical broad racial boosterism:
>
>> "The Green Pastures" will[,] no doubt, receive magnificent and glowing accounts in the Negro press . . . and unhappily so for the Negro public. . . . Negro newspapers on the whole have a false sense of values. . . . They seem to work from the premise that anytime a Negro appears in a play or picture which the whites have produced it should be applauded regardless of its merits. . . . This department goes on record as feeling that Oscar Micheaux, with his inferior equipment, would have produced a better picture.[16]

Ottley (here) and Matthews (elsewhere) insisted that no matter what the technical and stylistic problems, the only future for the production of black culture was through black people, and the only future for black films was through black filmmakers. What heretofore had been seen as technical problems and mistakes in the production values of race movies might then be seen instead as elements of style and texture, as, for example, the "rough" carving is now understood in the sculpture of Elijah Pierce or as the rough acting, dubbing, and general directing of many of Rainer Werner Fassbinder's films is understood to be integral to their artistic success:

No doubt [Fassbinder] was temperamentally incapable of working in any other way than he did, but this is to say that he was incapable of making anything but flawed films. . . .

The advantage of setting a furious pace was that no-one could get bored, and everyone was under tension, especially the actors. The disadvantage was that there would be a good deal of botching in every phase of making the film, from scripting to post-synchronizing.[17]

The criteria for "successes" and for failures would then have to be derived from a culture of twoness—from the culture of the maker (whether rural or urban, working- or middle-class, gay or straight), not from the apartheid and assimilationist Hollywood industry.

Judging the Films

It is not necessary to assume that the conventions of Hollywood cinema constitute the only valid basis for narrative cinema. What would a "good" black cinema look like, then, if it did not imitate classical white cinema? Actually, though scholars such as Pearl Bowser, Mark Reid, bell hooks, Ed Guerrero, Jessie Rhines, and Clyde Taylor have provided answers to this question, it should not be necessary to delineate qualities of good black cinema; students of world cinema are familiar with many styles of narrative cinema other than those of the classic Hollywood film. Many of those films have successfully reached supportive audiences, both mass and non-mass audiences, such as those who responded to Melvin Van Peebles's *Sweet Sweetback's Baadasssss Song* (1971). *Sweetback* made money as a black-produced independent film, but the movement it spawned, called "blaxploitation," consisted primarily of Hollywood-produced films. Such co-optation suggests that the problem for black independent producers lies not with their films or their audiences but rather in the machinery of distribution and exhibition, an issue that Roy Armes emphasizes in his book on Third-World cinema.[18] Black independent filmmakers can and do make movies in all sorts of ways, just as black musicians, ministers, painters, sculptors, and writers have created different kinds of improvisational music, oral jeremiad, visual art, and narratives, all of which could be understood by their own audiences and which were later celebrated by Eurocentric audiences as well. The contribution of these forms to art, pleasure, and understanding has often been the greater for their ethnic authenticity and has come to be seen as diminished by any forced concessions to classicism.

Since Micheaux did not necessarily assume Hollywood standards, his films may be based on assumed or invented syntagmatics unknown in the film industry. White cinema is important to Micheaux's work, both positively and negatively, but it is not determinant. Micheaux's style and production values were appropriate to his circumstances and can be considered to be artistically limiting only if we allow that the super-refined style and the high production values of *Gone with the Wind* (1939) are artistically limiting in their own way.

The Issue of Assimilation

Micheaux's treatment of racial or ethnic issues has received as much disapprobation as his stylistic artistry. When Cripps concluded that "race movies tended to acquiesce in segregation, place white cupidity off-limits as a theme, rehash many stereotypes . . . , set black against black, and imitate white movies,"[19] he characterized these attributes as failures, at least in Micheaux's films. As bell hooks has pointed out, however, Micheaux's films *interrogated* those issues, among many others.[20] Hollywood movies themselves certainly could not have been relied on to deal with those issues or with most of the other issues Micheaux explored; it is equally improbable that Hollywood's content and style could ever reflect such sensitivity to twoness and contradiction as do Micheaux's content and style.

According to Neal Gabler's thesis in *An Empire of Their Own,* Hollywood was constructed almost entirely by immigrants who wanted desperately to assimilate to the characteristics of the founding groups of Europe and New England. Hollywood created an empire of illusion that would do just that—turn immigrants into the image of the power elite, the American of "New England–Wall Street–Middle West money," through the ideals and aesthetics of Hollywood movies.[21] The fact that immigrant Jews created the "White Anglo-Saxon Protestant" cinema *par excellence* may seem to contradict any thesis about the importance of ethnically produced cinemas. It proves, however, very little in itself. It suggests the tendency of a group in power—such as white Anglo-Saxon Protestants in America—to be imitated and flattered; it suggests the power of such a dominant group to attract services from ambitious sub-dominant groups—such as immigrant Jews; and it exemplifies a solid basis for the fears of those critics who point out that even African-American cinema often seeks to look white. Nevertheless, the construction of an assimilationist Hollywood style by immigrant Jews disproves nothing about the value of cultural diversity and the need to encourage it.

Assimilation has had a strong economic impetus, owing to the radical fragmentation of the American labor and consumer markets during the development of mass production. The factories and urban centers were attracting new ethnic groups all the time, including southern blacks, who were in the midst of their greatest northward migration. D. W. Griffith and Micheaux were getting into filmmaking at about this time (c. 1908–1918). Hollywood, itself seeking a dependable mass market for its films, began trying to assimilate the new urban diversity. In order to cover over the (substantive) near-impossibility of such a job, Hollywood developed a (formal) style of gloss, illusionism, and closure that gave the appearance of a common system of values for all Americans, an appearance of unity that undoubtedly played a part in forming a broad exclusionism, one reflecting intolerance of difference and twoness.

Micheaux's style is sometimes better understood as a retaining of earlier film traits, from before the advent of glossy illusionism, rather than as a failed imitation of white assimilationist movies. His style is more closely related to the glossing of a *text* (such as African-American life) than to the glossing *over* of a rough surface (such as value differences among whites). A non-assimilative style that glosses a living struggle with twoness—a twoness that, as DuBois said, threatens the dark body with "being torn asunder"—can itself, as a style, be expected to reflect the turmoil of that struggle.

The Case of *The Girl from Chicago*

The Girl from Chicago (1932) serves well as an example of Micheaux's non-assimilative "crooked-stick" style, partly because it is not one of his better films, from the point of view of conventional Hollywood style. Since it is an extreme case, any diminishment of disdain for it, or any overlooked values that can be claimed for it, might strengthen the case for Micheaux's overall accomplishment. In *The Girl from Chicago,* Mary Austin is a middle-aged southern black woman who runs a boarding house in the small town of Batesburg, Mississippi (reminiscent of the Patesville of *The Conjure Woman,* 1899, by one of Micheaux's favorite black writers, Charles Chesnutt) and who wishes to send her sister north to seek her fortune as a singer; Austin's boarding-house savings have all been set aside for that purpose. When Norma Shepard, the female lead in the film, arrives in town to take up her position as a new teacher, she stays at Austin's boarding house. The boarding house is the setting for most of the action in the first half of the film, since it also temporarily houses the male lead, Alonzo White, who eventually captures the villain there, thereby saving Norma.

The first five minutes of the film are composed of some thirty short and medium-length shots—averaging about ten seconds each, with one take of about sixty seconds—of disturbing content (peonage and potential rape) and of disturbing style (flagrantly discontinuous matching, expressionistic shooting, some awkward blocking and acting, and some practically comic, but also illusion-shattering, audio glitches). Then there occurs a 'sequence shot' (an entire sequence of "shots" in a single take, with no edits—a 'long take') of over three minutes, in which Mary Austin, in medium shot, stands beside her sister, who, seated in the foreground at the piano, performs an entire song. The transition to this shot (the long take) is accented by a strong piano tone that is struck a fraction of a beat after the cut that begins the long take. Thus, the viewer springs, via syncopation, into this sequence-shot scene out of a previous scene that has been peculiarly and disturbingly fragmented by editing. Mary Austin's sister then sings "Blue Lagoon" in an impressive, but imperfect, light-operatic voice. Partly because the recording quality is poor, the voice seems to break up occasionally, and the humble, upright piano sounds tinny. The weak, single-point lighting and the hard, live acoustics seem consistent with the low production values and discontinuities in editing and with the amateurish, declamatory style of acting of the previous scene. The effect produced is bound to be excruciating or inappropriately comic to anyone used only to Hollywood production qualities.

Fig. 5. The long take (this single shot is about three minutes long) of Mary Austin (Eunice Brooks) in *The Girl from Chicago* as she admires her sister's rendition of "The Blue Lagoon" and wishes that she had the money to send her sister north to become part of the increasingly successful renaissance of African-American culture.

Yet for a viewer sympathetic to the economic status of the characters (characters for whom the viewer is meant to care and for whom there is no narrative reason not to care), this shot sequence appears realistic and is appealing. There is both hope and pathos in the desires of the two sisters, emotions that are articulated in the "grain" of the untrained but beautiful voice and in the "grain of the apparatus" through which that voice is presented. The "grain" of Micheaux's style is analogous in some ways to the grain of Panzera's voice, and the polished and perfect style of Hollywood is analogous to Fischer-Dieskau's voice, as characterized in Roland Barthes's famous essay "The Grain of the Voice."[22]

There is integrity in the unity of time, place, and action that sets this song apart as a vignette for special appreciation and as a stylistic haven from the surrounding "confusion." The title ("Blue Lagoon") and theme of the song reinforce the stylistic effect of haven. The hopes and fears in this scene are stylistically represented in the contrasts: the confusion of the previous editing vs. the unity of the long take; the roughness of the audio recording and of the untrained voice vs. the smoothness of the vocal talent and the self-confidence of the singer. These stylistic representations, whether conscious or not, are appropriate.

Even though there is pathos as well as hope, the scene is not pathetic. Pathos does not dominate, since Micheaux's audience would have been aware that some black singers much like Mary Austin's sister (as well as writers, dancers, musicians, and composers) were "making it" in Chicago and Harlem at the time. Jazz, blues, jazz dance, and the Harlem Renaissance were common knowledge in 1932. In the second half of *The Girl from Chicago,* most of the primary and secondary characters, in fact, move to Harlem. The line "Home to Harlem!," uttered by Alonzo in celebration of the move from Batesburg to Harlem, is a reference to the famous novel of that title by one of the leading lights of the Harlem Renaissance, Claude McKay. Many of those who succeeded during the Renaissance period were not "New Negroes" or eastern-educated "dicty"-style ("high-toned") artists, and many of those who were at least partly dicty were also loyal to their humble origins in the South, as was Zora Neale Hurston, for example. Mary Austin's sister's song of the blue lagoon is more dicty, certainly, than Bessie Smith's or Billie Holiday's songs, but it is not more dicty than some of Marion Anderson's or Ethel Waters's songs, and the very successes of people like Smith, Holiday, Anderson, and Waters would have lent credibility to the Austin family's hopes. Micheaux's scene represents the hopes and fears of the migration realistically, something which Hollywood had never done.

There are several possible objections to this scene. It is possible to object that the sister's voice is not a good one, that it breaks in places—but so did the voices of Louis Armstrong and Bob Dylan, although their styles were more ironic. Armstrong and Dylan were not always ironic, but to the extent that they were, it was part of what made them great. Mary Austin's sister, however, is not meant to represent greatness—she represents hope and pathos, and she may turn out to be unfortunate enough to learn irony too.

It is possible to object that the shot is too dark. But the darkness of the shooting in *The Girl from Chicago* serves its aesthetic purpose in representing an interior scene in a depression-era, lower-middle-class house of American Victorian or southern gothic origins, a house that would typically be dark, compartmentalized into small rooms, and run down. Its lighting loosely resembles the lighting in certain paintings by Micheaux's contemporaries, Thomas Hart Benton, Grant Wood, Edward Hopper, and Charles Burchfield. For Micheaux to have lit this scene strongly and from the classical three points would have given an inappropriately glossy effect. Had Micheaux had the money to shoot "correctly," the scene might have changed stylistically from realistically oppressive to reassuring, mediocre, conventional real*ism*. In avoiding such conventionality, Micheaux's work is a significant but overlooked precursor to Italian neo-realism, which changed the course of film style in the late 1940s.

It is possible to object that Micheaux's shot is grainy. Yet shots in cinéma vérité and in direct cinema, semi-documentary, neo-realism, new wave, and underground styles are often grainy. All those styles are accepted (though they were not originally accepted) as mature, purposeful, and effective. They became accepted stylistically as being appropriate to the circumstances of their production and to their representational systems, once those systems were understood. The grain in Micheaux's shot reflects lower-middle-class tawdriness and material thinness, approximating the economic status of the (diegetic) boarding house and of the (real-life) film's producer. Micheaux's interiors are reminiscent of the Farm Security Administration (FSA) photographs of the southern poor (those of tenant farmers, for example, by photographers Walker Evans and Russell Lee). The content represented in Micheaux is lower-middle-class instead of "dirt" poor—Mary Austin's boarding house is plain and run down but not dirty and falling apart, like the FSA tenant-farm houses. The style of Micheaux's shots is closer to the production style and aesthetics of his subjects than Evans's and Lee's style is to the style and aesthetics of their subjects, and thus, Micheaux's subjects are less set off, embossed, or foregrounded by the style of their representation. Micheaux's dark, grainy shots look like the faded, halftone newspaper and magazine art that decorates the sharecroppers' houses in Evans's and Lee's photographs. Evans and Lee reproduced those sharecroppers' interiors, but they represented those often messy, poverty-stricken interiors through the *artists'* styles of photography, which were often elegant and well-produced. Micheaux as a producer, however, was much closer to the economic status and the messy style of his lower-class subjects or to the respectable (rather than refined) values of his middle-class ideals than Evans and Agee were to the status and styles of their subjects.

It is possible to object that the piano in this sequence shot is tinny and out of tune and is presented as such without irony, thus making the scene ludicrous—yet the piano in one of Benny Carter's jazz groups, "Benny Carter and His Swing Quintet," is tinny and out of tune, and it is not used ironically. The instruments in Carter's "Waltzing the Blues" and "Jingle Bells" sound, in relation to earlier jazz, like the "original instruments" movement of Gustav Leonhardt and Nikolaus Harnoncourt in classical music today. A review of one of the major recording projects of the original-instruments movement points to some criticism of that movement that is reminiscent of the criticism of race music and race movies' amateurism and inexpensive production values:

> even sympathetic scholars could find the Leonhardt–Harnoncourt approach disconcerting, what with its clipped non-legato articulations, its rhythmic alterations and dislocations, its easily satirized dynamic bulges, its brusquely punctuated recitatives, its flippant tempos, not to mention the tiny forces, the green and sickly-sounding boy soprano soloists, above all the recalcitrant, sometimes ill-tuned "original instruments."
>
> Some were downright indignant at the loss of traditional scale and weight. The venerable musicologist Paul Henry Lang blasted the "frail performances with inadequate ensembles."

In defense of the original-instruments movement, the same review says the following:

> Mr. Harnoncourt's style has taken on attributes that "performance practice" alone could never have vouchsafed. They can only have come from those "contemptible" Lutheran texts and their unaccommodating polemic. His increasingly hortatory and unbeautiful way of performing Bach reached a peak about halfway through

the series, and the intervening decade has done nothing to lessen its power to shock—or disgust. If you seek contact with the essential Bach at full hideous strength, Mr. Harnoncourt's performances remain the only place to go.[23]

Analogously, if you seek contact with the essential African America at full "hideous" (unwhitewashed) strength, Benny Carter's style of jazz and Micheaux's style of race movies are "the only place to go."

There is no doubt about Benny Carter's ability to produce more polished music, since he has spent much of his career writing music and arrangements for very smooth orchestras, Hollywood films, and mainstream television programs and commercials. His choice of tinny original instruments for some of his recording sessions was consciously judged by him to be aesthetically legitimate, and it resulted in some of his most engaging work. Micheaux's performers and instruments were also legitimate, in spite of the fact that Micheaux's choices may have been less intentionally aesthetic, because they were more severely bound by economic and cultural constraints. In that sense, his films are comparable in style to the painting and sculpture of the great "outsider" or "self-taught" artists of his era, such as Grandma Moses (1860–1961), William Edmundson (c. 1870–1951), Horace Pippin (1888–1946), Elijah Pierce (1892–1984), William Hawkins (1895–1990), Sister Gertrude Morgan (1900–1980), Nellie Mae Rowe (1900–1982), and numerous others.[24] The question of whether Micheaux had the talent of a Benny Carter or an Elijah Pierce remains open, but it is not relevant to this point of style. The evaluation of Micheaux's accomplishment has hardly begun, and fundamental valuative criteria remain obscure.

After Mary Austin's sister's song ends, the sequence shot continues with Austin congratulating her sister on the perfection of her performance and lamenting the lack of financial resources that prevent Mary from sending her sister to Chicago to pursue a career. Austin strikes her open hand with her fist and says "If I only had a few more boarders, I could soon send you." Mary Austin's references to her own lack of financial resources can be understood to express the anguish of any "producer" or manager of talent—such as Mary Austin is in relation to her sister, or such as Micheaux himself is as a film producer. Micheaux's production values and style in this shot can be read as part of a representation of the desire for financial means; that is, Micheaux has presented Mary Austin as having a production problem similar to his own, and thus the production values and style of the film become themselves a contributing theme in the narrative. The question of Micheaux's rough style becomes itself a theme treated by the film, as does the struggle with twoness, which is inherent in the style of all race movies but absent from the style of the Hollywood films produced for black audiences.

The themes of production financing and representations of the struggle with twoness in this film might be pursued along avenues such as the following:

(1) There are several more set-piece singing sequences in the film, two of them in the boarding house in the first half of the film, the others in nightclubs

in Harlem in the second half. Each such sequence set in the boarding house is presented in a style different from the preceding one. Those three sequences might be understood as a progression, in which the stylistic changes and the narrative meanings constitute a development of underlying themes of the struggle with twoness and with uplift. In these three sequences, the style becomes progressively more upscale but also more fragmented. The intercutting becomes very confusing; the matching of the eyeline vectors of glances becomes complex and unorthodox.

(2) The direct glance is used with poignancy at several points in the narrative. When Alonzo and Norma declare their feelings for each other and conspire to keep their relationship secret, they look at the camera. When they discuss Liza Hatfield's lover in the second half of the film (the numbers-racket magnate, Gomez) during the 'rupture' in Liza's song (this scene is discussed below), they refer to him as furtive. While emphasizing the term "furtive," they speak directly to the camera. These direct glances may be seen as a representation of direct speech, of integrity and good faith, through a simple, pseudo-theatrical address to the audience. They can also be seen as part of a style that is less illusionistic and glossy than that of Hollywood, that does not stitch the implied viewer into the narrative through "furtive" continuity editing. Even if these glances toward the camera or "audience" are unconscious or unwilled by the filmmaker, even if they are "mistakes," they have a consistency of pattern that constitutes a breach of illusionism, an improvisation that tends to advance Micheaux's themes and to represent his enunciative directness. They represent an attitude toward making film and an address to film audiences that is fundamentally different from the classical, an attitude that is not so much anti-illusionistic as a-illusionistic.

(3) The whole production, so to speak, moves to Harlem in the middle of the movie. This might be considered a serious flaw in the film, because the displacement to the North seems to hack the narrative in two, and the Harlem story becomes a seemingly gratuitous second beginning for all the characters. Some story lines are tied off completely, while others are taken up again later. The extreme and messy break is not gratuitous, however, but is integral in ways related to both the theme of twoness and the theme of production financing. John Russell Taylor argues in a similar way in defense of the unity of Satyajit Ray's film *Aparajito* (*The Unvanquished*, 1957), whose title, interestingly enough, recalls Micheaux's first novel, *The Conquest*, and whose narrated struggles resemble those of Micheaux's characters and his "crooked-stick" style:

> Even many sympathetic critics feel that [*Aparajito*] is broken-backed and lacking in unity . . . and that at best it makes formal sense only as a hinge between the two flanking films [of the Apu trilogy]. I cannot agree with this. . . . What gives unity to it, despite *its apparent break in the middle* [emphasis added], when Apu and his mother return from Benares to the country . . . is the continuing theme of Apu's relations with Sarbojaya, and the tug between education and new experience on one hand and traditional ways of life on the other.[25]

In the case of *The Girl from Chicago,* the break in the middle represents the Great Migration itself, which broke apart black families and societies forever. That migration continued during the depression (when *The Girl from Chicago* was made), when thousands of ambitious African Americans moved from the agrarian, rural, poorly capitalized South to the industrial, urban, well-capitalized North. Like Ray's rural people, Micheaux's southerners went to northern cities to get jobs. In the terms of the claims of this study about Micheaux's discourse on production values, such migrations can be seen as related to production. The job seeking was literally an act of personal and household financing, and the seeking of fortunes by artists and entrepreneurs were searches for production opportunities and corporate financing. Mary Austin and her sister, as well as Alonzo and Norma, are among the characters in *The Girl from Chicago* who go north to "refinance" their personal and productive lives.

(4) There are several production numbers in the second half of the film, the most important of which features the girl from Chicago herself, Liza Hatfield, as the lead chanteuse of a jazz band. Liza Hatfield represents the "wrong" approach to the twoness problem and to production values and style, in comparison with the "right" approach, which is represented by the earlier, more amateurish "production number" in the boarding house (discussed above). Narrative anticipation builds around Liza's production number as the film's male lead, Alonzo White, in conversation with Norma, calls Liza exotic and strange, partly because Liza is reputed to be returning from a successful career in Paris and is of unknown African-American origin. Liza's production number is temporally interrupted by a cut-away from the lead-in music to another long discussion of her by Alonzo and Norma (at their nightclub table). The cut-away is the kind of time-extending, non-continuity edit found in the naive style of early films, such as Edwin S. Porter's *The Life of an American Fireman* (1903), and in Sergei Eisenstein's (non-naive) avant-garde style of the 1920s. When Alonzo and Norma's discussion ends and we return to the production number, the music continues from the same point at which we left it, the timeline of the production number having been suspended. The scene then continues from there as a long take without further interruption. The song, "Love is a Rhapsody," is intended to be seductive and polished. Although the production number recalls Mary Austin's sister's performance in some ways—it is a long take of a female vocal performance—Liza's number is carefully distinguished from that of Mary's sister. Since Liza turns out to be the central, and eponymous, problem in the film, her relation to explicitly high production values—those of Paris and of the Radium Club where she sings in Harlem, higher production values by far than those of the good characters in the boarding house—suggests a definite attitude toward the issues of production financing for African Americans struggling with twoness and uplift. The glossier production number, though it is enjoyed by the protagonist, Alonzo, and is meant for the enjoyment of Micheaux's film audience, is nevertheless located explicitly in a realm of villainy, furtiveness, and seduction.

Conclusion

Micheaux surely did not intend all the rougher aspects of his style explicitly in the ways suggested above, but his style is nonetheless appropriate to and worthy of his situation and his themes and issues. That in itself indicates that his accomplishment may have been greater than has been recognized. Micheaux's style has served important themes, such as the financing of African-American culture, and has provided a complex but worthy approach to the dilemma of twoness. Micheaux has represented the hope for, but also the dangers of, assimilation. He has compared the hopes of one *amateur* singer and the accomplishments of one *professional* singer and has incorporated ideas about the production and stylistic values of each. The relatively high financing and stylistic values are associated with Liza Hatfield, a virtual prostitute; the lower production values are associated with the hopes of a character with undeveloped talent but with personal integrity. Micheaux associated his own underdeveloped style and personal integrity with *both* these modes, as a hope and a fear. He might have liked to have been able to assimilate himself into "high" aspects of the American culture, but he represented such assimilation as dangerous, as well as attractive, for African Americans. The idea of a *dangerous attraction* is a dilemma. It is but one reflection of the struggle with twoness in African-American uplift, a struggle embodied in a style "whose dogged strength alone keeps it from being torn asunder."[26]

4   Negative Images

The historical project of uplift has always deployed both positive and negative images of "the race." The efficacy of such images has been hotly debated. Black middle-class conservatives have, on the one hand, sometimes used negative images to chastise certain perceived characteristics or behaviors of some African Americans as detrimental to uplift and have, on the other hand, sometimes chastised artists who themselves used negative images for the same purpose. Some critics have called for the use of only positive images, eschewing self-criticism as unnecessarily unpleasant, redundant, or unintentionally supportive of white racist arguments and perceptions.

Addressing such concerns, Richard Grupenhoff has stated the following:

> Rarely, if ever, did Micheaux depict members of his race in a negative light. That is not to say that his films lacked negative behavior. Micheaux's films were often melodramatic, and as such presented a world of good vs. evil, with its obvious heroes and villains. *The Girl from Chicago* (1932), for instance, is a tale of exploitation, greed, and murder. *Swing!* (1936) is a proto-feminist critique of middle-class black male behavior. Still, while there are negative characters in Micheaux's films, there are not negative stereotypes held up to ridicule.[1]

It is certainly true that Micheaux always worked to advance his race, but there is no doubt that he also did "depict members of his race in a negative light." He was criticized throughout his career by the black press, black film critics, the Young Communist League, the National Negro Congress, and others for his negative portrayals of black people.[2]

Micheaux's negative images cannot be explained by reference to the genre of melodrama, as Grupenhoff has tried to do in the quotation above. Micheaux's use of genres and of modes such as melodrama was always radically impure. Eclecticism and contradiction are marks of his style, making it difficult to single out any particular genre as safe ground for an explanation of his work. He is famous for ignoring accepted systems of coherency, such as continuity editing and illusionistic mise-en-scène. To the extent that negative characters can be explained by their place in the melodramatic formulas, one still needs to explain Micheaux's perennial choice of such formulas.

Racial Slur

Micheaux mounted a persistent, career-long critique directed at perceived character traits in people of his own race. In *The Girl from Chicago,* during a romantic exchange, the hero (Alonzo, the black government agent) and the heroine (Norma, the northern-trained, southern school teacher) reveal to each other their mutual low esteem for other members of their race:

> NORMA: I had begun to think that there were no such men as you.
> ALONZO: I hardly expected to meet anyone down here, or anywhere else, like you.
> ... You see, this inspires a new confidence in me with regards to our women.[3]

In another part of the narrative, Norma reports to Alonzo that she saw a "dirty old Negro" spying on them. The "dirty old Negro," who is the henchman of Ballinger (the melodramatic villain), has a shuffling walk and clownishly exaggerated facial expressions, including bugged eyes and a dropped lower lip. Another character, Cornbread, a numbers runner for Gomez, the Harlem numbers banker of the second half of the film, hangs around tap dancing while waiting for a new assignment from his crime boss. Cornbread also walks with a shuffle and responds to complicated situations by scratching his head and contorting his face like a buffoon. At one point, he boisterously exclaims, "Well, I'm a monkey's grandpa!" Here, it seems, Micheaux is endorsing a common racial slur, using it against a sector of the community he finds unsavory. Any irony or playfulness intended in this type of deprecation is weakened by Micheaux's consistent application of such terms ("dirty Negro," "Cornbread," "monkey's grandpa") to characters he does not like. The terms are meant to hurt. He seems to be saying to his ethnic group that some of them deserve these terms. Micheaux's treatment of his good leading characters is also devoid of irony; they all invest their racial pride in middle-class values without any sense of contradiction.

Micheaux's negative stereotyping, however, usually differs from that of Hollywood, but not always. One extended scene in *Lying Lips* (1939) employs a quite standard Hollywood "coon." Two black detectives (the hero, Benjamin Hadnott, played by Carmen Newsome, and Detective Wanzer, played by Earl Jones) take a murder suspect to a "haunted house" to scare a confession out of him. This suspect is a dark-skinned man with a penchant for drinking, lying, and stealing. He has a paralyzing fear of anything that appears to be supernatural, and he dissolves into a trembling, eye-rolling, and pleading coon stereotype when exposed to the possibility of being left by himself in the haunted house. He is also henpecked and unable to think without the castrating supervision of an equally unsavory dirty-dealing black woman.

Micheaux's ridicule seems to run throughout his films. *Swing!* opens by drawing a graphic picture of the man-supported-by-his-woman stereotype, as discussed in a previous chapter. Mandy (Cora Green), not wanting to get up in the morning to go to work, has an altercation with her alarm clock. The fact that she does get up (and presumably does every morning, since she is a responsible character) contrasts with the behavior of her man, who comes home about the same time she is rising. He is a fancy dresser who has been carousing all night. Mandy supports him financially, a relationship that is elaborated, but not changed, by the action of the rest of the film.

In a different vein, when Lena (Dorothy Van Engle) attempts to get Mandy a job by misrepresenting Mandy's qualification, Mandy comments "Us colored folk are just natural born liars." This remark is mitigated by the fact that the lie itself is harmless (since Lena knows she can help Mandy do the job in spite of Mandy's lack of experience) and by the fact that it is delivered as a joke. The lie is a charming example of the depths to which a good character will stoop to help a deserving member of her race. However, it remains uncharming as a racial slur, unnecessary to the plot, and typical of Micheaux's scripting. In the same film, one of Mandy's women friends describes all black men as cheating and no-account, concluding that since a woman must have a man, "as long as they're just no 'count, we can put up with it." This remark is not directed at any melodramatic villains; it is a racial slur that Micheaux means to be interpreted as such by "a certain class" of his own people.

In *Underworld,* Dinah, the black gangster's moll and central female character, first appears with a black eye, which has been given to her (justifiably, the film implies) by her man. Soon afterward, we are treated to a lingering scene of a fight between Dinah and another black woman in a Harlem nightclub. Later, when Dinah feels she has been wronged by Paul (the black college graduate she has been leading astray), she says, "I'll do my worst; the dirtier the better." Here, Micheaux creates a vamp who embodies behavior he sees as typical, posing a problem that his college-graduate male lead must overcome. In doing so, Micheaux presents the familiar black sex siren described by critics of black stereotypes. (Donald Bogle, for example, discusses Nina Mae McKinney as playing the first black whore to whom almost "every black leading lady in motion pictures, from Lena Horne in *Cabin in the Sky* to Lola Falana in *The Liberation of L. B. Jones,* owes a debt."[4]) Two other versions of the vamp occur in *The Notorious Elinor Lee* (1940): one evil woman, daughter of the notorious Stacker Lee from folk legend, hires a younger woman to vamp a worthy, black boxer to tempt him to throw a fight.

Micheaux's ridicule is often directed at what he perceived to be a lack of business sense and intelligence in African Americans, shortcomings he presents as general group traits. The following quotations from three characters in *God's Stepchildren* exemplify the texture of the slurs that upset many African Americans. When the hero discusses his business plans, Eva, the heroine, says:

> Why is it that so many—most all of our men—when they go into business, its got to be a crap game, or a numbers bank, or a policy shop? Why can't they go into some kind of legitimate business—like white people?

Jimmy responds thus:

> They could . . . , but they've made no study of economics. Their idea of success is to seek out the line of least resistance. The Negro hates to think. He's a stranger to planning. . . . After viewing the failure of our group—for we are failures—it seems that we should go back to the beginning and start all over again.

Soon after this exchange, a black racketeer named Copper comes up to the couple and makes Jimmy an offer of gambling partnership, which Jimmy refuses. Copper responds:

> I thought that when I told you how much money there was in it—quick money, and easy money . . . and the Negro is so simple and falls for any kind of game.

All three of these characters express disdain for perceived tendencies in the "black race." The difference is that the racketeer intends to exploit group weaknesses, whereas Jimmy wants to set an example for group improvement.

More of the standard racist stereotypes are to be found in Micheaux's work, such as male dancers who overtly "coon" to the approval of leading characters and of (usually) black audiences within the films. *Swing!* contains the most egregious example: a boy dancer and a young male pianist are brought in off the streets of Harlem for a special audition before the black producer of the black show (who corresponds to Micheaux, the producer of race movies). The boy sings and dances with a painfully artificial grin, putting on an enthusiastic "coon" act. The producer, whom we are expected to take as a model of black manhood, approves the act and asks the duo to return the next day. (There are also, on the other hand, many black performers in Micheaux's films who work in black idioms but who do not "coon.") Another stereotype used by Micheaux is the beautiful, fair-skinned woman (Donald Bogle's "tragic mulatto").[5] But that stereotype is used in untypical ways; this character appears as a black man's romantic, pre-Raphaelite ideal in *The Exile,* as a tragic figure in *God's Stepchildren,* and as a paragon of virtue in *Veiled Aristocrats* and *Lying Lips.*

Determining whether there are "toms," "mammies," and "bucks" (Bogle's other stereotypes) in Micheaux's films is also problematic. Some viewers might feel that Micheaux's male leads have a more or less palpable tom-ness simply because of their attitudes toward white skin, white culture, and some white people, such as the white theater owner at the end of *Swing!,* whose intervention allows the show to go on. Anyone who feels that there was a strong element of "tom" in Booker T. Washington is likely to see toms in all of Micheaux's male leads, since they are often Micheaux's embodiments of Booker T. Washington's ideals. Washington's ideals were undergoing a radical critique in portions of the black press throughout Micheaux's career. Though Micheaux's ideal African American was not modeled solely on Washington, Micheaux never abandoned his original admiration of Washington's qualities and accomplishments—never considered Washington an Uncle Tom—and thus, Micheaux attracted criticism from both the black-nationalist and the integrationist quarters of the black press.

More recently, J. Hoberman has characterized one of Micheaux's leading characters, Jimmy in *God's Stepchildren,* as "fatuous," a deprecatory term that, in the context of Hoberman's critique, is related to tom-ness:

> A light-skinned foundling is raised . . . by the overpoweringly virtuous Mrs. Saunders. When the child, Naomi, runs away from "colored school," and attempts to enroll

in "white school" (i.e., tries to obtain "white" opportunities) she is punished and incarcerated in a convent. Upon her return, Naomi falls in love with her fatuous older foster-brother, Jimmy. (Jimmy has hithertofor [*sic*] demonstrated his supposed virtue with his infamous "only one Negro in a thousand can think" statement.)[6]

Jimmy and his mother, Mrs. Saunders, are characterized as representing an attitude toward segregation that might be called collaborationist. The idea of collaborationism is consistent with Booker T. Washington's strategy of emphatic and explicit compromise toward social segregation, and thus, Jimmy can be seen not just as fatuous but also as a Booker T. Washington–type "tom." The perception of fatuousness in some of Micheaux's leading characters is related perhaps to a perception that Micheaux's orientation toward the middle class is thoroughly bourgeois, in the Marxist sense.

The Issue of Skin Color

Understanding Micheaux's use of negative images requires some analysis of one of the most controversial aspects of Micheaux's rhetoric, one of the perceived problems of race movies in general—the use of light and dark skin tone to represent a system of racist values. There is no doubt, from the evidence of the extant films, that Micheaux tended to favor light-skinned, Caucasian-featured actors. This has sometimes been received as a racial insult.

The deployment of skin color in Micheaux's films does not, however, constitute a scheme or template. The tendency to favor light-skinned actors is only a tendency and is not consistent throughout his films. A cursory survey of important characters in the films viewed shows that about 75 percent are light and 25 percent are dark. Of the dark-skinned characters, about half of them are good (constructed to evoke sympathy and identification), and half of them are bad. Of the light-skinned characters, about two-thirds of them are good, and one-third of them are bad. Of the sub-Saharan African-featured characters, about half of them are good, and half of them are bad. Of the Caucasian-featured characters, about two-thirds of them are good, and one-third of them are bad. Of the light-skinned characters, about one-third of them have significant sub-Saharan features, and of that third, a little under 60 percent of them are good, favored characters.

Some African-American viewers and critics have felt sure that Oscar Micheaux was himself light-skinned, and that he was, through his narrative "color schemes," disparaging other African Americans who were not so "fortunate."[7] This assumption may have led to misreadings of some of his films. It is high time to establish the fact that Micheaux was a dark-skinned man who was unambiguously recognizable as an African American. In a private phone conversation (April 26, 1996), Oscar Micheaux's grandniece, Mrs. Mildred Micheaux Lewis, who lives in Columbus, Ohio, stated that Oscar was "fair-skinned" and that all of his brothers and sisters were fair-skinned except for

Fig. 6a. These two men in *Underworld* match fairly well the bourgeois, white-like ideal caricatured on the barbershop window behind them.

Fig. 6b. The hero of *Underworld*, Paul, is one of the lightest-skinned of all Micheaux's heroes; he looks like the Arrow shirt man. But, though he might be thought of as a kind of ideal, he is not so different-looking from the villains on the right. All three are visually close to a bourgeois "ideal," so Micheaux is not equating an aesthetic ideal with character and valorization.

Fig. 6c. Here, Micheaux's "Arrow shirt" black hero from *Underworld* is shown with an appropriately white-like, light-skinned African-American female counterpart. But she is not the heroine; she is the villainess. Again, skin tone is not an indicator of character or valorization.

Fig. 6d. This dark-skinned character in *The Exile*, Jango, is indeed unsavory. But his unsavoriness arises entirely from his association with the light-skinned villainess. Also, there are saving aspects of his character in that his rash act of violence is motivated by black African racial pride (he is a Haile Selassie supporter), which Micheaux shares, and by a justifiable impulse to punish the villainess.

Fig. 6e. The same dark-skinned actor who played the unfavored Jango in *The Exile* plays the most favored man in *Veiled Aristocrats,* Frank Fowler.

Fig. 6f. In *Veiled Aristocrats*, the most visually idealized light-skinned pair are brother and sister, Rena and John Walden. However, they are passing for white and are considered racially disloyal. Rena will reject skin-color valuation and find her "ideal" lover in the dark-skinned man in figure 6e.

Fig. 6g. This glamour shot of Naomi in *God's Stepchildren* might seem the sort of glorifica-tion of light-skinned fetish that the Communist Party com-plained of when it demonstrated against the film in 1938. But Micheaux portrays this character as a very "bad girl" because of her obsession with her own "whiteness."

Fig. 6h. This "beautiful couple" in *God's Stepchildren,* foster brother and foster sister Naomi and Jimmy, are, like Rena and John Walden in *Veiled Aristocrats,* somewhat incestuous. These light-skinned paragons are por-trayed by Micheaux as vaguely tainted. Many of the other danc-ers, such as the woman on the left, give them a cutting gaze (see also figures 15b and 15c).

Fig. 6i. One of the reasons *God's Stepchildren* was boycotted by the Communist Party was the portrayal of Naomi's overt revulsion at being coerced into marrying this dark man.

Fig. 6j. However, Micheaux portrays the good people in the film, Jimmy (*second from left*) and Naomi's and Jimmy's mother (*right*, played by Alice B. Russell), as admiring the man, whom they welcome into the family group. His dark skin means nothing to them, but it means everything to Naomi. It is her fetishistic values that will be punished by the filmmaker.

Fig. 6k. Naomi's mother warns her in no uncertain terms that her light-skin fetish will destroy her. This sentiment, expressed here by the Alice Russell character, is also Micheaux's sentiment. The film is a cautionary tale.

Fig. 6l. Micheaux's so-called white-looking heroes, such as Jimmy in *God's Stepchildren,* when placed beside "real" whites, such as this doctor, look like the 1930s middle-class Negroes they are intended to be. Micheaux was not hiding black people behind white veils; he proudly set them off.

Fig. 6m. This motley crew in *The Symbol of the Unconquered* is exotic but generally light-skinned. But they are as villainous as they come; they are plotting here to "white cap" the black hero by forming a Ku Klux Klan–like terror campaign to drive him off his oil-rich land.

Fig. 6n. Perhaps the lightest of all Micheaux's actors is one of the most evil, the peonage boss in *The Girl from Chicago*.

Swan. Mrs. Lewis said that it was commonly understood in Micheaux's extended family that he was not dark. However, the evidence of photographs and films of Micheaux suggests otherwise. Clearly, most scholars and critics have assumed that Micheaux was relatively dark, certainly dark enough not to be considered fair or light. This assumption was confirmed by a discussion between African-American Micheaux scholar Learthen Dorsey and Harley Robinson at one of the public sessions of the third annual Micheaux Film Festival in Gregory, South Dakota, in August 1998. Robinson, who is a cousin of Micheaux's and who knew him personally, characterized Micheaux's skin tone as brown. Dorsey, in trying to refine this further, asked Robinson if Micheaux had been Robinson's color, which is dark brown, a skin tone that Dorsey considered "dark" in the context of the debate over Micheaux's famous "color scheme." Robinson said, "Yes, he was my color." Viewers may judge Oscar's skin tone for themselves in the films in which he plays bit parts (the larger detective in the shot in which detectives are shown staking out the house in Westchester in *Ten Minutes to Live* and the larger detective in the scene in which the murdered woman is examined in *Murder in Harlem*).

Micheaux was a relatively dark-skinned man, and evidence of his confident bearing suggests that he was proud of it. Clearly, however, Micheaux did (inconsistently) somewhat favor light- and Caucasian-featured actors. The com-

Fig. 7a. Oscar Micheaux (*far right*) had a cameo role as a detective in *Murder in Harlem.*

Fig. 7b. When seen beside other African-American characters in the film, such as the night watchman (*left*) and the other detective in this frame, Micheaux's relatively dark, African features are distinct.

Fig. 7c. The only other known instance in which Micheaux appeared in his extant films is another cameo detective role in *Ten Minutes to Live,* included here in spite of the photo's poor quality so that readers can identify the shot when viewing the film. (Thanks to Edward Luna Brough for these "Micheaux spottings.")

plexity of the evidence, however, suggests that questions of correlation between skin color and cultural values and of any motives that Micheaux might have had for such correlations need further analysis. Also, those questions would need to take into account the general prevalence of light-skin favoritism in the other race movies of the era. Even more telling might be the incidence of light and dark skin color in Micheaux's films in comparison with the incidence in the African-American population in Micheaux's time. Without such analyses, it is hard to judge what Micheaux is actually saying, since meaning derives from articulated difference. Is the incidence of skin color in Micheaux's films different from the incidence of skin color in real life? If so, how? The critical discussions in the literature are often passionate on this subject but are frequently impressionistic. Grupenhoff's section on Micheaux in his book *The Black Valentino* significantly illuminates the issue of color favoritism; it is the only extended analysis so far that recognizes the complexity of the phenomenon, and it is an important contribution.[8]

Conclusion

Micheaux's films do contain stereotypes, which raises the following questions: To what extent had he assimilated them? And to what purpose and effect did he use them? It matters very much that Micheaux intended these films for black audiences, which suggests that his "racial slurs" were expressly intended for the improvement of "the race." Maybe his intentions justified his means, but the means sometimes seem to retain their character as racial or ethnic slurs.

It is very clear, however, from Micheaux's work that though he might have used the term "race" to describe his ethnic group, as virtually everyone did at that time, he did not ever mean it as a signifier of biological determinism, certainly never in the racist sense of biological hierarchy and inherent inferiority of races. This is beyond doubt. Micheaux's emphatic message was that a "black man [and woman] can be anything."

The next six chapters of this study will suggest that Micheaux used negative images, including stereotypes, not to exploit and thus strengthen them but rather to mount a complex, nuanced, extended critique of racist stereotyping. Micheaux's unabated indignation toward what he considered flaws in his group is clearly one of the central themes of that vision. His frankness may be disturbing to some, but he considered frankness essential to progress, as he implied in the following statement (from the Philadelphia *Afro-American* in 1925): "It is only by presenting those portions of the race portrayed in my pictures, in the light and background of their true state, that we can raise our people to greater heights." His frank use of caricature served his purposes of analyzing, revising, interrogating, and eradicating caricature; his use of caricature was balanced by the equally frank indignation, directed at white racist causes of caricature, that Micheaux demonstrated throughout his literary and cinematic career.

5 The Middle Path

> The Afro-American spokesperson who would perform a deformation of mastery shares the task of Sycorax's son [Caliban], insofar as he or she must transform an obscene situation, a cursed and tripled metastatus, into a signal self/cultural expression.
>
> . . .
>
> *A merger of . . . African-American cultural anima and Western high culture, Negro masses and Negro thinking classes* is the sounding result of this rending of the Veil. . . . Such [are] fruitful and empowering mergers of long-standing dualities. [Emphasis added]
>
> —Houston A. Baker, Jr., *Modernism and the Harlem Renaissance* (pp. 56, 57)

In the face of polemical structures and virulent systems of race and class, Micheaux advocated and practiced negotiation. He articulated, in *The Girl from Chicago* and other films, a modulation away from the "middle passage" via a middle path toward the middle class. The middle path had to be navigated between the dangerous and indeterminate poles of twoness. Micheaux's work reflects in its style the dilemmas of African-American community and class mobility in a white-dominated world; his films treat these dilemmas as issues not only at the level of art but also at the level of economics, not only at the level of his fictional characters but also at the level of the production values of his own films. His constant purpose was to show, through art and through business, the capacity of African Americans to overcome American adversity, as the titles of his first novel (*The Conquest,* 1913) and his fourth film (*The Symbol of the Unconquered,* 1920) suggest. The inexpensive production values that inform his difficult predicament and his difficult style reflect, and also *represent,* adversity. Micheaux's noted insouciance toward mainstream production values indicates a curiously elevated perspective with respect to such adversity. Micheaux was using production values in such a way as to make them an issue in the problematics of uplift and the drama of self-reliance.

The idea of a dangerous attraction in high production values, as discussed in preceding chapters, reflects Micheaux's middle-class goals and criteria, which are deeply rooted in American Calvinism, which is itself complicitous in the entrepreneurial capitalism that was Micheaux's chosen (and inherited) economic mode. Micheaux's rhetorical ideals were certainly middle-class, and they were in some ways bourgeois, based as they were on acceptance of capitalist economics; his actual style, however, is harder to classify. On the one hand, if Micheaux, like the Calvinists, considered entrepreneurial economics so fundamental to uplift that personal dignity depended on economic success (as a sign of divine favor for the Calvinists; as a sign of citizenship for Micheaux), then creating high production values might have mattered very much to Micheaux as an indicator of successful progress toward his main goal of class mobility. There are, in fact, signs of such material values in his style; his favored characters are provided with the material properties of dignity, such as business suits, evening wear, and decent houses and apartments. In that sense, the high production values of Hollywood may have been an attraction for Micheaux and for African-American cinema, as Thomas Cripps assumes they were.

There are also, on the other hand, signs that contradict such a conclusion. Micheaux's disdained characters are often more lavishly attired and domiciled than his favored characters. More suggestively, the incommensurability of the scales of Micheaux's actual production budgets, when compared to those of the bourgeois (not middle-class) norm developed in Hollywood—a norm based on production values a hundred times more expensive than those of Micheaux—ought to have worried Micheaux more than it did, as critics both then and now have not hesitated to point out.[1]

How exactly was Micheaux using low production values—as a necessary vehicle for a climb to a higher production level or as an apparatus inseparable from a complex, conscious discourse of class? Insouciance toward production values has been an important *positive* element of several progressive styles, including Italian Neo-Realism, the American underground cinema, and Third Cinema. Such styles, however, are seldom in contradiction with their content, as Micheaux's style seems to be. The American avant garde—Marie Menken, Willard Maas, Maya Deren, Stan Brakhage, Ken Jacobs, Carolee Schneemann, Sidney Peterson, Andy Warhol, and Hollis Frampton—are perceived as rebels from the middle class, not as aspirants to the middle class, such as Micheaux. So, if Micheaux considered high production values to be dangerous to his cinema, it appears he considered them such in a different sense than did the avant garde. It may be, however, that if the term "middle class" is understood more broadly, in accordance with William Julius Wilson's Weberian usage (which emphasizes material expectations), for example, then Micheaux, the American underground, and other progressive movements may be seen as having more in common than might be supposed. All of those movements were, for example, anti-bourgeois, but none was anti-middle-class in Wilson's sense. Even avant-garde bohemianism is technically a middle-class position in Marx's, Wilson's, and Weber's terms.

Was Micheaux attempting to use production values for purposes of assimilation or rather for purposes of separation from mainstream American culture? Speaking to similar issues, Amiri Baraka has celebrated the bebop era as a period manifested by the restoring to black jazz (after the intervention of white swing) of "its *valid separation* from, and anarchic disregard of, Western popular forms [emphasis added]."[2] It is not easy to ascertain to what extent Micheaux was expressing, on the one hand, a valid separation of black cultural production from white and to what extent he was aspiring, on the other hand, to a kind of cultural assimilationism that Baraka has disapprovingly called (and that Duke Ellington approvingly called) "citizenship." Micheaux produced more African-American cinema more autonomously than anyone else has ever done; he was also, however, accused of racial self-hatred. Baraka's description of how the bebop artists reestablished the valid separation of their cultural production from the mainstream indicates that aspects of style, such as "jaggedness," comprise an important element of that separation:

> [The bebop musicians] have used the music of the forties with its jagged, exciting rhythms as an initial reference and have restored the hegemony of blues as the most important basic form in Afro-American music. They have also restored improvisation to its traditional role of invaluable significance, again removing jazz from the hands of the less than gifted arranger and the fashionable diluter.[3]

It is tempting to compare the jaggedness of bebop style with the jaggedness of Micheaux's scripting, shooting, and editing, especially in a film like *The Girl from Chicago*. Another way Baraka distinguishes bebop from swing is by reference to tonal characteristics relating to musical form: "What [Ornette] Coleman and [Cecil] Taylor have done is to approach a kind of jazz that is practically nonchordal and in many cases atonal (meaning that its tonal 'centers' are constantly redefined according to the needs, or shape and direction, of the particular music being played, and not formally fixed as is generally the case—what composer George Russell has called 'pan-tonality')."[4] An equally important distinction, according to Baraka, is the difference between the smoothness and commercialization of swing and the lack of those characteristics in early blues, early jazz, and bebop. Such references, and the reference to "the less than gifted arranger and the fashionable diluter," imply a hierarchy of low and high production values in which low production values are favored. Again, it is tempting to consider Baraka's attribution of such a value system in jazz as analogous to the hierarchy of production values found in Micheaux's films.

The analogy between music and film is, however, imperfect. Jane Gaines has pointed out that such an analogy must consider the differences in economic scale between the production of music and the production of film. Discussing production values *as an element of style* in cinema has the advantage, at least, of implying precisely Gaines's important question regarding the economic scale of production and of implying also the issues of class that follow from economic scale.

Production Values as an Element of Style

As was shown in chapter 3 in discussions of *The Girl from Chicago* (1932), Micheaux portrayed the Great Migration as a flight from conditions of peonage in the American South to the Harlem Renaissance of New York and as a rise in class and in production values. The first musical production numbers in *The Girl from Chicago* were shot on location in a southern boarding house; the shots are grainy, dark, crudely lit, and crudely sound-recorded. When the characters move north to Harlem, they do so to seek better conditions, not only in their domestic lives but also in their professional work, particularly as producers of entertainment. In that respect, they resemble Micheaux as the producer of the film. In comparison to the amateurish production numbers that take place in the South, the Harlem production numbers, especially that of Liza Hatfield, the "girl from Chicago," employ and represent higher production values; those production numbers look more sophisticated, more urban, more European, and more expensive. Since Liza Hatfield also represents furtiveness, disloyalty, violence, and prostitution, high production values are portrayed not only as attractive and entertaining but also as undesirable. High production values are a dangerous attraction.

The Girl from Chicago, Continued

Further analysis of *The Girl from Chicago* indicates how middle-class, as opposed to high-class, values were deployed in narrative and how they informed Micheaux's attitude toward production values. Alonzo White, the hero of the film, is presented as a middle-class black man who is employed by the white establishment, untypically enough by the "Secret Service," an agency of the federal government that in actuality probably would not have employed him in 1932. Even within the fantasy world of this film, Alonzo's position implies extraordinary trust from the white regime. And, though it seems hard to credit the reality of a black Secret Service agent in 1932, the strikingly ironic name "White" for a black investigator indicates that Micheaux is alluding to an important historical event—Walter White's extraordinary investigations of lynching throughout the South between 1918 and 1928, during which time White successfully passed for a white reporter. By the time Micheaux borrowed his name for this film, Walter White had been secretary of the NAACP for two years and was famous. In addition to all this, Micheaux's character, Alonzo White, is associated with the Eastern establishment in America through his close connections with the European infrastructure, exemplified by his recent assignment to Scotland Yard and by the symbolism of his crossing on the luxury ocean liner *Europa*. The film opens with a shot of the ship on the ocean. A title card reads: "Four days out of Southampton, aboard the Europa, Alonzo White, of the U.S. Secret Service, after several months with Scotland Yard, was returning to New York." A close shot of Alonzo reading something is interrupted by an insert shot of a telegram addressed to him on shipboard; the telegram reads: "Call on George Saunders room 97L6 Empire State Building immediately arrival New York stop Wants you handle bad case of peonage Batesburg Miss/Van Cleve/US Secret Service." So, Alonzo's association with American and

British reigning classes is a close one, and it ignores or defies the actual racism of those upper classes, particularly in America, at the time the film was made.

That tight association with the upper classes, however, does not elevate Alonzo above the middle class. He remains an agent working for the ownership class, for the bureaucracies of both capitalistic and vestigially aristocratic governments, a class condition that would also serve to characterize many other fictional heroes in American cinema. Micheaux emphasized Alonzo's middle-class position by placing him carefully between overlapping lower- and higher-class contexts. The telegram he receives confirms not just his close working relationship with the upper classes who sent the telegram; it also refers to the lower classes, the "bad case of peonage" that is his next assignment for the Secret Service, thus bracketing him, neo-feudalistically, between the lords above and the serfs below.

A Middle Position between Lords and Serfs

The southern peonage and tenant farming systems were historical extensions of slavery, and slavery was in 1932 a sore subject for a film about the black middle class. Micheaux was criticized, on the one hand, by some elements of the black press throughout his career for dealing with distasteful and demeaning subjects; on the other hand, he was criticized by other black critics for presenting a kind of bourgeois pipe dream that avoids presenting problems of white supremacism. In fact, as the example of Alonzo's position shows, Micheaux mixed realism and idealism in the same films, even in the same sequences. And since his fictions of black autonomy were laced with often unwelcome criticisms of black *foibles* (here Micheaux was reproached by black and leftist critics for being too realistic) in addition to the also often equally unwelcome fictions of black *sovereignty* (here Micheaux was reproached for being too fantastic), Micheaux's hybrid style and faceted perspective served as answers to both these polarized criticisms. And, though Micheaux's fictions of African-American sovereignty have been accused of ignoring problems related to white-supremacist oppression of blacks, to the contrary, it is precisely issues of white oppression that *are* often present at several levels of Micheaux's content and style, even after extensive white censorship. In emphasizing an African-American position that is high enough on the social scale to criticize its group's own failures (aiming downward) and also high enough to criticize a higher oppressor (aiming upward)—i.e., a *middle* position—Micheaux was refusing to accept an *inferior* perspective, even when dealing directly and critically with issues of white supremacism.

Returning to the *Europa,* in the opening sequence of the film, the reference to slavery (in the telegram) through the term "peonage" lends another small hint of Europe to the connotational aura of the adventure, since the term "peon" relates historically to feudalism. As already mentioned, however, peonage was much more familiar to readers of the black press as the *current* condition of many former slaves in the South at the time that Micheaux made his film. By the year 1932, Micheaux had been traveling regularly for almost two decades through the rural and urban South, selling his books door to door, distributing his films from movie theater to movie theater, and, as he dramatized in his second novel, *The Forged Note* (1915), studying the character and conditions of black southerners. The black South and the large, newly migrated black communities of the urban North were his principal markets at the time he made *The Girl from Chicago*. Through his extensive travels and constant person-to-person engagement in the South, Micheaux was in a position to know firsthand about the problems of peonage and tenant farming and also to understand them as systems that replicated slavery. Tenant farming was to become infamous in the late 1930s and early 1940s, even to white people, through the photographic documentary and promotional programs of the Historical Section of the Farm Security Administration during the New Deal. But well before that time, both tenant farming and peonage were common knowledge to black audiences, since the black press and the NAACP had made a high-priority issue of them for decades, at least since 1910.[5]

Farming and Tenantry

Micheaux was sensitive to the plight of tenant farmers long before the white establishment representatives, Margaret Bourke-White and Erskine Caldwell, made sure the public had "seen their faces" and before James Agee and Walker Evans had made sharecroppers famous.[6] Tenant farmers and former tenant farmers who had migrated north to escape the tenant and peonage systems actually comprised many of Micheaux's readers and audiences. Micheaux himself had grown up on a family farm in southern Illinois, just within shouting distance of the South, and he had also later sought his fortune as a young man through entrepreneurial farming in South Dakota. These farming experiences provided the setting and subject of his early books and films and provided expert knowledge that Micheaux deployed in several novels and films. Farming country is the primary setting for the three novels that deal with Micheaux's own biographical farming experience—*The Conquest, The Homesteader,* and *The Wind from Nowhere.* Extant films that refer to farming (all favorably) include *Within Our Gates* (Sylvia's father is a tenant farmer who, as he is about to become independent, is lynched; the lynching story is set in the context of a tenant-farming system that punishes economic transgression); *The Symbol of the Unconquered* (the hero is a farm-owning prospector out West; he relives the horse-trading scam that Micheaux's hero suffered on the homestead in the novel *The Conquest,* and he helps his homesteading neighbor work her subsistence garden); *The Exile* (the hero becomes a successful western homesteader whose visits to Chicago temporarily corrupt him); *The Girl from Chicago* (the peonage system under discussion in this chapter); and *God's Stepchildren* (the hero buys a large farm and wants his stepsister to marry the farmer next door to curb her extravagant urban-white desires).

Farming is an aspect of the polarity of an urban-vs.-rural ethos that pervades both Micheaux's work and the whole period of the African-American migrations from the rural South.[7] Micheaux's employment of a quintessentially urban and federal "District of Columbia" agent, the black Secret Service hero, to deal with a quintessentially rural and regional problem, black peonage in the South, reverses the racist dialectics of minstrelsy noted by Houston Baker, Jr.:

> The continuation of such "darky jokes"—of what I call *sounds* of the minstrel mask—flows from the [story from Booker T. Washington's *Up from Slavery* of his] mother as chicken thief . . . through a condemnation and mockery of Afro-American professionals in the chapter [in *Up from Slavery*] on Reconstruction. In its drama of condemnation, this chapter also presents a deceived body of Afro-Americans who reside in the nation's capital and have been victimized by their removal from southern "country districts." These urbanites have suffered the false guidance of higher education. . . .
>
> [Booker T. Washington's] Epic [of a whole race beginning to go to school] gives way to pastoral; a black *nation* is displaced by a deceived urban sector in need of redemption. Implicit in the drama of condemnation is the real theme of the piece: the aspirations that characterized a *federal* period of Reconstruction (metonymically signaled by the District of Columbia) must be relinquished. More realistic goals are necessary to meet incumbencies of a new *regional* (the New South) era in which blacks will cast down their buckets where they are and seek advice and counsel from southern whites.[8]

Consciously or unconsciously, Micheaux's visions of uplift revised the strained relations between Washington, D.C. and Washington "B. T.," as described by Houston Baker. In *The Girl from Chicago,* the hero is working for Washington, D.C., coming to the aid of those who are "casing down their buckets" per Washington, B.T. The comparison of Tuskegee-era peonage with slavery is made explicit by the characterization of the peonage master, the town boss Jeff Ballinger, as a light-skinned, Caucasian-featured black man dressed in the traditional white linen suit of the southern white aristocrat. Ballinger serves as a surrogate antebellum slave master. The reference (in Alonzo White's telegram from the Secret Service) to a bad case of peonage is not just a convenient villainy for the hero of the melodrama to set right; peonage also resonates with the vestiges of American slavery, and the surrogate whiteness of the villain graphically reinforces that resonance. And Micheaux's idea of the way up from that slavery, though it includes farming, remains epical; it is not pastoral. The titles of Micheaux's stories of farming are heroical—*The Homesteader, The Conquest, Symbol of the Unconquered, The Exile,* and *The Wind from Nowhere.*

The Middle Passage and the Inferno

The allusions to historical slavery in the film make plausible a related set of epical connotations. The idea of the "middle passage" is very strong in African-American culture. It is the title of Charles Johnson's novel, which won a National Book Award, about the psychic trauma of the slaving ships that brought blacks to the Americas.[9] The middle passage is a harrowing vision that may have occupied a place in the cultural imaginations of African Americans that was as significant as the place that Dante's Christian vision of hell has occupied in the imaginations of European Americans. Dante's *Divine Comedy* begins not only with that hell (Canto I of *The Inferno*) but with the famous opening phrase "Nel mezzo del cammin": "Midway through the journey." Similarly, Micheaux's film opens midway through an Atlantic crossing that is pointedly different from the middle passage but that nonetheless resonates, through the telegram about peonage in the American South, with the slave trade and the possibility of the infernal. On the one hand, references to the middle passage and to Dante's famous opening lines seem unlikely to have been consciously intended by the filmmaker; on the other hand, Micheaux was as Eurocentric as he was Afrocentric, and he was widely read. And, as William Uricchio and Roberta Pearson point out in a recent discussion of the Vitagraph film *Francesca di Rimini* (1908), there was a

> veritable Dante craze . . . at the turn of the century at least among a restricted segment of American society. A set of Dante postcards, "A Visit to Hell with Dante—the Italian Poet," (circa 1900) cost 50 cents for twenty-five "views." . . .
> . . . the passion for Dante to some extent transcended social barriers. While Dante enjoyed nothing approaching the broad cultural permeation of Shakespeare, absent from school curricula for example, his appeal was not limited to the purchasers of elegant calendars and relatively expensive postcards.[10]

The middle passage is a plausible connotation, even if it is an unconscious one, and Dante's "Nel mezzo del cammin," while remaining unproven as a direct allusion, can nonetheless serve for comparative purposes as a Eurocentric evocation of the sort of impasse of the heaven-and-hell bracketing of spirit that Micheaux's characters are made to negotiate in a secular, African-American context. The "mezzo" of "nel mezzo" is as crucial to Dante's metonymical and metaphorical situation as the "middle" of the "middle passage" is crucial to the African-American situation. And both "nel mezzo" and "middle passage" resonate with Micheaux's idea of the difficult negotiation of a middle path through dangerous attractions in a vertical force field of race and class.

The southern peonage problem that Alonzo is assigned to handle would be merely a conveniently heroic professional task for the protagonist to negotiate, except for the fact that he is a black American. Given the American racial attitudes and white-supremacist actions of Micheaux's time, Alonzo's task entails a general, inescapable jeopardy. Alonzo is midway in a professional journey, a life journey, and a cultural journey, surrounded by metonymical horizons—literally fore (his next assignment in the South) and aft (his recent assignment at Scotland Yard), metaphorically past (slavery) and future (uplift). Alonzo is, at the same time, bracketed by a corresponding vertical hierarchy of social class based on "race," which constitutes the paradigmatic class condition of all the characters.

Micheaux's "Narrative Situation" as a Film Producer

Alonzo's vertical and horizontal, metaphoric and metonymic, narrative situation reflects the analogous positioning that was faced by Micheaux as the producer of the film. Regarding production values, Micheaux was caught in a matrix similar to that of his heroes. Recognizing Micheaux's own economic bracket in real life helps explain the double consciousness, or twoness, of his style, which so directly reflects honorable and indefatigable struggle. For example, in the opening scene from *The Girl from Chicago* (discussed above), Micheaux attempted to produce high production values to represent the economic status of a luxury liner; he obtained an image of a great ship, then the images of Alonzo reading the telegram were inserted to suggest that the latter images were shot on board that great ship. The desired effect of high production values, however, is mitigated by visual evidence that the on-board shooting, the medium shots of Alonzo reading the telegram, were filmed on a lesser ship (probably something like a Staten Island ferryboat). Also, any effect of luxury is virtually destroyed by the recurrent images of the great ocean liner bobbing like a cork (along with the entire ocean in which it sits!) because of the placement of Micheaux's camera on a minuscule bark that was being tempest tossed by the tiny harbor waves. Thus, Micheaux's style itself represents—reluctantly, but also somewhat insouciantly—a kind of middle passage toward uplift in the depression of the 1930s, bracketed by high and low production values as well as by a concomitant high and low artistic status.

This bracketing of artistic status produced incongruity that in a superficial viewing sometimes causes laughter in the wrong places; for example, the bobbing of the ocean liner is funny because of the contradiction of the ship's mightiness and the shot's flimsiness. That laughter, however, diminishes with increased experience and understanding of such films, as did the derision surrounding the advent of race music. Viewers steeped in underground or Third-World cinemas (and music) learn to appreciate such styles without condescending to them, without treating them as "camp."[11] Clyde Taylor reports that "Gaston Kabore, Burkina Faso director of *Wend Kuni,* explains . . . the much more restrained use of cinema apparatus in African films as reflecting 'appropriate means'," and that "African film directors have so far been satisfied to establish a look in their films consistent with the actual level of development in African societies, unlike their Euro-commercial counterparts."[12] And viewers steeped in film history recognize that Micheaux's production values are an index of his own economic and ethnic predicament as a filmmaker at the time, which, finally, was not funny.

Production Values *as* Signifiers

So, to summarize, since production values are usually tied directly to economic expenditure, since expenditures are often conscious signifiers of artistic value in mainstream cinema (as discussed by Janet Staiger in *The Classical Hollywood Cinema*[13]), and since high production values are thus an index of wealth and high social status, so production values as deployed by Micheaux may be significant throughout this film in relation to the high-and-low bracketing structure identified in the narrative positioning of the characters.

Signifiers *of* High Production Values

Furthermore, since Micheaux was not able to deploy high production values *as signifiers* because he could not afford them, he deployed *signifiers of* high production values, somewhat in the manner of the ancient Japanese notion of *nazoraëru:*

> to substitute, in imagination, one object or action for another, so as to bring about some magical or miraculous result.
> For example: you cannot afford to build a Buddhist temple; but you can easily lay a pebble before the image of the Buddha, with the same pious feeling that would prompt you to build a temple if you were rich enough to build one. The merit of so offering the pebble becomes equal, or almost equal, to the merit of erecting a temple.[14]

For example, in the opening sequence of *The Girl from Chicago,* the facsimile of the telegram, Alonzo's processed hairstyle, his suit of clothes, and the inserted segments of classical music on the soundtrack are all signifiers not just of the economic status of the character in the world of the story but also of the production values in the world of the filmmaker. The classical music is pointedly taken from the world of bourgeois aesthetics, interpretable as "dicty" in African-American culture. Since the music is not from the world of the story, it can easily be associated with the world of the filmmaker. Further, this classical music was deployed by Micheaux much as Godard has since deployed musical quotations from a late Beethoven quartet in *Two or Three Things I Know about Her* and as Jean-Marie Straub and Danièle Huillet have deployed fragmentary musical quotations from Bach in *Machorka-Muff* and *Not Reconciled.* Though Micheaux certainly was not attempting to be avant garde (neither were Straub and Huillet, for that matter), Micheaux was, nevertheless, like Godard and Straub and Huillet, consciously *signifying* to his audience through the musical quotations. The emphasis on signifying is common to all these filmmakers. Their conscious decisions, including those of Micheaux, not to "wallpaper" the whole film or even whole sequences with background music but rather to foreground the insertion of musical "sound bites"—something like an insertion of Hearn's *nazoraëru* pebble—emphasized rather than papered over the real world outside the story, the world shared by the filmmaker and the audience, thus indicating, again, an attitude toward filmmaking that is more presentational, and less naturalistic, than the classical. The threshold of entry into illusion is higher in Micheaux's films than is prescribed by the Hollywood standard or by the Institutional Mode of Representation in Noel Burch's terms, and that places

Micheaux's films in a category that includes the avant garde. Though Micheaux surely did not intend to make avant-garde or even modernist films, it is important to understand these de facto alignments as parallel alternative practices that tend to corroborate each other.

Musical Quotation and Reception

As is the case with the race music of Micheaux's time, there is considerable space in Micheaux's films for experiencing overtly the labor of the artist, and there is also space for intervention by the audience. Since, in the case of *The Girl from Chicago,* Micheaux was inserting a fragment of classical music and was choosing a specific narrative moment for the insertion, he could anticipate the conscious, real-world effect of that insertion on a viewer who, upon hearing the fragment, might say to himself or herself, "That piece of music has been inserted; and it is dicty music. That probably means this character, Alonzo, is middle-class, and the filmmaker is signaling something to me about this man and perhaps about himself and the audience he is addressing." If the classical music had been seamlessly woven into the film, the viewer would more likely have remained sutured into the illusion of the story world, immersed in and only unconsciously aware of the middle-class reference and the signifying aspect of the choice of music. In fact, the viewer would have been in a virtual middle-class world, not in the non-virtual presence of a *reference* to a middle-class world.

Micheaux's willy-nilly association with the modernist avant garde could also be extended to include concerns of the postmodern era—after all, Micheaux did not own the classical music he used, since he could not afford to pay for it. Instead, he *appropriated* a quotation of "someone else's" classical music in order to mark the place of high production value and high status in his own middle-class work, just as postmodern conceptualists might mark the place of a complex event (as Yvonne Rainer in *Lives of Performers* marks the place of a dream sequence by simply using slow motion—a cinematic cliche signifying "dream sequence"—of a little girl bouncing a ball) or might appropriate other artists' or corporations' work in order to mark its place in their own art, or might, as rap musicians do, use samplings appropriated from existing work to generate their own critical and signifying music. These all employ presentational as well as representational modes.

It is tempting to propose that Micheaux's appropriation of certain elements of mainstream styles—that disjointed appropriation that is so characteristic of his whole dilemma of assimilation and the problematics of twoness—was an anticipation of the appropriational reaction of the postmodernists against the mainstream of art and society in the 1980s, the era of Ronald Reagan and NWA ("Niggas wit Attitude") and of Margaret Thatcher and hip hop. However, Micheaux's use of musical quotation probably arose from the technical problems related to an inability to mix multiple soundtracks, owing to his probable inability to afford mixing equipment and professional expertise. That fact really changes nothing except the level of intentionality of Micheaux's self-reflexiveness. If Micheaux's signaling of the act of signifying (through the fragmentation of background music into quotations) is best characterized as having been unintentional, then the term "a-illusionistic" better serves to characterize the technique than the more common term "anti-illusionistic." Either way, Micheaux's double level of signification requires and rewards creative and interpretive skills that are analogous to those of self-reflexive, avant-garde cinemas. That interplay of levels of signification accounts for some of the pleasure of repeated viewings of Micheaux's work and of other race movies and inexpensive cinemas, just as the quotational signifying, appropriation, and irony in jazz provide some of the play of meaning that has long spoken to and pleased aficionados of race music. Micheaux's narratives can be read, like modernist texts, in multiple registers, and, like postmodernist texts, in the context of "signifying" quotation and "epic" enunciatory situation.

Negotiating Hierarchy

A scene that continues the sequence of Alonzo's sea passage, discussed above, introduces the female lead, Norma Shepard, and places her carefully within the hierarchical brackets already introduced through Alonzo's complex narrative positioning. Norma is placed in a beautiful garden, where she is seen admiring hydrangeas on a bright sunny day. She is tastefully dressed as a middle-class young woman. She is visited by an older woman, who is dressed in a somewhat more expensive fashion, who speaks with an Eastern-establishment accent, and whose whole bearing signifies wealth and breeding. She could represent a white benefactress of black protegees, a figure something like the patroness who Zora Neale Hurston, Langston Hughes, and Louise Thompson all shared for a time during the Harlem Renaissance in New York. Hurston called this patroness her "Godmother," which would also be an appropriate term for Norma's visitor, Miss Warren. Miss Warren, played by Micheaux's second wife, Alice B. Russell, a light-skinned black woman, is possibly meant to be a surrogate white, or she may represent the black upper-middle class in the world of the story. As such, the term "Godmother" is still appropriate, since her function in the story is to take Norma under her wing by giving her good advice and by finding her a good job as a teacher at a black school in the deep South.

White or black, Miss Warren is carefully constructed as a signifier of economic status and cultural capital—of wealth and worth. Her dress, bearing, accent, skin tone, and her words of advice testify to her status. She is also associated with high cinematic production values in the same way as is the hero, Alonzo. For example, not only are all the above qualities—dress, bearing, complexion, accent—choices of production (mise-en-scène), but Micheaux also carried the western classical music (from the *L'Arlésienne* suites, by Georges Bizet) from the *Europa* scene over into the garden scene, using that music to help characterize Norma, Alonzo's leading woman, and also using that music to "launch" the formidable Miss Warren.[15]

"Launch" is an appropriate term, since Miss Warren enters the frame from the left in a stately manner, moving very slowly and steadily in the same direction as Alonzo's ship was moving just a few shots before; the ship continues to move in the same way in the two insert shots of the ship that were edited, emphatically and intrusively, into the conversation between Miss Warren and Norma. These inserts serve the narrative purpose of reminding the viewer of the hero's continuing ocean crossing, and they serve to associate that crossing with Miss Warren's intervention in Norma's life. Both the ship, which bears Alonzo, and Miss Warren, who bears class and wisdom, move with the same dignified speed and screen direction. Miss Warren's movement toward Norma is intercut with the movement of the ship, which implies that the ship bearing Alonzo is also moving toward Norma, an implication that eventually is made explicit when Alonzo and Norma meet in Batesburg. Alonzo, like Miss Warren, is bearing dignity and class but also the authority, agency, and ability to help Norma navigate through the vestiges of slavery that will soon threaten her. His motion toward Norma on the ship, which is itself an image of a revision of the hated, African-American middle passage, continues in a screen-right direction until Alonzo meets her in the boarding house in Batesburg and begins his mission to redeem her from the continuing effects of the historical middle passage into slavery and peonage. This line of action, while interrupted by numerous intervening actions, is maintained and reinforced absolutely consistently by the screen direction of Alonzo's and Norma's movements, much in the manner of the cinematic figure of the "line of action," first fully developed in D. W. Griffith's Biograph films.[16]

One of the scenes that forwards this metonymic line of action also continues to demonstrate the metaphoric operation of the vertical hierarchies and their associated high and low production values. When the leading woman of the film, Norma Shepard, finally arrives in Batesburg by train, she is observed by the town boss, Ballinger. Moments later, as Norma is walking along a sidewalk with her suitcase, in a continuation of the slow, screen-right line of action, she meets a polite working-class black man, Wade Washington, and asks him the directions to Mary Austin's boarding house. He offers to show her the way. Just as he is about to carry her bag for her, Ballinger (the surrogate-white villain) arrives and gives Washington the evil eye (a castrating glance similar to Abe Lincoln's in John Ford's *Young Mr. Lincoln*), causing Washington to back down and withdraw. Ballinger is dressed in a white linen suit and addresses Norma in a pronounced pseudo-British or New England accent, possibly intended to suggest an aristocratic white southern dialect. His accent is stilted, and along with his dress, it signifies class and status. He tells Norma that Mary Austin cooked for his family for many years and that he will gladly take Norma to Mary Austin's boarding house in his car. His car is an expensive convertible. Norma's response is emblematic of the film's ethical and economic values. She draws herself into a proud posture and says, with disdainful significance, "Thank you, I'd

Fig. 8a. The image of a giant ocean liner bobbing like a cork in the film frame because it is being filmed from a small, wave-tossed craft stands in for Alonzo's "SS EUROPA AT SEA" in *The Girl from Chicago*. Like other movements in this and the following scene, the vessel faces screen right.

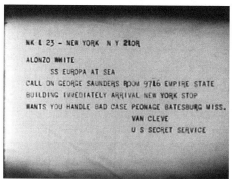

NK L 23 - NEW YORK N Y 210R

ALONZO WHITE
      SS EUROPA AT SEA
CALL ON GEORGE SAUNDERS ROOM 9716 EMPIRE STATE
BUILDING IMMEDIATELY ARRIVAL NEW YORK STOP
WANTS YOU HANDLE BAD CASE PEONAGE BATESBURG MISS.
                              VAN CLEVE
                              U S SECRET SERVICE

Fig. 8b. The telegram Alonzo receives on shipboard during his ocean passage explicitly connects the moving ship with Alonzo's goal, his next mission in Batesburg, Mississippi, which lies thousands of miles "off screen" to the right, in the heart of historical slavery and contemporary peonage. This configuration suggests an investigatory revisitation of the middle passage in the cause of uplift.

Fig. 8c. After reading the telegram, Alonzo moves off purposefully and with concern to screen right . . .

Fig. 8d. . . . and the ship seems to do the same.

Fig. 8e. The next scene seems to "launch" the formidable patroness, played by Alice B. Russell (*left*), who moves in a stately ocean-linerish manner toward screen right to her objective, the same objective as Alonzo's—the leading woman, Norma (behind the hydrangea bush on the right) . . .

Fig. 8f. . . . until they meet in a two shot.

Fig. 8g. The above series inter-cuts the screen-right-moving ship and patroness, then cuts to a screen-right-moving train that takes Norma to Batesburg, where this peonage boss, facing screen left, seems to be waiting for all this screen-right movement to come to a rest at "his" railroad station.

Fig. 8h. Norma does arrive on the train and does encounter the unwanted, pseudo-aristocratic propositional courtesies of the boss . . .

Fig. 8i. . . . but she disdainfully rejects them and continues her screen-right progress toward the safe haven of the middle-class boarding house, where Mary Austin is striving to save money, where Austin's sister is shown practicing her singing, and where Alonzo will eventually arrive (after all *his* screen-right travels) to help Norma and the whole striving enclave to stay the course toward uplift.

rather walk," and continues her interrupted line of action by walking screen-right out of the frame.

The hierarchy of status noted above—in the discussion of Alonzo White's metonymical retracing of the middle passage and his vertically bracketed, purgatorial situation, a middle position between European aristocracy and southern American slavery—is reproduced here as a choice for the leading woman. In the above scene, Norma is faced with a figure of high status and is offered a chance to partake, but she recognizes in the offer an attempt to "proposition" her. Her judgment in this regard later proves to be reliable, since Ballinger is shown soon afterward in a seamy relationship with Liza Hatfield (the "girl from Chicago") and is also shown to be the leader of the peonage racket that Alonzo has been assigned to clear up. Ballinger represents not only very high status but also the very low institution of slavery, since he is the boss of the peonage system and a surrogate-white vestige of the plantation system. In being faced with an invitation from Ballinger, Norma is being bracketed with the same high-and-low structure that confronted Alonzo. She firmly maintains the metonymic line of action established compositely by the ship, Alonzo, Miss Warren, and her own resolve to be a schoolteacher. She walks screen-right through the vertical hazard, taking the *middle path* and avoiding the dangerous attraction of an artificial, unearned elevation founded in her own slavery.

High Production Values as a Dangerous Attraction

The potential attraction in Ballinger is partly in his high production values; his car, his accent, his light skin and Caucasian features, his tonsorial sophistication—all signs of high class. In his first novel, *The Conquest,* Micheaux explicitly stated his ethical judgment of such expensive style. When in that novel Micheaux's autobiographical protagonist, Oscar Devereaux, goes to seek his fortune in Chicago after leaving his family, he visits his older brother. He describes the encounter as follows: "He was not enthusiastic concerning my presence in the city and I had found him broke, but with a lot of fine clothes and a diamond or two. Most folks from the country don't value good clothes and diamonds in the way city folks do and I, for one, didn't think much of his finery." Micheaux went on to reinforce this judgment and to give an indication of where his values lay:

> He went along, wearing his five dollar hat, fifteen dollar made-to-measure shoes, forty-five dollar coat and vest, eleven dollar trousers, fifty dollar tweed overcoat and his diamonds. I found my way to church alone and when I saw him sitting reservedly in an opposite pew, I felt snubbed and my heart sank. However, only momentarily, for a new light dawned upon me and I saw the snobbery and folly of it all.[17]

Micheaux's "Epic Situation": Hierarchy in Production Values

Micheaux was expressing disdain for such spectacle, and thus, he may be expected to have disdained the cinematic production values that contributed to spectacle. He did, however, value material success, and thus, some production values could be expected to have mattered to him. Material success was essential to but not sufficient for uplift (cf. Gaines, *Uplifting the Race*, "Introduction"). Micheaux's narrator did seem to know all the prices for the pieces of his brother's outfit. And Micheaux himself owned a chauffeur-driven car that he used in his distribution circuit. He was proud of his material accomplishments, including his car, all his life, but his pride was grounded in his own productive competence, not in spectacle and display for its own sake. His car signified his material success but also his productive work, since his car was actually a tool of his business, which involved virtually continuous travel for the promotion and distribution of his novels and films.

In the structures of class and status that Micheaux created, Ballinger's grand, master-and-slave, *leisure*-class style can be seen to be in opposition to Micheaux's moderate, middle-class, *work*-oriented style. Ballinger's style, like the Hollywood style, represents spectacle, seduction, and mastery. For Micheaux as filmmaker, to have accepted Hollywood style would have been truly capitalistic and bourgeois, a capitulation to the most problematical aspects of white assimilation and to false ideas of class mobility. For Norma, in the film's story, to have accepted Ballinger's style and his offer of a free ride would have represented the acceptance of an ethos of material elevation without struggle, without productivity, without a substantive association with autonomous action. Her status would have been superficial and unstable, inappropriate to her history and epic situation; it would have required submission to a kind of slavery, almost literally in the sense of "white slavery."

The Middle Path

Norma, however, does the right thing by taking the middle path through this dangerous attraction, thus avoiding both an *artificially high* style and a *genuinely low* degradation (both inherent in the capitalistic bourgeois style) and demonstrating part of Micheaux's answer to some of the dilemmas of twoness. She, preferring to walk (screen right), and Micheaux, preferring moderation, remain on their path to a genuinely black, unassimilated, and self-made middle class.

6   Middle-Class Cinema

The goal of uplifting the race has commonly been portrayed as the attainment of middle-class status for African Americans. The term (and idea) of a middle class is employed here and retained throughout this study despite its semantic vagueness. The difficulties of its application to African Americans are notorious. Kevin Gaines says, "The consequence of th[e] . . . interpretation of the history of black oppression and liberation focusing on the private, depoliticized space of family and emphasizing cultural and behavioral explanations for black poverty, was a self-lacerating middle-class ideology that often pitted black men and women against each other, internalizing prevailing antiblack and misogynist attitudes," and "in light of their tragic plight within a racist social formation, it is more accurate to say that many blacks, or whites, for that matter, were not middle-class in any truly material or economic sense, but rather, represented themselves as such."[1] A term other than "middle-class" might have been chosen, but, despite philosophical and semantic problems, none seems as appropriate. The term "middle-class" needs to be reclaimed in the advanced bourgeois era, an era in which "bourgeois" means upper-class, not middle-class. In the developed world, most citizens, even oppositional filmmakers and writers, are middle-class.

Micheaux's may be the only philosophically and financially middle-class cinema in the history of American film. Since most inexpensive art cinema is anti-bourgeois and anti-middle-class, and since most Third Cinema is leftist, those cinemas are financially middle-class but not philosophically so. Conversely, Steven Spielberg's *E.T.* (1982) and Lawrence Kasdan's *The Big Chill* (1983) are philosophically middle-class (their values are, respectively, suburban and yuppyish), but these films are not financially middle-class—their production values are quite high and, therefore, very expensive. Micheaux's unusual combination of middle-class philosophic values ("uplift") with middle-class production values has been a widely but unfairly denigrated recipe for filmmaking.

A Standard of Moderation

Early chapters of this study have demonstrated that low, inexpensive production values have been the major reason for the negative critical assessments of Micheaux's accomplishment since the era of silent cinema. Micheaux himself treated the problem of underfinancing in his own cinematic discourse, arguing that low production values are an aesthetic issue, because high and costly production values are inherently exclusionary. The uneven conflict between high and low production values in the aesthetic realm reflects the uneven conflict between rich and poor in an American society, a conflict well illustrated in Micheaux's critique of Griffith's films. The causes of the "problem" of low production values are the following: the successful establishment, by D. W. Griffith and Hollywood, of high production values as the principal standard of cinematic beauty throughout *all* classes of western society; the claim, by successful producers, to the ownership of the (high) minimum standard of the means of production; and the corollary implied claim, by successful producers, exclusively to represent not only the class that has the wealth necessary for high production values but all material estates.

Micheaux's critique of Griffith can be understood as a debate between exclusive vs. inclusive social policy—Griffith's "oneness" vs. Micheaux's "twoness." Micheaux was more moderate, more open-ended politically and formally, and more dialectical in his approach to art, which are characteristics of twoness; Griffith was more extreme, more closed-ended formally (e.g., the last-minute rescue with converging "single-point" parallel editing), and less dialectical, which are characteristics of oneness.[2] Though Micheaux, like Griffith, had to fight political censorship, Micheaux also recognized high production values as the stylistic trait that most limited his access to classical aesthetic values because of its direct connection to money.

Micheaux saw high production values as an attraction but also as a danger. Since high production values were just as dangerous as very low production values, Micheaux recommended, and tried to follow, a middle path between them. Just as the good characters in his movies always chose a middle path between elevation and degradation, moderation was also the path Micheaux reckoned would allow him, in real life, to proceed toward his own goal of class mobility through the business and art of cinema.

Micheaux treated the ethics as well as the pragmatics of production values. In his cinematic portrayals of exploitational social relations, a character's fascination with extremely elevated status represented a desire for unequal and exploitative relations with other people. Micheaux recommended moderation. His philosophy of egalitarian social relations was directly linked with production standards lying somewhere between those of the blues and those of the "Great White Way."

Micheaux's critique of white-produced black stereotypes and caricatures is consistent with his reasoning about production values. Concerned that some African Americans had identified with the lower-class roles and with the degradation defined for them by the materially and aesthetically exclusionary processes of the cinema of high production values, Micheaux pointed out not only the danger in high production values, per se (the fragility of falsely elevated status), but also the converse danger in their concomitant degraded roles for those who were excluded from the expensive aesthetic standard (falsely degraded status). His criticism, in *Veiled Aristocrats*, of false aristocracy (see chapter 11) as a response to such general degradation illustrates the dangers of excessive assimilation of the white standards of social class, standards founded on a principle of exclusion that was not in the interests of African Americans.

Micheaux argued for a black middle class founded on meritorious accomplishment rather than a black upper class founded on extra-meritorious assets, such as skin color and family origin. Again—in the face of the bracketing dangers of artificially low (caricature) and artificially high (imitating aristocracies) class position—Micheaux recommended a middle course between the extremes.

Micheaux's film *Murder in Harlem* (1935) demonstrates why moderation in production values and in material estate has structural integrity in the face of a class system and a classical aesthetics; to seek *upper* class position would be to insure the perpetuation of *lower* class position, which is, in the context of the aggregate class actions of all participating African Americans, counterproductive. And since class *conflict* was impractical for African Americans,[3] Micheaux judged that the middle class constituted a goal that was structurally attainable not just by anyone but by everyone and was, thus, a goal with structural integrity.

Whiteness has been said to be inherent in Micheaux's middle-class ideals. To the contrary, however, white avant-garde artists in all media, including film, have tended to be outspokenly anti-middle-class while remaining, as the theorists of Third Cinema point out, economically and ideologically embedded in bourgeois relations of production. White-produced film art ranges from the popular Hollywood model, in which lower-, middle-, and upper-class visions are created by materially upper-class producers, to anti-bourgeois and anti-middle-class visions (art film), which are created by materially middle-class producers. Micheaux's category of middle-class visions created by middle-class producers is under-represented among white cinemas. In fact, Micheaux proposes, in *God's Stepchildren* (1938), to exclude the element of whiteness from his vision of an explicitly black middle class (see Green, *Visions of Uplift*, forthcoming). Micheaux proffered a philosophy of racial loyalty and of partial self-sufficiency for African Americans in the face of white supremacism.

Micheaux was able to create a new species of film, which today would be recognized as postmodernist, by crossing existing species. Analysis of Micheaux's films gives evidence of Micheaux's ability to improvise by using materials from the hybrid American popular culture. Micheaux's deployment of music in *The Exile*, for example, shows that his middle-class position allows for the assemblage, on an equal footing, of various styles of music, both black and white. The lack of exclusive commitment to any one musical estate produced a style of collage, improvisation, signification, and ideological positioning that is comparable in some ways to the race music of his time but that is also surprisingly comparable to the dramaturgic style of Brecht and the cinematic styles of Jean-Luc Godard, Jean-Marie Straub and Danièle Huillet, and Yvonne Rainer. The importance to current cinematic concerns (including those in the realm of representation as well as aesthetics) of a style that encourages hybridity helps explain the reemergence of interest in Oscar Micheaux's films.

The moderate production values evident in Micheaux's films have most often been either regretted or excused. Micheaux probably indulged in both of those responses himself; he also, however, treated them as the stuff of life and of art that required a balanced, progressive attitude. His optimistic but hard-nosed struggle with the standards and realities of high and low production values was part of a dialectical praxis that extended to other aspects of his work. Micheaux blazed a middle path through a forest of vigorously contending and vitally important issues. In this study, that complex and sometimes contradictory path will now be followed through issues of upper and lower classes, master and slave ethics, falsely degraded and falsely elevated entertainment caricature, assimilationist or separatist racial policies, DuBois's and Booker T. Washington's philosophies of intellectual vs. vocational forms of education, and classical and alternative aesthetic styles. The moderate production values displayed in his films are a manifestation and representation of the roughness of his struggle as well as of the efficacy of his decision to keep to a middle path. In continuing to make such films for three decades, Micheaux revised the idea of middle-class cinema; he also attained a middle-class life and created a dynamically balanced vision of African-American citizenship, addressing directly some of the disturbing issues of black middle-class ideology.

Micheaux's extended critique of the standards of production values as an element of film style and as an analog to the material foundations of a lifestyle may be his most original contribution. Through a discourse on production values (a praxis), Micheaux illustrated how beauty and truth are tied to the economic and social relations inherent in cultural production. It is not easy to name another filmmaker of Micheaux's era who mounted such a critique, even in the Soviet and European avant garde of the late 1920s and the related social documentary movement of the 1930s. Micheaux's creation of cogent cinema out of poor means, like that of Soviet, Italian, French, and British filmmakers, is inventive, improvisory, and transformative. In the right hands, such "crooked sticks" can deliver a "straight lick." And, as the following discussion tries to show, Micheaux's discourse on those poor production values transcends the work of his time—and transforms his crooked stick into Aaron's rod.

The Logic of Production Values—An Ethics of Keeper and the Kept

Micheaux's stories suggest not only why low production values were (and are) necessary given the task of uplift, they also suggest, more philosophically, that low production values are more ethical than high production values. Micheaux demonstrated how extreme economic differentials in one of the characteristic blues configurations of "keeper" and "kept" were unethical, and he suggested that such economic relations were analogous to the relations of production in the entertainment industry. Micheaux's story about black productions on Broadway, *Swing!* (1938), treats those issues using the main characters as surrogates for Micheaux himself and for his wife, Alice B. Russell, who acted as his producer under the name A. Burton Russell. Micheaux in this way analyzed the relations of production in race movies. In spite of Micheaux's commitment to entrepreneurial capitalism, his analysis of his own socioeconomic situation can be understood as a critique of the deleterious effects of monopoly capitalism on character and, therefore, on uplift.

Not surprisingly, given Micheaux's attitude toward high production values, Protestant ethics were central to Micheaux's values, just as they were in the old Eastern-establishment values and in the values of ascendant Europe, as discussed by Max Weber in *The Protestant Ethic and the Spirit of Capitalism.* Weber pointed out that "[u]nlimited greed for gain is not in the least identical with capitalism, and is still less its spirit" and that "Capitalism *may* even be identical with restraint, or at least a rational tempering, of this irrational impulse."[4] Weber was speaking of capitalism of the sort propagated by America's Calvinist founders, colored by the deep historical significance Weber brought to that same moment in Europe.

Micheaux, in his first novel, *The Conquest,* described his reaction to America's founding families through the reaction of his main character, Devereaux, to the city of Boston:

> By this time I had seen nearly all the important cities in the United States and of them all none interested me so much as Boston.
> ... the passenger yards were right at the door of the fashionable Back Bay district ... not three blocks from where the intersection of Huntington Avenue and Boylton [sic] Street form an acute angle in which stands the Public Library, and in the opposite angle stands Trinity Church, so thickly purpled with aristocracy and the memory big with the tradition of Philip Brooks, the last of that group of mighty American pulpit orators, of whom I had read so much. ...
> The mornings I spent wandering around the city, visiting Faneuil Hall, the old State House, Boston commons [sic], Bunker Hill, and a thousand other reminders of the early heroism, rugged courage, and far seeing greatness of Boston's early citizens.[5]

Clearly, for Micheaux, the Protestant ethic and the nation's founders provided an example to emulate. If, as Weber said, "modern" capitalism was characterized by restraint and not by greed, it also was "identical with the pursuit of profit, and forever *renewed* profit, by means of continuous, rational, capitalistic enterprise."[6] Weber preceded Micheaux by one generation, flourishing while Micheaux developed; Micheaux would have been breathing the atmosphere of Weber's influential ideas of capitalism, though probably not reading Weber. Micheaux, in other words, developed his theme of uplift in the philosophical atmosphere of a restrained and "rational" capitalism. Though his was the age of tycoons and of the often brutal suppression of the labor movement, Micheaux's formation occurred before the world wars, before the Soviet revolution, and before the anti-capitalist negative dialectics of the Frankfurt School.

Capitalistic as it was, Micheaux's own discourse on the ethics of production reflects the African-American dilemma of twoness. By founding the possibilities of black class mobility on the Calvinistic and capitalistic work ethic, Micheaux was advocating a lifestyle that white supremacists claimed exclusively for their own race. In that sense, though he was becoming "more white," he was at the same time becoming transgressive by poaching on white methods of up-lift that were already proven and closely held.

In keeping with the values of that transgression and that uplift, Micheaux criticized the socioeconomic structure and the ethical implications of the blues. He characterized the figures of "keeper" and "kept," for example, as a negative aspect of blues culture, one that was analogous to master and slave, respectively. By extending the idea of keeper and kept to the financial circumstances of black cultural production—such as black musical theater on Broadway and white-financed race movies themselves—Micheaux accounted for ethical contradic-tions in African-American uplift in the context of petit-bourgeois capitalism. As Charles Burnett was to do in a much later film about the black middle class, *To Sleep with Anger* (1990), Micheaux examined those issues in the context of the blues.

The Blues

The blues form is potentially attractive to proponents of alternative, anti-bourgeois art, in part because of its transgressive content, but also because its homespun production values challenge those of mainstream art forms. One of the qualities that high production values conceal is the labor required to pro-duce value. The seamless perfection of highly produced music, whether popular or classical, suggests an effortless, natural grace. That grace, and its relation to the labor that produces it, is analogous to the lifestyles of the leisure class and their relation to the invisible "dead labor" of capital itself. The same kind of invisibility of labor defines the continuity editing system and the glossy surface of Hollywood film. The 1970s poststructuralist film theories of Metz, Dayan, Oudart, Commoli, Baudry, Burch, and Heath claim that the hidden "film work" underlying the seamless style of mainstream, high-production-value cinema—analogous to the "dream work" in Freud's explanation of the realistic effect of dreams—produces the famous "reality effect" of cinema that is, equally fa-mously, illusionistic. The absence of overt evidence of the labor of production is necessary to the success of the dream state in Freud and of the state of illu-sionism of mainstream cinema in poststructuralist theory.

According to 1970s film theory, the absence of any evidence of labor, of struggle, and of politics is central to the workings of classical Hollywood cinema. The famous essay on John Ford's *Young Mr. Lincoln,* by the editors of *Cahiers du cinéma,* clarifies how the film work relates to dream work, how the film work analogously creates a reality effect with the goal of producing artificial ideology that appears to be natural.[7] The blues, however, is an entirely different form, with essentially different relations to its production and to the representation of its production. The blues arose from, among other sources, rural African-American work songs produced by workers on the job. The sounds of work can be heard in the labored blues style (especially in so-called primitive blues); in the strained but strong voices of the singers with their grunts, moans, and vio-lent articulations of pent-up lung power (see, for example, Robert Johnson[8]); in the singers' "scoops," "falls," and breath interruptions (see Gunther Schuller's analysis of Bessie Smith's style[9]); in the powerful beat of their instrumental accompaniment, corresponding to a pick or hammer (Robert Johnson's guitar); in the two-line repetition at the beginning of each three-line verse, suggesting treadmill manual labor; and in the unsung lines, left open for vocal or instrumental response, reminiscent of call-and-response shouts used by labor gangs and in marching exercises in the military. A blues-like style in cinema might be expected to show analogous effects, giving evidence of the hard work and tough conditions that generated it.

Micheaux's style might be examined for evidence of its proximity to hard work. Micheaux, however, though he was formed by the early hard work of farm, factory, and railroad, was also intent on making a transition out of hard manual labor and into the service and professional sectors of the middle class. And as a film producer, Micheaux was competing with highly capitalized corporations. It would be interesting to pursue Micheaux's own social position and his related film stories in the context of Weber's and Theodor Adorno's analyses of class in relation to the basic split between manual and mental labor. For the latter two individuals, that split was fundamental in the development of the Enlightenment, of capitalism, of reification, and of modern class relations. Perhaps in those terms, uplift, whenever it occurs in modern times, is a phylogenic recapitulation of the ontogeny of the "original sin," the basic division of labor between manual and mental. In any case, since Micheaux was a newcomer to the middle class and a self-made independent producer, it would be likely that he would create neither a rural (peasant) or working-class (proletarian) style nor a slick (bourgeois; upper-class) style but rather a "middle-class" or even petit-bourgeois style, one consistent with the values of uplift that are, in fact, reflected in the Protestant ethic and in the Booker T. Washington–like themes of Micheaux's films.

Micheaux's *Swing!* (1938) does examine the working-class roots of black entertainment, represented by the blues, in relation to the upper-middle-class goals represented by the historical invasion of Broadway by black musical theater (see next chapter). The title itself, *Swing!*, suggests the central dilemma of black entertainment culture, since swing music was a white middle-class appropriation of black working-class musical forms and thus an overt exploitation of artistically successful black cultural work. *Swing!* focuses on black producers of musical theater, but it also represents the dilemma of all black producers, including producers of race movies like *Swing!*

Swing!

Ted and Lena, the principal male and female characters in *Swing!*, are, as were Micheaux and his wife, New York producers of black entertainment. The film begins, however, with the story of Mandy, a black working woman in Birmingham, Alabama, who cooks for a white family (not portrayed in the film) and supports "her man," a "no-account" dandy. The significant secondary characters in the Birmingham sequences include a railroad man, who supports a lazy woman who steps out on him with Mandy's no-account man. After Mandy discovers the deception and catches her man with the other woman, she starts a brawl that marks the end of the Birmingham sequence, and the story then moves abruptly to New York. This migration is announced by a title card that accompanies a scene of a variety-show rehearsal in Harlem. The lead characters of the Harlem sequences, Ted and Lena, become a couple, but they are also, respectively, the producer of the show and his assistant producer. Thus, they are professional associates—partners in a small company, as it were—like Micheaux and his wife, Alice B. Russell. After the above characters and their activities are established, each of the main characters from the Birmingham sequences gradually reenters the story in its new Harlem setting. As in *The Girl from Chicago,* the disorienting effect of the great black migration to the urban North is handled by a jolting transition in the middle of the film.

The Migrations in *Swing!*

The migrations were jolting in more ways than are implied by the profound inconvenience associated with pulling up deep roots and moving to a new territory, new climate, new economic system, and new urban environment. David Levering Lewis has emphasized that the consequences were also potentially deadly:

> DuBois joyously shared [the] confidence [of migrating black laborers], writing in *The Crisis* that the Afro-American worker "will soon be in a position to break any strike when he can gain economic advantage to himself." With 250,000 workers locked out or on strike in Chicago in late July 1919, the city was primed for the race war touched off by the drowned boy in Lake Michigan. . . .
> . . .
> Those who harbored doubts about *braving genocide* [emphasis added] in 1919 were already searching for a less heroic role for the New Negro to play in defending the rights of his people. . . . The Red Summer had shown that most white Americans, North and South, were in no mood for generosity, and that outright conflict was a course pointing to almost certain doom.[10]

On the positive side, Lewis portrays the euphoria of migration:

> King Solomon Gillis, the protagonist of "City of Refuge," a short story by one of Harlem's most promising novelists, Rudolph Fisher, was a southern peasant born to buy the Brooklyn Bridge twice. Exiting from the Lenox Avenue subway stop at 135th Street, Gillis exclaimed, "Done died an' woke up in heaven."[11]

Micheaux makes use of Harlem as the Mecca of migration. As is the case with *The Girl from Chicago,* a noticeable motive for the migration from the rural South to the urban North in *Swing!* is the need to *make a living producing entertainment* during the height of the depression and in the fading light of the Harlem Renaissance. A host of the people seen in the Birmingham sequences show up again in the Harlem sequences. The orchestra in Ted's show in Harlem is the same as the one that plays at the roadhouse in Birmingham, where Mandy discovered her man stepping out. The woman who solos on the trumpet at that roadhouse in Alabama later auditions for Ted's show in Harlem. Lena herself, who as Ted's assistant plays a part in producing the Harlem Renaissance–like culture, is from "Alley C" in the Birmingham neighborhood that Mandy knows so well. When the Alabama railroad man's woman appears in the Harlem scenes, it is as Cora Smith, the star of Ted's show. Both she and the railroad man play their parts in the production of the Renaissance—when the railroad man appears in the Harlem scenes, he appears as the owner of a nightclub called the Autumn Leaf Social Club. He also remains Cora's keeper, as he had been in the South, but now he is also her manager in a public sense; they are both part of a larger and more urban movement and predicament.

The Migrations as an Upgrading of Cultural Production

It is important to recognize that the migrations are not a digression or rupture in the narrative (nor in this chapter on the ethics of production in the vision of uplift). Within the wrenching dialectics of the migrations, Micheaux made use of the idea of Harlem and the Harlem Renaissance for his story about class mobility and its relation to black entertainment. The Renaissance was, as the name implies, a rebirth for the migrators as well as for the Harlem literati, a proof that uplift was possible.

If Harlem and the Renaissance were the Mecca of uplift, they were also, however, geographically and socially distant from most African Americans. Recognizing the profound split that North and South represented for all African Americans—one that embodied the multiple dialectics of twoness—Micheaux represented the blues as southern and uplift as northern. Lena, the young assistant producer in *Swing!*, is from Birmingham, as is virtually every other character in the Harlem of this story. When Lena recognizes Mandy, who has come north after the breakup of her blues-like relationship of keeper and kept, Lena tries to help Mandy by getting her a job on the stage production as a seamstress and wardrobe designer. Cora Smith, the two-timing, kept woman from the Birmingham sequences, shows up in Harlem as the star of Ted and Lena's production; they call her their "blues singer and mammy lead." The producer Ted, who loosely represents Micheaux, refers to Cora as the best blues singer in the Negro race. Historically, there were several important female blues singers named Smith to whom Micheaux might have been alluding, including Clara, Mamie, and Trixie. There was also, to match Micheaux's Cora Smith by first names, Cora Green, one of the first commercial blues singers, whom Alberta Hunter described as having "an 'in-between voice, between sweet and jazz'."[12] Micheaux's Cora Smith, however, was probably a direct reference to the most obvious figure, Bessie Smith. Ted's reference to the Cora Smith in *Swing!* as the best blues singer in the Negro race could only apply to Bessie Smith, who was called the empress of the blues. And Bessie Smith was from the South, and, to some extent, she equated her qualifications as the blues empress to her southernness—Bessie

Smith's denigration of Ethel Waters's lack of blues talent was capsulized in Smith's term for her, "northern bitch."[13]

The dialectic of North and South was not just the dialectic of blues vs. swing in the aesthetic contexts of talent and cultural authenticity, or roots. It was also a dialectic of capital vs. labor. The North was historically more capitalized than the South; thus, the migrations were (though extremely complex in motivation, as James Grossman has explained in *Land of Hope*[14]) in part a pursuit of capital to fuel aspirations of class mobility. King Solomon Gillis, the "southern peasant" in Rudolf Fisher's story "City of Refuge," implies as much: "'In Harlem,' he reflected, surveying the Lenox Avenue scene, 'black was white. You had rights that could not be denied you; you had privileges, protected by law. And you had money. Everybody in Harlem had money.'"[15]

Urban Blues—Capital and Labor

The southern blues ethic of keeper and kept could, with northern financing, transform itself into an ethic of capital and labor. In *Swing!*, Cora's man, the railroad worker who was keeping Cora financially and domestically in Birmingham, has become petit-bourgeois in Harlem, the owner of a nightclub called the Autumn Leaf Social Club. More importantly, he is the manager of Cora's career. When Cora, the "mammy lead," behaves like a prima donna and jeopardizes the show, the former railroad man discovers her behavior and disciplines her, precisely in the manner of a manager. Thus, the railroad man, with his social club and his "talent agency," and Ted and Lena, with their show, are now producers in the sense of Weber's modern capitalism; their relations of production *produce capital* in a way suggested by the following quotation from Karl Marx: "A singer who sells her song for her own account is an unproductive laborer. But the same singer commissioned by an entrepreneur to sing in order to make money for him is a productive laborer; for she produces capital."[16]

Producer and Produced

Micheaux's image of himself as an entrepreneurial producer must have grown more important to him as his durable career continued, decade after decade. The preceding chapter indicated that the theme of entertainment production is important to a movie like *The Girl from Chicago*, even though the main characters are neither producers nor entertainers themselves. Later chapters will extend the production theme to Micheaux's other show-business films, such as *The Darktown Revue* (1931) and *Ten Minutes to Live* (1932), and even to the murder mysteries, such as *Murder in Harlem* (1935). The concern in *Swing!* for the realm of production is so pervasive that the idea of production extends to the ethos of life in general. All the primary and secondary characters in the film are either producers or they are "produced" in their private or professional lives. The most important secondary couples are Mandy and her no-account man and Cora, the initial mammy lead of the show, and her railroad man. These are complementary and perverted relationships of "keeping." Mandy keeps her man, supplying him with money, fine clothes, and a modest room and board through her job as a cook for white people. The railroad man keeps his woman, supplying her with money, fine clothes, jewelry, room and board, and a car, through his railroad job. Given the context of the primary theme of the film—the production of a New York show—and given the message of the film—that the show's success depends on the authenticity of the lead performer's relationship with the blues, an authenticity that springs directly from domestic relations—then the phenomenon of keeping can be understood as a relationship of production. To keep someone is to *produce* him or her as an object of love and desire, even an object of (sexual) entertainment, analogous to an actor or a singer in the entertainment industry.

Though the connection is not made explicitly, one reason Mandy can be promoted and "produced" by Lena (later in the film) as a seamstress and wardrobe producer for the show is that Mandy has already gained experience, through her real-life blues background, as a "wardrobe designer" for her man. Her man is a dandy, a clotheshorse, a spectacle, and as such, she has long since been "producing" him as a walking manikin. When Lena is touting Mandy's qualifications as a seamstress to the show's producer, Mandy is worried that Lena is lying about Mandy's actual professional experience. Lena feels compelled to explain later how her love for Mandy, her feeling of indebtedness for past kindnesses from Mandy (in Birmingham), and her racial loyalty (all powerful motives) justify her lie. The deeper logic of the film tells the attentive viewer, however, that Lena is not lying. Mandy is qualified. The same love and desire that motivated her keeping of her man also explain her competency at wardrobe production. The very same love and desire also explain Mandy's authority as a blues singer later on in the story. Later, when Cora falls down a flight of stairs while drunk and breaks her leg, the show is saved when Lena realizes that hard-working, hard-loving Mandy will make a perfect replacement, in the mammy lead, for Cora Smith. Mandy "just lubs dat man," "dat man" being the dandy from Birmingham, who has come north in order to resume exploiting Mandy. The implicit logic of the narrative is that if Mandy is so in love as to put up with such a no-account man, then she obviously understands the blues. The show then receives a godsend in the form of financial backing from a white investor, but this investor makes two demands: that Mandy star and that the show's title be changed to "I lubs dat man!" Mandy's star quality, and thus her (modestly) elevated status as spectacle—and her exchange value—come directly from her marginal life of everyday struggle, which in this film is not masked by slick production values and is identified as the working position, in real life, of the stereotype of "mammyhood," a position directly related to the blues.

Stereotypes as Denial of Labor

As Micheaux aimed at the higher financing that uplift required, he certainly had to face the potential contradictions of producing the stereotypes demanded by more mainstream entertainment, the stereotypes Micheaux has been accused of producing himself (as discussed in chapter 4). Those stereotypes have dominated most previous discussions of race movies and of Hollywood's treatment of black characters. And those stereotypes are part of the apparatus of masking the contributions that labor makes to any classical style, as Ed Guerrero has pointed out.[17] As usual, Micheaux chose a middle path, but he also constructed a discourse complex enough to include dialectic and irony. *Swing!* works to qualify the stereotype of the mammy not just by supplying the evidence of struggle, which is often concealed by the mammy caricature, but also by treating the mammy specifically as a role, but as a role that has an understandable and even honorable basis in the love and desire that occur in the everyday life of the blues. Micheaux's use of the mammy stereotype is self-reflexive; since the mammy role is a role in the nightclub show within the film, it is explicitly treated as a kind of "signifying" (the demonstrating of a contextual understanding superior to the role) in a way that is different from those mammy roles discussed by Donald Bogle. Bogle has shown how the actresses in mammy parts were "signifying" in spite of the producers of the films in question. The producers of the Hollywood films Bogle discusses were not black and were intending to produce straight stereotypes; those stereotypes, Bogle shows, were undermined by the ingenious signifying skills of the actresses.[18] Micheaux, however, found a film director's way to signify that is analogous to the signifying of Bogle's actors and actresses. Thus, Micheaux, like Bogle's signifying performers, helped to transform the damaging stereotypes of the mainstream culture. Chapter 10 will show how Micheaux's self-reflexive signifying of stereotypes connected entertainment to everyday life. In all these ways, Micheaux made an early and sophisticated, if not widely recognized, contribution to film culture, which badly needed oppositional tactics and strategies.

Micheaux's contribution was as important to African-American cultural politics as it was to the art of cinema. His conception of a leading role, even a "mammy lead," is informed, among other things, by a work ethic, and that ethic informs the production ethics of Micheaux's story. Micheaux's "hero" producer makes a decision to replace a *fake* lead—the grandstanding but lazy Cora Smith, who is living the Broadway life—with a *true* lead—the modest but hard-working Mandy, who has been living the life of the blues that she is asked to portray in the show. According to Marx, all value, no matter how great or remunerative, ultimately must rest on a foundation of quotidian work. Micheaux seems to have believed that such work must be part of any effective, transformative vision of uplift. The work should not be hidden by the role playing, spectacle, and production values, all of which comprise comparatively fragile props to class elevation.

Exaggerated Production Values

Micheaux produced a demonstration of the fragility of such elevation in having Mandy's man and the railroad man's woman—the male and female epitomes of spectacle, role playing, and exploitation—step out together. The two lavishly produced, kept love objects are attracted to each other, thus going against their keepers' express wishes but ironically following the logic of their keepers' exaggerated domestic "production values." The keepers/producers of the two kept/produced objects of desire cannot afford even to participate directly in the style they create for their kept/produced objects. The economic and stylistic division between keeper and kept creates a relationship that is inherently unstable, a state of affairs that is analogous to the relation of the middle classes to Hollywood movies and of athletes and sports fans to professional sports. It makes sense that Micheaux's two kept characters would be repelled by the styles of speech and dress of their own keepers and that they would instead be drawn toward each other, seeing their highly produced, slick style as more appropriate and more desirable than the styles of their inelegantly laboring keepers in the working class. The same can be said for actors and producers in relation to their middle-class movie audiences and for athletes and owners in relation to their fans—stars and filmmakers, athletes and owners are slick; fans are ordinary stiffs. (So who are the keepers and who the kept?)

As in *The Girl from Chicago* (see chapter 5), Micheaux has constructed in *Swing!* a vertical bracket system of high and low values. This time a *working class,* comprised of the railroad man and the cook, forfeits a potential *middle-class* position by financing an *upper-class* style for its objects of desire. The style with high production values—denoted by the car, the clothing, and the leisure of the kept lovers in *Swing!*—is an inappropriate style for any middle-class producer, according to the logic of the film. And that same logic suggests that if it was inherently unstable for a lover to keep her love object at a higher level than the keeper could afford for herself, then it was also unstable for a film producer, such as Micheaux, to produce films with production values that radically exceeded what that producer and his audience could afford. The possible consequence in both cases was the reversal of the evident goals of the producer; instead of possession, loyalty, satisfaction, respect, pride, gratitude, and freedom, the probable return on investment was alienation, betrayal, denial, disdain, shame, ingratitude, and slavery. Micheaux felt that the same returns on investment awaited any potential or hypothetical black producers of a Hollywood-like cinema.

Relations of (Cultural) Production

The kept couple is epiphenomenal to its keepers in ways that anticipate Louis Althusser's description of base and superstructure: "on the one hand, *determination in the last instance by the (economic) mode of production* [base; keepers]; on the other, *the relative autonomy of the superstructures and their specific effectivity* [superstructure; kept]."[19] According to that analogy of Micheaux's keeper/kept and Althusser's base/superstructure, the autonomy of the kept couple is illusory in the same way as is the autonomy of the superstructure. An ultimate dependency on the keepers as economic base structurally contradicts the seeming freedom of the superstructural kept. Micheaux demonstrates such structural contradictions. When Mandy's man is explaining to Mandy his perception of their contract, he corrects her English, telling her not to say "Co'se I does," because, he says, the dialect "sounds so dumb." He is acting here, like the kept woman discussed above, in an inversion of his kept relationship. He is ineffectually trying to do what real capitalists do, to *reverse the relations of production,* to manage (or "produce") his keeper, his source of capital: i.e., to manage the labor force so as to extract surplus value. He is acting with a "dicty" freedom that, since he is dependent on his laborer, is artificial, incompetent, and, finally, untenable. He is as bad a producer here as the railroad man's woman is when she attempts the confidence game of deluding her keeper. For one thing, it is obvious that Mandy's man cannot hope to change Mandy; for another, he would be incompetent to do so, since he himself, a few lines later, uses an egregious equivalent of the dialect he had corrected in her. He is also a bad producer, according to the logic of Micheaux's version of the entertainment industry, since the denouement will show that any correction of Mandy's dialect is a misguided attempt to reshape a style of speech that has historical relations with the blues. Thus, he is trying to correct the very style that will make Mandy well suited for the "mammy lead" in the big show. And what is more, he is damaging a style that is directly related to his own talent as a piano player, a talent that will eventually get him a part in the show as well, in spite of his counterproductive interventions.

In contrast to Mandy's man, Lena, the producer's assistant, will have seen the value in Mandy's dialect, and Ted will have had the good show-business sense to believe Lena and to incorporate her insight into his show. Lena and Ted are the most perspicacious producers in the film; the poor judgment of secondary characters in the film helps to set off the wisdom of Lena's production ideas and of Ted's production decisions. The "good judgment" Micheaux portrays in Ted and Lena is based on a middle position between blues and swing, a position that accurately reflects the economic foundation (base) for their show (superstructure). Ted's recognition of Lena's competence as, literally, an assistant producer is also clearly an autobiographical tribute by Micheaux to his wife, who is credited as producer of *Swing!* and of other films by Micheaux ("A. [Alice] Burton [B.] Russell Presents"). *Swing!* is, thus, a proprioceptive film about the pragmatics and ethics of producing black entertainment and, more broadly, black culture; these pragmatics and ethics amount to middle-class cinema.

"Producing" the Ideal Couple

The illusory autonomy of superstructure is best dramatized in the scenes in which the kept love objects of both couples come together as an "epicouple." An implicit comparison is then made between the two keepers and their respective kept lovers, a comparison that emphasizes production competence itself. This comparison is prepared for by scenes involving each of the separate keeper/kept couples. As the railroad man is leaving his apartment for a three-day run, he sits on the bed beside his supine lover, who claims she is sick but who is discernibly faking. He offers to get her a doctor, but she says no: it is just a headache. He is suspicious, which is to say that she is producing a fiction that the railroad man does not believe; that makes her an incompetent producer. He recites the contract between them, telling her that he is "doing for her" and that if he ever catches some loafer looking at her, he will kill him. She looks truly worried and tells him that though she wants him to love her, she doesn't want him to kill anyone for her. The viewer knows she is thinking of her fancy back-door man. The railroad man reiterates his position while assuming a physical position that marks his claim on her, almost strangling her in the process of kissing her goodbye. An analogous scene occurs between Mandy and her man, though Mandy's threats are more solicitous and more financial than physical. Each of these keeper partners is trying to *produce* in the respective kept partner a type of character on whom he or she can rely, with the keeper finally maintaining the upper hand by economic purchase and sheer force.

In spite of this seemingly one-sided relationship of power and relative competence of keeper over kept, Mandy's no-account man and the railroad man's no-account woman make much of their individual autonomies. Cora, for example, boasts to her back-door man about her relative competence in the altercation discussed above, which, from the film viewer's privileged point of view, had apparently been resolved in the railroad man's favor, not in Cora's. Mandy's man, in like fashion, claims he is better than Cora at making his keeper, Mandy, do just what he wants.

The scene in which the railroad man recites the contract, and a later scene in which Mandy's kept man explains how he understands the relationship he has with Mandy, demonstrate that all *four* of the characters are acting as producers of fictional states of affairs. The keepers, though better at producing their desired results than are the kept, are nevertheless also producing incompetently in a different way. The keepers are better at it than the kept, because they have the financial means that lends material substance to their production; they are the "base" in the base/superstructure analogy. The fiction (superstructure) produced by the kept is essentially a confidence game without material substance. The fictions produced by the keepers are more than confidence games; they can purchase "goods" in a market relationship that is equivalent to "johns'" solicitations of prostitutes. Their fictions are backed up by money, which is produced by their own labor. The confidence games of the "ideal" kept couple, however, (Cora's ruse about her headache) are ultimately inadequate in the face of the material substance of the keepers (the railroad man's reiteration of his financial support and, thus, his claim on Cora). Again, the material substance of the keepers is equivalent to Althusser's economic base, and the confidence games are equivalent to the superstructure.

Micheaux reveals the idealized, unrealistic nature of the epi-couple by constructing what, in the light of poststructuralist theory of the 1970s, amounts to an inversion. In Althusser, the base/superstructure figure represents capital supporting culture; in Micheaux's keeper/kept figure, labor supports a culture that masquerades as *capital*-supported, not labor-supported—an ideal couple. That is, the railroad man and Mandy have jobs, which under capitalism ought to put them in a dependent and dialectical relationship with capital. Instead, they are throwing up a mask of production values, financing Cora and the no-account man, respectively, which disguises labor as capital. This is an aspect of their fiction that does not work. The upper-class lifestyle of the epi-couple is a farce. Such masking of economic relations is not conducive to uplift in Micheaux's films, and it is not difficult to see why. The kept figures represent an illusion of capital and uplift, not the real thing. Real capitalists are sustained by accumulated capital, Marx's "dead labor." The railroad man and Mandy are financing a vision of a leisure class through their own living labor. They are not capitalists, and they are investing their lives, love, and desire in a fragile construct that they will not be able to control.

An Ethics of Production Values

The relationship that is fragile is also unethical, since it masks personal relations that replicate the master/slave imbalances of power discussed in Hegel, Marx, and Althusser; keeper and kept are persons who are "producer" and "produced" to each other, a Pygmalion syndrome. There are many other instances of this film's concern for such ethics of production, including the following:

(1) The exchanges of the keepers and the kept are not just conversations involving give and take, listening and responding, arguing cases, developing common points, and the like. Rather, each person's rhetoric is an attempt *to direct* another person's action and style. These domestic exchanges represent acts of production that mimic many of the functions of film producing: financing, oral contracts, negotiation, bargaining, grievances, and direct orders. The general condition of domestic keeper and kept also mimics acts of direction, as in a film, such as costuming, dialogue coaching, "talent" management, and blocking. Thus, Micheaux's film characters perform flagrant acts of mise-en-scène and redaction on each other's persons.

(2) The keepers, as producers with mere material values, are not able to produce true confidence—love, loyalty, and stability—no matter how strong their will to work, to fight, and even to kill. The kept, as producers of mere confidence values, are not able to extend their game beyond the contract and cannot use their "conned" materials, their production values and sense of high style, autonomously. Like labor under capitalism (and like superstructural culture "over" basic capital), the kept remain ultimately an epiphenomenon of the keepers' game.

Since the construction of an adequate representation of the black middle-class couple is a primary concern of Micheaux's, the epiphenomenal state of the kept couple is a problem. According to Micheaux's ethical values, the "good" ideal couple (the Broadway-bound show's producer and assistant producer, Ted and Lena) serves as an instrument for the production and perhaps for the accumulation of wealth and culture; the "bad" ideal couple (the falsely elevated, kept couple in *Swing!*) serves as an image of unearned, "premature" accumulation and of direct, covert exploitation of a lower class of workers. Micheaux makes covert exploitation visible. In that sense, the relation of the pyramid of couples—the kept couple standing on the shoulders of the keeper couple—is an ethical model of structurally exploitative class relations. It is an almost literal image of false, unstable uplift.

(3) Micheaux's own ethics of moderation are narratively corroborated, in that neither set of producers—the keepers or the kept—has chosen a middle ground or middle way from which to negotiate, at the appropriate level, for the most valued things of life, whether these be material or spiritual. Inappropriately high production values are an aspect of the imbalance and the poor judgment of the keepers, which reflect an underlying imbalance in the relations of production.

Conclusion

The dilemma of production values in relation to uplift is historically implicit in the title of the film *Swing!*. The exploitation of blues and jazz in the creation and development of swing music—an often overproduced white adaptation of blues and jazz—raised confusing issues of race and class, of status and community; swing created an ethical dilemma for black producers. The self-made quality of Micheaux's success undoubtedly affected his attitude toward that dilemma. High status was one of the goals of uplift. High status was desirable in Micheaux's ethical system, but only when it was earned; it was dangerous and unstable when it was unearned. Also, Micheaux's stories about the middle path and the message of the film *Swing!* affirm that personal, racial, and artistic autonomy could be maintained and strengthened through earned status, or true class mobility, but would be jeopardized by unearned status, or false class mobility.

When applying such stories as those in *Swing!* to the circumstances of Micheaux's professional life, it is clear that the elevated style of Hollywood, with its highly capitalized corporations, might have been appropriate for its rich producers, but it was inappropriate, illusory, and threatening to the autonomy of an independent producer like Micheaux and was threatening to most African Americans as well, as Micheaux repeatedly demonstrated to his audiences. Unlike Hollywood's style—including the style of Hollywood-produced films made for black audiences, such as *Hallelujah!* (1929) and *The Green Pastures* (1936)—Micheaux's style, with its middle-class production values, was appropriate to the economic class and status of his films and of their intended audience. His style reflected work—both manual and mental, both lower- and middle-class—in contrast to the mainstream styles, which tended to erase the work that produced them. Micheaux sensed that the erasure of work in the representation of uplift would misrepresent the realities of class advancement, creating false perceptions that would tend to keep audiences in their place, and he made stories about what he sensed. Micheaux's stories and their style both reflect uplift at the same time that they reflect work, in part by representing an African-American reality that is, interestingly enough, not defined exclusively by manual labor. In that sense too, this reality is middle-class.

Any tendency by critics to see Micheaux's emphasis on earned status as overly conservative and quietistic in relation to late-twentieth-century issues—such as the welfare state or affirmative action—should perhaps be tempered not just by historical context but also by reflection on Micheaux's lifelong parallel critique of racist obstruction of the status that actually *was* earned by African Americans and by reflection on Micheaux's consistent tendency, in the interest of real politics, to take—as many of us from the middle class (broadly defined) have done—a middle but progressive path between extreme positions.[20] Micheaux's critique and his tendency to take a middle but progressive path between extreme positions yielded a rare example of oppositional cinema that is middle-class in both its philosophic and economic values, thus providing a model of the middle class as a position from which social progress—in Micheaux's case, race, class, and gender emancipation—can be pursued with integrity in the context of cultural production, which is structurally impossible in the film industry.

7   White Financing

The following blues was written by [Broadway's] Porter Grainger and sung by [blues empress] Bessie Smith:

Put It Right Here or Keep It Out There

I've had a man for fifteen years, give him his room and board;
Once he was like a Cadillac, now he's like an old, worn-out Ford.

—Amiri Baraka (LeRoi Jones), *Blues People* [bracketed material added]

Between the Blues and the Great White Way

If one of the horns of the dilemma of twoness was assimilation, then surely the need for and the danger of white money was one of the great trials in the pilgrim's progress of uplift. Micheaux had to negotiate a middle path through the dangerous attractions of false uplift and white assimilation, including the dangerous attraction of white financing. That same negotiation continued to characterize the style and content of his films *after* he had chosen to seek the white financing that became necessary in order for him to make the expensive transition from silent to sound film. His continuing goal of uplift without the sacrificing of autonomy required that he not exceed a minimum budgetary standard, which caused him to seek a middle path between Broadway and the blues.

Swing!, Continued

Micheaux's fourteenth sound film, *Swing!,* discussed in the previous chapter, is a parable of decisions such as those described above, since the central event of the plot is the production of a Harlem variety show. The main characters are Lena and Ted, the show's producers. Their narrative problem does not center on their personal relationship with each other, which is idealized and devoid of conflict, but rather on whether they can bring the show to final production and make it succeed when it gets to the stage. The central action of the film is cultural production itself. The biggest problem with the show is the star, Cora Smith, "the best blues singer in the Negro race." Her stardom itself causes the problem and threatens the entire venture. She has gotten "too big" for the situation. Her keeper, who serves as her manager, is able to control her professional arrogance when he discovers it, but he cannot discipline her daily life, for she eventually gets drunk and breaks her leg. She becomes an example of the danger of inflated production values. Mandy—an example not of the kept but of the life of daily struggle that historically gave rise to the blues—replaces Cora Smith as the star.

A Pep Talk for Moderation

Micheaux prepared the ethical and economic basis for the lesson of Cora's grandstanding behavior and the narrative centrality of its consequences by having Ted, the film's hero and the show's producer, give an overtly didactic lecture to his cast and crew:

> Alright folks, gather round. Hear what we'll have to say. I hope you like it folks, but these are only rehearsals. I want you to remember that. If we go to falling in love with our own efforts, often only to be let down so hard after the first night until the heart is taken out of everybody by the bad press notices they get the morning after [sic]. And we don't want that to happen to our show. You know and I know that while a colored show may be and is supposed to stay within a certain prescribed scope, we must, if we hope to get anywhere, deliver something within that scope that the public will like and come to see, that is entirely different from what that audience has become accustomed to seeing and hearing. That, my people, is what I'm hopeful of giving them. So I want all of you to do your best. Unbend, relax, give me all that's in you. But don't, oh please don't begin thinking how good you are and all that. *Just hope you're fair and try to get better* with every rehearsal. And then the show will get over, and the public will like and come to see you. [Emphasis added]

This set piece follows a quintessential opening sequence that establishes the blues-life characters of the keepers and the kept. Ted's speech could serve as the summary statement of Micheaux's strategy of the middle path—to a life leading out of that blues life—"just hope you're fair and try to get better." Ted, Micheaux's surrogate for himself as film producer, gives a pep talk for moderation (the oxymoron of "pep" and "moderation" notwithstanding). To some viewers, the speech may appear middle-class in the worst sense of the term, characterized by reduced ambition, low expectation, and middling self-esteem. The strategy is, nonetheless, Micheaux's considered compromise as a producer, a compromise that allowed him to produce African-American films all his life and to envision and demonstrate a middle-class position for African Americans. Micheaux received "bad press notices . . . the morning after" for much of the second half of his career, but he learned to accept the limitations in technical and production quality that generated such notices. The semi-quietism of that policy and of Ted's speech can be balanced against the historical success of the strategy and the lack of success associated with more naive strategies for producing race movies. Micheaux's only comparatively successful competition in the production of black-produced cinema was the career of Spencer Williams, and Williams's strategy, though less fatuously stated perhaps than Ted's speech, was similarly middle-class in its mode of production. The grander attempts to produce race movies, such as Emmett Scott's "challenge" to Griffith, *Birth of a Race,* failed utterly. And quite possibly, Ted's/Micheaux's statement is not fatuous from the lower-middle-class perspective of the characters, the filmmaker, and the intended audience of this film.

Ted's speech is stylistically similar to the speech by Nevsky, a surrogate Joseph Stalin, at the end of Eisenstein's (and Stalin's) production of *Alexander Nevsky* (1938). Micheaux, however, did not place his lecture as a coda at the end of the story. Instead, Micheaux went on to offer further narrative illustration to support the rhetoric of Ted's pep talk. A few scenes later, Cora comes to rehearsal late and drunk; grandstanding outrageously, she unwittingly provides a dramatic demonstration of the wisdom of Ted's call for moderation. This scene is concluded by the appearance of Cora's manager, who deals out explicit punishment for her behavior. Mandy, on the other hand, exuding humility, conforms perfectly to the ethics of Ted's speech—and saves the show.

Bessie Smith vs. Ethel Waters

A historical perspective on Micheaux's intentions can be gained by substituting from real life the functionally equivalent figures of Bessie Smith and Ethel Waters, respectively, for Micheaux's fictional Cora Smith and Mandy. The front page of the Pittsburgh *Courier* of May 23, 1931, featured a large leading headline on the release of Micheaux's "first big venture in [the] dramatic talking field," *The Exile.* On the same front page, coincidentally, is another large headline that reads "Bessie Smith accused of deserting company down in Wheeling, W. Va." Such headlines regarding Bessie Smith appeared often in the black press. The following general observations about Smith (by one of her biographers) emphasize the headstrong autonomy of her personality:

> If I try to conjure up Bessie's presence, in wig and feathers, ready to go on stage, she rises before me, a large-framed woman, with a quick temper, used to resorting to violence when crossed. She was strong enough to fell a man; and she didn't always wait to be attacked before using her fists.[1]
>
> . . . she was capable of behaving with complete irresponsibility. She might leave the whole troupe behind and set off for New York in a temper. Or get so drunk that the police in some small town would have to lock her up, and the show would have to go on without her. An angry manager would dock a whole day's pay from everyone for such behavior; and to make things more difficult, Bessie often failed to pay for hotel rooms before disappearing.[2]
>
> She had always alleviated the exhausting business of being on tour with liquor, parties and promiscuous love-making.[3]
>
> . . . Jack [Gee, Bessie's first husband] began to look into her business arrangements a little.[4]
>
> For his part, Jack needed to establish some kind of husbandly control over his wife.[5]

Jack was stronger than Bessie, and she respected him most when he challenged her physically.[6]

All of the above observations apply also to Micheaux's character Cora Smith. Moreover, not only do Cora Smith and her keeper-manager pretty accurately replicate Bessie Smith and her husband-manager, but Cora Smith's relation to Mandy in the movie also parallels Bessie Smith's relation to Ethel Waters in real life, as the following quotations suggest:

> Bessie's empire extended more widely than Ma [Rainey]'s, but she never aspired to widen it in the way Ethel Waters was able to. . . .
> Ethel was a singer with talent. . . . Born in a slum in Chester, Pennsylvania, she was brought face to face with poverty and squalor at least equal to anything in Bessie's childhood. But her grandmother was hard-working and determined that she wanted a better life for her children. It was her voice which urged Ethel towards cleanliness and moderation in her drinking.
> . . .
> Ethel Waters went on to star in Broadway musicals, and to act in Hollywood. Neither world opened to Bessie.
> . . .
> . . . [Ethel] made herself the deliberate antithesis of all Bessie stood for. . . .
> Bessie sensed this opposition instinctively, and was jealous of her. . . .
> Ethel Waters did not hold this against Bessie, in whom she recognized both spirit and greatness. And she did not challenge Bessie, though she was willing to fight hand to hand herself. She had a much stronger need to be liked than Bessie. It was only in the world of show business that she found solace and camaraderie.[7]

Despite the fact that Ethel Waters came from the North (and, as discussed below, that she was "whiter" than Bessie in appearance and behavior), she could in several ways serve as the real-life equivalent of Micheaux's character, Mandy. Mandy and Cora are rivals in Micheaux's film in much the same way Feinstein describes Ethel and Bessie to be rivals in real life at the time of Micheaux's sound films. Mandy does not challenge Cora's greatness in Micheaux's film, but she is "willing to fight hand to hand" and does just that in the roadhouse when Cora tries to steal Mandy's man. In addition, Mandy, without challenging Cora, eventually succeeds on Broadway, just as Ethel Waters succeeded without challenging Bessie. Micheaux's Cora Smith does not succeed on Broadway, just as Bessie Smith did not in real life.

Black Cultural Production

Micheaux's deployment, in surrogate form, of these two exemplary public figures and their perceived relation to whiteness allowed him to explore in his art the production of black culture in white America. During Micheaux's career, the whiteness of the Great White Way was being broached for the first time by black performers, producers, composers, and lyricists. The first production of a black musical theater that transcended minstrelsy and used black performers rather than whites in blackface was *The Creole Show* (produced by Sam T. Jack, 1890), and it "created something of a sensation in New York when they edged up to the 'Broadway zone' by playing at the old Standard Theatre in Greeley Square."[8] The first black producer of black musical theater, John W. Isham, inspired and instructed by the success of *The Creole Show* (which employed him as an advance man), created the successful touring show *The Octoroons* in 1895.[9] It is surely no accident that Isham was aided in his work as an advance man for white producer Sam Jack and aided in his effort to create the first successful black-produced musical theater by the fact that he was light-skinned enough to pass for white. Thomas Cripps's thesis of the "slow fade to black" was true not just of cinema but of all African-American cultural production. Isham's success, in turn, set up the first black intervention on the Great White Way itself (i.e., Broadway), with Will Marion Cook's *Clorindy, the Origin of the Cakewalk* and Bob Cole's *A Trip to Coontown,* both in 1898.

After the idea of black musical theater on Broadway became a reality, the next project for black producers was to transform the caricatures of minstrelsy and of the "coon songs" into something resembling the realities and potentialities of African Americans from an African-American point of view.[10] The landmarks of that transformation up to 1930 can be found in James Weldon Johnson's *Black Manhattan.*[11] All of those landmarks—including the Cole and Johnson collaborations, the Williams and Walker team, the "darktown" revues, the Sissle and Blake and Miller and Lyles productions, and the Lafayette Players—comprise an important context for Micheaux's treatment of production issues in his sound films, especially in a film *about* musical theater, such as *Swing!.* A paradigmatic opposition of production strategies already existed in the two approaches of the producers of the two 1898 successes, Cole (*Coontown*) and Cook (*Clorindy*). Alan Woll has pointed out that those two producers

> had radically different notions of the Negro's proper role in American musical theatre. Cole believed that blacks should strive for excellence in artistic creation and must compete on an equal basis with whites. . . . Cook, however, felt that "Negroes should eschew white patterns" and not try to do what "the white artist could always do as well, generally better." Negroes should look to themselves for the wellsprings of creativity, developing artistic endeavors that reflected the soul of black people.[12]

Cole and Cook were fighting out one of the dilemmas of twoness, cultural assimilation vs. cultural autonomy. Cole and Cook's struggle with each other often took rough forms, as did Micheaux's style, since the struggle arose from what DuBois characterized as "two unreconciled strivings; two warring ideals."[13] James Weldon Johnson emphasized the raw style this conflict took in real life between these two gifted artists:

> Our room, particularly of nights, was the scene of many discussions. . . . The opinions advanced and maintained, often with more force than considerateness, were as diversified as the personalities in the group. However, the only really bitter clashes were those occurring between Cole and Cook. Seldom did they meet and

part without a clash. . . . Both these men tended toward eccentricity, both were hot-tempered. . . . Cook never hesitated to make belittling comments on Cole's limitations in musical and general education; he would even sneer at him on a fault in pronunciation. Cole was particularly sensitive on this side, and Cook's taunts both humiliated and maddened him.[14]

Cole and Cook represented separate commitments to opposing sides of the "unreconciled strivings" that were present, according to DuBois, in many African Americans. Their debate not only reflected a dialectical paradigm with which African-American cultural production is still struggling, but its personal roughness and bitterness also represented the style the debate often took within the work of a single artist, like Micheaux, who was struggling internally with those same issues.

The opposition between the lifestyles and artistic styles of Bessie Smith and Ethel Waters is also a manifestation of that struggle. One of Micheaux's contributions to cinema is to have drawn his examples from blues artists and the world of musical theater entertainment and then to have meaningfully extended those lively worlds into cinema. Micheaux's cinema is enriched by his tendency to treat the common concerns among musical theater, blues, and cinema not just as stories, not just as issues of African-American cultural production, but also, explicitly, as issues of ethics and politics in daily life.

Blues Culture

The issue of whiteness as a horn of the dilemma of twoness arises at every stage of African-American culture, even in the blues. Blues is a fundamental touchstone of African-American culture, as the works of Amiri Baraka and Houston A. Baker, Jr., have shown. Baker's metaphor for the elemental quality of the blues is more complex than the metaphor of the touchstone; for him, blues is the matrix of African-American culture:

> The guiding presupposition . . . is that Afro-American culture is a complex, reflexive enterprise which finds its proper figuration in blues conceived as a matrix. A matrix is a womb, a network, a fossil-bearing rock, a rocky trace of a gemstone's removal, a principal metal in an alloy, a mat or plate for reproducing print or phonograph records. The matrix is a point of ceaseless input and output, a web of intersecting, crisscrossing impulses always in productive transit.[15]

Amiri Baraka's formulation of a fundamental twoness within the blues itself is particularly useful for the study of Micheaux's strategy of the middle path:

> Blues is the parent of all legitimate jazz, and it is impossible to say exactly how old blues is—certainly no older than the presence of Negroes in the United States. It is a native American music, the product of the black man in this country: or to put it more exactly the way I have come to think about it, blues could not exist if the African captives had not become American captives.[16]

Whiteness

Whiteness is discussed here in the context of Micheaux's concern for ethical social relations in general and also in the context of his corollary concern for black autonomy in the face of the professional necessity of white financing. Issues of class (position with respect to the means of production; creative autonomy), race (caste position), and status (position in the hierarchy of material rewards) are so entangled that they cannot be separated without difficulty.[17] African Americans obviously face whiteness in a way that is different from the way Catholic or Jewish Americans face Protestantism under the pluralism of America and in a way that is different from the way Asian Americans must face whiteness. African Americans are not immigrants and did not choose the dialectics of the pluralistic experiment.[18] The bitterness and roughness of African-American cultural production—as evidenced in the conflicts of Cole and Cook, of Bessie Smith and Ethel Waters, and of Micheaux's characters and production values—are appropriate as a reflection of the bitterness of the struggle with whiteness and twoness.

The whiteness of the Great White Way refers literally to the white limelight and marquees (production values as they relate to publicity and fame) and figuratively to the spectacle and status of the Broadway theater district in New York City; but it can conveniently refer as well to the white racism of Broadway and American musical theater. Racism on Broadway was no secret conspiracy in the 1920s. White supremacy was broadly assumed and was a matter of public discussion among whites as well as blacks, as a contemporary theater review by Heywood Broun indicates: "When I see a Negro child two or three years old come out and dance better than anybody at the New Amsterdam or the Winter Garden I grow fearful that there must be certain reservations in the theory of white supremacy."[19] Allen Woll's chapter that analyzes Broadway's response to the success of black musical theater begins with reference to a popular song from the (white) *Ziegfeld Follies of 1922* that includes the following lines:

> We used to brag about the Broadway white lights,
> The very famous dazzling White-Way night lights.
> They used to glare and glimmer,
> But they are growing dimmer;
> . . .
> Yes, the great white way is white no more,
> It's just like a street on the Swanee shore.
> It's getting very dark on old Broadway.[20]

Such reports of the death of whiteness on Broadway were greatly exaggerated, of course. Woll has demonstrated how black producers of musical theater were cheated and manipulated by white producers; how those white producers then cheated black composers, lyricists, and performers out of their salaries and royalties; how white theater owners exploited and rejected black producers; and how white reviewers criticized black shows that were too "ambitious" (meaning not "darky" enough). Woll has concluded that "while many authors claim that *Shuffle Along* opened new doors for black musicals on Broadway, it actually opened them only a crack."[21]

Of the black and black-cast productions that slipped through that crack in the 1920s, the most successful were the black revues. Revues resulted from the discovery that the elimination of the "book" (the plot that had provided the narrative matrix for the production numbers in black musical theater) produced more positive critical responses: "Critics praised the songs, the choreography, and the performances of the new black musicals, but the libretto often came under intense, and frequently harsh, scrutiny."[22] Revues were strings of musical and comedy numbers with no book and, thus, with highly attenuated or completely abandoned narrative continuity. Micheaux produced a film version of that genre in 1931 called *The Darktown Revue.* He has also been accused by critics and scholars of letting his plots become so attenuated in his other early sound films that those feature films became a string of production numbers, most notably in *Ten Minutes to Live* (1932). On the contrary, Micheaux always kept his narrative form firmly in hand, as will be demonstrated throughout this study. The only film in which the narrative matrix is not dominant over the music is, for generic reasons, *The Darktown Revue,* and in that film, a quite decipherable rhetoric exerts perfect control over the deployment of production numbers.

Twoness within Twoness: No Essentialism

The opposition between Bessie Smith and Ethel Waters, between the blues and Broadway, is an aspect of the struggle of twoness, as is the paradigmatic Broadway-centered struggle between Cole and Cook and their creative offspring. Twoness, however, as shown above, was already inherent on each side of such struggles; twoness was inherent in the blues, on the one hand, and in African-American assimilationist approaches to Broadway, on the other hand. The opposition between Smith and Waters was a split also between South and North, rural and urban, and lower-class and upper-class African-American cultures.

In the face of this matrix of dilemmas, Micheaux tended to protect and negotiate his autonomy in order to produce class mobility and social worth. He looked to whites for models of behavior only when he could approve of that behavior; and he condemned white behavior when he disapproved of it. He seems to have been just as likely to do either. In Micheaux's film *Within Our Gates* (1920), white people are responsible for generous philanthropy as well as lynching and rape, and black people are responsible for altruistic self-sacrifice as well as deceit, disloyalty, and buffoonery. Blacks remain the central actors at every point of the narrative, even though they must address and respond to socially, politically, and economically dominant whites whose behavior includes explicitly racist actions. Whiteness is an overt issue in much of Micheaux's work, often for its "good" qualities, those associated primarily with middle-class character and success, but just as often for its cruelty, stupidity, dominance, and injustice.[23] Micheaux extensively treats oppression, primarily that engineered by whites but including that created by blacks, and class mobility (and immobility), primarily that of blacks but including that of whites. Many of Micheaux's films and novels emphasize black initiative over white oppression, but whiteness and blackness are never essentialized.

Micheaux was overtly and publicly considering the issue of placing specifically black productions on Broadway in his film *Swing!*. In spite of his own practical and principled choice of independence from Hollywood (the Great White Way of cinema), Micheaux's sophisticated treatment of the ethics of production values was surely in aid of the development of understanding among black people about the strategies and implications of taking the blues to Broadway, of taking black culture into mainstream America, and of African-American uplift in general. Micheaux was portraying the road to Broadway—the great "white" way—as a highway equivalent to the highways of the migration from South to North, the *literal* roads that signified the progress from cultural stagnation to mobility in real life. The dialectical oppositions within black life that arose from the migrations (oppositions that can be broadly extended to include dialect, literacy, dress, codes of honor, status, and so forth) carried with them a full spectrum of positive and negative feeling. African Americans were, individually, both happy and sad to leave the South; the countryside and the network of social relations in the South bound them and gave them a sense of place. Rural blues (Robert Johnson, Bessie Smith) reflected primarily the sadness, but it remains famous also for its sense of humor and hope. Conversely, urban jazz (Duke Ellington, Ethel Waters) reflected primarily the happiness, though it was infused also with despair and rage. Finally, the positive aspects of the migration must be allowed, in historical balance, to have outweighed the negative, otherwise the migrations would not have become the irresistible force they did become during the first half of the twentieth century. James Grossman's detailed description and analysis of the positive and negative forces that generated the migrations to Chicago and Nicholas Lemann's more general study of the northward migrations have both been given titles that reflect the positive side, *Land of Hope* and *The Promised Land*.[24]

In his film *To Sleep with Anger*, Charles Burnett sacrificed the blues figure on the altar of uplift—the Danny Glover character slips and falls, dying on the suburban middle-class kitchen floor. If Micheaux, too, in *Swing!* sacrificed the Bessie Smith figure, Cora Smith, on that altar (she slips and falls "downstairs"), there may be consequences for Micheaux's message about black culture and for his own artistic accomplishment. Artistic standards are at stake here, since the blues and the major jazz movements that have arisen from blues are perhaps the greatest contributions Americans have made to world culture. Hardly anyone sensitive to vernacular music would be willing to give up the historical figure and the actual accomplishments of Bessie Smith or her continuing influence on music. Micheaux, however, was not suggesting any such thing. His surrogate for himself in the film, the producer Ted, continues to consider Cora (Bessie) Smith "the best blues singer in the Negro race," even after Cora has virtually scuttled Ted's show and destroyed herself as a performer through her low-down lifestyle.

Ted's problem, as the producer of the show within Micheaux's film, is basically a practical one of not being able to rely on his star. Metaphorically and rhetorically, however, that sense of practicality had implications that are so far-reaching for Micheaux that some concept of pragmatics virtually comprises his message and describes his style. He was saying that if a people cannot rely on their stars, on their top cultural representatives, in the practical world of American capital and American norms, then such people must accept that they will be stuck in something like the blues forever. Many African Americans today, in fact, have very little interest in the blues except as a historical accomplishment; the audience for traditional and urban blues today is mostly white. African Americans tend to be more interested in urban jazz, soul, gospel, fusion, rap, or classical music, depending on age and circumstance. This hindsight confirms the general direction Micheaux was suggesting, though that in itself says little about the artistic and cultural value of the musical forms of the blues, per se.

Beyond the Blues Condition

In any case, Micheaux did not sacrifice the blues as a cultural accomplishment when he sacrificed the Bessie Smith figure for the Ethel Waters figure; he sacrificed the lifestyle that generated the blues. Most blacks (and whites) have done the same, or would prefer to do so if they could, like the family in *To Sleep with Anger*. That willing sacrifice of the blues style and its accompanying hard and dangerous lifestyle does not entail giving up roots any more than does the move from the South to the North or from country to city. It entails attempting to leave the roots in the soil and growing upward from those roots toward necessary light and air. Roots become roots only if they have a plant above them to nurture. The power and accomplishment of today's rap is no doubt owing in part to the violent conditions out of which rap grows; but the greatness of some rap music is no justification for those conditions and that lifestyle. If rap depends on those violent conditions, then the sooner rap dies, the better, so that another great but less violent black music can replace it. Micheaux must have had similar feelings about the blues and the lifestyles of people like Bessie Smith.

Bessie Smith and the Blues

Like the Danny Glover character in *To Sleep with Anger* and like the Cora Smith of *Swing!*, Bessie Smith, in fact, did not live an entirely admirable life. Her promiscuity and drinking were virtually compulsive; she was unfaithful to people she loved deeply and that she knew she was hurting; she was profligate in her spending on herself and on display and luxuries; and she was not dependable in her professional arrangements, sometimes in petty and unattractive ways. Conversely, she also had excellent qualities of material and spiritual generosity, extraordinary physical and moral courage and candor, racial pride and loyalty, and sexual freedom and love. She resembled such flawed cultural heroes as James Agee and Jackson Pollock and such flawed fictional heroes as Sweet Sweetback and Thelma and Louise; one may admire them ferociously, but one might hesitate to encourage one's children to emulate them.

Micheaux's rejection of the Bessie Smith–like character in *Swing!* is understandable in the historical context of uplift. He left himself open for the criticism, however, that he was choosing not just uplift from the blues life but also assimilation and whiteness, since Bessie Smith's career can be interpreted as a struggle against whiteness. Feinstein and Albertson, in their respective biographies of Bessie Smith, use the term "whiteness" to refer to a family of qualities that Bessie Smith rejected and that Ethel Waters adopted in order to broaden her audience. Albertson says, for example:

> Black Swan, was founded in 1921 by composer W. C. Handy and Harry Pace, Handy's partner in the music-publishing business. It was the first black-owned record company. . . . Black pride notwithstanding, the company rejected the very black sound of Bessie Smith when she auditioned for Black Swan in 1921, while recording the "whiter" sound of Ethel Waters extensively.[25]

In the long but illuminating quotation below, Feinstein sets up the difference between Bessie Smith's and Ethel Waters's relationships with blackness and whiteness as a central defining idea of her biographical treatment of Bessie Smith:

> To succeed in the entertainment business of the time, Bessie's most significant disadvantages were her size, the African cast of her features and the unfashionable blackness of her skin. The chorus line was expected to look as if tanned golden-brown and to have a slender build; and beauty was supposed to lie in small, European features. Bessie's early full-lipped loveliness was unacceptable. Irvin C. Miller (himself black) had her thrown out of the chorus line for not meeting these standards, which must have bruised her awakening confidence, but did not check her determination. The scar remained, and probably accounts for her lifelong dislike of "Northern bitches" with skins much lighter than her own. People have to love themselves if they are going to survive, and Bessie was a survivor. If she was black, then black was good. And all her life she preferred men who were as dark a black as she was.
>
> Bessie's empire extended more widely than Ma's, but she never aspired to widen it in the way Ethel Waters was able to. At the height of her fame Bessie played to white audiences in the South, as well as in night clubs in the North, but never saw the white audience as an opportunity. Ethel Waters was sharper about what was to her advantage. It was partly because she came from the North, and was bewildered to find how much blacks in the South were afraid to seem uppity. . . .
>
> Ethel was a singer with talent; she was also pretty and (for much of her life) slender; hence her nickname, "Sweet Mama Stringbean." . . . Born in a slum in Chester, Pennsylvania, she was brought face to face with poverty and squalor at least equal to anything in Bessie's childhood. But her grandmother was hard-working and determined that she wanted a better life for her children. It was her voice which

urged Ethel towards cleanliness and moderation in her drinking. It was her grand-mother who taught her to imagine God's eye on her. And although her temper was as violent as Bessie's in her childhood, and she was familiar with local whores and all the crime and vice of a slum ghetto, she had more interest in her schooling than Bessie.

Ethel Waters went on to star in Broadway musicals, and to act in Hollywood. Neither world opened to Bessie. [Waters] never liked the appurtenances of white life that went along with success, such as caviar and expensive European food, but she enjoyed the success. And even though she found many white people joyless, she liked the society of successful writers, and was able to discuss books with them and ideas for interpreting roles.[26]

Rejecting the Bessie Smith–type character and accepting the Ethel Waters–type character in Micheaux's *Swing!* might be seen as rejecting blackness and accept-ing whiteness. However, neither Ethel Waters in real life nor Mandy, her surro-gate in *Swing!,* can be interpreted as representing whiteness. They both started out and remained just as "black" as Bessie Smith, who recognized Waters as a Northern and urban black. From Bessie Smith's point of view, Waters was al-ways a "Northern bitch," but there was no claim that she was "white." And in *Swing!,* the Bessie Smith figure is actually lighter-skinned than the Ethel Waters figure; the emphasis for Micheaux is more on the behavior than the "racial" characteristics of these two versions of black stardom. It is probable that the differences in the sounds and styles of Bessie Smith and Ethel Waters had less to do with ideas of blackness and whiteness (which were undergoing dynamic change in the period of time under discussion) and more to do with rural and urban cultures and, concomitantly, with class distinctions. The migrations themselves gave rise to a volatility of styles and values among black people that could account for a considerable amount of confusion about what blackness and whiteness entailed.

Duke Ellington and Swing

Since the title concern of Micheaux's film is swing music, the common criticism that Micheaux was advocating a move toward "whiteness" needs to be considered in the light of the whiteness of swing as well as in the blackness of blues. Duke Ellington is a perfect male version of Bessie Smith's idea of a north-ern bitch. His middle-class sophistication, dicty manners, dress and accent, and the smoother tone and more predicable organization of his music (despite his famous "jungle" style) were precisely the qualities Feinstein suggests were anathema to Bessie Smith. Ellington was what Baraka has called a "citizen," a black American who had moved beyond the status of post-slavery and post-freedman, whose music, "was 'the detached impressionism of a sophisticated Negro city dweller.'"[27] Bessie Smith probably wanted to be a citizen as much as she wanted anything (both Albertson and Feinstein say she wanted accep-tance, in spite of her aggressive behavior), but for her, both citizenship and ac-ceptance had to leave plenty of room for her country manners—her southern working-class identity. Ellington grew up in Washington, D.C., and identified with upper-middle-class manners and values. Citizenship in the centers of culture and commerce was easier for him to attain.

In the case of the reception of Ellington, the ideas of blackness and whiteness are thoroughly confused with ideas of class. In spite of such difficulties, Baraka has used "whiteness" and "blackness" throughout his discussion of blues people to characterize the direction that black music was taking during the evolution of jazz. He has said, for example, that "Duke's sophistication was to a great extent the very quality that enabled him to integrate so perfectly the older blues traditions with the 'whiter' styles of big-band music."[28] Baraka, however, used the idea of whiteness in concrete historical terms, so there is no temptation to essentialize blackness and whiteness. Though Baraka has explained that the blues was culturally half-white from its beginning, he could also say that "[t]he idea of a white blues singer seems an even more violent contradiction of terms than the idea of a middle-class blues singer."[29] Whiteness may have been part of African-American cultural production, such as the blues, from the beginning—nevertheless, Baraka has said, only blacks can produce the blues: "The materials of blues were not available to the white American, even though some strange circumstances might prompt him to look for them."[30]

Duke Ellington helped move the idiom of blues toward the idiom of jazz, and in doing so, he could be said to have helped make a black idiom more white. In fact, Baraka has said that Duke Ellington, in perfecting the big jazz band, contributed to the ascendancy of swing music, which, unlike blues and virtuosic jazz, white musicians could understand and play and, thus, exploit. In one sense, such contributions implied citizenship for black artists; in another sense, since that citizenship was second class, it simply restaged the continuing conflict between black and white. While the wide acceptance of swing music was an opportunity for "uplifting the race," it simultaneously created the conditions for white exploitation of black accomplishment. Nonetheless, swing music was also the staging ground (in the sense of Hegel's supersessional stages) for a new black separatist subculture, bebop. History and blackness and whiteness are dialectical and dynamic. Micheaux, as will be seen, made films that were infused with such dialectics. Micheaux's (and a few others', such as Spencer Williams's) race movies were a staging ground for the black films of the civil rights movement.

Classic Blues

In narratively rejecting the Bessie Smith character, Micheaux was certainly not eschewing blackness from black musical theater or from race movies as a means of storming the Great White Way. Even Bessie Smith, in spite of her staunch loyalty to and affinity for blackness, cannot serve neatly as an impregnable fortress of black blues. Baraka has pointed out how Bessie Smith was rejected for her blackness of style by early race music producers (the Black Swan record company), but he has also emphasized her movement away from the separateness of primitive blues and toward the assimilationist classic blues:

Classic blues is called "classic" because it was the music that seemed to contain all the diverse and conflicting elements of Negro music, plus the smoother emotional appeal of the "performance." . . . it represented a clearly definable step by the Negro back into *the mainstream of American society*. . . .

The emergence of classic blues indicated that many changes had taken place in the Negro. His sense of place, or status, within the superstructure of American society had changed radically since the days of the field holler. . . . Now large groups of Negroes could sit quietly in a show and listen to a performer recreate certain serious areas of their lives.[31] [Emphasis added]

Even Bessie Smith was actively moving toward a more theatrical big-band music toward the end of her career and was doing so cheerfully and successfully. As race music was dying, Bessie Smith was moving toward the more assimilative styles of jazz. Clearly, then, one must be careful not to oversimplify by using historical figures such as Bessie Smith and Duke Ellington to represent essentially correct or incorrect attitudes toward the idea of blackness and whiteness.

In the face of such dynamics, it has been hard for critics and viewers to be confident in a reading of Micheaux's film treatment of the issues of African-American cultural production. *Swing!* seems to extend the idea introduced in *The Girl from Chicago* that high production values, such as stars and expensive mise-en-scène, may be attractive but are nonetheless problematic according to Micheaux's ethos of moderation. The expensive look of the classical Hollywood film of the mid-1930s, Micheaux's nemesis, is represented in *Swing!* by the analogously expensive productions of Broadway (white midtown theaters); Broadway is the goal of Micheaux's fictional producer, Ted. Ethel Waters, in her first autobiography, recognized the same goal for black producers and for herself:

About that time in Harlem they were casting a show they were calling *Mayor of Jimtown*. Miller and Lyles and Sissle and Blake were writing and producing it and were also going to appear in it. They hoped to send this show downtown. When Broadway finally saw this all-colored production it had the title *Shuffle Along,* and it was the fast-moving musical that made theatrical history and opened the trail for all the successful Negro musicals and big revues that followed.

I was trying to get a job in that show. I wanted to get away from smoky night-club work for a while, even if I was only to go in the chorus or in a walk-on part.[32]

The Great White Way was not to be sought by Ethel Waters with impunity, however:

Frank said he could use me in blackface comedy. That meant working in burnt cork. The name of his show, I think, was *Hello, 1919!* I sang and did a crow-jane character with Brown of Brown and Gulfport. In this I played a sort of blind-date bride whose groom refuses to marry her after getting a good look at her face. I also did a dance in the show. The white audiences thought I was white, my features being what they are, and at every performance I'd have to take off my gloves to prove I was a spade.[33]

In making it to Broadway, Ethel Waters had to play "crow-jane" in burnt cork in a confusion of identity that left her having to reestablish her blackness.

The Issue of White Financing

The White Way was not to be sought with impunity in Micheaux's world either, not in the styles of his films' characters nor in the style of Micheaux's films themselves. The goals of Micheaux's valued characters—Mandy, Ted, and Lena—may seem similar in some ways to those of Ethel Waters, and they may seem to imply compromise with white money (getting to Broadway required white financing) and with whiteness itself (the characters in black plays on Broadway had to be acceptable to white audiences). Nevertheless, Micheaux recognized those problems, treating them narratively and stylistically. Certainly Micheaux needed white financing to make sound films. In fact, as will be seen, he was supported financially by Frank Schiffman, the white manager of the Apollo Theater, so he was tied financially into the world of the black musical theater that he portrayed in *Swing!*[34]

The fact is, however, that in spite of white financing, Micheaux's progressive contribution to the fight against white racist caricature and stereotype throughout a career of several decades and dozens of films is so great that it is hard to understand why it has not been given the critical attention it is owed. Perhaps Micheaux has been ignored or underestimated for so long partly because he split his audience. The portion of his audience interested in his middle-class goals may have been unhappy with his "incompetent" filmmaking; for example, some of the recent film school–trained black filmmakers have been critical of Micheaux's lack of cinematic skills. Conversely, other black filmmakers interested precisely in the untrained, alternative, and inventive aspects of Micheaux's style have been unhappy with his "bourgeois" goals. Some critics, such as J. Hoberman and Jane Gaines, while aesthetically and rhetorically impressed with Micheaux's films, have questioned such bourgeois values.

It is difficult to say what Micheaux would have done if he had had the chance to produce films with the higher production values that would have satisfied one side of his split audience. On the one hand, he showed little inclination to work in Hollywood. He considered himself to be in a fight against Hollywood. An offer to make a grand Hollywood spectacle of something like the story of Mandy, as Spielberg did with the story of Celie in *The Color Purple* and as Spike Lee did with the history of Malcolm X, might have been rejected as inappropriately grand. Micheaux's favored characters, like Norma in *The Girl from Chicago,* refused that sort of ride. Micheaux may have had an aversion to the values of Hollywood, based on his own lifelong commitment to middle-class values that are closer to the Calvinist work ethic than are the values of Hollywood. Criteria that would accompany an expensive style might have been incompatible with Micheaux's sense of integrity and offensive to his sense of propriety. He might have seen them as threatening to his autonomy as a cultural producer.

Moreover, as Cripps and others have pointed out, Micheaux had practical reasons for avoiding high production values and for counseling moderation as an avenue to status; his actors would be ruined, for example, for use in autonomous black productions if their status exceeded that of the middle class. Micheaux's exploitation of actors has been exaggerated, as will be seen, but his resistance to the star system was real and strategic. He felt he (and, thus, his actors) simply would have been driven out of the film business if he allowed stardom to be inflated as a production value. The star system is a major component of the classical cinema. Race movies could not afford stars as luminous as the white stars of Broadway and Hollywood—neither the black audience nor the black producer could support such a scale of production and still maintain their autonomy. Race movies *could* accept white financing and remain autonomous, however, so long as they followed Micheaux's principles of moderation.

On the other hand, the narrative climax of *Swing!* presents a serious challenge to any pat conclusion about Micheaux's ethics of production. In that climax, a white Broadway theater owner intervenes soon after Mandy replaces Cora in the mammy role, offering to feature Ted's show in his theater and to provide financing with a profit-sharing deal. The black producers, Ted and Lena, who loosely represent Micheaux and his wife as producers of the film, accept the deal with alacrity and seemingly without qualms. The entry of this "white angel" has the feel of *deus ex machina* and seems to belie the idea that receiving big money for a big production was against Micheaux's principles. There are, however, other ways to understand this scene. In one of the most important senses, in spite of any discomfort felt at the narratively abrupt and artificial "rescue" of a black production by a white angel, the scene is nevertheless historically realistic. After the sound era began in cinema, virtually all independent black films had to be financed to a significant degree by white producers. Mark Reid, working from Cripps's discussion of the race movies' transition to sound, has emphatically pointed this out:

> Micheaux's move in the late 1920s from Black independent film to Black commercial film signaled a 40-year pause in Afro-American independent film production. In *Black Film as Genre,* Cripps writes that "after 1931, Blacks raised capital from Frank Shiffman of Harlem's Apollo Theatre, Robert Levy of Reol, and white Southern distributors like Ted Toddy and Alfred Sack. By the end of the decade . . . all white prevailed."
>
> It is absurd, then, for film historians and critics to call Micheaux's post-1931 films "Black independent cinema," for these films herald the start of two decades of Black-directed, white-financed, low-budget, commercial films made outside of Hollywood.[35]

Setting aside for a moment the question that is the principal concern of Reid's essay—that of the historical definition of black independent filmmaking in the face of white financing—Reid and Cripps both help to clarify the import of the "white angel" scene in *Swing!*. The white financier is to be properly understood as an *intrinsic* rather than an extraordinary element of race movies of the sound era, since the white financier was an absolute necessity of production for black producers in the 1930s. The figure of $10,000, mentioned by the white financier as the advance he will make to the black producers of the show, is a figure that is often mentioned by scholars and filmmakers of race movies as the nut (the minimum financing needed to insure day-to-day survival in production mode) that Micheaux previously would have needed to produce a feature film. Thomas Cripps confirmed in a telephone conversation that this figure is commonly used. He also pointed out that other figures were used also, including amounts as high as $50,000. Cripps felt that $15,000 to $20,000 would be a good guess for Micheaux's nut during the depression.

The climactic scene with the white theatrical investor in *Swing!* represents the pragmatics of black production in 1938. There were virtually no black investors to whom black filmmakers could turn when outside financing became necessary (with the advent of sound). David Levering Lewis has stated that in Harlem during the Harlem Renaissance, "[w]hites owned more that 80 percent of the wealth."[36] Mark Reid has suggested that Micheaux's post-1931 films of the sound era should not be called black independent film at all since they were white-financed and commercial.

Reid also, however, incidentally uses the term "low-budget" in the same observation. The prevailing context that Reid notes of low-budget production in race movies is certainly true of *Swing!* and of Micheaux's other sound films, the ones that Reid considers commercial rather than independent. Though the $10,000 offer at the end of *Swing!* does represent a saving stroke, it is still modest and the show still inexpensive. And inexpensiveness is significant in its own right. The white financiers in Micheaux's film and in Reid's history do not foreshadow or imply production values as expensive and inappropriate as those of *The Color Purple* and *Malcolm X*. White financing of race movies certainly did not represent anything like the expensiveness of Hollywood production.

The white financier in Micheaux's film does, however, still seem to represent a compromise or even a contradiction of the idea of African-American authorial autonomy because of the demands the financier makes about the show's billing. Those demands seem to exploit racist stereotyping, since he insists that the show emphasize Mandy's "mammyness" and dialect. If this is, in fact, a compromise or contradiction of Ted's, and Micheaux's, autonomy, it would support Reid's thesis that Micheaux's sound films should not be considered independent black cinema. Reid does not mount such supporting evidence in his own argument, perhaps because scenes such as this one seem so clearly supportive of white meddling that no emphasis is needed.

But there are at least two other ways to interpret this scene so that no compromise or contradiction is implied. First, Micheaux can be understood to have been directly signaling the intrusion of white capital and pointing straight to the kinds of inflections it would cause, such as mammyness and stereotyped dialect[37]—he could have been "signifying" both in the sense of "In your face," "a standard Signifyin(g) retort, meaning that by which you intended to confine (or define) me I shall return to you squarely in your face"; in the sense of "enouncing" a "sense of difference by repetition with a signal difference"; or in the sense of "making fun of a person or situation."[38] For black audiences, there is the satisfaction of seeing the white producer parted from his money; in addition, the tom-fool changes he demands are placed in "signifying" quotations so that the movie audience knows how silly they are. It is the white producer who draws laughter, for it is his act of stereotyping that is held up for ridicule, not the stereotyped actors or characters themselves.

Second, the white investor's insistence on featuring Mandy, who has been established by the narrative as a blues person in her daily life, and the white investor's insistence on renaming the revue "I Lubs Dat Man" could signify the affirmative retention of an "authentic" black style (blues) rather than the compromising insertion of white caricature (mammy stereotype and minstrel dialect). Mandy, after all, really does represent the blues within the connotative meanings of the film. Baraka has similarly compared the authentic blues content of the southwestern dance bands to the swing bands of the northeast:

> Bands like Bennie Moten's from Kansas City, Walter Page (and his Blue Devils) from Oklahoma City, Charlie Creath from St. Louis, and Troy Floyd from Texas had "books" that were jammed with blues numbers, and all were bands that developed in relative isolation from the whiter orchestral styles. Negroes in the Southwest still wanted a great part of their music to be blues-oriented, even if it was played by a large dance band. And the music of these great Southwestern orchestras continued to be hard and swinging, even when a great many large Negro bands in other areas of the country had become relatively effete. It is said that when Ellington's and Henderson's bands traveled through the Southwest, the musicians there were impressed most by their musicianship and elegance, but they did not want to sound as "thin" as that.[39]

Perhaps Micheaux was also marking the place of a kind of blues integrity in upwardly mobile, black musical theater. The special requirements of the white investor are, in fact, consistent with the roots of the blues—"I lubs dat man" is in fact close to the way Mandy talks. Even if the dialect that the white man wants emphasized can be seen as exaggerated and as a lower-class aspect of Mandy's style, it can also be seen as the roots of black culture that Micheaux wanted represented and valorized in a higher venue. Uplift, in that case, would not mean whiteness and rootlessness. Approached thus, the Great White Way could be a highway to a kind of African-American cultural citizenship that did not necessarily deny its black, country, and blues origins.

Conclusion

The above interpretations are each possible, but they contradict each other. Micheaux's intentions remain unclear, but they need not be inferred to represent a cynical ceding of black autonomy to white capital. Micheaux was moving away from the blues and toward the mainstream, but always in his own considered and proprioceptive way. He showed little evidence of compromise with white racist intervention from his financiers in any of the extant sound films that might have been subject to such influence. The middle path he advocated from blues toward the Great White Way favored authorial and ethnic autonomy. Even if his message in the ending of *Swing!* includes serious compromise (which there is reason to doubt), his own film practice demonstrated integrity, consistency, focus, and tenacity—anything but serious compromise.

Mark Reid was surely correct in saying that independence of production mode and the possible compromise of that independence associated with white financing are crucial issues. So far, however, no critic has shown that Micheaux was influenced by white investors, either directly or indirectly, in any way, much less in ways that affected the integrity of Micheaux's films, novels, or cultural goals. In fact, the above analysis of *Swing!* suggests that the more Micheaux worked under the conditions of outside financing by whites, the more clearly he understood and the more carefully he considered the ethical as well as practical consequences of a costly style.

8 Stereotype and Caricature

The last scene in *Swing!* warns that white financing of race movies, while structurally necessary in the sound era, threatens uplift through the possibility that it might insinuate racist stereotyping and caricature into black culture through white financial control. Whether or not such controls actually occurred in Micheaux's case—and there is no textual or contextual evidence that it did—there is also no doubt that stereotyping and caricature were chronic hindrances to Micheaux's principal goal in life, uplift. Micheaux dealt directly with these hindrances throughout his career. This chapter explores the foundation of caricature in economics and its maintenance through violence.

Legitimate Foundations for Productive Life

In *The Exile* (1931), when Micheaux's male lead Jean (pronounced almost like "John") rejects Edith, the matron of the Southside Chicago "social club," he is rejecting, most fundamentally, the underworld as a production site and a way of life. He is not, however, rejecting the underworld as a site of nightlife and entertainment. He is as willing to go to a "club" (i.e., a speakeasy) as the average urban middle-class person clearly is. But he is not willing to operate a club. He is siding with the "legitimate" economic world. His professional identity lies with legitimate, not with underworld values. These realms of "legitimate" and "underworld" relate respectively to positive and negative imagery within the ideology of uplift, and negative imagery manifested itself as racist caricature.

The Value in Production Values

Micheaux's strong association of personal values with the realm of production suggests the relative significance for him of production (over consumption) in the struggle for class advancement. In the films he made (and the stories that were set) after Prohibition, Micheaux associated legitimate production relationships with small clubs and with swing and hotter jazz music, but he never allowed his heroes or heroines to associate themselves directly with the illegitimate activities that clustered around the phenomena of clubs and jazz. Micheaux's ethics of film production suggested a formula of integrity and moderation in the realm of production, even when they implied a certain disdain or insouciance in the realm of consumption. His films are numerous and they have integrity, but for the consumer, their availability and integrity come at the "expense" of production values. In order to have a prolific black cinema—a film-production arm of the black community as a means of producing a black public sphere—in the 1930s, the audience almost had to identify with the black producer as producer. Micheaux's production values and their concomitant ethics implicitly admonished the unrealistically and self-indulgently demanding consumer, who refused to understand the realities of class mobility, who merely wanted to be served without taking account of who profits and thus gains class advancement in the production–consumption cycle.

A scene with an unusual parallel edit, near the end of *The Exile*, points directly to Micheaux's deepest concern. After Edith and Jean have decided to marry after all (after Jean's decision not to risk miscegenational marriage with his "white" neighbor in South Dakota), one of Edith's former lovers, an Abyssinian university student named Jango, comes into her room upstairs, and there follows a long, degrading argument between them. During a particularly squalid exchange, there is a cut to Jean at his cabaret table in the part of Edith's Southside Chicago house that serves as the social club. Jean is watching the floor show, but the edit makes it appear as if he is watching the "show" between Edith and Jango, which is going on elsewhere, out of his view. Jean laughs out loud, as if at a comedy team. There is no cut to show what he is really looking at, and there is no sound of the jazz band or the floor show that are presumably in progress right in front of him. The unnatural absence of sound helps hold the viewer's attention on Edith and Jango's argument, the "show" going on upstairs, not on the musical show that Jean is really watching within the diegetical continuities of space and time. Micheaux was thus referring pointedly, and with unconventional editing style, to some hilarity that is not in the floor show but is embedded in the narrative, and embedded analogously, as he saw it, in black life.

This surprising and disconcerting edit marks one of Micheaux's top priorities in his overall strategy for attaining class mobility—the criticism and exorcism of caricature (the topic of the next chapter). The seemingly mistaken cut to Jean watching the floor show, in which Edith and Jango *become* the floor show by editorial implication, is an example both of Micheaux's sharp ridicule and of his rhetorically purposeful and inventive editing style.

The jump cut from Edith and Jango to Jean, turning Jean, figuratively, into an observer of ethnic caricature and degradation, helps explain what Micheaux really cared about in the complex of issues introduced in the opening scenes of this film. Contrary to some readings, there was no simple opposition between urban and rural, between sweet music and jazz, drink and work, or jubilee and jazz. There was, rather, a warning that the world of the underworld rackets—of easy profits, sordid exploitation, and insouciant sex—as a foundation of productive life was not just morally wrong and socially unacceptable but was also the cornerstone of white disdain and a confirmation of white racial caricatures and stereotypes of blacks. Micheaux was saying that if blacks chose the underworld for their realm of economic productivity, they also chose it as their identity, and they thereby confirm an aspect of white racism. When Edith and Jean are discussing their plans, just before they decide to separate in the early scene de-

Fig. 9a. Jean Baptiste, the leading man in *The Exile,* is shown watching an amusing floor show . . .

Fig. 9b. . . . but the scene is edited in such a way that he seems to be watching this private domestic squabble in an upstairs room.

scribed above, Edith says, in response to Jean's disgust: "I appreciate your point of view, Jean, but we do not have to be wicked because of the nature of our business." What becomes clear in the later scene, in which Jean laughs at Edith and Jango's vaudeville-like "skit" of international domestic violence, is that it is not primarily wickedness that concerns Jean but rather dignity.

Jango, in fact, is an Abyssinian exile of high birth who has lost his dignity through his sordid relationship with Edith. Abyssinia, or Ethiopia, was important to blacks in America as the avant garde of black nationhood. Roi Ottley treated Ethiopia as his principal example of black nationhood in his chapter called "The Apostles of Race":

> the Ethiopian struggle [had a] profound effect upon the American scene. . . . Negroes first became aware of the black nation back in 1919, when Ethiopian dignitaries arrived in the United States on a diplomatic mission. . . . While staying in New York at the old Hotel Waldorf-Astoria, they received a delegation of Harlem citizens. From the Waldorf the group journeyed to the Metropolitan Baptist Church in Harlem, where addresses of welcome were made, not only in the name of Harlem but in the name of Black America. . . .
>
> . . . to encourage the migration of farmers, mechanics, engineers, physicians, dentists, and scientists, in an attempt to modernize the ancient empire, Emperor Haile Selassie offered them free land and high wages. Several hundred went to Ethiopia and in 1930 the Emperor appointed an American Negro, Doctor John West, of Washington, D.C., as his personal physician; made another American Negro, John Robinson, a Chicagoan, his personal aviator; and a number of World War veterans were given commissions in the Ethiopian Army. Even Negro missionaries were welcomed. As the United States tumbled further into the depression, it is very likely that numbers of other Negroes would have migrated to Africa, had not the war interrupted.[1]

As a matter of biographical fact, one of Micheaux's respected middle-class financial backers, a celebrated African-American pilot, was appointed by Haile Selassie as commander of the Ethiopian air force. In *The Exile*, Jango's lost Ethiopian-based dignity is made the more poignant by his discovery of a newspaper announcement of Ras Tafari's (Haile Selassie's) accession to the throne, a great point being made of the fact that Tafari's lineage is traceable back to King Solomon and the Queen of Sheba. Jango had been about to leave Edith's apartment to commit suicide, but upon seeing the article on Ras Tafari's accession, Jango remembers his birthright and decides to kill Edith instead, to rid himself and the world of someone capable of so egregious an effect on racial duty and ancient dignity. Jango, though a minor character, is nevertheless one of the significant exiles in the film, a film whose title, *The Exile*, refers most particularly to Jean Baptiste's sojourn in the wilderness of South Dakota, but also refers more broadly to his place in the African diaspora.

Thus, Jean is—by Micheaux's editorial implication in the scene that intercuts between Jean's lighthearted enjoyment of the cabaret show downstairs and the violent "domestic farce" upstairs—laughing at the caricature that Jango and Edith are making together. Micheaux was ridiculing behavior that he felt was intrinsic to the illegitimate businesses of the "darktowns" of Prohibition, behavior he felt was also too common in the black community and that was, thus, broadly threatening to the dignity of all people of African descent.

Micheaux's concern for dignity was not a desire for materially empty middle-class status; he was addressing a specific politico-economic situation. At the time this film was made, Prohibition offered a rare opportunity for blacks to cash in on a contradiction in white-imposed racial relations. Nathan Huggins has explained why that opportunity might be a hard temptation to resist; he also has explained, however, that other more legitimate options were available:

> Harlem meant still another kind of opportunity. With such a large concentration of Negroes it provided a market for business and professional men. Negro lawyers, doctors, and dentists could anticipate for the first time a large potential clientele. Of course, it was not easy for the professions. Negro doctors found it impossible to use white hospitals until the Harlem hospital was built on 135th Street and Lenox Avenue. Lawyers' cases with Negro clients were not the most rewarding, and the field was too crowded for good business. Yet there was the chance.[2]

The kernel of the argument between Jango and Edith is Jango's claim that Edith has kept him from pursuing his education and becoming a doctor or a lawyer. Edith expresses the cynical opinion that there are too many black doctors and lawyers already and that most of them have to serve the illicit trades associated with Prohibition anyway—black lawyers getting prostitutes out of jail and black doctors performing prostitutes' abortions, for example. Micheaux, in other films, such as *Murder in Harlem* (1935), was sympathetic to the argument that blacks were overeducated and underemployed—he was often in agreement with Booker T. Washington and in disagreement with DuBois on this point. Micheaux, however, would never have chosen an undignified solution to that problem. He consistently favored characters who resisted the easy rackets, who persisted and invented, who worked through failures and worked with socially legitimate business projects over the long term, just as Micheaux did in his own life. In *Within Our Gates,* made twelve years before *The Exile,* Micheaux's hero is, in fact, a professional, an optometrist, who has few clients but plenty of time to read widely, to support good causes, and, thus, to reflect dignity on the race.

Huggins has supported the view that legitimate choices were available at that time, even for women:

> As to many a young girl, white or black, New York offered womanhood. . . . But Harlem offered something more. While there, she was on the crest of a creative wave that would surely define the New Negro, and let her know her self through her race.
>
> . . .
>
> . . . And as early as 1918, Madame C. J. Walker had become a millionaire, and had bought a mansion at Irvington-on-the-Hudson, as a result of her processing and treatment of the hair of Negro women. Harlem meant opportunity and promise for all kinds.[3]

Edith's story was not that of a Madame C. J. Walker, a different kind of urban "social leader." Micheaux's use of caricature in his portrayal of the demise of Edith was consistent with both his middle-class values and with his ethnic loyalty, the most salient feature of which was a tough critical stance toward the refuge of white-sanctioned illegitimate realms of production that were the foundation for racist caricature.

Stage Fright

Micheaux's highlighting of stereotype and caricature in *The Exile*, his concern for the erosion of the dignity of African-American identity by minstrel-based entertainment, and its perceived relation to African-American life are related to a general American condition that particularly affected African Americans at the turn of the century. It might be called stage fright, since America was a new leading player on the global stage. Vast numbers of immigrants and migrants were filling the new cities and the newly opened farmland. The newness of the American cities and lands themselves plus the newness of urban life and of farming in an industrial economy plus the newness of the ethnic melting pot, where one's language and social instincts could be a constant liability, were all frightening. For the petit bourgeois and nouveaux riches, there was fear of social ineptitude and non-acceptance. The middle class feared derision by the American upper classes. The upper classes feared derision from the older European upper classes.

More seriously frightening, however, than any of those possibilities was the fear that had to be faced by the working classes in the socioeconomic game of American capitalism. Along with the land of opportunity came the "opportunity" to fail to measure up to the minimum employment standards that might be set by one's boss or by competition with one's neighbor or another ethnic group. The range of consequences of not measuring up included extinction, poverty, or mediocrity, all of which were seemingly "deserved," having been measured out in open competition under the rules of an economic meritocracy, the rules of which were maintained and supervised by plutocrats.

Rube Movies

The fright associated with the dramatic ethnic competition, in particular, that characterized the American rise to economic prominence may be found in a number of important permutations of early cinema. Thematically, one sees fear of failure expressed in ethnic terms in rube movies, which were common during the emergence of cinema. Rube movies include *Rube and Mandy at Coney Island* (1903), and Uncle Josh movies, such as *Uncle Josh at the Moving Picture Show* (1903), and *The European Rest Cure* (1904), in which a nouveau-riche American cannot even competently negotiate a European vacation. Not all of these examples pose their rubes as specific ethnic types, but those films that do employ racial stereotypes and slurs may be seen as the most extreme case of a general tendency toward ethnic specificity in the rube theme. The implicit presence of ethnic prejudice, perhaps free-floating and unspecified, can be understood in the derivation of the term "rube" from "Reuben," a proper Germanic name. "Rube" denotes an awkward, unsophisticated person and is also explicitly a nickname for "Reuben"; thus, the term always connotes ethnicity. Charles Musser has pointed out the formative influence of ethnic prejudice in his discussion of Edwin S. Porter's childhood:

> Growing up in Connellsville [Pennsylvania], Porter apparently adopted the strong prejudices that his family and friends held against many immigrant groups. During the 1880s the town's native white population developed a deep-seated antipathy for Eastern European immigrants. The first explosion of hostility came in February 1883, when an open letter accused the "Hated Hun" of barbaric acts. . . . Such hostility focused on the "not overly clean habits and queer customs" of the "Hated Hun." Native workers were disturbed by a common sight: "their women in a state of semi-nudity at work in the . . . blinding dust of a coke yard forking the product of the ovens." By 1886, 25 percent of the cokers were Poles, Hungarians, and Bohemians, while another 10 percent were Germans and Prussians. These workers were initially seen as the tools of the operators who brought them to their mines. During the strike of 1886, however, they proved to be more militant and radical than their domestic counterparts. When they rioted to maintain the effectiveness of the strike, the "Hated Huns" were characterized as lawbreakers and dangerous radicals.[4]

Musser goes on to point out that the attitudes exemplified in this passage were translated into Porter's films (made for the Edison Manufacturing Company from 1901 to 1909) and, as such, were an accurate reflection of the ethnic and racial prejudices of most native-born white Americans.

One way to read the hatred of the "Hun," from evidence such as that above, is as fear of an employment competitor. The image of women's coke-covered breasts and legs exposed to the factory ovens may have offended the native workers' sense of "propriety" in senses other than that of morality. The Eastern Europeans were behaving as if economic success meant not "onward and upward" but "down and dirty." Their radical strike behavior may have threatened the native-born workers' assumptions that the American worker's dreams were tied safely to the dreams and successes of the factory owners. The aggressive strike behavior of the "Hated Hun" accepted rules that were brutally realistic. The immigrants made the game of ladder climbing suddenly less like a game; the cost of losing was livelihood and sometimes life itself.

The place of an Edwin S. Porter in such a native-born, white-American sensibility actually took the form of conspiratorial association: "Porter was almost certainly a member of the nativist Order of United Mechanics, which sprang up to challenge the disruptions caused by the protracted, violent strike of 1891. A member of this secret beneficial association had to be a native-born American, of good moral character, believe in a supreme being, favor the public school system, oppose the union of church and state, and be capable of earning a living."[5] Conspiracy, more along the lines of the Ku Klux Klan conspiracy in *The*

Birth of a Nation, was also advocated in a Porter film of 1905, called *The "White Caps,"* which portrayed a Klan-like vigilante organization that rid the community of "undesirable citizens."[6]

Among the criteria listed for the secret society to which Porter probably belonged—criteria that included precepts based on aspects of patriotism, morality, religion, and constitutional democracy—was the criterion of holding a job. That criterion was not necessarily based on the work ethic; the secret society did not say that a member must "be no stranger to hard work" or must "do his best" but that a member must "be capable of earning a living." In other words, he (probably not "she") must succeed in the competitive job market. Incompetence in the labor market was possibly the deepest fear (pace Freud) informing ambient racism and was undoubtedly the dominant issue of white-supremacist conspiracy.

The rube movies articulated the sense of awkwardness and the lack of sophistication of many Americans, including the kind of social awkwardness that country people might feel upon going to the city, or that immigrants might feel among native-born Americans, or that African Americans might feel among white compatriots upon moving to the more integrated employment situations in the North. The rube theme might also appeal to the middle class and even the newly rich class of Americans, who obtained economic status before obtaining social class, and who thus did not know how to behave at the dinner table. Underlying such fears was the question of competence, always important but made preeminent by the American experiment of plutocratic meritocracy. Rube movies proliferated not only because of fear of ethnic difference but also because of fear of incompetence. Americans had to be psychologically prepared to accept that they were just "not good enough" to merit attention, honor, or, at worst, even survival. Rube movies continue as a genre throughout the history of American cinema, defining the careers of artists such as Buster Keaton, Jerry Lewis, and Steve Martin. The converse of the rube movie—films about those who *are* good enough—constitutes another continuing theme, defining the careers of directors such as Howard Hawks, Clint Eastwood, and Sylvester Stallone.

Laughter was a release from the anxiety about competition; it could be a comfort in that someone other than oneself or one's own group was the target of laughter. Rube movies played on the hopes and fears surrounding competency in numerous ways. One of the least subtle ways was through caricature and stereotypes, such as Uncle Josh or Reuben, especially the long-lasting stereotypes used as a broad rhetorical device to rigidly define groups that could be preemptively struck out of the competition or written off. The minstrel caricatures of African Americans were such stereotypes.

Stereotyping—or Writing Off—African Americans

Along with the serious problems of virtual absence from the public eye and blocked access to the paid jobs that would place black performers before the public, there were few problems for African Americans that were more important than those of stereotype and caricature. Any autonomous effort by African Americans to engage in serious performance, to work out their own identity as American citizens and thereby to provide a realistic and autonomous model of African-American citizenship through public spectatorship, was constantly blocked by the pervasiveness of ethnic, rube-like images. Nothing was going to get done until that problem was dealt with. Micheaux made it a top priority throughout his career and the main theme of his only concert film, *The Darktown Revue* (1931).

The Darktown Revue features a "dicty" (high-toned, upper-class) chorus that interacts with several vaudeville performers. Micheaux's handling of production numbers in *The Darktown Revue* is an example of the "positive image" figure in race movies, a figure meant to counter the negative rube stereotypes. The first song in *The Darktown Revue* is sung by the full chorus, perhaps a dozen men and women, most of them black but one man light enough to be white, facing the camera. The chorus leader, Donald Heywood, is conducting the chorus from a front podium, a little below the chorus, with his back to the camera. The camera is positioned for a slight downward angle, so that all ranks of the chorus as well as the chorus leader can be seen. The title of the first song is "Watermelon Time," and, though it had been composed as caricature in the tradition of minstrelsy (it was one of Ernest Hogan's "coon" songs, discussed below), it can be classified in this arrangement as popular, pseudo–folk music of the sort written by Stephen Foster. The style of Heywood's musical arrangement is not folk but rather a commercial, "sweet" multi-part harmonizing, reminiscent of barbershop quartets, though, unlike typical barbershop music, it is mixed in gender and larger in scale than a quartet. This "Watermelon Time" is a musical hybrid, combining black, rural, folk melody and lyrics with white, urban, popular harmony and voice training. The voice training includes elevated (dicty) diction, so that the effect is of white bourgeois diction superimposed over black rural dialect.

More striking than the positive, dicty images in *The Darktown Revue* is Micheaux's use of familiar negative images of black caricature and stereotype. The positive-image song just described is followed by a vaudeville act that is performed in "coon" caricature by Tim Moore and Andrew Tribble, two veterans of the black musical stage, each of whom, along with Amon Davis, who appears later as a caricature of a "hard-shell" preacher, receives multiple entries in Henry Sampson's chronology of blacks in show business.[7] Their tableau in *The Darktown Revue* is a typical vaudeville dialogue, with a straight man and a fool, titled "Why Leave by the Window?" Their act includes ethnic stereotyping, clichéd references to laziness, and gratuitous racial naming slurs, such as "Blondie" and "me and another Hawaiian boy."

The explicit dialectic between positive and negative images invites comparison with Micheaux's other extensive dialectical constructions—such as the dangerous attraction of easy but false class elevation—and with Micheaux's articulations of DuBois's fundamental condition of twoness. Micheaux seems explicitly to have made an issue of African-American twoness in his directing decisions. He chose an art deco stage set and dressed his chorus in upper-class evening clothes. The chorus members look like the college-aged sons and daughters of a long-established black bourgeoisie who are accustomed to ownership and cultural sophistication. They are easy in each other's presence; there is a working relationship between them and the chorus leader, who occasionally steps off the conductor's podium to join them or to play piano accompaniment. Most tellingly, they are confident in their judgment of the "lower" forms of life that intrude upon and become ironically displayed in the otherwise high-class performance. When examples of lower-class black culture appear, in the form of vaudeville acts such as the "cooning" dialogue by Tim Moore and Andrew Tribble and the burlesque parody by Amon Davis (of a shouting preacher), the upper-class chorus members feel no need to demonstrate their superiority; that superiority is simply obvious. The politeness of their aloofness in the face of the outrageous racial caricatures that come before them is impressive.

A Historical Timeline for Early Black Music

It is hardly possible to begin an interpretation of the political meanings of these "racial" acts, as deployed by Micheaux, or to understand their potential importance as a paradigm that runs throughout Micheaux's work without first placing the music and the acts in historical perspective. Alain Locke provides a historical taxonomy of African-American music that is useful not only for its own sake but also because it was written in 1936, near the height of Micheaux's film-producing career. Its historical perspective on black music would likely have been about the same as Micheaux's. Under the rubric of "Ages of Negro Music," Locke lists the following:

Before 1830—1. *The Age of Plantation Shout and "Breakdown."* Dominated by African Reminiscences and Survivals.
1830–1850—2. *The Age of the Sorrow-Songs: The Classic Folk Period:* The Great Spiritual and the Folk Ballads.
1850–1875—3. *The First Age of Minstrelsy:* Stephen Foster and the Sentimental Ballad.
1875–1895—4. *The Second Age of Minstrelsy:* Farce and Buffoonery;—the "Buck and Wing," the "Coon Song," the "Folk Blues."
1895–1918—5. *The Age of Ragtime:* Vaudeville and Musical Comedy.
1918–1926—*The Jazz Age:* The Stomp, the Artificial Blues and Dance Comedy.
1926 to date—*The Age of Classical Jazz;* with the dawn of Classical Negro Music.[8]

According to that map, Micheaux's parents were probably born just before the first age of minstrelsy (Micheaux's father was born c. 1847) and were coming of age in the second age of minstrelsy (Micheaux's father and mother were married c. 1872). Micheaux was born in the middle of the second age of minstrelsy (1884), came of age in the middle of the age of ragtime (c. 1905), wrote and published his early novels in the last half of the age of ragtime (c. 1912–

1917), made his silent films in the jazz and early classical jazz ages (1918–1929), and made his sound films in the age of classical jazz.

Locke's timeline is not the only historical perspective imaginable, but it is nonetheless useful in identifying layers of musical history in a film like *The Darktown Revue;* and since *The Darktown Revue* is a set piece, a musical short subject intended to present a series of performances, it is a relatively stationary specimen for such an analysis—each performance is mounted, not unlike a science or forensic exhibit.

Darktowns

The title of the film probably belongs historically to the first and second ages of minstrelsy and the age of ragtime. The film was actually made later than the title implies, during the later jazz age, which was a significant transition period in the usage and implications of the term "darktown." Nathan Huggins introduced his first chapter of *Harlem Renaissance,* titled "Harlem: Capital of the Black World," by making a distinction between the emergence of Harlem and the previous development of other "darktowns," or black communities, even in New York City:

> Harlem had thus freshly become a great concentration of blacks—not peasant but urban—within the most urbane of American cities then just feeling its youthful strength and posturing in self-conscious sophistication. No wonder Harlemites felt that they and their community were something special; *not just another darktown.*[9] [Emphasis added]

The term "darktown" may have come to prominence between the collapse of Reconstruction—which was ensured by the election of Rutherford B. Hayes in 1876—and the expansion of the urban black communities in the North and South at about the time of the migrations surrounding World War I. Books on black entertainment show that the term "darktown" was used commonly in titles of books, songs, theater pieces, performance companies, and clubs but that the high incidence peaked well before the turn of the century. Sampson lists the tour of A. G. Allen's Minstrels in Virginia in 1908 as featuring two numbers that contained the term "darktown" in their titles: "Last act—'Outing of the *Darktown's* 400', [emphasis added]" and "Billy Kersands makes a big hit with his new out-of-doors production entitled 'The *Darktown* Fire Brigade'" [emphasis added].[10]

One important significance of the term "darktown" is its association in entertainment with Micheaux's nemesis, the indignities of clowning and caricature, as indicated by Nathan Huggins's analysis of Billy Kersands, who represents an extreme style of "coon" performing:

> Some black performers attempted to achieve the distance between the stage character and themselves by the very extremities of the exaggeration. Grotesques, themselves, could allow black men, as they did white men, the assurance that the foolishness on stage was not them. Thus Billy Kersands, popular with Negro as well

as white audiences around 1911, made himself into a freak entertainer. Claiming to have the largest mouth in the world—"If God ever wanted to make my mouth any bigger, He would have to move my ears"—did a dancing act with two billiard balls in his mouth. And the very popular Ernest Hogan pushed the *darky* characterization to the limits of unction and denigration. Neither he, nor anyone he could have known, ate watermelon the way his stage character claimed to.[11] [Emphasis added]

As African Americans entered the world of minstrel entertainment, replacing whites in blackface, they had to inhabit white-created discourses of "darky" characterization. But, in addition to having to face an understandable "stage fright," they also were physically circulating among whites, putting their bodies in jeopardy outside the "darktown" ghettos. At least in those real darktowns, i.e., the black communities, there was the possibility to move outside the white-created *idea* of the darktown, even to begin gradually to find the strength and support to propagate a revision of that idea. bell hooks has said that "[t]hose of us who remember living in the midst of racial apartheid know that the separate spaces, the times apart from whiteness, were for sanctuary, for reimagining and re-membering ourselves."[12]

In order to propagate revision of the idea of darktown, those acts of reimagining and re-membering had to be taken outside darktown, outside of sanctuary. The danger inherent in that required the adoption of a bit of the darktown caricature as protective coloration, which required great skill and a complex discourse of irony. Billy Kersands's trope of performance can be related to Donald Bogle's thesis of reluctant but great ironic portrayals of caricature roles in Hollywood movies. Bogle says of Stepin Fetchit (Ed Lee), for example,

> Fetchit was able to tie together all the disparate elements to create a stylized character. As if aware of his own effect, he gave performances that were often a series of extravagant poses. When he sang and danced in films, it was hard for audiences not to respond to the precise control of his body. "Mr. Fetchit's feet are like chained lightning as he performs," wrote one critic. Even when his characters were flamboyantly exaggerated, the master Fetchit was economic and in command of his movements. Never was there a false footstep. Never was there excessive excessiveness.[13]

Not only could great caricaturists such as Fetchit claim the dignity that comes with great performance, but they also developed a refined sense of irony:

> Fetchit's dimwits never had to acknowledge the inhumanity that surrounded them. They were inhabitants of detached, ironic, artistically controlled worlds. The ambiguity in Fetchit's work was so strong that audiences often asked, "Can he be serious?" That was something never asked of later black comics, and it was this aspect of Fetchit's work that distinguished him and made him more than just a stereotype figure.[14]

Ironic tropes of ethnic caricature can be a kind of reclamation of competency, identity, autonomy, and even dignity:

Fig. 10. The grotesque caricaturing of the minstrel comedian Billy Kersands.

to recognize a fool makes one not a fool any longer; and that is very pleasing. Surely this is true of ethnic humor, whether on or off stage, especially as it is performed by members of the characterized group. For the comic accepts a demeaning characterization of his group, assuming to improve upon it with his claim of authenticity. Thus, he becomes superior because his perspective allows him to judge himself and his people and because his pose places him above even those who had disdain for him to begin with.[15]

Adoption and adaptation of caricature, a form of "Signifyin(g)," as defined by Henry Louis Gates in *The Signifying Monkey,* is not a new idea. Signifyin(g) is related, as Gates has pointed out, to Harold Bloom's idea of misreading as a central literary mode consisting of Oedipal struggles of influence between poet heroes. There is more at stake, however, as Gates has also pointed out, in black adoption and adaptation than in Bloom's "misprision."[16] Bloom has made a case for misprision as a struggle for the soul, something that has deep psychological, cultural, and philosophical implications for the antagonists of the drama of producing great western literature. But Nathan Huggins has shown that black performers such as Kersands were in a larger game than were Bloom's poet heroes, since the stakes included both soul and body:

> The black mask of the minstrel—its most figurative representation of the ethnic stereotype—was a substantive shield protecting more than self-esteem. The mask was a means of survival—only by wearing it in some form could black entertainers find work—and, even more, it was a defense against violence.[17]

"The mask as a means of survival" helps explain why certain descriptions of caricature, such as those in Marlon Riggs's film *Ethnic Notions* (1989), are so psychologically disturbing. Huggins presents a photograph of Billy Kersands with his mouth wide open; this image, as with similar images presented by Riggs in *Ethnic Notions,* is so grotesque as to verge on the expressionistic (see fig. 10). Such images may engender revulsion rather than the laughter intended by their original producers. The Kersands photograph has a more apparent kinship with Edvard Munch's *The Scream,* with contemporaneous expressionist works, and with Weimar "degenerate" art (so called by the Nazis) than it does with the American musical theater.

If the terms "darktown" and "darky" (denoting grotesque caricatures epitomized by Kersands and Hogan) derive from the period just after the collapse of Reconstruction, when the newly free blacks were conspicuously vulnerable, then the frightening quality of the Kersands photograph may be a direct expression of the frightening quality of black life in white America. Seeing through to the extremity of a Kersands or a Hogan demonstrating a "darky" or a "coon" caricature can reveal a difference between fear of criticism (stage fright, fear of failure) and fear of bodily harm or death through enforced poverty or assault. In black musical theater of the second age of minstrelsy, those two fears were confused with each other.

9 Revising Caricature

The goal of uplifting the race required that the negative images of caricature be faced directly. In the context of that historical project, Micheaux's film *The Darktown Revue* is political in the same way that the Fisk Jubilee Singers were a political act during the period when Micheaux was growing up.

The Fisk Jubilee Singers

The Fisk Singers had already lived an exhilarating moment when the potential for their full citizenship was being demonstrated publicly in a new way. When the Jubilee Singers set out from the recently founded black Fisk University in Nashville in 1871 to tour the eastern part of the country, the ground was prepared for them by civic and religious leaders in the major northern cities. The apprehensive white audiences who attended their concerts, drawn by the entreaties of their trusted ministers, did not know what to expect from black performers, except minstrelsy. The Fisk Singers astonished them with their sophisticated middle-class musicality and social demeanor, and the tour netted a huge $20,000 in revenue for the university. The leaders at Fisk were carving a niche for their ethnic group that would be a reference point of progress both culturally and financially.

Fisk University's political strategy included propagation of their group (the $20,000) and propagation of their cause, which included the idea of ethnic uplift. The Fisk tour worked as propaganda, because the clean-cut, educated, and musically sophisticated qualities of the Fisk students genuinely surprised white audiences. The Fisk Singers engaged in the kind of public relations and promotion that Huggins has discussed in his book on the Harlem Renaissance: "The Negro had to be 'sold' to the public in terms they could understand. Not the least important target in the campaign was the Negro himself; he had to be convinced of his worth. It is important to understand this, because much of the art and letters that was the substance on which the New Negro was built and which made up the so-called Harlem Renaissance was serving this promotional end."[1]

The success of the Fisk Jubilee Singers undoubtedly contributed to the slipping of the yoke of caricature and to the evolution of a more liberated black musical theater. Alain Locke placed the heyday of the farce and buffoonery—the "Buck and Wing," the "Coon Song," and the "Folk Blues"—in the second age of minstrelsy that ran from 1875 to 1895, but it is clear from other sources that caricature performances characterized by farce and buffoonery were well estab-

Fig. 11a. This group portrait–like shot of the middle-class chorus in *The Darktown Revue* from 1931 . . .

Fig. 11b. . . . is reminiscent of this photograph of the Fisk Jubilee Singers, the frontispiece to the 1883 book on the Singers' first two great tours (*The Story of the Jubilee Singers with their Songs*, by J. B. T. Marsh).

lished before this period. G. D. Pike, in his account of the first tour (in 1871) of the Jubilee Singers, made reference to a tradition of caricature performance:

> Good people understood full well that the singing of the Fisk students was sufficiently enjoyable before they reached New York; but did the large class of Christians, who would scarcely patronize negro concerts, deem it respectable to attend those of the Jubilee Singers? Was there not so much odium attached to negro concerts, as represented in burnt cork minstrels, that people of taste and character did not think it becoming to rush in crowds to a paid concert given by negroes?[2]

This statement is drawn from a paragraph that reports how Pike answered a question at one of his public lectures after the tour; the question inquired about the reasons for the success of the tour after it reached New York City. In his answer above, Pike identified two audience groups and two categories of black performance. The term "good people" referred to the cadre of white liberals and African-American middle classes in the North, the kind of people who helped organize and promote uplift and black educational institutions of the South. The "large class of Christians," on the other hand, were the rank-and-file white middle-class and lower-middle-class people who were not necessarily liberal and progressive but who were not depraved or debauched, as the "lower class" might be. This target audience would loosely approximate the native-born whites of the sort that formed the patriotic secret society of which Edwin S. Porter was a member, as discussed by Charles Musser. Pike implied that this "large class of Christians" would have shied away from negro entertainment because of the association with previous burnt-cork genres, which rank-and-file Christians found offensive. The challenge, as Pike explained it, was to get the word out to this audience that the Jubilee Singers represented a different kind of "negro entertainment."

Changing the Joke

Another look at Pike's explanation of the Jubilee Singers' strategy for building an audience clarifies how the leaders of Fisk University, and later Micheaux, deployed bourgeois values, including caricature, to help "change the joke and slip the yoke." Pike pointed to the success of a performer, who he suggested served as a model for Fisk's plan for audience development:

> John B. Gough is said by some critics to owe his wonderful success largely to the fact that he is an "Evangelical comedian," and people who dare not patronize the theatre, and do not know what acting is, go and laugh safely at his lectures. Although this criticism is unjust, it suggests to me that there may be such a thing as supplying a wholesome demand for entertainment to a class of persons who have too much principle or taste to accept the popular entertainments that come within reach.[3]

Pike's example of Gough was intended to demonstrate a rhetorical trope: the packaging of propaganda ("Evangelical") within entertainment ("comedian") or, conversely, the packaging of entertainment in propaganda ("supplying a wholesome demand . . . to . . . persons who have too much principle"). To the sort of audience who would go to see a comedian, propaganda could be delivered as well. To the sort of audience who would go to see evangelism, entertainment also could be delivered. In the former case, the propaganda might be a surprise, but it would be an acceptable one if it was entertaining. In the latter case, the entertainment might be a surprise, but it would be a welcome one if it was not degrading. In both cases, the audience was potentially expanded to include the numbers of people who might attend for *either* of the two motives. The fitting together of the two realms of discourse made audience development possible.

Oscar Micheaux used the same trope in *The Darktown Revue*. Micheaux's talent as an entrepreneur has seldom been questioned, and it is often contrasted with his alleged artistic failings. Such a perception of Micheaux's accomplishment would probably accept the interpretation that Micheaux's use of a sophisticated, middle-class jubilee chorus in formal attire was a case of employing bourgeois values to sell entertainment. If that were a fair criticism, then Micheaux's priority would be seen to be entrepreneurial business rather than artistic or cultural production, which would be in line with a common critical perception of Micheaux's motives and accomplishment. Within such a characterization of the film, the bourgeois values that Micheaux employed were inherent in the kind of music sung, the elegant appearance of the performers, the stylish stage set, and the relatively high production values of the film. These values would have helped to sell the film, which was, according to this line of criticism, Micheaux's principal purpose and the nature of his business.

The converse of that trope, however, is equally defensible. Micheaux worked all of his life, he said, to prove that a black man could be anything. It is true that Micheaux wanted to be successful in the businesses of his choice, that he had to prove his competence (and that of his ethnic group) in a plutocratic meritocracy by saving money, building capital, investing in land, farming intelligently, writing and selling novels, and producing films that would return profits on their investments. Success in such complex realms necessarily occupied his energies and affected his values. But it is equally true to say, more generally and simply, that Micheaux wanted to be successful *specifically as* a middle-class American, and he wanted to be accepted and valued as such. As a filmmaker, he had to sell his films in order to have any chance of such success, but that would not have been enough. To be accepted by American audiences as a good and valued colleague and citizen was a deeper rhetorical challenge than to be accepted as a good salesman or entrepreneur. Micheaux, as a matter of fact, emphatically rejected the entrepreneurial success that might have come from mounting entertainment based on white-majority-conceived stereotypes of blacks. Micheaux did use such stereotypes, undoubtedly knowing that they would help sell his films even to black audiences, but selling was not his priority. Selling was primarily a means to the rhetorical end of a full citizenship that would require an outright and effective contradiction of those stereotypes.

Citizenship was his true priority, both for himself and for his ethnic group, and cultural production was his means; it was to that end that he used caricature and stereotype against itself.

The Evangelical Comedian

Pike's prior strategy (using John B. Gough) foreshadows the ways in which Micheaux may have used entertainment to sell values, as well as values to sell entertainment. Pike considered the disdainful implications of the term "Evangelical comedian" an unjust criticism of Gough. Not only was it inappropriate as a criticism but the term "Evangelical comedian" was positively suggestive of a worthy strategy. It is true that the term was indeed negatively suggestive of a kind of entertainment that Pike found unacceptable, the burnt-cork minstrels. That is undoubtedly the reason Pike considered the term "Evangelical comedian" to be a criticism rather than a neutral description (the unsavory connotations were associated with the "comedian," of course, rather than with the "Evangelical"). It is not clear from the remainder of Pike's explanation what role the comedian aspect of Gough's success might have played in the strategy and the success of the Fisk tour. Elsewhere, Pike may also have masked possible references to an element of comedy by using terms that were more general than "comedy," terms such as "entertaining" and "enjoyable." He also made it very clear throughout the book that the principal attraction and value of the Fisk concerts, and the most common impression left with the audience, was the uplifting quality of the songs and the singing. The following extract, from a Cincinnati paper, quoted at length by Pike earlier in his report, is typical of Pike's documentation of audience responses:

> The music was strictly devotional, and was preceded by a prayer from the pastor of the church . . . and accompanied by explanatory remarks by him and Professor White [the choir leader of the Fisk Singers]. . . . The hymn that followed was the masterpiece of the evening; rough in language, it was richly melodious, and showed that analogy between the feeling of the slaves at the South and that of the captive Israelites, upon which Mrs. Stowe has dwelt so much in her Uncle Tom's Cabin. . . . "O, redeemed, redeemed, I'm washed in the blood of the Lamb," was sung beautifully by the rich, clear voices. . . . The unaffected, simple fervor, breathing forth the soul, were remarkable and touching qualities of the performance.

Soon after this quotation, Pike used another newspaper notice to demonstrate the rhetorical problem faced by the Fisk tour: "The following item appeared [in a city paper]:—'A band of negro minstrels will sing in the Vine Street congregational Church this morning. They are genuine negroes, and call themselves "Colored Christian Singers".' But no matter how the crowd was called, when once under the magnetism of their music, prejudice melted way, and praise of their performance was upon every tongue."[4] Pike was, of course, objecting to the characterization "band of negro minstrels." A related point is made more colloquially by an earlier anecdote:

On reaching the musical department, Professor White requested Miss Sheppard to play Annie Laurie, with variations upon the piano. Almost at once a crowd gathered, and exclamations were heard on all sides, "Only see! she's a nigger." "Do you see that?" "Do you hear that? Why, she's a nigger." On being invited to sing, the troupe gave "Star-spangled Banner," with "Red, White, and Blue," "Away to the Meadows," and other favorites, every note seeming to increase the crowd, till it became so great one could scarcely tell where it commenced. Wherever the Singers moved the crowd followed, with an admiration entirely new to these people, who, for many years, had no rights a white man was bound to respect.[5]

The audiences the Fisk Singers were trying to reach had little or no experience with black performers who claimed middle-class legitimacy. Audiences were genuinely amazed that black performers were not necessarily caricatures that could be adequately rendered by whites in burnt cork. Pike insisted that the energetic promotion of the Fisk tour by key members of "good" society in New York, combined with the serious spiritual and aesthetic qualities of the music and the performers themselves, caused the tide to turn toward success in New York for the 1871 tour.

Pike never returned in his speech to an explanation of the significance for the Fisk strategy of the "comedian" aspect of the Gough example, which he had used early in his lecture. He did hint, through the use of such terms as "entertaining" and "enjoyable," that there was something more than strictly devotional music in the formula that turned the tide toward public acceptance of the Fisk Singers in New York. The anecdote of Miss Sheppard's variations on Annie Laurie and the choir's renditions of "Red, White, and Blue" and "Away to the Meadows" indicate a direction the Singers were taking that was not strictly devotional but was, rather, more secularly popular. Such extensions would not be surprising, being largely in the spirit of American optimism and patriotism; they were not different in sentiment and in style from the devotionals.

There were other elements, however, in the Fisk entertainment that are described elsewhere in Pike's book and that suggest that the reference to Gough's Evangelical comedian might have been more literal and less figurative than Pike had yet implied. Pike mentioned a performance from early in the tour that may have been an experiment, not just in theatrical characterization but also in a kind of caricature:

It was at this concert that Mr. Dickerson [one of the Fisk Singers] made his first appearance in the Temperance Medley. He is described as standing out in front of the others, with a long rusty coat and mutton-legged pants, by far too short for him, with low-quartered shoes. The whole class were said to have been trembling for him, while his knees knocked together like chattering teeth, but, under his magnetism, the audience seemed to lose their identity, and swayed to and fro like trees in a tempest.[6]

To be sure, this skit would have been in the interest of the temperance message, but it may have exploited caricature. If this example seems tenuous, a later example is more explicit: "Georgie [a little fellow who found his way into camp, hungry and nearly naked] . . . also joined the company. His ability in declamation and song, considering his age, was indeed wonderful. His rendering of the 'Hard-Shell Sermon,' 'Sheridan's Ride,' and 'The Smack in School,' was simply inimitable. The audience seemed never to have enough of it."[7] Clearly there was something going on in the Fisk tour that was more than strictly devotional music. It is possible, from the description of Georgie's act, to see elements of farce and buffoonery (the "Hard-Shell Sermon") as well as of vaudeville and musical comedy that characterize what Locke calls the second age of minstrelsy and the age of ragtime.

Revising Caricature, Sixty Years Later

This view of the Fisk Jubilee Singers' act would make this act quite similar to the act presented, sixty years later, by the performers in Micheaux's *The Darktown Revue*. *The Darktown Revue* also presented a spoof on the "hard-shell" sermon, a skit performed by Amon Davis, who had made the act famous on the vaudeville circuit during the age of ragtime, twenty years before his appearance in Micheaux's film. One might question why Micheaux returned to the form of the jubilee choir, the success of which, though confirmed in the Fisk tour of 1871, was grounded in a sensibility that ran backwards deep into slavery, at least into the age of the sorrow songs, around 1830. And one might question why Micheaux returned to the form of the vaudeville skit, "The Hard-Shell Sermon," whose success was confirmed at the turn of the century but the sensibility of which is grounded in the farce and buffoonery associated with the second age of minstrelsy, around 1875. Why should he make, and why should critics today be interested in, a film like this at all, when sophisticated cultural sensibilities had already passed triumphantly through the age of jazz, the era of the New Negro, the Harlem Renaissance, and the Roaring Twenties and were, according to Alain Locke, negotiating the age of classical jazz and the dawn of African-American classical music?

In answering these questions, it is useful to look again at the historical context of *The Darktown Revue*. If, as seems the case, the Fisk Singers had been incorporating into their act in 1871 some of the caricatures from their age and previous ages, there are various ways they might have been using those caricatures. Their caricatures might have been benignly entertaining and thus simply an attraction, though it is hard to imagine such a simplicity or benignity surrounding those particular skits, the titles of which suggest a minstrel theme. The caricatures might have been malignantly entertaining and thus an attraction in the way minstrelsy was attractive, though any such malignancy must have been more subtle than the skits of minstrelsy, since the audience appealed to was the relatively refined, even devout, middle class.

On the other hand, the caricatures might have been carefully assimilated into the uplift message of the Fisk project, playing a part in that progressive rhetoric. If the latter is most probably correct, then the Fisk project may have been using caricature to confront the problems of racism, if somewhat diffidently. They were not just putting themselves forward as well-dressed, well-behaved models of non-caricatured, upright Americanness; they may also have been "signifying" on white caricatures of black Americans. For example, the inclusion of the skit of the hard-shell sermon invites a comparison with the more sober "sermons" of the Fisk tour and with the sermons of the non-hard-shell clergy who supported the tour throughout the country. The Fisk entourage and the sermons of their middle-class hosts were favored in such a comparison. Rhetorically, the Fisk Singers would be saying, "here is a caricature of ethnic religious behavior that you will recognize; notice that we are not like that, but that we are black. We African Americans from Fisk are more like you and your ministers than we are like this hard-shell caricature. We are more like you than you thought we were." Fundamentally, the rhetorical import of this use of caricature would have been a polite request to be allowed into the ranks of the American middle class.

In the pursuit of this request, such a strategy selectively denies and exploits aspects of ethnic vernacular discourse. It denies, for example, through caricature, the hard-shell sermon; it exploits, through refinement, the sorrow song. Convincing explanations of the choice of the sorrow song for development as a middle-class crossover genre can be found in Rawn Spearman's article on the success of the African-American spiritual—alongside the Baroque and early Classical songs, the German lieder, and the songs of the Romantics—in the repertoire of western-trained black singers, like Roland Hayes, during the Harlem Renaissance; similar explanations can be found in Georgia A. Ryder's essay on the music of black composer R. Nathanial Dett, who developed vernacular spirituals into western musical theater and classical oratorio.[8] There must be many other reasons for those choices of vernacular adaptation, and there must be many other similar choices by this group and other groups, choices that are beyond the scope of this study to pursue.

But where does all that leave Oscar Micheaux, who was apparently making strategic choices in 1931 that were virtually identical to those made by the Fisk Singers in 1871? After all, the great migration and the Harlem Renaissance had intervened, presumably changing everything. There was a much higher level of black sophistication and a greater acknowledgment of it by the white establishment. The very success of the Fisk Singers three generations before would surely itself have changed for the better the middle-class society for which the Fisk strategy had been specifically designed.

Micheaux's Historical Situation

Micheaux's historical situation can, however, be characterized differently. The Fisk Singers did perhaps live an exhilarating moment when the potential for their full citizenship was being demonstrated publicly in a new way through their acceptance by certain doyens of the white establishment. The leaders at Fisk were carving a niche for their ethnic group that would be a reference point of progress, not just culturally but financially as well. A mere five years later, however, Rutherford Hayes was in the White House, Reconstruction was in retreat, and lynchings and Ku Klux Klan activities were on the rise. With the great migrations a few years later came race riots in the northern cities, as white competitors at the lower end of the meritocracy reacted to the influx of low-cost African-American labor.

Micheaux was developing his early work through some of the worst of these setbacks. The great migration of blacks from the South occurred during the first world war; at the same time, Micheaux was traveling and writing his second novel. The most famous of the post-war riots occurred in East St. Louis in 1917 and in Chicago in 1919, just as Micheaux's film career was getting under way in Chicago. The earliest of his films that has survived, *Within Our Gates* (1919), was made partly in response to the Chicago riot; it deals directly with the subject of lynching and was consequently subjected to censorship in Chicago and was censored, banned, or rejected for screening in many venues.

Into this historical scene stepped D. W. Griffith. Soon after Micheaux had published his angry and ironic books about the failure of his entrepreneurial homesteading enterprise (*The Conquest,* 1913) and of black enterprise in general (*The Forged Note,* 1915), Griffith scored an epic conquest over any progress in the African-American condition that might have been made since the time of the Fisk Jubilee campaign. *The Birth of a Nation* (1915) was a sophisticated film production, convincing enough in its techniques of realism to inspire the president of the United States, the former president of Princeton University, and a respected historian (all in the person of Woodrow Wilson) to call it "history written in lighting." Wilson's judgment notwithstanding, Griffith's sophisticated film production contained not a grain of social, political, or economic illumination. The idealism that defines the white protagonists—produced with Billy Bitzer's famous soft-focus, backlighted portrait technique, in the case of the Lillian Gish, Miriam Cooper, and Mae Marsh characters, and with the editing strategies for which Griffith is celebrated—is thoroughly illusionistic.

Minstrel "Realism"

Any realism contained in *The Birth of a Nation* breaks down completely around its portraits of blacks, blacks played by white men and women in blackface, actors whom Huggins has characterized as "merely playing minstrel types." Griffith's minstrelized "realism" arose in Micheaux's adulthood. That in itself would justify the continuing need for promotional and critical strategies such as those pioneered by the Fisk Singers forty-five years earlier. But the situation was even worse than that, since Griffith's legacy of black minstrel characters in realistic settings has continued into our own time with a rather shocking literalness. That the genre that combines animated cartoons with live-action cinematography is a small one makes it all the more surprising that a high percentage of the best known of such films deal with African-American material. In *Song of the South* (1946), the trickster figures of Gullah storytelling are rendered as literally caricatured, i.e., they are cartoon figures representing the imagination of a live-action black storyteller, Uncle Remus. In *Who Framed*

Roger Rabbit? (1988), members of the exploited and oppressed ethnic group are called "toons," which is short for "cartoons." And since the ghetto where the toons live is called "toontown," a near-homophone of "coontown," a parallel is inferable between "coon" caricatures and "toons." The association of animated cartoons, as a genre, with ethnic caricature may not be too far-fetched as a conscious intent in *Roger Rabbit,* and it may be an unconscious equation in some other films. Some of the other more notable experiments in extreme realism in animated films, and in the association of animation with live action, are Ralph Bakshi's *Heavy Traffic* (1973) and *Coonskin* (1975), which deal extensively with black ethnic material. These films demonstrate little or no artistic integrity with regard to the issue of ethnic caricature; they merely reflect a continuing tendency in mainstream cinema. Mickey Mouse himself was born as a minstrel in a matrix of early jazz and is probably passing for white even today.[9]

Such minstrel caricatures, including those of Griffith, that were represented as inhabiting "real," even hyper-real, geographical and social landscapes "would have been funny . . . had it not been distorting *real* history and had it not provoked horrible fantasies about the political future of the northern communities following the migration of southern blacks."[10] The backwardness of *The Birth of a Nation* is indistinguishable at many levels from the reigning attitude of that period among the American populace and its administrative apparatuses. The following passage from Thomas Kochman's study of black styles of communication gives a sense of the period of Micheaux's early career and suggests what Micheaux was up against:

> In November 1914, Monroe Trotter, an educator and equal rights activist, led a black delegation to the White House to renew the protest against the segregation of federal employees that had become widespread for the first time during Woodrow Wilson's administration. President Wilson indicated that the intention of such segregation was to avoid friction between black and white clerks. Trotter disputed this, saying that white and black clerks had been working together for fifty years in peace, harmony, and friendliness and that it was only after Wilson's inauguration that segregation was to a drastic degree introduced in the Treasury and Postal Departments by Wilson's appointees. Trotter's rebuttal brought about the following exchange:
>
>> *Wilson:* If this organization is ever to have another hearing before me it must have another spokesman. Your manner offends me.
>> *Trotter:* In what way?
>> *Wilson:* Your tone, with its background of passion.
>> *Trotter:* But I have no passion in me, Mr. President, you are entirely mistaken; you misinterpret my earnestness for passion.[11]

In spite of the emergence of the New Negro, any change going on in the historical situation in Micheaux's time seemed to be change for the worse. The film industry had absorbed the success of *The Birth of a Nation* into its genetic materials. Black independent filmmakers fought back with "positive image" films, such as *The Birth of a Race* (1919), which emerged stillborn from the Booker T.

Washington staff's efforts, and *The Trooper of Troop K* (1916), from the Lincoln Company. All such films failed rhetorically or financially. The National Association for the Advancement of Colored People (NAACP) fought against Griffith and Hollywood through various means, including an unsuccessful attempt at a co-production with Carl Laemmle. The NAACP made no headway until 1942, when it reached an agreement with a group of Hollywood studio heads; that agreement, which was considered a breakthrough, was so small a concession as to hardly be an occasion for celebration. Micheaux, in fact, was faced with a more violent racial climate than that with which the Fisk Singers had been faced in 1871.

In one sense, the historical knowledge of the resurgence of racial violence helps explain how Micheaux might have been pursuing oppositional artistic practices similar to those of the Fisk Singers three generations earlier. The dialectics of twoness and of high and low status that were complexly negotiated by Fisk are also characteristic of Micheaux's work; in fact, the construction of those dialectics in *The Darktown Revue* is explicit, schematic, and paradigmatic in relation to Micheaux's other films, as will be demonstrated below. Micheaux's usual proposal of a middle path through such dialectics can be seen in his portrayal of the kinds of music produced by the chorus in *Darktown Revue*—that "positive-image" middle class of African Americans—music that, as far as Micheaux is concerned, can include hot jazz as well as dicty operatic songs.

In *Darktown*, however, in spite of the sympathetic portrayal of the middle path—of semi-white, semi-black hybridity—Micheaux's emphasis is noticeably focused on one element of the dialectic of twoness. The force of the film's signifying is not deployed primarily along a middle path but forcefully *against the negative* images. Micheaux's emphasis is complementary to that of the Fisk Singers, who stirred the world with their positive images of African Americans while soft-peddling and signifying on negative, minstrel images. Micheaux's shift in emphasis can be explained in part by analyzing the developing role of stereotype and caricature directly in relation to the historical pressures of the great migration surrounding World War I.

Violence and the Migrations

One of James Grossman's initial premises in his book on the first wartime black migrations to Chicago is helpful as we attempt to gain the perspective of those southern African Americans who were migrating. Grossman argues that the "push and pull" theories for explaining the migration, though important, are inadequate. The "pull" theories state that the better racial conditions and economic opportunities of Chicago (and the North) attracted southern blacks and thus were a cause for the migrations. The "push" theories state that the poor racial and economic conditions in the South repelled blacks and thus were a complementary cause for migration. Grossman does not dispute the realities of the push and the pull, but he complicates the notion of how they might be causes for actions. Grossman posits a complex "web of [racist] social relations" that is countered by considerable black ethnic autonomy and agency in the events of the migrations. His argument provides a series of close-ups that allows some access to the African-American migrant's point of view, and that point of view suggests that a general apprehension about violence was a prime mover:

> The physical abuse that sent many migrants North assumed a variety of forms, from mistreatment by law enforcement officials to rape and lynching. The fear of such violence could induce flight as easily as the acts themselves. Blacks from Florida told investigators that they had gone North because of "the horrible lynchings in Tennessee." . . . Chicago Urban League workers found that after a lynching, "colored people from that community will arrive in Chicago inside of two weeks." . . .
> . . . The black Houston *Observer* offered a poignant recitation of dissatisfactions:
>
> > Take some of the sections from which the Negro is departing and he can hardly be blamed when the facts are known. He is kicked around, cuffed, lynched, burned, homes destroyed, daughters insulted and ofttimes raped, has no vote nor voice, is underpaid, and in some instances when he asks for pay receives a 2 × 4 over his head. These are facts.[12]

The story of the Florida migrants responding to Tennessee lynchings shows how far climatic conditions could reach to effect outlook and motivation; the story from the Houston *Observer* presents factors that affected that climate. Grossman has attempted to approach the migrants' own understanding of their actions:

> A Mississippian tried to explain the problem:
>
> > Just a few months ago they hung Widow Baggage's husband from Hirshbery bridge because he talked back to a white man. He was a prosperous Farmer owning about 80 acres. They killed another man because he dared to sell his cotton "off the place." These things have got us sore. Before the North opened up with work all we could do was to move from one plantation to another in hope of finding something better.[13]

The presence of violent intimidation in the daily lives of black Americans and of the deadly violence reported regularly "in the grapevine" and in the public media was a hindrance to black autonomy, one against which any strategy for advancement would have to struggle. Merely doing a good job and adopting the dominant American values was not an adequate strategy for advancement, especially in the South:

> After fifty years of "hoping against hope," the *AME Church Review* observed in 1917, black southerners had learned that "neither character, the accumulation of property, the fostering of the Church, the schools and a better and higher standard of the home" had brought either respect or the chance for substantial mobility. "Confidence in the sense of justice, humanity and fair play of the white South is gone." . . . One Tennessee black newspaper reported in 1909 that a black farmer's "signs of prosperity" could attract "nightriders" who would drive him from his

land. Working hard as an employee was equally unlikely to bring advancement; most black southerners were well aware of the "Dixie limit" beyond which no black could advance. . . . Little had changed since Reconstruction, when, as W. E. B. Du Bois later argued, the white South had feared black success above all else.[14]

Such a reality or web of social relations gave rise to the kind of "success" that Billy Kersands and Ernest Hogan forged with their development of exaggerated caricature.

Violence and Caricature

Nathan Huggins has explained the role this violence played in the evolution of the ethnic caricatures of the second age of minstrelsy and the age of ragtime:

> The black mask of the minstrel—its most figurative representation of the ethnic stereotype—was a substantive shield protecting more than self-esteem. The mask was a means of survival—only by wearing it in some form could black entertainers find work—and, even more, it was a defense against violence. The veteran comic Tom Fletcher recalled that many of the small southern towns his company performed in were so hostile to Negroes that violence was always threatening, murder seemed in the shadow of white men's eyes. Signs which warned, "Nigger, Read and Run" chilled the hearts of Negro performers who played there. Yet, they hit upon a way. They would enter such towns in private Pullman cars, which were parked at a siding. Then, with their band, the entertainers would parade from the railroad car to whatever served as the theater; and after the performance, they would strike up the band and parade back to their Pullman. Whatever the number of shows—if there was a matinee or two-day stand—they would march to rousing music or they would not be on the streets of that town. And they seldom had doubt, Fletcher reports, as to what tune would do them the most good. "As soon as all the members of the company were on the ground we would start playing '*Dixie.*' No matter how many different tunes we had in our band books, we could play that song in any key." It was as if the *modus vivendi* depended on the Negroes continuing to play their parts, off stage as well as on. *And these black performers knew that their very existence depended on their never pretending to be other than their stage characters.*[15] [Emphasis added]

The trick that black performers played was to inhabit these stereotypes as a survival niche and to develop and sometimes revise the stereotypes while under their protection. Huggins and others explain that this trick was dangerous, because it was easy to become deformed by inhabiting such a niche. Numerous great performers, nevertheless, were willing and able to take the risk of inhabiting the rube joke in order "to slip the yoke." Kersands and Hogan "prided themselves on playing at its most extreme what the audience wanted," and that playing of the extreme "could be a personal insulation."

Nevertheless, Huggins has said, the assumption of the mask was damaging to the performer and to the audience. Though some of the performers believed their work to be progressive, not just protective, Huggins has discounted the progressive effect, emphasizing instead the psychological damage:

> Doubtless . . . [t]he white man could be put at his ease, "to take us as we really were." At least, so it would appear, but the profound question was never asked and never answered: who were these black men *really?* It was just possible that the trick had been too perfect; *legerdemain* had undone itself in a disappearance act where the self had vanished, but also the incantation to call it back again.[16]

A strategy that required loss of ethos and loss of self, though perhaps temporarily necessary for survival under extreme conditions, was ultimately not adequate or honorable. The adoption of caricature as a refuge had to be transformed from a tactic of survival to a strategy of revision toward a level of citizenship that would require the eradication of caricature.

Among the more daunting questions Micheaux took upon himself to address in his career was the one Huggins has posed, "Who were these black men *really?*" There is little question that one of Micheaux's principal missions, as stated above, was to show "that a colored man can be anything."[17] This career commitment was a historical extension of the efforts of the Fisk Singers and of Booker T. Washington, to whom the book is dedicated from which Micheaux's statement is cited. The Fisk mission in 1871 was (to paraphrase the Micheaux quotation) to show that a "colored man" could be something; the Booker T. Washington mission in 1900 was to show that he could be useful; the Micheaux mission in 1913 was to show that he (and she) could be anything. Some critics have considered this position naive and insufficiently oppositional in light of white oppression. Micheaux, as usual, chose a middle position that included some uplift rhetoric and some protest.

Ethnic Self-Criticism

Micheaux considered ethnic self-criticism to be, however controversial, just as high a priority as criticism of white oppression. This priority should be understood in part as a function of his address primarily to a black audience throughout his career. He would presumably have changed his critical priorities if he were aiming primarily at white audiences. On the one hand, his racial loyalty, demonstrated in his lifelong interest in the stories and goals of his own people, would not have allowed him to focus primarily on black shortcomings if he had been addressing a white audience. On the other hand, some evidence exists that Micheaux was capable of running down elements of his own ethnic group, even in the presence of a white audience. Such instances may seem to be betrayals, but they cannot be construed to characterize Micheaux's general practice or critical objectives.

Micheaux's strategy differed from that of the Fisk Singers, who could make their point simply by doing a good job of presenting ethnic music in a middle-class style and by using prevailing caricatures as aspects of their evangelically uplifting entertainment. By the time Micheaux started to work, doing a good job was not enough, and caricature had, against expectation, become resurgent rather than attenuated. As discussed above, for southern whites, African-American achievement itself was the most feared consequence of emancipation. Similarly and more generally, material achievement by competing ethnic groups was for native-born whites such as Edwin S. Porter the most feared consequence of immigration. Micheaux's strategy, like Fisk's, in this instance, assumed middle-class values. Micheaux pitted the middle-class values against various negative values in the African-American community that he perceived to resemble the minstrel caricatures.

Caricature was perceived by Micheaux as a prime obstacle for black advancement; thus, cultural production was an important battleground in the uplift movement. Blacks in the performing arts, such as Micheaux, needed to shed the caricature being used as a shelter. For many, the devolving climate of racial violence was transforming the foxholes of minstrelsy into permanent retrenchments. At the same time, however, the emergence of the New Negro and the Harlem Renaissance suggested that the time was right to go over the top.

Using Caricature to Critique Caricature

Micheaux's engagement with his objective took the form of presenting caricature for the purpose of criticizing it. There are more- and less-pure examples of Micheaux's use of this tactic. At the pure end of the spectrum are explicit caricatures, minstrel figures directly from the world of performance and entertainment. Such caricatures occur in Micheaux's films that include music and performance as subject matter, such as *The Darktown Revue, Ten Minutes to Live, Swing!, Lying Lips,* and *Birthright.* At the less-pure end of the spectrum are characters who are fully embedded in the plot—not in production numbers or skits—who nevertheless have characteristics comparable to minstrel caricatures. Such characters occur in *Within Our Gates* (the snitch who spies incompetently on the murder of the white aristocrat), in *Body and Soul* (the church congregation at the preacher's shouting sermon), in *Birthright* (the character called the Persimmon, who is another snitch), and in most of the other extant films.

By far the purest example of Micheaux's use of minstrel caricature is *The Darktown Revue,* since it is in fact a staged bit of black musical theater. The minstrel caricatures provided by three vaudeville veterans—the team of Tim Moore (who later became Kingfish on the television series *Amos and Andy*) and Andrew Tribble and the solo act of Amon Davis are very broad "coon" caricatures worthy of Kersands or Hogan. It is not evident that either act had the kind of redeeming self-referentiality or pathos that must have been perceived in the work of Bert Williams and George Walker—the famous vaudeville team—and in the work of Williams after Walker's death in 1911. The acts in *Darktown Revue* are old-fashioned, antebellum, and post-Reconstruction caricatures. Though they are in themselves unregenerate, they are nevertheless meant to entertain and to impress a black audience. The two acts in Micheaux's film are not untypical of race movies in that respect, and both acts are very good. The second, Amon Davis's rendering of a shouting preacher, is a brilliant ironic transformation of the letters of the alphabet into a seemingly passionate spiritual jeremiad. Davis's act would stand up well today if it were not so painfully redolent of "ethnic notions."

The audience for *The Darktown Revue* was invited to stand above these caricatures in spite of their enjoyment of them. The chorus in *Darktown Revue* serves as a surrogate audience; they stand behind and above the preacher so that their pseudo-serious and mildly amused and bemused expressions can be read as a commentary. Lest the facial expressions seem too subtle a commentary, the music sung by the chorus is more explicit—after the Moore and Tribble skit, the chorus sings "Ain't it a Shame?" and the framing song that the chorus sings before and after the sermon skit is the rhetorically titled "Is that Religion?" The implied answers to both those songs' questions are that Moore and Tribble's skit *is* a shame and that Davis's hard-shell preaching is *not* respectable religion. Also, when the preacher leaves, there is sexual innuendo in his parting word to the "sisters," and he does not bother to address the men in the "choir." The lyrics of the chorus's song then explicitly critique this sort of religion and these sorts of deacons and ministers.

A = Legitimacy, B = Caricature

In the $ABAB^1AB^2AB^n$-structure of this revue, the recurring A figure (the chorus) represents black middle-class legitimacy and the series of B, B^1, and B^n (the vaudeville skits) represent various illegitimate ethnic caricatures, such as "coons" and (for Micheaux) hard-shell preachers. The $ABAB^n$ structure is *paradigmatic* and is used repeatedly by Micheaux as a narrative form for his cinematic, class-based critique. As a paradigm of Micheaux's critique, the A figure represents (consciously or not) middle-classness and is the term upon which the positive values for critique are founded; it is the normative reference by which the qualities of the caricature series $B–B^n$ are found wanting.

In the light of this paradigm, it is easy to see why Micheaux has been accused of racial self-hatred and white racism. Ethnic criticism, however, for the purpose of ethnic development, is not necessarily racist. The A figure in Micheaux's paradigm is dialectical and complex and cannot automatically be equated with whiteness, with the pseudo-white, or with any unproblematized notion of middle-class or bourgeois values.

Complicating the A Figure

It is important, for example, that the A figure in *Darktown*—represented by the chorus and its director—present beautifully produced, upper-middle-class persons for the audience to identify with, along with perfectly superior but not quite condescending behavior toward the caricatures. It is important that the chorus members sing barbershop harmonies and pseudo-operatic "jazz,"

Fig. 12. The paradigm shot of the cutting gaze: the upper-class chorus is a surrogate critical audience for lower-class caricature in *The Darktown Revue.*

which establishes their abilities and potential popularity for a white, mass audience, just as the Fisk Singers had done. It is equally important, however, that the A figure also present hot jazz. A competent brand of hot jazz is heard over the opening and closing credits, and good improvisatory jazz piano, played by the chorus leader Donald Heywood, is interlarded with some of the high jinks of the chorus during transitions in their plantation-song numbers and in the vaudeville caricature acts. The positioning of hot jazz, privileged through both mise-en-scène and editing, complicates the A term and the bourgeois image of the chorus in a way that is consistent with Micheaux's other work. The hot jazz urbanizes the A figure, contributing to the sophistication of the chorus and its leader; at the same time, it endorses the roots, accomplishments, and the implications of the jazz phenomenon. Since it is the chorus and its leader who introduce and endorse jazz, their representation of middle-classness is understood to include an artistically impressive African-American ethnicity. Hot jazz was not only invented, developed, and marketed by blacks as "race music," but it was also difficult for whites to perform. In 1931, on the one hand, few whites had distinguished themselves in hot jazz; only Bix Beiderbeck was considered the equal of black performers, and some would debate that. On the other hand, the jazz age was a general condition of urban life, and classical musicians and white critics of serious music were occasionally expressing admiration for African-American jazz. Micheaux, however, can nevertheless be judged ethnically loyal and unusually self-confident for presenting hot jazz as a positive value within his middle-class norms, because the jazz age had really only occurred in the sophisticated urban environments, such as New York and Chicago. Most of the country's middle class were listening to sweet jazz, pop music played by Paul Whiteman and lesser white groups, who were adapting black music for the mass white market.

All these uses of music, with their historical and ideological associations, are important to any analysis of Micheaux's artistry, including its critical thrust. Underlying those uses, however, remains the paradigmatic ABAB schema that represents Micheaux's dialectics of high and low, of spirituals and jazz, of swing and blues, and of white and black, including the condition of twoness (having to negotiate both poles of those dialectics). Those same dialectics provide the framework for Micheaux's related ideas of moderation, the middle path, and the middle class.

The Cutting Gaze

At the same time, however, those dialectics also provide the framework for a cinematic "surgical" procedure in relation to the gaze. Micheaux presented a simple configuration of shot and edit that implies the "cutting" of the B figure by the A figure. When the minstrel and vaudeville performers, or B figures, are introduced in the same shot with the chorus members, or A figures, the B figures are gazed upon by the A figures in a way that implies reprobation. When the film cuts analytically from such establishing shots to separate detail shots of the B figures or to and from detail shots of the A figures and the B figures, the "cutting" gaze of the A figures becomes the surrounding context for the film's suggested critical reception of the B figures' show. The A figures continue to hold the stage and the screen, while the B figures pass in "revue" and are, in effect, assessed, found wanting, and then excised. Thus, the very title of the film, *The Darktown Revue,* is rendered explicitly critical.

The last B figure in *Darktown Revue,* the hard-shell preacher, is an exemplary manifestation of this search-and-destroy operation. Micheaux, of course, particularly despised black ministers, especially jackleg charismatics such as the one Paul Robeson plays in *Body and Soul.* The vaudeville skit of the hard-shell sermon is appropriate as a final target for Micheaux's exorcistic revue. One wonders if the Fisk Singers included a cutting gaze in their presentation of the evangelical comedy of their hard-shell preacher. Probably—but film is better suited for such a rhetorical trope, since it can control the viewer's attention through shooting and editing, not just mise-en-scène.

Negative Images

Micheaux's cutting gaze is an example of what has already been discussed (in chapter 4) as Micheaux's focus on negative images. The cutting gaze is also, however, a formal foundation for an intensely critical cinema, and as such, it contributes to uplift by criticizing the obstacles to uplift—negative images—and by figuratively excising them. Micheaux's figure of the cutting gaze represents at least a step beyond the related uplift strategy of the Fisk Singers, since the great focus at Fisk was on the A figure itself, the positive image of African Americans, which was surprise enough for the white world. Micheaux's cutting gaze is also different from Fisk's evangelical comedy, because Micheaux was addressing a psychologically internalized relationship with caricature and stereotype, as pointed out by Huggins. Thus, Micheaux's vision of the cutting gaze functions as an exorcism, a sort of cinematic "cure."

It would be misleading not to point out that Micheaux must have savored the actual *presentation* of the caricatures in *The Darktown Revue*. In a sense, he was having it both ways. He wanted his audience to enjoy as much as he did the actual ridiculing of those aspects of his ethnic situation that he felt invited ridicule. If he hated preachers, then he probably loved to see them portrayed as fools on the screen.

Micheaux's concentration on certain negative qualities that he found identifiable as African-American qualities is common to ethnic groups in the American melting pot. It is related to the rube joke and the rube movie, though the versions of the rube associated with racism are especially violent and virulent. The fact that such negative images would be nurtured *within* the stereotyped group is not surprising, given the pressures to assimilate. A passion of certain Jews to assimilate helped to form the valuative paradigms of Hollywood, with all its rube figures and stereotypes.[18]

Negative images that developed within the African-American community need not be read as evidence of self-hatred, however, as social critic Shelby Steele has shown:

> Sam's persona amounted to a negative instruction manual in class identity.
> . . . It never occurred to us that [Sam] looked very much like the white racist stereotype of blacks, or that he might have been a manifestation of our own racial self-hatred. He simply *gave us a counterpoint against which to express our aspirations.* If self-hatred was a factor, it was not, for us, a matter of hating lower-class blacks but of hating what we did not want to be.
> Still, hate or love aside, it is fundamentally true that my middle-class identity involved *a dissociation from images of lower-class black life* and a corresponding identification with values and patterns of responsibility that are common to the middle class everywhere.[19] [Emphasis added]

Conclusion

For better or worse, Micheaux's abuse of negative characters—analogous to Steele's Sam—recurs throughout his work. The fact that Micheaux made *The Darktown Revue* and *The Exile* a year after the success of *The Green Pastures* on Broadway also suggests that Micheaux was not just criticizing his own group but rather was critiquing white-produced negative stereotypes such as those in *The Green Pastures*. The fact that *The Exile* would never become a hit itself, in spite of the complex integrity of its vision and in spite of its uncompromising sense of African-American dignity, is consistent with the obstinate toughness of Micheaux's attitude toward caricature.

The complexity, dignity, and toughness toward caricature of *The Exile* reflect an independence of spirit that could only be maintained in a relatively inexpensive cinema, where Micheaux could, at the expense of commercial marginality, "afford" to say what he believed. Micheaux's commercial marginality, however, did not fool Roi Ottley; writing about the film version of *The Green Pastures* in the *Amsterdam News* in 1936, he declared:

> "The Green Pastures" will no doubt, receive magnificent and glowing accounts in the Negro press . . . and unhappily so for the Negro public. . . . Negro newspapers on the whole have a false sense of values. . . . They seem to work from the premise that anytime a Negro appears in a play or picture which the whites have produced it should be applauded regardless of its merits. . . . This department goes on record as feeling that Oscar Micheaux, with his inferior equipment, would have produced a better picture.[20]

10 Interrogating Caricature
as Entertainment

The most famous insult to the discourse of uplift is the white racist "n" word. That word has a complex association with entertainment. Micheaux applied the tactic of the cutting gaze not just to the "n" word (and to racial caricature generally) within entertainment but also to entertainment within the meaning of the "n" word.

Murder in Harlem

The Darktown Revue, because it is short and because it is uncluttered with competing narrative incident, is a relatively pure example of Micheaux's surgical use of shooting and editing related to negative characters such as Steele's Sam. In other Micheaux films, the cutting gaze is deployed in more complex narrative and ideological contexts that expand its usefulness and transform its simplicity into elegance. The cutting gaze—the ABAB paradigm of middle-class observation of lower-class behavior—operates this way throughout, for example, *Murder in Harlem* (first released as *Lem Hawkins' Confession*; 1935).

A scene in which the female lead, Claudia (Dorothy Van Engle), vamps Lem Hawkins (Alec Lovejoy), one of the less than admirable black characters who is caught in the machinations of white intrigue, contains a set of variations on the paradigm of the cutting gaze. The setting is a large apartment living room that is used as a "buffet flat," an informal nightclub where one can dance, buy illegal drinks, listen to live jazz, and watch floor shows. According to Bessie Smith's biographer, Chris Albertson,

> Buffet flats—sometimes referred to as goodtime flats—were small, privately owned establishments featuring all sorts of illegal activities: gambling and erotic shows, as well as sex acts of every conceivable kind. These buffet flats were usually owned by women, who ran them with admirable efficiency, catering to the occasional thrill-seeker as well as to regular clients whose personal tastes they knew intimately.
> . . . Buffet flats were always located in private homes or apartments. Bootleg liquor was plentiful, and a different "show" was usually presented in each room.[1]

The clientele at the buffet flat in Micheaux's film are portrayed as respectable and middle-class. They are dressed in impeccable evening clothes, and their manners are polite and reserved, in spite of their obvious enjoyment of the evening and in spite of their drinking and some frivolous party hats. Albertson has emphasized the class-based legitimacy of the daring entertainment at buffet flats:

> Buffet flats had a reputation for being safe, and reports of violent incidents and thefts were rare. Originally set up for the benefit of Pullman porters . . . whose travels, contacts with the white world, gentlemanly manners, and good income gained them much respect in the black communities—these establishments served as models for the outwardly legitimate "high-class" night clubs where tuxedoed maître d's discreetly provided "important persons" with sexual liaisons that suited their tastes.[2]

When Lem Hawkins shows up at the door of this high-class establishment, he is greeted by the owner of the flat, "the Catbird" (Bee Freeman), who compliments him on his attire and offers to take his hat and cane; she tells him that he looks "hot" tonight and that she would not mind making a play for him herself. The audience might be inclined to take these compliments at face value if this sequence had not been introduced by a scene in which the Catbird and her male partner discuss what a fool Hawkins is and how they are going to trick him out of his newfound wealth at the buffet-flat party that night. Also, Hawkins looks out of place, even though he is dressed up. He is wearing a brown, ill-fitting suit with a lighter colored vest; he is unfashionably overweight and, though he is smoking with a fancy cigarette holder, he is handling it as if it were a cheap cigar. The other clientele are dressed in perfectly fitting evening clothes, many in black tie or evening gowns; their physiques are fashionably trim, and they urbanely smoke cigarettes. Micheaux's introduction of the explicitly lower-class Hawkins into this upper-class environment is an extension of the A/upper-class, B/lower-class structure of the cutting gaze, manifested in its purest form in *The Darktown Revue*. In *Murder in Harlem*, the ABAB paradigm is integrated into a more complex narrative, and the idea of the entertainment stereotype as inhabiting the class relations of daily life is elaborated.

When Hawkins calls the waiter to bring a drink, he uses the impolite phrase, "Say, dark man," as if he were drinking with other commoners in a bar. There is no interpreting this remark as a color prejudice on the part of the filmmaker, since there is no indication that Micheaux identified himself with Lem Hawkins nor that he wished the film viewer to do so. In fact, the waiter is dark, but so is the would-be slanderer, Lem Hawkins, and so are some of the higher-class clientele with whom the audience is meant to identify. The dark-skinned waiter is seen in the background of most of the shots of Hawkins and Claudia, talking to the bartender, who is himself not only noticeably lighter-skinned but who is also a friendly companion to the "dark man." There is no invidious distinction between those two based on their skin color.

The skin-color scheme in this scene is consistent with Micheaux's other films and can be summarized as follows: darkness and lightness of skin sometimes affect perceptions of beauty in Micheaux's work in the sense that lighter skin is often preferred for characters representing the "beautiful people"; Micheaux's beautiful people, however, are not always his good people. In addition, the equa-

Fig. 13. Lem Hawkins is out of place at this upscale buffet flat in *Murder in Harlem*. He is dressed in light colors, not in evening wear, and he handles his cigarette holder as if it were a cigar, knocking ashes on the floor.

tion of lighter skin with beauty is associated with a widely shared convention that many prominent race leaders felt was, while unfortunate, temporarily unavoidable owing to the cultural hegemony of the white majority.[3]

In Micheaux's work, both beauty and goodness of character are to be found in very dark people as well in light-skinned people. The issue of skin tone is debated in the literature and is discussed elsewhere in this study; suffice it to say here that Micheaux himself was relatively dark. Also, several of his heroes are dark and several of his villains very light. As Pearl Bowser has pointed out, Micheaux had to work within the conventions of skin tone in race-entertainment circles—conventions that explicitly favored light skin—and consequently, it is difficult to generalize today about the ultimate meaning of Micheaux's choices of skin tone.

The issue of skin tone aside, Micheaux's "dandy," Hawkins, has made a triple error in the context of this refined, middle-class African-American entertainment venue of the buffet flat—he has invoked an invidious (and, in this scene, clearly false) class distinction based on skin tone; he has expressed it rudely; and he has invoked it unwittingly against himself. These mistakes are themselves evidence of lower class status. The waiter, after being called so rudely, approaches Hawkins and Claudia very slowly, having exchanged concerned and disgusted glances with both the bartender and his boss, the Catbird. On approaching the table, the waiter gives Hawkins the evil eye—a cutting gaze—then turns slowly and gives Claudia a big smile, thus making a clear distinction between Hawkins and Claudia regarding their worthiness of his regard.

The fact that Hawkins has made an earlier distinction between himself and the waiter based on skin tones; the fact that Hawkins has not considered the implication of that distinction for himself, since Hawkins is darker than most of the clientele in the room; the fact that Hawkins does not realize he is insulting all dark people within range of his voice; and the fact that Hawkins has spoken in a loud and public manner place him in a certain class that is not only below that of the clientele but below even that of the entertainers and servants, whom Micheaux portrays as respectable, accomplished, and attractive in their own right. It is no accident that the waiter adopts a slow-moving caricature routine that is, in fact, very much like that of a blackface entertainer. He is signifying an appropriate response to Hawkins's behavior by alluding to a racist entertainment stereotype of "unwarranted" ostentation that Hawkins appears to have invited and inhabited.

The waiter and Hawkins become part of a cinematic demonstration of the close connection between embarrassing public behavior and the persistence of harmful caricatures in white (and black) entertainment. Micheaux felt that such entertainment figures were hurting the African-American citizenry and hurting in a special way precisely the entertainers who practiced the vestiges of minstrel caricature.[4]

In the world of the story, Lem Hawkins is not actually an entertainer; small connections, however, throughout the scene in the buffet flat tend to weave Hawkins into the fabric of the buffet flat's featured entertainment. The spectator of the film is invited to interpret Hawkins's behavior as performance and to distinguish him from the other clients at the buffet flat, who comprise an audience for performance. Hawkins is dressed more like the entertainers and the servants at the party and is recognized by them as a member of their class. Also, in the background of several of the shots of Hawkins, the leader of the band can be seen singing; dark, round of face and figure, and broadly smiling, he somewhat resembles Hawkins, and both of them somewhat resemble the ultimate African-American entertainer, Louis Armstrong.

A scene that almost immediately follows corroborates Micheaux's probable intention to invest Hawkins with the worst characteristics of the world of race entertainment. A man dressed in dark pants, a dark pullover, and a light porkpie hat appears at the door of the buffet flat. The maître d' tries to explain to the man that he is not welcome, which generates an exaggerated exchange that resembles the vaudeville routines of, for example, Williams and Walker. In fact, the interloper looks enough like Bert Williams and the maître d' enough like George Walker that black audiences, who venerated the Williams and Walker team, might have made that connection. The interloper (the Williams figure) has been gotten up, like Williams had been, in something approximating blackface tradition. In that sense, he signifies the appearance of minstrel caricatures that masquerade as realistic characters in such rube movies as *The Birth of a Nation*. Micheaux makes the absurdity of white minstrel entertainment itself—and its legacy in such figures as the slow-moving, eyebrow-wiggling northern valet in *The Birth*—the butt of the joke, instead of the African Americans themselves. He reverses the rube joke and turns the rube movie inside out.

The Bert Williams–like interloper enters the buffet flat in spite of the maître d's efforts to reject him. Since he is a lower-class caricature of a fool from the entertainment world, one expects him to go looking for his friend among the entertainers or servants, but instead he pays special attention to Hawkins, who is technically a client of the social club. The interloper moves very slowly toward and around Hawkins's table, giving Hawkins a long stare, much like that of the "Hey, dark man" incident. The interloper then asks if Hawkins has seen a very black man with one eye and a crooked nose, a man called "bogeyman." Hawkins and Claudia laugh at him, and slowly he leaves, still staring at Hawkins. Hawkins has again been fixed with an emphatic, vaudeville-derived gaze and has thus been singled out for inclusion in a discourse of fools and caricatures, drawn explicitly from on-stage routines but presented as part of the *off*-stage story.

Here, Micheaux was not denigrating entertainers or entertainment in general, which was, after all, his own profession. He was interrogating non-entertainers who inhabited the caricatures of a specific form of racist entertainment, and, intrinsically, he was interrogating the entertainment that produced those caricatures.

Identifying with Entertainers

Standard format for Hollywood musicals calls (1) for diegetic non-entertainers *to behave as if* they were entertainers, to break into song without seeming to interrupt the diegesis (the world of the film's story), as Fred Astaire might do in the middle of a love scene or as Ann Miller does in the Museum of Natural Science in *On the Town* (1949); (2) for diegetic non-entertainers *to become* diegetic entertainers, as Al Jolson does in *The Jazz Singer* (1927); or (3) for diegetic entertainers themselves *to be the main characters* of the diegesis *as* entertainers whose lives are followed by the narrative both on stage and off, as in the films of Fred Astaire and Ginger Rogers.

Whereas all of those combinations typically produce positive images by associating diegetic amateurs with diegetic professional entertainers, Micheaux's combination produces a negative image. The diegetic amateur (non-entertainer), such as the dandy Lem Hawkins, is *degraded* rather than elevated by his association with professional entertainers, and entertainers themselves are placed loosely in a class with or below servants. For example, in Micheaux's *Veiled Aristocrats* (1932), the servants always provide the film's song-and-dance numbers.

As Jane Feuer has pointed out, professional singers are often used by Hollywood to portray amateurs:

Fig. 14a. On the left is another character in the buffet flat who will associate himself particularly with Lem; he seems to form, through his farcical interaction with the service class, a recognizable vaudeville team act, not unlike the well-known Williams and Walker or the duo act in *The Darktown Revue.*

Fig. 14b. Lem gets the evil eye from waiters . . .

Fig. 14c. . . . and from entertainment figures, thus effectively becoming identified with the service class and with entertainment routines.

Fig. 14d. In contrast, the leading woman of the film, who is slumming with Lem in order to gather information that will eventually save her brother's (and probably Lem's) life, is treated with respect by the same waiters . . .

Fig. 14e. . . . and entertainment figures.

For a movie genre which itself represents professional entertainment and which is also frequently about professional entertainers, there seems to be a remarkable emphasis on the joys of being an amateur.

. . .

No performer in the Hollywood musical had more talent than Judy Garland, and no performer more frequently portrayed the amateur, a girl who sings for love instead of money. Judy Garland's child-like qualities were exploited in her films in order to lend an amateur feeling to all her performances. Eve[n] her vocal quality is kept within an amateur range; music critic Henry Pleasants has observed that Garland's singing voice had "a sound innocent of anything that smacked of artful management." [5]

Feuer's insight concerning the contradictory use of professional entertainers to celebrate amateurism is an important contribution to the workings of Hollywood illusionism, showing how the commercial traffic in joy and talent constructs an idea of itself as explicitly *non*commercial joy and talent. A certain dilute Brechtian strain within the professional world of Hollywood has even played with anti-illusionistic ideas such as Feuer's. When Joshua Logan, for example, selected non-singing actors such as Jean Seberg and Clint Eastwood to play singing parts in *Paint Your Wagon* (1969), he reversed the Hollywood convention of selecting professional singers to portray amateurs. Since the audience could have been expected to know that neither Seberg nor Eastwood was a professional singer, the audience would understand the eruption of these actors into song to be a parody and a reversal of the standard conventions of the musical genre spelled out by Feuer. Since the singing is patently awful (though charming), the audience can discern the reversal with their own ears, even without any knowledge about Seberg's and Eastwood's professional resumes. The effect of this distanciation from the standard conventions of Hollywood illusionism—the replacement of the professional amateur by the amateur professional—fits well into Logan's extended comparison between *Paint Your Wagon* and Brecht's own anti-illusionistic, Wild-West musical, *Mahagonny*. The anti-illusionism in the professional–amateur reversal was further extended by the non-diegetic knowledge that many viewers would have had, in the case of Jean

Seberg, of the fact that this star was not even a professional actress in the usual sense, since she had been created by Otto Preminger twelve years earlier by a "talent search" conceived to promote Preminger's production of *Saint Joan* (1957). Thus, Logan was able to produce anti-illusionistic statements about both the Hollywood musical genre and Hollywood cinema in general.

Such anti-illusionism is not so unusual in the Hollywood cinema. Fun is had with the non-diegetic knowledge that the character played by Irene Dunne is treated by one of the other characters as an incompetent amateur singer in *The Awful Truth* (1937), when fans were perfectly aware that the non-diegetic (and diegetic character, for that matter, as the evidence of her singing demonstrates) Irene Dunne has a trained operatic voice. Similar fun is available in Elvis Presley's movies and other vehicle genres.

All those examples come from white cinema and are perhaps largely limited to white entertainers. The formula may not easily extend to African-American cinema or to black entertainers meant for black audiences. For example, Micheaux's association of amateurs with the realm of entertainers is not meant to emphasize joy and talent but rather foolishness and low class. The strategies of mainstream musicals that Feuer has described and the strategy of Micheaux in this case are based on opposing values: white mainstream-movie viewers are expected to identify with entertainers; black race-movie viewers are asked by Micheaux's film to identify with non-entertainers who wanted to be *consumers* or even *producers* of entertainment.

This set of identifications has implications for class position. White viewers may envy the performance talent of the lower-class performers in mainstream movies; Micheaux has encouraged black viewers to envy the material power and social esteem of the higher-class consumers of entertainment in his movies, such as cabaret patrons. This can be seen explicitly in the scenes in which Micheaux invites the black film audience to identify with the elevated and cool, cutting gaze of diegetic audiences rather than with the disdained foolishness of those characters whose actions are being laughed at as if they were the entertainment.

Identifying with Producers

Micheaux's black viewers may have identified with performers at times, but primarily (according to Micheaux's paradigm) as a means to class mobility. There is little evidence in the films of envy of talent per se. Micheaux apparently did not expect the black audience to wish that they could just burst into professional song like Judy Garland or Ethel Waters. He seems to have expected them to wish that they could produce and own the show that presented Judy Garland or Ethel Waters or to wish that they were among the "swells" in the audience on the night a Garland or a Waters was introduced. Of the several films in which Micheaux presented a diegetic producer with whom the audience was expected to identify, the most obvious is *Swing!*. The main character is the producer of a show that eventually makes it to Broadway. As in all analogous characters in

Micheaux's films, the producer character is a surrogate for the filmmaker himself, and he is supposed to represent an appropriate figure of uplift and to be above reproach. While entertainers were to be enjoyed in a critical way and not often as objects of identification, producers of entertainment (as well as businessmen and women, teachers, professionals, independent farmers, and property owners) were to be identified with wholeheartedly.

Whether Micheaux was right about who his audience would identify with is another question that cannot be answered without (badly needed) studies of the reception of Micheaux's films. The fact that Micheaux encouraged such identification is beyond doubt, and it is an important point, since it interrogates a common perception that African Americans have until recently seen the field of entertainment—whether in performing arts or athletics—primarily as an opportunity for stardom. Micheaux saw it, and created visions of it, as an opportunity for class advancement and for increased control of the entertainment image and, thus, as a means by which to defeat ethnic caricature.

Identifying with Critical Spectatorship

Returning to the scene from *Murder in Harlem,* Claudia suggests that she and Lem Hawkins dance. She compliments Hawkins's dancing, but it is clear to the film viewer that Hawkins is a juke-joint dancer rather than a nightclub or ballroom dancer, such as the patrons who surround him. This shot is composed so that such a comparison is unavoidable, since Claudia and Hawkins, alone in the foreground, are surrounded by elegant, dancing couples in the background. The elegant dancers not only form a virtual audience for the performance in the foreground, but *they behave explicitly like an audience* watching the "show" in front of them. These sophisticated dancers watch Hawkins just as the sophisticated chorus in *The Darktown Revue* watched the vaudeville skit of the hard-shell preacher—and they do so with the same disdain. One of Hawkins's observers runs his eyes up and down Hawkins in casual disbelief at the foolish spectacle, replicating precisely the actions of chorus members in *Darktown Revue.* The dancers in *Murder in Harlem* and the chorus in *Darktown Revue* are functioning as commentators on the action, precisely as did the chorus in classical Greek drama.

The similarity between the composition and meaning of the shot in *Murder in Harlem* and those of the shot of the chorus observing the minstrel caricatures in *Darktown Revue,* and the similarity of the *Murder* scene and scenes such as Jean Baptiste's spectatorlike relationship with the combination of domestic violence and a floor show in *The Exile* suggest the reprise of the paradigm of the cutting gaze—the middle-class look of disdain upon lower-class behavior. It also suggests a non-incidental relation of the diegetic cutting gaze to critical spectatorship in entertainment. The application of the *Darktown* shot as a paradigm in the scene in *Murder in Harlem* reaffirms not only Micheaux's critique of minstrel caricature but also his intention to make an explicit connection between

Fig. 15a. The paradigm shot of upper-class observation of lower-class behavior as it occurs in *Murder in Harlem*. The dancers behind are, like the chorus in *Darktown Revue,* an audience enjoying an entertainment.

Fig. 15b. In *God's Stepchildren,* the paradigm shot is used again with emphasis . . .

Fig. 15c. . . . but is aimed at a different target, a light-skin-proud woman who disdains her race (see also figure 6h).

the caricatures of African Americans prevalent in entertainment and lower-class black behavior in everyday life.

The "N" Word and Entertainment

The idea that blacks in everyday life might be considered by whites to be minstrel entertainment is not far-fetched. G. D. Pike noted (in 1873) the surprise of white audiences in their reception of the Fisk Singers' sophisticated, non-minstrel entertainment. Even in Micheaux's time, a distinguished black novelist and editor, Jessie Fauset, reported the following sentiment on the part of a friendly white journalist:

> the sort of attitude instanced by a journalist the other day who thought colored people ought to be willing to permit the term nigger because it carries with it so much *picturesqueness* defines pretty well, I think, our position in the eyes of the white world. Either we are inartistic or we are picturesque and always the inference is implied that we live objectively with one eye on the attitude of the white world *as though it were the audience and we the players* whose hope and design is to please.[6] [Emphasis added]

Fauset's observation, made in 1922, describes the audience-vs.-entertainer structure inherent in caricature and relates that structure to daily life; the "n" word seemed to the white journalist unobjectionably to imply "entertainment." In 1935, Micheaux described just such an audience-vs.-entertainment structure in his paradigmatic shot composition, with the "entertainment," Lem Hawkins, dancing in the foreground and the "audience" dancing in the background, explicitly registering its amusement. Micheaux left little doubt about which group, the audience or the entertainers, he favored—the audience was cool, and Hawkins was a fool.

Thus, Micheaux placed not just entertainers but also middle-class spectators within the film, like a Greek chorus, for his black audience to identify with and to be guided by. In that sense, he suggested an African-American context for the same uplift policies previously developed in white cinema by the Eden Musee, the Motion Picture Patent Company, and D. W. Griffith. It might seem cruel of Micheaux to have emphasized class difference in a way that invites comparison with D. W. Griffith's racist derogations, in a way that recalls early rube movies and that invites laughter and disdain toward a class-bound "brother" by treating Lem Hawkins as caricatured entertainment. However, as pointed out in the introduction to this study, the point for Micheaux was not cruelty. The point was to defeat caricature.

Defeating Caricature

Murder in Harlem is not a rube movie. Micheaux was not using caricature as a platform for elevating himself, at the expense of another, through a strategy of class distinction. His strategy of uplift was directed not primarily at an existing African-American middle class, since that class, unlike the white middle class addressed by Griffith, was too small to support a cinema of its own. Micheaux also had some disdain for the contemporary manifestations of the black middle class, who, he said, were too concerned with status and seldom read books. Micheaux was, in fact, primarily addressing the class below, with the intention of goading them out of their class condition, as expressed in the often-quoted remark from his first novel: "One of the greatest tasks of my life has been to convince a certain *class* of my racial acquaintances that a colored man can be anything" [emphasis added].[7]

That statement is representative of Micheaux's purpose and is fundamental to his integrity. The common observations by critics and scholars that denigrate Micheaux's career by emphasizing his genius for self-promotion, confidence games, manipulation, showmanship, and assimilationist imitation of white culture are not convincing. It is true, however, that some of Micheaux's caricatures are perhaps too pleasurably painful, which might indicate that there is some meanness, or at least thoughtlessness, in them (sadism or cruelty would be too strong a characterization). Micheaux, however, felt that the difficulty of his mission required tough, unrelenting criticism of his own group, as he stated in an open letter that appeared in several African-American newspapers:

> I have always tried to make my photoplays present the truth, to lay before the race a cross section of its own life, to view the colored heart from close range. . . . It is only by presenting those portions of the race portrayed in my pictures, in the light and back ground of their true state, that we can raise our people to greater heights. I am too much imbued with the spirit of Booker T. Washington to engraft false virtues upon ourselves, to make ourselves that which we are not. Nothing could be a greater blow to our own progress.[8]

Tough Interrogation Pays Off

It is true that Lem Hawkins was portrayed by Micheaux explicitly according to white racist stereotype as a kind of caricature from the world of entertainment, though Hawkins has no *literal* entertainer's role in the world of the story. However, a major narrative and rhetorical reversal occurs later in the film when the leading man, Henry Glory, a striving middle-class black attorney (and an explicit surrogate for Micheaux himself), subjects Hawkins to a tough interrogation on the witness stand. Micheaux places him on the stand to interrogate him *as* caricature and *as* entertainment. Just before that scene, Glory tells his client (the framed night watchman's sister, Claudia, who has retained Glory to handle her brother's defense) that he knows how to make Hawkins talk. The way Glory makes Hawkins talk is by badgering and ridiculing him on the witness stand, which causes the (mostly black) courtroom audience to laugh. Glory turns the poor Hawkins into a caricature in front of an audience; Micheaux was thus emphasizing the paradigm from *The Darktown Revue,* the literal, material connection between the African-American class predicament and black entertainment.

Glory's diegetic interrogation of Hawkins is a key to Micheaux's position on class and on his relationship with his audience. Glory loosely represents Micheaux himself, since when Glory is first introduced in the film, he is selling his own self-published novel door-to-door in the black community, which is precisely how Micheaux had made a living before and even during his film career and is also closely analogous to the way Micheaux distributed his films. Glory's tough attitude toward Hawkins's buffoonery thus replicates Shelby Steele's Sam and Micheaux's own vision of the perceived behavior of African

Americans "of a certain class." The key, however, to understanding and appreciating Micheaux's position in this state of affairs lies in the *results* of the courtroom interrogation.

The first few sequences, representing Hawkins's testimony under interrogation, reaffirm Micheaux's intention to connect Hawkins to entertainment caricature. In the depiction (in flashback) of Hawkins's testimony about the crime, the white manager flips Hawkins a coin, which causes Hawkins to go into a happy shuffle routine in front of the factory door. That "insert coin, get shuffle" trope practically turns Hawkins into a white man's living "juke" box. When the attempted rape and supposed murder are occurring, Hawkins, trying to spy on the rape, tiptoes around the boss's office like a buffoon, accompanied by comic-movie music. Those scenes would fit comfortably in an Abbott and Costello movie or in the *Amos and Andy* television series.

Such examples suggest that the African-American attorney, Henry Glory, is fighting not just a specific injustice instantiated in a specific murder intrigue but also the broader injustice of a social matrix that engenders both black caricature and lackeyism as generalizable traits.

In the courtroom interrogation scene, Micheaux's class hero, Glory, is in dramatic (and humorous) conflict with a representative of the proletariat, Hawkins. Such a reading, as far as it goes, would support criticisms of bourgeois identification leveled against Micheaux over the years (including official denunciations by the Communist Party in the 1930s). Such criticisms, however, were (besides being shockingly unskilled in terms of elementary hermeneutics) too simple. Micheaux's class hero is clearly *also* fighting white racism and bourgeois capital, since those interests are represented by the white factory manager, Brisbane, who forces Hawkins into complicity in the crime and pays him for it and who is thus primarily responsible for Lem Hawkins's immediate predicament.

Micheaux's emphasis on Hawkins's caricatured buffoonery does, in fact, continue through the first half of the courtroom testimony, to the amusement of the African Americans who make up the courtroom audience. Even the part that reveals Brisbane's manipulations of Hawkins, with its "hilarious" images of Hawkins crying and playing the helpless victim, is treated explicitly for laughs, in spite of the distinctly unhilarious predicament Hawkins finds himself in—being implicated in the rape and murder of a white woman.

At that point, however, the narrative discourse begins a crucially significant modulation of its enunciation of Hawkins's character. Hawkins begins to reveal an impressive proletarian intelligence, and he begins to be recognized by the white boss, Brisbane, as potentially oppositional and as a dangerous adversary. Brisbane, and Micheaux's intended film audience, get a good look at the well-developed survival skills underlying Hawkins's caricature act.

Wit and Its Relation to the Unconscionable

The modulation of Hawkins's character in this scene is the most important reversal in the film in relation to issues of class and race. The whole gist of

Fig. 16a. When Lem, at his place of work, is given a coin by the white plant manager in exchange for cooperation in a sexual harassment adventure . . .

Fig. 16b. . . . Lem, like a human juke, does the proverbial shuffle.

Fig. 16c. As the white plant manager makes his move on the white woman employee behind closed doors, Lem tiptoes to the keyhole to the accompaniment of comic, Abbott and Costello–type movie music.

Glory's middle-class critique of Lem Hawkins is mitigated by Hawkins's revelation—under the pressure of Glory's courtroom interrogation—of Hawkins's own subjection by the criminal white manager. Even more important is Hawkins's revelation of his own proletarian intelligence in the face of that subjection. After all the song and dance by Hawkins about his helplessness and inability to understand the intricacies of the plot in which he is becoming implicated, Hawkins shows that, without a doubt, he understands it all perfectly; thus, his song-and-dance routine had been "artful," in the old sense of the term.

Fig. 17a. The literal interrogation in *Murder in Harlem* . . .

Fig. 17b. . . . is intercut with the courtroom audience enjoying the interrogation of caricature as entertainment.

The first indication of Hawkins's perfect understanding comes shortly after Brisbane (the factory manager) has pulled the incriminating note that he has been dictating to Hawkins out of Hawkins's hands, saying, "You'd never understand." Brisbane orders Hawkins to write another one, but Hawkins plays dumb, and Brisbane says "write another *note*, dumbbell." Hawkins responds with heavy irony, "Oh, write another note, *dumbbell*." The irony of Hawkins's response indicates that he is not a dumbbell, and the dialogue that follows explicates and embellishes Hawkins's irony and his intelligence:

> Brisbane [dictates the second note to Hawkins]: "That tall Negro did this. He will try to lay it on the night . . ."
> Hawkins: "'He will try to lay it on the night . . .' I understands. The night, that's me [Hawkins is night watchman]. You mean, he will try to lay it on me. I understands it all now."
> [Hawkins nevertheless writes the dictated note; Brisbane nods his approval.]
> Hawkins: "Ah, I got it now, Mr. Brisbane. . . . You did it, but you want them to think that Vance did and these notes will make them think that Vance did, but Vance, he tryin' to make 'em think that I did. 'Course you know I didn't, and you won't let 'em arrest me, but Vance, he be here tonight and if he finds her and calls the police, they goin' arrest him and maybe lynch him quick, then they ain't goin' never find out who killed her. Huh, I understands."
> Brisbane: "Yeah. You understands too damn much."[9]

After this impressive display of plot explication, Hawkins's irony escalates to sarcasm:

> Brisbane [reads the note and hands it back to Hawkins for a correction]: "Here, rub that 'a' out in 'Negro' and make it 'e.' "
> Hawkins [looks at the note]: "Uh, it seems to me that, that you ain't spellin' it like they calls it nohow. There should be an 'i' instead of an 'e' and there should be two 'g's instead of one." [Hawkins raises his eyes in a gesture of overtly fake innocence.] [Brisbane shifts uncomfortably, but says nothing. Hawkins finishes the note and Brisbane takes it with an approving gesture.]

Admittedly, Hawkins's analytic intelligence is perverted and distorted by the history of racial oppression and by his immediate predicament. And admittedly, Hawkins's resistance to Brisbane is not radically oppositional, since Hawkins accepts payment of $250 and reverts to caricature at the end of the scene. Nevertheless, the reversal of Hawkins's otherwise unmitigated buffoonery and lackeyism reveals his "darky" caricature as a cover—a dangerous cover—that has nothing to do with the essence of racial identity and everything to do with both economics (the flipped-coin payoff; the $250 payoff) and the necessities of survival under white oppression. And the reversal reveals that under the right circumstances, such as Glory's forensic (and Micheaux's cinematic) interrogation, a race-based and class-based oppositionality that is disguised by the "joke" of caricature can show itself and threaten ethnic political action that would not be funny.

Thus, Micheaux's treatment of caricature in lower-class figures is less cruel than it might seem, because his interrogation also leads to a payoff: freedom. In the case of Hawkins, Glory's interrogation leads to Hawkins's release from white manipulation and possibly from prison, execution, or lynching. Hawkins has already figured out that Brisbane's manipulative "syllogism," which begins "You did it, but you want them to think that Vance did and these notes will make them think that Vance did [it]," includes the term "Vance, he tryin' to make 'em think that I did [it]." Thus, Hawkins is explicitly at risk in Brisbane's syllogism and in the white judicial system. For this, he must at least be paid well.

The original title of the film, "Lem Hawkins' *Confession*" (emphasis added), specifically refers to the courtroom interrogation. The importance of the interrogation is reconfirmed in recent scholarship on Micheaux by a seeming coincidence of language that links the interrogation of Hawkins with the critical approach to race and class (and gender) that bell hooks has discovered in one of Micheaux's other films:

> *Ten Minutes to Live* exploits all the conventions of simplistic melodrama even as it *interrogates* on multiple levels issues of representation. Nothing appears on the screen to be as simplistic as it often seems in everyday life. The capacity of individuals to discern good and evil, to distinguish that which is desirable and that which threatens, is *interrogated*.[10] [Emphasis added]

Micheaux's approach to caricature and stereotype was one of interrogation, and in *Murder in Harlem,* that interrogation is made literal.

Conclusion

As hooks has implied, and as demonstrated above, the middle-class position for which Micheaux was working was neither a cabin in the cotton nor a mansion in the sky; it was not even a house in the suburbs. It was a critical, hard-nosed, working position. From that position, Micheaux interrogated entertainment as a function of class—not just in the self-reflexive ways of modernism that take entertainment as a secondary, cultural representation of a political situation; and not just in the Althusserian Marxist sense that takes entertainment as the secondary, sociocultural superstructure constructed on a primary base of political economics—but in a direct way that takes entertainment to be a literal, not just representational, sociopolitical condition inherent in the Rube joke; inherent in the idea of American "stage fright" (lack of experience on the world stage is "funny"); and inherent, as Hawkins signifies to Brisbane, in the racist "n" word. Micheaux chose not to ignore such negative images; for thirty years he gave audiences visions of a working position from which to change the joke and slip the yoke.

11 Interrogating False Uplift

If Micheaux's middle-class position was a place from which to fight a battle against class degradation, and if Micheaux launched an unrelenting critique from that position against certain aspects of "lower-class behavior" and against the entertainment caricatures provided for that class to inhabit in real life, then what was Micheaux's relation to the upper class of American society? Was he complicitous with the upper class? Partly through confusion about his rough treatment of caricature in relation to lower-class position, Micheaux has been criticized for being not just middle-class but also bourgeois and "white."[1] As is seen, however, in *Murder in Harlem,* Micheaux's hero, Glory, not only interrogates and wins freedom for the African-American lower-class figure, he also interrogates and indicts characters who are significantly bourgeois and white. Micheaux's hero does not interrogate only the African-American lower-class figure; the upper-middle-class white corporate manager's perjury and, subsequently, the true but totally unsuspected white murderer—the dead woman's white-supremacist-type, Leopold-and-Loeb-type boyfriend—are also exposed by Glory's tough critique.

If Micheaux's middle-class treatment of lower-class figures is less antagonistic than it might seem because his interrogation frees that class, Micheaux's treatment of the upper-class figures in the film is also less complicitous than it might seem, because Glory's interrogation leads to their indictment. Brisbane's exposure represents an indictment of whiteness, but Brisbane also represents the large chemical company that is shown in the film's opening shot, which establishes the main setting for the entire story. As such, the discredited Brisbane may represent accumulated capital and the bourgeoisie. His treatment by Micheaux suggests that the assertions by some critics of Micheaux's identification with bourgeois values and with whiteness have been too simple, since Micheaux was interrogating and indicting racism and classism directly.

Micheaux's refusal to favor the values of the bourgeois classes and of whiteness within the realm of entertainment has already been demonstrated. The speech given to the performers of the stage revue by the African-American theater entrepreneur in *Swing!* urges middle-class moderation rather than bourgeois excess. That film is an elaborate parable of false class advancement within the context of entertainment. Nevertheless, against such parables one could still set the argument that Micheaux continuously referred to his films and his actors as cognates of the white, bourgeois movie system in America. His genres were often similar to established white genres, such as musicals and gangster movies, and his actors were sometimes exploited as black versions of white stars.

Lorenzo Tucker, for instance, who starred in *Veiled Aristocrats* (1932), was called "the colored Valentino," and Bea Freeman, the heavy in *Lying Lips* (1939), was called "the sepia Mae West." The rush to judge such evidence as proof of Micheaux's intention to make bourgeois or white movies is, however, premature. First, such exploitation of black stars and movie genres was a general convention within the world of race movies, not a "white-like" invention of Micheaux's. Second, Micheaux was a master at ironically "signifying on" the white genres and identities he referenced in his films. Third, Micheaux always publicized his films and casts as "all colored," placing the emphasis on the African-Americanness of his work. And fourth, Micheaux worked to keep his films within the class confines of his African-American audience and to keep his actors from indulging in pretensions to an African-American star system inspired by Hollywood or to an African-American color-caste system based on values borrowed from white racism.

That Micheaux's goal of racial uplift was, despite his efforts to the contrary, tainted by bourgeois values and whiteness goes without saying, but only in the sense that any culture is influenced by association with prior and dominating cultures. American democracy is informed by European patriarchy, aristocracy, Christianity, and capitalism. Nevertheless, its differentiation from those older systems—its revolution, its version of freedom, its independence and separateness, its "exceptionalism" (refusal to consider socialism), and its current, virtually consensual leadership role in the world—are all real as well, for better or worse. Questions remain as to what, exactly, was Micheaux's position with respect to the ruling bourgeois and white classes (not to mention the ruling patriarchal, heterosexual, and religious groups, which have been addressed in the Micheaux literature less often than have the socioeconomic and racially defined groups) and as to how Micheaux regarded the entertainment system of the ruling group.

Identifying Whiteness

In assessing Micheaux's critique of the lower socioeconomic classes in *Murder in Harlem,* it is useful to sort out and isolate the elements of whiteness lodged in lower-class identity and behavior. Micheaux helps by isolating just such elements in the scene in which Lem Hawkins himself identifies, through ironic signifying, the white racism "hidden" in the plot to implicate African Americans in an entirely white rape and murder incident. Lower-class position and behavior in African Americans are shown to be, in part, white defined and white maintained. Micheaux identified two causes for Lem Hawkins's class position: white racist hegemony and Hawkins's "willing" complicity in that hegemony in the face of alternative choices that were open to him (and to other African Americans in similar circumstances), such as entrepreneurship, education, and the other tactics of strategic uplift founded in middle-class values.

Veiled Aristocrats

In other films, such as *Veiled Aristocrats* (1931) and *God's Stepchildren* (1938), Micheaux isolates the specific quality of whiteness more overtly than he does in *Murder in Harlem*. In *Veiled Aristocrats,* there are two strong male African Americans who are vying for the most valued of prizes—the most desirable woman in the film, Rena. The contest will be won by the man who can offer the socio-economic position in life that is most worthy of her. Thus, the prize is to be won or lost based on a contest of *uplift*. The first male lead is the thoroughly self-confident, attractive, and successful attorney John Walden, who is a new member of the *white* aristocracy of a neighboring region, a position he has gained, as a light-skinned black man, by passing for white under the name John Warwick. The second strong male is the thoroughly self-confident, articulate, and ambitious construction contractor Frank Fowler, a darker-skinned black man who is a member of the local *black* aristocracy and who is both too dark and too ethnically loyal to pass for white. The literal contest for class advancement between Frank Fowler and John Walden is the narrative core of the film.

Passing for White

The issue of passing for white represents one side of the conflict in the above-mentioned contest. The other side of the conflict sets itself against the idea of class mobility achieved through the method of passing for white. Frank Fowler describes the nature of the conflict between himself and John as, indeed, a challenge between two strong individuals. He characterizes individuals, however, as being specifically constituted within a problematics of political and economic class struggle: "Times have changed, and it's up to the Negro race now to individualize his efforts, by which I mean that each and every one of us must make a concerted drive toward success along the many individual lines."[2] Frank goes on to lay out his plan to become a leading construction contractor, using borrowed capital; he ends his statement of purpose by comparing the solidity of his "individual" plan with the relatively easy and dishonest plan of Rena's brother: "By the time your brother's conquest for you on the other side [i.e., the white world] has ended, I hope [indecipherable] to be [indecipherable; 'laying tiles on the dome'?] [lacuna; 'of the capital of'] the state of North Carolina, a monument to honesty and determined effort."

In Charles Chesnutt's original novel *The House Behind the Cedars,* on which Micheaux's film is based, the conflict between John and Frank is much more uneven, since the darker man, Frank, does not have the competence or driving ambition in the novel that the same character does in Micheaux's film. Frank's class position in Chesnutt's novel is so low as to make a match between him and Rena virtually unthinkable, whereas the same character in Micheaux's film is a respected member of the local black aristocracy, in spite of the fact that he is darker than most of the other aristocrats. And in Micheaux's film, Rena never wavers in her love for the darker man. Micheaux's elevation of Frank Fowler from lower- to middle-class African American with no change of skin tone is an implicit affirmation of class mobility in the face of darkness of skin, and an affirmation of Micheaux's own ambitions, as he was a darker man himself. Micheaux's insistence on the possibility of the entry of a dark-skinned man into the black aristocracy might be counted as one of Micheaux's supposed lapses into fantasy, since light skin color is known to have been a common, and often virulently restrictive, criterion for membership in the black aristocracy. Micheaux's insistence on the compatibility of dark skin and class mobility is, however, more accurately characterized as an argument than as a fantasy.

Color and Class

Micheaux was weighing in for a fight that was already under way in the black community:

> One of the most extensive discussions of the black class structure occurred in 1896, when the editor of the Indianapolis *Freeman,* W. M. Lewis, invited Richard W. Thompson, a well-known black journalist, to respond to the question: "Do you think the interest of [black] society would be promoted by drawing lines, not based upon color, but in the same manner as instinct draws them in the race around us?" . . . Thompson began by asserting that class lines already existed among blacks and that these lines had been established as a result of the working out of the "natural order." He emphatically denied that social stratification of blacks should be based on criteria different from those prevailing in the white community because "the Negro lives under the same civilization as his Caucasian brother." Thompson also distinguished between authentic class criteria, such as "character, worth, morals [and] conduct," and transient, superficial considerations, ranging from "the accidental possession of money or position" to the "color of skin and texture of hair."[3]

Thompson, the editor of the *Freeman,* went on to call for a vigorous upper class that would "grant labor its dignity" and that would not "leave the race behind." To ignore such warnings, Thompson said, would lead to "a false aristocracy." Micheaux, in *Veiled Aristocrats,* is making the same argument narratively that Thompson had made journalistically—Frank Fowler's exposition about "determined effort" matches Thompson's point about "granting labor its dignity," and Fowler's point is made, like Thompson's, in the context of setting an example for the race and of proving the inefficacy of concern for accidental qualities of skin color and hair texture.

The debate continued in later issues of the Indianapolis *Freeman,* and similar points were perennially discussed in other black publications. Additional complaints were lodged against the black aristocracy for its pretentiousness, conspicuous consumption, disdain for manual labor, and its "'whims, vanities and tomfoolery:'" "'The highest expression of the social tastes of the aristocracy,' [Dr. J. M. Henderson] observed, 'is the exclusive dance and the exclusive party.'"[4]

The arguments deriding the "whims and vanities" of the black aristocracy are not unusual, and they anticipate E. Franklin Frazier's classic debunking of that class in *Black Bourgeoisie*[5] and William Greaves's more balanced and more positive critique in his film *Still a Brother: Inside the Black Middle Class* (1968). Henderson's critique of the aristocracy (quoted above) led, finally, to a defense of a middle class as distinct from an aristocracy:

> The fate of the Afro-American, according to Henderson, rested with the emerging middle class, which was vigorous, enterprising, aggressive, and intimately identified with the race and its collective welfare. . . . [The "tiny class of effulgents" and the "few puny accidental colored exquisites"], always preoccupied with promoting themselves as "an exclusive social set," would in *the judgment of history* [emphasis added] go largely unnoticed while the robust middle class would force its way to the front.[6]

As in the ending of James Weldon Johnson's novel of passing, *The Autobiography of an Ex-Colored Man* (discussed below), the idea of "making history" informs the argument. In *The Autobiography,* to pass for white was to abdicate a historical mission; in Henderson's article (above), the effulgent black aristocracy was abdicating a historical mission that was being taken up by a more vigorous black middle class. Since "effulgency" means brightness, and since "bright" means light-skinned, and since most of the black aristocracy was light-skinned (and some manifestations of that aristocracy were exclusively so), certain parallels with "passing for white" can be drawn. Henderson was implying that the lightness criterion of black aristocracy, and other criteria *that are complicitous with white racism,* would lead the black bourgeoisie toward a small place in white history rather than toward a larger place in black history, just as Johnson concluded would happen with passing for white at the end of *The Autobiography.*

In *Veiled Aristocrats,* Micheaux represented that debate explicitly, and he placed his bet on the middle class. Frank Fowler is a dark-skinned member of that "more vigorous" group, and he wins the contest (with John Warwick) for class mobility, for economic security, and for Rena. But, as is utterly consistent with Micheaux's methods, the issues are as complex for Micheaux as they were for Thompson and Henderson in the discussions in the black press. Frank Fowler is a member of the vigorous middle class; that class is *not* pitted against the black aristocracy in this film but rather against light-skinned passing. Since Fowler is himself a member of the black "aristocracy," and since he has not, at the beginning of the film, yet succeeded in his business plan, it must be inferred that the black aristocracy of Fayetteville has no virulent phobia concerning hard work or dark skin; they have welcomed Frank in spite of both. Micheaux, himself dark-skinned, entrepreneurial, and nouveaux middle class, had personal as well as group interests at stake.

Micheaux's account of the black aristocracy is thoroughly embedded in the issues already raised by Thompson, Henderson, and others. Micheaux's aristocracy has wealth but admits the less wealthy; it is light-skinned but admits the dark-skinned. Micheaux's black aristocracy admits the classes that are still working out their destinies and who are making history; but it is also as sophisticated as any urban elite, as the scenes of its dances and parties indicate. One of the hostesses of the elite group, played by Micheaux's wife, Alice B. Russell, introduces a "famous contralto" singer, Madame Bernadine Mason from Boston, who sings light-operatic song, accompanied by Cordawin Alexander "at the pi-ah-no." After the song is over, the music returns to sophisticated, urban 'sweet jazz.' The wealth and urbanity of the black aristocracy are manifest also in their employment of black servants, who provide an environment not only of service but of good, though lower-class, jazz-age entertainment—race music, jazz dance, and vernacular humor.

While this portrait of a lifestyle may be problematic in many ways, it also addressed many of the points of the discussion about class, a discussion that was ongoing in the black press. Micheaux was arguing for a leadership class that was inclusive rather than exclusive, that did not focus on accidental traits such as skin color, that was not trying to pass for white, and that was lively, entertaining, and culturally creative. He was arguing for a leadership class, somewhat like DuBois's talented tenth, that would, in Thompson's words, "not leave the race behind" and that would not turn into a "false" aristocracy.

False Uplift

The idea of a false aristocracy is imbedded in the central conflict of Micheaux's film; it is, in fact, inferable in the title, *Veiled Aristocrats*. The film drives home the comparison between false and true ideas of aristocracy (or of a leadership class) by having the hostess of the upper-class social gathering tell a story to her guests, a story that clarifies the differences between false and true aristocracy with regard to the issues of skin color and of passing for white. When Frank and Rena meet at night to discuss John's plan to take Rena with him across the line into the white aristocracy, a title card announces: "While nearby, at the home of Dr. Hubert Waring's, the select and elite colored of Fayetteville, were making merry that night." After the title card, the film cuts to that social gathering, where a guest asks why Frank Fowler is not present and is told that Fowler is with Rena Walden. The hostess then entertains her guests with the story of the Walden family. There follow several intervening cutaways to scenes of John Walden spelling out his plan to his mother, of Frank Fowler reacting to the news of that plan being told to him by Rena Walden, of the announcement and performance of the song and piano accompaniment at the social gathering, and of Frank and Rena's continued discussion.

After all this, and just after remarks by Frank that John's plan for Rena to pass for white is "vain and impossible" and that it won't make Rena successful or happy, there is (finally) a cut back to the aristocratic hostess, who is telling the story she had promised. The hostess then relates that the Walden brother, presumably John, would not speak with (former?) slaves, "especially the dark ones," and that he "didn't have anything for dark people to do, [and] said they were evil." The last line about dark people draws loud laughter from the listening party guests. The film then cuts back to Rena and Frank's discussion, in

Fig. 18. In *Veiled Aristocrats,* the hostess of the black upper-class community—a community that respects and welcomes the dark-skinned, striving hero, Frank Fowler (not present here)—tells a funny story that denigrates the Walden family for light-bright fetishism and for passing for white. The black elite, many but not all of them light themselves, laugh disdainfully at the Waldens' foolishness—at overvaluing skin color.

which Frank is about to tell Rena what he will be doing while she is obeying (dutifully and properly) her brother and passing for white. Before he is able to explain his plan, the film cuts back to the hostess telling her story. She says: "That's the story; now how's that for scandal in this little old bitty town?" A guest answers, "I'll say!" The film then cuts to John and his mother, who are continuing their discussion of John's plan to "make Rena a white lady."

Though the aristocratic hostess does not actually tell the Walden family story on camera, it is quite clear from the implications of associative editing (the story takes the form of cutaways and inserts) that she is, in fact, telling about John's color phobia and about his passing for white. Color phobia and passing are what she calls a "scandal." The effect of the story, told to other black aristocrats who are expected to concur, is to place the black aristocracy firmly in the camp of Frank Fowler's approach to uplift, one that is firmly opposed to John Walden's (alias John Warwick's) color phobia and his passing. The effect of Micheaux's editing—cutting from the hostess's story to Frank's remarks about vanity and then to John's ongoing pursuit of such vanity—strengthens the interpretation that John's plan, based on identifying with whiteness, is ludicrous and disloyal and that Frank's plan, based on hard work within the black community, is a reasonable, even noble, alternative to such nonsense.

That relatively complex editing (the story inserts are not literally inserts; they are "simply" changes of venue) further suggests that this group of socially sophisticated, entertaining, and right-minded people is part of what Frank has to offer Rena. It is no wonder that Rena is upset when she enters her brother's white aristocracy later on. She is not only concerned with avoiding a disastrous faux pas in her brother's scheme of passing, but she is also anxious to get back to everything that Fayetteville has to offer her. It is Rena's concern for and desire for her mother that provides the final motive for her return, but her desire for Frank and for the securely founded, ethnically honest, middle-class society he represents has also been on her mind.

True Uplift

That desire, on Rena's part, for the black community is one of the significant changes that Micheaux made in Chesnutt's original story, in which, on the contrary, Rena was quite happy to go into the white world with her brother, very much in love with the aristocratic lover she finds there, very nervous—though not hesitant—about going home to her sick mother, and completely distraught at being found out for what she "really is" by her white lover. The distraughtness in Chesnutt's Rena remains a condition from which she never fully recovers, a condition to which she succumbs tragically later on—she is never able to reconstitute her life and her identity because of constantly disturbing interventions from the white and the black worlds.

Micheaux thus gave Rena a genuine class mobility that Chesnutt did not allow her. Rena's successful mobility in Micheaux's version is based on black entrepreneurship. In Chesnutt's version, however, her unsuccessful, even tragic, mobility is based on whiteness, per se, and her resultant fate is consistent, in Chesnutt's novel, with the white racist stereotype of the tragic mulatta. In Micheaux's rewrite, Rena's mobility means all the more because it takes as its goal the black aristocracy of Fayetteville, a class of people who are generously inclusive; who reject neither blackness nor whiteness, neither darkness nor lightness; who reject phobia; who embrace desire and all sorts of non-degrading entertainment; who respect hard work and accomplishment; who seek and enjoy wealth, but also spend it within the black community; and who "elevate" themselves, but who do not "leave the race behind." Micheaux, using many of the elements of the debates of his times, drew a picture of an attractive society that black people of the 1930s might rightfully and properly strive for and hope to join or to build. That is Micheaux's picture of a leadership class.

Aristocracy vs. Middle Class

Micheaux's ideal class was actually founded on a middle class, not on an idea of aristocracy. Aristocracy, per se, was not a model for class mobility, since aristocracy had no engine of locomotion, and uplift required such an engine. Micheaux's engine of class mobility was that of individual ambition, but it was not a vision that included Marxian alienation, since it was not an ambition that "left the race (or the lower classes) behind." The contradictions raised by Marx's linking of individualism and alienation go unexplored in Micheaux's work, since Micheaux's vision never separated legitimately ambitious individuals from society. Micheaux's individuals were always constituted as representatives of the race, and their individual ambition was always constituted as community ambition.

Similarly, bell hooks has often insisted that there need be no contradiction between individual ambition and active communalism. Also similarly, hooks offers a vision of a black middle class that prefers to "live simply in safe comfortable multiethnic neighborhoods rather than in mansions or huge houses," that has "no desire to be well-paid tokens at ruling-class white institutions"; a black middle class that could maintain "aspects of black life and experience that [they] hold sacred and are not eager to commodify or sell to captive colonized imaginations."[7] hooks's conditions for a communitarian middle class could be applied to improving the idea of a white middle class as well; the fact that an excess of competitive individualism tends to drive out communalism is perhaps a significant aspect of the (ill-defined) social category of "whiteness," and as such, it is certainly part of the larger problem faced by the project of African-American (and white) uplift.

Making History

For all the complexity of Micheaux's class and race discourse, his picture of a black leadership class does not adequately address the horrors of a reality such as that portrayed in Richard Wright's work and in other protest literature, even though Micheaux knew that work and commented on it in his novels. Nonetheless, the project of building a black middle class—with the qualities suggested above by hooks—was for Micheaux a great project of history, and it remains so today. Passing for white, whether literal or figurative, by definition, could play no part in such a project. Passing for white was a way into an already established white middle class, a class whose historical mission had already been and continued to be prodigious, but one that might be assumed to be very different from that of a black middle class. For an African American to enter, literally or figuratively, the white middle class or the black aristocracy of "effulgency" was false uplift. It was to leave the race behind, to abdicate history making, and to deny twoness, thus inviting confusion and destructive contradiction.

12 Passing and Film Style

If black filmmaking was going to play a part in the historical project of building the black middle class, how was it to do so? Are there film styles that can be specifically associated with the middle classes? If so, what are those styles? Do they all approximate the style of Hollywood and mainstream cinema? Did Micheaux merely fall short of producing a Hollywood mainstream cinema with African-American content? In *Slow Fade to Black,* Thomas Cripps judged that Micheaux did fall short of a Hollywood style; he qualified that judgment substantially in *Black Cinema as Genre* but revived it again in *Making Movies Black.* Is there a putative style that would have been produced if Micheaux's economic circumstances had been different? How can such a putative style be assessed? What is to count as good filmmaking? This line of questioning may not produce satisfying answers, but it represents a legitimate quandary that filmmakers and critics have long faced.

Fundamentally, artistic critique of any film cannot begin until stylistic values can be related to class position, since socioeconomic class is always linked directly to stylistic traits, and since class is commonly used, consciously or not, as a criterion of artistic quality, or taste (see Appendix 1). If Henry Glory in *Murder in Harlem* is fighting a class war on two fronts—in the face of the degradation below and the oppression above—perhaps those two fronts represent the Marxian dialectic of lower (working) and upper (bourgeois) classes, but perhaps they also represent the dual consciousness, or twoness, identified by DuBois and discussed earlier in this study as an underlying condition of Micheaux's "difficult" style. If such a representation exists and if the dilemma of twoness, as characterized by DuBois, is the mind split between African-American realities and values, on one hand, and white American values, on the other hand, then, following the dominant, white-supremacist norms in America, the African-American values of that split would be looked for in the lower-class front of the class war (the "degradation below"), and the white values would be expected to reside in the upper-class front (the "oppression above"). Simply stated, class position would follow racial identity, with the dominant race at the top of the class ladder.

Verticality of class position was integral to DuBois's initial formulation of twoness: "this double-consciousness, this sense of always looking at one's soul by the tape of a world that looks on in amused contempt and pity." Contempt and pity imply an elevated, vertical prospect, a "looking down on." It is the verticality in twoness that provides the stakes that make twoness such an important issue, that cause an emotional and spiritual imbalance in the soul that makes conflict between classes necessary, struggle inevitable, and fission and fragmentation the hallmarks of artistic styles that are related to this struggle. The style of Weimar expressionism, for example, with its obsessional dopplegangers (or twonesses) and its stylistic tawdriness and analytical fragmentation, was an appropriate response to the forces of the totalitarian nationalisms of its time and place.[1] Those totalizing nationalisms included both the recent German monarchy and emerging Nazism, with their slick, monumental, synthetic, and seamless artistic styles. The artistic triumph of Weimar style is founded in its oppositional relationship to monism, to a "higher" order of oneness, of singleness of purpose, an order that suppressed "lower" orders of life. The lower-order style itself is a kind of return of the repressed; it bears the marks of extreme pressure and of violent conflict necessitated by its emergence from beneath a more dominant style. Hitler called such styles degenerate.[2]

Assimilation vs. Separation

Any latent or manifest lower-order class that struggles to emerge, that places itself in conflict with "the tape of the world that looks on in amused contempt and pity," has, basically, an unenviable framework of choice between the extremes of assimilation and separation. Either extreme involves struggle and conflict as long as the vertical class structure obtains, so the style of its expression would presumably reflect struggle no matter which path is chosen. The path of assimilation for African Americans in the realm of filmmaking would lead to Hollywood, where, as already noted, the rhetoric and aesthetics have been designed by and for those who have already settled any potential problem of twoness in favor of a dominant "whiteness." Any minority, whether lower-class or not, attempting to assimilate to Hollywood style will have to make major compromises in terms of its own style in favor of the dominant and majoritarian style. Thus, the artistic progress of any emerging assimilationist style would be judged in comparison with Hollywood films and by Hollywood criteria of aesthetic success.

That was the initial route recommended by Thomas Cripps as he judged the merits of Micheaux's films, as discussed earlier in this study. Since the dilemma of twoness formulated by DuBois implies a class structure, an assimilationist approach assumes the need for uplift. Assimilationist uplift, however, would be aiming necessarily at a class position, the standards of which were characterized by whiteness. In stylistic terms, assimilation, which Cripps recommends, would result in what Cripps characterized pejoratively as imitating white cinema, or "mirror-image films."

No one knows for certain what Micheaux's stylistic goals were. Some critics have felt that he was so hampered by lack of funds that he was never able to realize any approximation of a style he might have wished for. Others celebrate the fact that he was able to produce and distribute many times more hours of finished film than had any other black American and feel that the resultant style is relatively unimportant or best left unmentioned. A few critics recognize Micheaux's accomplishment as not just an entrepreneurial feat but as an artistic success superior to most of its natural competitors, superior especially to white-produced competitors such as *The Green Pastures.*[3]

A Putative Micheaux Aesthetic

In the search for an understanding of Micheaux's stylistic intentions, or putative aesthetic, attitudinal clues can be found in the narrative content of Micheaux's films and novels. For example, in his film *The Girl from Chicago,* the fact that Micheaux narratively favored an amateur singer over a more sophisticated professional nightclub singer indicates his possible sympathy for amateur film styles and his distrust for polished styles. The fact that Micheaux directed his leading man and woman along middle paths that avoided any unearned claims on white-established territory indicates that Micheaux favored a *sui generis* black style that was commensurate with the level of black wealth. That point is narratively extended when the surrogate-white, southern town boss in *The Girl from Chicago* offers the leading woman a fast track to a higher station in life, which she refuses. In the film *Swing!,* Micheaux makes it clear, again through the narrative arrangements, that black-produced theater should not aim for expensive production values. In *The Exile,* analysis of both the narrative and the stylistic deployment of identifiable types of classical and jazz music indicate that Micheaux was associating the adoption of the stylistic trappings of high society with the urban Roaring Twenties, with its drinking, gambling, and illegal rackets; he was denigrating aspects of the dominant culture. In *The Darktown Revue,* Micheaux focused critical attention on the problem of racial stereotype and caricature by forging a paradigmatic comparison between upper-class and lower-class African Americans who were performing entertainments on the same stage (and in the same shots). The representatives of the upper classes can perhaps be characterized as mirror images of whites in terms of their dress, manners, and in some of their performance numbers. Micheaux was careful, however, to anchor their identity in *African* Americanisms, such as spiritual- and gospel-based choral music and even hot jazz, so that there could be no misapprehension that they were intending to pass for white through their high-class style of mise-en-scène. And the denouement of *Murder in Harlem* demonstrates the efficacy of a middle path through the vertical hazard of lower-class protective coloration (caricature) and upper-class assimilative coloration (with its complicity in white-on-black oppression). The middle-class black attorney in *Murder in Harlem* is no mirror image of whiteness, for if he had chosen that option and had behaved like the whites, he would have been in a poor ideological position to implicate the white oppressors and to free the black victims.

Narrative *content,* then, has served throughout this study as a guide to Micheaux's attitude toward mirror images of whiteness, and that attitude may extend to Micheaux's sense of film *style,* though the legitimacy of such an extension remains unproven. If, however, Micheaux had a goal of making films that looked like white films, if that were his standard of excellence in film style, then some indication of that attitude might be discoverable in his attitude toward a particularly appropriate figure of behavior—passing for white. If Micheaux felt strongly that upward mobility depended on approaching and attaining white ideals of personal and social style—represented by details of accent, dress, housing, neighborhood, skin color, facial or bodily feature, gentlewomanliness, choice of marital partner, ethnic and class exclusiveness, and cultural refinement—then passing might represent the ultimate and most desirable accomplishment of those ideals. And if Micheaux felt so about personal and social style, he might be expected to feel the same about his film style. Conversely, if he were emphatically opposed to the idea of passing, then that evidence would tend to counter the idea that Micheaux was aiming, ineffectively, at a style of cinema that mirrored white cinema. Two of the surviving films of Micheaux do, in fact, focus almost entirely on passing—*Veiled Aristocrats* (1932), discussed in the preceding chapter, and *God's Stepchildren* (1938), discussed in *Visions of Uplift* (forthcoming).

Veiled Aristocrats, Continued

Veiled Aristocrats is a remake of a silent film made by Micheaux in 1927, which was called *The House Behind the Cedars* and which was itself based on a famous novel of the same title by the fine and widely respected African-American novelist Charles Chesnutt. Micheaux's earlier film based on Chesnutt's novel has not survived, but *Veiled Aristocrats* has been rediscovered. The other existing film on passing, *God's Stepchildren,* is based, according to its credits, on a story of unknown origin called "Naomi Negress," and it treats the infancy, childhood, school days, coerced marriage, motherhood, and fugitive passing-for-white of a light-skinned African-American woman.

The attitude toward passing in *Veiled Aristocrats,* on the face of it, seems simple and entirely supportive of one of the working theses of this study—that Micheaux thought high style, either in life or in film production, should be considered a dangerous attraction. The following plot can be deduced from the fragments of the film in the collection of the Library of Congress and from the more extensive fragment of the film discovered in 1992.

The respected Judge Straight, of the white aristocracy of the deep South, adopts as a protégé (for reasons that no existing remnants of the film reveal but which are clear in Chesnutt's novel) the light-skinned African-American son of one of his black servants, Molly Walden. The Judge sends John Walden, under the assumed name of John Warwick, off to a white school to be educated as a white boy. Warwick returns twenty years later, having become a dapperly dressed and successful white lawyer, to his mother and sister, Rena. With the complicity of his mother, he concocts a plan to take Rena back with him to his new venue and introduce her into white society, hoping to marry her to an upper-class white man. In order to accomplish that, he must first separate her from her fiancé, Frank Fowler, who is, according to Rena's mother, a good boy, but a very dark-skinned one. When Rena tells Frank what is being planned, he takes the position that, for reasons of Rena's future happiness, the two of them should make sacrifices in order to avoid an open breach with Rena's mother and brother, both of whom Rena loves very much. Rena, for her part, in spite of her family loyalty, is willing to marry Frank immediately. But Frank says no, he is not ready, for he also has a plan for class advancement that he proposes to pursue in direct competition with Rena's brother's plan. Frank's explanation of his plan serves as a short, transparently expository set piece on black self-improvement:

> Some of the white people, to encourage us, have been telling us we've made the most wonderful progress of any race in the world in the years since we have been free. Result, [lacuna] permitted the grass to grow beneath our feet and wake up to find we are almost lost in the shuffle, holding the bag on all sides. Times have changed, and it's up to the Negro race now to individualize his efforts, by which I mean that each and every one of us must make a concerted drive toward success along the many individual lines [lacuna]. He has given me some money. The bank has loaned me some more, even though [lacuna], and by the time your brother has begun to build [lacuna] society over there, Frank Fowler hopes to be well on his way to success as one of the leading builders and contractors of Fayetteville. My [lacuna]. So that's my story, Rena. By the time your brother's conquest for you on the other side has ended, I hope [indecipherable] to be [indecipherable; "laying tiles on the dome"?] [lacuna; "of the capital of"?] the state of North Carolina, a monument to honesty and determined effort.[4]

Rena has confidence in Frank's ability but wishes to remain with him to help realize his ambition. Frank insists that Rena must submit to her family's wishes for a period of time in order to convince them that passing is not the right choice for her. So Rena goes off with her brother, and she is eventually courted by a respected white man, George Tryon, who asks her to marry him. She refuses, leaving him discouraged, whereupon John convinces him to regard her refusal as a mark of her admirable naivete and shyness. At the same time, Warwick and Tryon discuss their family backgrounds and finally concur that the marriage is possible, in spite of certain irregularities in the pasts of both families. They agree to give the courtship more time.

Rena becomes homesick and concerned about her mother's well-being. She also is reaching the end of her ability to deal with the stress of passing, which she explains to her passing-for-white brother in the following way:

> When Judge Straight sent you away to school as a white boy, you were young and unburdened and no environment had settled upon you and shaped you for another life as it has me. You grew up and went through school as a white boy, so that by the time you were old enough to go with girls you had forgotten your childhood days sufficiently to feel at home. It wasn't a case of being suddenly picked up and placed in a new and strenuous environment as you have placed me.
>
> All this frightens me. I'm afraid to talk, to smile, to do anything for fear that I will make a mistake that will embarrass you. [lacuna; "This Mr."?] Tryon that you are so interested in. I imagine he is wonderful. But, oh John, I . . . I haven't known men like him. I'm afraid that . . . I don't know what to do or what to say, or how [sic] to turn. I am not vain, but, but I find it so, so hard to talk to him. And then another thing; always when in the presence of these people—Mr. Tryon, and all the

rest—I am constantly thinking of who I am, and who they are, and how they would hate me and despise me if they knew the truth. How they would scorn and look at me and point their fingers at me and call me that unspeakable name. John, John. [She breaks down in his arms.]

Rena then telephones her dark-skinned lover, Frank, and talks him into letting her return to Fayetteville and to the life of a young black woman.

The moral of the story, from Rena's point of view, is that passing is a lie, is personally harrowing, and does not work. The moral from Frank's point of view is the same, with the corollary that "honest and determined effort" by a dark-skinned black man is preferable to passing for white by a light-skinned black man. This corollary is proven by the fact that Frank's honesty, effort, and manly sacrifice win the greatest prize of the film, Rena's loyalty.

Passing cannot ever have served as a model for racial uplift and class mobility for all blacks, of course, since only the lightest-skinned can ever have availed themselves of such a model. The opinions in the black community about the morality and efficacy of passing have been varied and sometimes complex, but they have generally tended strongly toward the negative side. The tragic out-comes of stories such as Chesnutt's *The House Behind the Cedars,* Nella Larsen's *Passing,* and Oscar Micheaux's *God's Stepchildren* are not untypical and could be expected to be related to the stereotype of the "tragic mulatta."

The Tragic Mulatta

Donald Bogle has suggested, however, that the negative attitude toward the tragic mulatta must be apprehended in context in order to assess its import. Peola's remorse at the end of *Imitation of Life* can be seen as a punishment not just for passing but also for non-passive resistance to white oppression:

> Originally, Peola had been conceived as a tragic mulatto type, the beautiful girl doomed because she has a "drop of Negra blood." But as played by Fredi Washington, Peola became a character in search of a movie. With eyes light and liquid and al-most haunted, Miss Washington made Peola a password for non-passive resistance. "Mama," she cried, "I want the same things in life other people enjoy." The line was the film's great one, its simplest, its most heartfelt. To obtain the equality she wants, Peola has to rebel against the system. Peola was the New Negro demanding a real New Deal. But as *The New York Times* pointed out in its review of the film: "The photoplay was content to suggest that the sensitive daughter of the Negro woman is bound to be unhappy if she happens to be able to pass for white."

Bogle's point is that to perceive only the stereotype of the tragic mulatta, caught between appearance and reality, or to perceive passing *only* as a lie and a denial is to miss the strongest progressive point of an otherwise flawed film: "The ex-planation [by the *New York Times*] for Peola's rebellion is simply that she wants to be white, not that she wants white opportunities. Her weeping by her mother's casket was Hollywood's slick way of finally humiliating her, its way of finally making the character who had run away with herself conform to the remorseful mulatto type."[5] Bogle may imply, by his critical reference to Holly-wood, that a black film producer might not have dismissed the poignancy of Peola's desirable goals in a rush to portray the poignancy of the fearful conse-quences of her pursuit of those goals.

The reason that characters like Peola have been considered quintessentially tragic is based on the dominant white perception that an attraction to whiteness by a black person is a kind of hubris. The narratives of stereotype tend, arti-ficially, to punish such attraction. For example, Peola, in accordance with the formula for such narratives, returns to her mother's funeral thoroughly chas-tened and assumes the role of a young black woman with "appropriately" lim-ited expectations. Stories written by black artists such as Nella Larsen and James Weldon Johnson, however, avoid that formula or use it in a different manner. Micheaux's *God's Stepchildren* would appear to be "the colored *Imitation of Life*," and its tragic mulatta figure, Naomi, could have been advertised as "the sepia Peola," if that is not a tautology. Micheaux, however, represents Naomi's relation to whiteness and her tragedy in a way that ironically signifies on the message of films such as *Imitation of Life*. Clare, in Nella Larsen's *Passing* (Naomi and Clare are discussed in detail in *Visions of Uplift*), is another example of such African-American re-construing of the white, racist stereotype.

James Weldon Johnson

In his novel *The Autobiography of an Ex-Colored Man*, James Weldon Johnson does not feel any narrative compunction to punish his protagonist for any wrongdoing connected with passing. In fact, Johnson's character, somewhat in the way Houston Baker has emphasized the idea of economic sophistication in slave narratives,[6] sympathetically represents the attitudes of blacks toward skin tone and passing as a practical matter of economics:

> I have seen advertisements in newspapers for waiters, bell-boys, or elevator men, which read: "Light coloured man wanted." It is this tremendous pressure which the sentiment of the country exerts that is operating on the race. There is involved not only the question of higher opportunity, but often the question of earning a liveli-hood; and so I say [the evolutionary tendency of blacks toward lighter complexion through marriage selection] is not strange, but a natural tendency. Nor is it any more a sacrifice of self-respect that a black man should give to his children every advantage he can which complexion of the skin carries than that the new or vulgar rich should purchase for their children the advantages which ancestry, aristocracy, and social position carry.[7]

By placing the issues of skin tone, and the issue of passing, in the realm of prac-tical self-interest, Johnson lightens the moral implications of racial identifica-tion. When the narrator in *The Autobiography* decides to pass for white, he tells himself the decision is like other big decisions that any sovereign being has a right to consider: "I argued that to forsake one's race to better one's condition was no less worthy an action than to forsake one's country for the same purpose."[8]

Getting Ahead vs. Making History

Johnson's narrator, in his claim to have strong interest in both blackness and whiteness, with no fears or loathings of either blackness or whiteness, and in his ability to chose either whiteness or blackness as an identity for himself is in the same relatively free position as Nella Larsen's Clara. Johnson's narrator, however, adds a crucial element to the pros and cons of passing, which is his profound admiration for specifically African-American uplift, as exemplified by the historical mission of Booker T. Washington:

> Several years ago I attended a great meeting in the interest of Hampton Institute at Carnegie Hall. The Hampton students sang the old songs and awoke memories that left me sad. Among the speakers were R. C. Ogden, ex-Ambassador Choate, and Mark Twain; but the greatest interest of the audience was centered in Booker T. Washington, and not because he so much surpassed the others in eloquence, but because of what he represented with so much earnestness and faith. And it is this that all of that small but gallant band of coloured [sic] men who are publicly fighting the cause of their race have behind them. Even those who oppose them know that these men have the eternal principles of right on their side, and they will be victors even though they should go down in defeat. Beside them I feel small and selfish. I am an ordinarily successful white man who has made a little money. They are men who are making history and a race. I, too, might have taken part in a work so glorious.[9]

Johnson's narrator harbors feelings of regret at having opted for the life of an average white man. Like Larsen's Clara, he feels the attraction of the black enterprise, the road not taken:

> My love for my children makes me glad that I am what I am and keeps me from desiring to be otherwise; and yet, when I sometimes open a little box in which I still keep my fast yellowing manuscripts, the only tangible remnants of a vanished dream, a dead ambition, a sacrificed talent, I cannot repress the thought that, after all, I have chosen the lesser part, that I have sold my birthright for a mess of pottage.[10]

One of the pleasing ironies of Johnson's novel is that the very thing that his narrator regrets is precisely the thing that James Weldon Johnson himself, in actuality, could feel good about—making history. Johnson, the author behind the unnamed first-person narrator, did *not* let his manuscripts about black folk culture deteriorate in a little box as "the only tangible remnants of a vanished dream, a dead ambition, a sacrificed talent"; he did not sell his birthright for a mess of pottage by passing for white. One can open any book on the Harlem Renaissance or any text on black music and find evidence of the place in history that Johnson claims, the place that his narrator, who passed for white, could not claim. For example, a standard text on the history of African-American music says:

> In 1901 Cole and the [James Weldon and J. Rosamond] Johnson brothers signed with Joseph W. Stern and Company a three-year contract that included guaranteed monthly payments. . . . This, apparently, was the first contract ever made between black song writers and a Tin Pan Alley publisher. . . . The Cole-Johnson trio wrote music for exclusive Klaw and Erlanger productions . . . and saw their songs published in the *Ladies' Home Journal*. . . .
> The Cole-Johnson combination was dissolved in 1906 when James Weldon was appointed a United States consul to Venezuela.[11]

Clearly, Johnson was himself making history even as he was also portraying in his fiction a complex African American who, understandably but regrettably, opted out of history by passing for white.

The quotation from the history text above could serve as a source for a typical story or film by Oscar Micheaux. The quality in Micheaux's films that some critics have called unrealistic fantasies about black men and women, the tendency for his heroes to be placed in unrealistic positions of social responsibility—such as the Secret Service agent in *The Girl from Chicago* and the producer of Broadway musicals in *Swing!*—is indistinguishable from the real-life story in the history text about James Weldon Johnson. Johnson, during the same period Micheaux was making films, *was* in fact a luminary on Broadway and a respected government diplomat; he was the hero of Micheaux's films, so to speak.

In an even more telling and little-known example of the real-life potentialities of Micheaux's stories, one of the child actors in *The House Behind the Cedars* (Micheaux's lost precursor to *Veiled Aristocrats*) was Oliver Hill. Hill may have been perceived by some critics to be acting in one of Micheaux's deluded fantasies of black potentiality; but in real life, Hill grew up to fulfill the ambition of one of the principal characters in Micheaux's "fantastic" story, the ambition "to be a lawyer." And like James Weldon Johnson, who in real life accomplished several of Micheaux's fantasy careers in one lifetime, Oliver Hill not only became a lawyer, but he served with Thurgood Marshall on the elite team that won, before the United States Supreme Court, the greatest civil rights victory in American legal history—*Brown v. Board of Education*. And when Hill appeared on a panel at the Virginia Film Festival in 1991 to discuss the childhood film experiences he had had with Oscar Micheaux, he was taking time from his responsibilities as an elected city council member in Richmond, the state capital of Virginia. To recount such details from Hill's resume begins to sound not only like the duplication of John's accomplishments through passing for white in *Veiled Aristocrats*, the remake of Hill's film; such details sound also like the non-passing, striving Frank Fowler's prediction for himself in the same film: "I hope [to be laying tiles on the dome of the capital of] the state of North Carolina." Oliver Hill, like James Weldon Johnson, was a Micheaux actor, but he was also a Micheaux-type hero in real life.

The choice of whether or not to pass for white in *Veiled Aristocrats* is inflected by the same issue that remains narratively unresolved at the end of *The Auto-biography of an Ex-Colored Man.* Any African American who is light enough or culturally white enough to pass can be seen as representing *any* black person who has the power to make a choice of whether to take a large role in black history or to accept a smaller role in white history. To make the choice of white-ness (whether literal or figurative) is understandable, but it nevertheless is to make a choice that bypasses, or even denies, the problem of race. That choice also bypasses the mission of one's group, and in that sense, it is to pass out of history.

Conclusion

Veiled Aristocrats suggests, by analogy, what Micheaux might have thought about creating films that were mirror images of white films, if he had had the money to do so. Mirror-image films would have constituted a cinema that was passing for white and thus would have denied twoness (by denying the effects of racism) and abdicated the historical mission to build an African-American middle class. The following chapter explores some of the ways Micheaux's novels and films stand up to strong charges of passing for white.

13 Racial Loyalty

The whole project of uplift has perennially and understandably faced criticism for, on the one hand, avoiding the issue of racism than firmly holds down uplift efforts and for, on the other hand, aligning itself with a bourgeois cultural whiteness that seems to require black "racial" or ethnic disloyalty.

Joseph A. Young takes this position in his book on Micheaux's novels, *Black Novelist as White Racist* (which at this writing is still the only book of criticism on Micheaux).[1] Young's argument provides an opportunity for a point-by-point review of the ways in which Micheaux's films and novels answer potentially damaging anti-uplift-ideology critiques. Whether Micheaux's "answers" would satisfy a more sophisticated anti-uplift critique, such as Kevin Gaines's recent *Uplifting the Race,* is an important open question.

Young has spelled out Micheaux's attacks on perceived African-American characteristics in great detail, providing contextual discussions to clarify Micheaux's positions and concluding that negative values in Micheaux's work are overwhelmingly associated with black people and with blackness and that positive values are associated with white characters, with Anglo-type black characters, and with whiteness. Micheaux's values, as analyzed by Young, work constantly to contradict Micheaux's own "racial" characteristics, racial heritage, identity, and interests, leading to Young's charges of white racism and self-hatred on Micheaux's part and to charges of the artistic disarticulation and cultural retrogression of Micheaux's novels and films.

In spite of my own extensive listing (in chapter 4) of Micheaux's use of negative images and racial slurs, it must be said that Young's even more extensive list of such stereotypes is ill-considered, owing to the unrelentingly negative, even hostile, argument by which Young's list of slurs is contextualized. Micheaux's attitudes and art are more complex than Young's assessment has suggested, and a more dialectical critical position is called for.

Before critiquing Young's argument, however, the importance of his book should be acknowledged. It is not only the first book on Micheaux, but it is also the only extended work on his novels. Micheaux's novels are the key to most current biographical knowledge, speculative though much of that knowledge must be. The novels are also a key to Micheaux's worldview and intentions, since they are richer in authorial voice than even the most autobiographical of the films. Young has done considerable work on decoding Micheaux's romans à clef–type figures, places, and cultural phenomena. Most of the few scholars who have read Micheaux's neglected novels will have figured out some of the name changes, such as Ora Thurston for Zora Neale Hurston, *Nature's Child* for Richard Wright's novel *Native Son,* and Atalia for Atlanta, Georgia. Some may have gone so far as to refer to Jack London's novel *Martin Eden* to help explicate the implications of Micheaux's naming one of his heroes Martin Eden, and some may have followed up references to some of the books of the day, such as Thomas W. Lawson's *Frenzied Finance* and Ida M. Tarbell's *The History of the Standard Oil Company*; some may even have identified the real-world versions of plays that Micheaux's characters attend in Chicago, such as Bisson's *Le Femmin X* (1909), which Micheaux calls *Madam X*. Young has done all of these things and more; thus, he provides a great deal of information.

Young has also provided Micheaux scholars with the most extended and the most forcefully stated interpretive argument regarding Micheaux's "anti-African-American" qualities. Since the argument about racial negativity has hounded Micheaux's critical reception from the very beginning of his career, Young's statement provides an opportunity here to address Micheaux's alleged racial self-hatred in breadth and depth.

Young's perceptions are too one-sided. They ignore or undervalue the positive intent of Micheaux's racial imagery. Young's diagnosis of terminal racial self-hatred does not fit a man who was himself quite black culturally and physically, who saw himself as black, and who did not see himself as inferior to anyone, black or white, including the major leaders of his day. Young's central critique of Micheaux's use of negative images of black people has been addressed in previous chapters of this book, which explain Micheaux's critical uses of racial slur and his commitment to employ critical honesty with his black audience "for their own good." Though Young, and other readers, may continue to find Micheaux's work offensive, nevertheless, each claim of Micheaux's hatred for his own people must be subjected to Micheaux's own intentions.

The Charge of Assimilationism

Young's charge that Micheaux advocated assimilation (pp. 19, 54, 79, 95, 117, 134, 148, 150)[2] takes several forms, some of which have been answered in the discussion above. Young has implied that Micheaux's work suffers because it does not address "the finest tradition of Western humanism" or "a truly black aesthetic philosophy" (pp. x, xi). The spectrum of work suggested by the poles of Western humanism and black aesthetics seems peculiarly academic and somewhat out of place in Young's argument, which so emphatically rejects colonialism, whiteness, and the middle class. The finest tradition of Western humanism has, after all, buttressed slavery, racism, classism, and sexism for centuries; and aesthetics (black or otherwise) is itself, according to Clyde Taylor in *Mask of Art,* profoundly Western, anti-African, and colonialist. The fact that Micheaux might not always be working in such traditions could be a point in his favor.

In general, assimilation, since it is an aspect of DuBois's idea of twoness, seems likely to be a difficult problem for any African American. Micheaux was no exception, as this study has sought to demonstrate. Young, however, in his advocacy for the radically African side of the dilemma of twoness, has not done justice to the struggle defined by DuBois and elaborated by virtually all black cultural figures since DuBois. Young has presented confusing criteria. Young accuses Micheaux of "adopting Anglo-Saxon myths, Anglo-Saxon values, and Anglo-Saxon philosophy" (p. ix); Young then, on the very next page, demonstrates that his own critical criteria are similarly implicated in Anglo-Saxon values— "[Micheaux] unwitting[ly] illustrat[es] . . . how oppressive myths have been forced on Blacks, especially black [sic] novelists who as artists should have been writing in the finest tradition of Western humanism or of a truly black aesthetic" (p. x). If Young wants black writers such as Micheaux to transcend twoness, Young must show the way by somehow coming to terms with twoness in his own criteria, which he never does. It seems to be alright, under Young's criteria, to work in either the tradition of Western humanism or of a black aesthetic, but these traditions are not defined, nor is it explained how they can be kept separate, nor is it explained why an artist could not work effectively and progressively somewhere between these two poles, exploring them both.

Young continues paradoxically to invoke Western values while calling for a non-assimilationist black artistic accomplishment; for example: "Micheaux does not concern himself with either the actual or the possible. His concept of 'shocker' determines that his efforts will contradict what Aristotle or any sensible theorist believed to be possible or probable or necessary" (p. 107). This criticism is accompanied by a footnote that fully explains Aristotle's aesthetic criterion and invokes its authority. Young, thus, has founded his radically separatist criteria partly on the most conservative core of Eurocentric aesthetics of narrative.

Young claims that Micheaux advocated the most extreme kind of assimilation—passing for white, cosmetically or culturally (p. ix). Micheaux, on the contrary, was an individualist who counseled against any kind of passing. Micheaux told the story in his first novel, *The Conquest,* of a light-skinned black family whose members were neighbors of his on the prairie. Micheaux's main character wants badly to get to know them, since they are the only other blacks in the vicinity—but they are passing, they are Negrophobic, and they will only associate with whites. Micheaux deplored this self-deception and found it socially ineffective and personally pathetic. Furthermore, in his films *Veiled Aristocrats* (1932) and *God's Stepchildren* (1938), Micheaux devoted whole plots and their attendant values to the tragic folly of passing for white. Young's interpretation of the latter film is misleading in a way that tends to favor Young's larger argument, leading Young to imply that the film was rightfully picketed and forced out of circulation because it "centered on racial rejection" (p. 70). Young reports that the main female character, Naomi, who passes for white, "rejects Blacks up to her end [suicide]," implying that Micheaux also advocates such rejection of blacks. The clear message throughout the film, however, is exactly the reverse. In fact, Naomi's continuing misery and final suicide are caused by her self-exile from her own black community. There can be little doubt that Micheaux's position on passing was always emphatically negative.

Cultural passing is a more complex matter by far. The final sequence, for example, of *God's Stepchildren,* in which Naomi commits suicide, includes several shots of Naomi's brother's family at home in their living room. These shots are practically emblematic of middle-class happiness, a happiness Naomi is denied because of her passing. Somewhat like the Cosby Show version of this happiness that became popular a half-century later on television, Micheaux's family is not only middle-class, but also consciously, beautifully, and happily black. If Young is implying that middle-class American life is itself a kind of whiteness and that middle-class aspirations are a kind of cultural passing, he never does justice to the difficulties of negotiating that implication, difficulties owing to the vast repository of middle-class values in the emerging mass culture of Micheaux's time. Young has not recognized Micheaux's explicit attempts, in films such as *Veiled Aristocrats* and *God's Stepchildren,* to isolate and purge the damaging qualities of whiteness from his idea of the American middle class. Young's analysis never comes to terms with the complexity of black assimilation in America, especially in regard to class, and, thus, Young's definitive statements about Micheaux's assimilation are poorly anchored.

Identification with Whites

Young states repeatedly, directly and indirectly, that Micheaux identified primarily with white people (pp. xi, 10, 35, 98, 140). There is plenty of evidence that Micheaux identified with some qualities of white people, but there is also considerable evidence that he rejected other qualities. Micheaux would have agreed, even with as racist a character as Thomas Dixon's abhorrent male lead in *The Leopard's Spots,* that blacks should be made to compete with whites, for their subsistence, on level ground. It is even true that Micheaux sometimes downplayed, as did Dixon, the history of oppression that prepared blacks for failure rather than success in any such competition. But Micheaux downplayed it for very different reasons. Dixon felt blacks were inherently inferior and were doomed to perpetual subjection, and he wanted the Reconstructionistic obstructions to that "natural" subjection removed. Micheaux felt that blacks were capable of moving forward—gradually on a broad front and dramatically in individual cases. Micheaux felt that blacks were hindering themselves in numerous ways that deserved his criticism. He was fed up with what he regarded as the rhetoric of complaint, or protest, as Young, Bone, and Gayle have discussed it. Micheaux felt that the rhetoric of protest dominated the attitude of African Americans and tended to excuse their lack of progress. He was not excusing victimization, as Dixon was, and he was not blaming the victim, as Young states. He was goading the victim not to be a victim any more and not to sound so much like a loser. In doing this, he may have been insensitive to black experiences such as the kind Richard Wright describes in *Black Boy* (1937), but in these cases, Micheaux is not identifying with white people.

Micheaux did identify with whites when their perceived qualities were, in his view, worthy of respect. When Young says that "Micheaux had an almost boundless faith in the omnipotence of Anglo-Saxons" (p. 140), one can agree in at least two senses: Anglos had oppressed blacks for generations and were continuing to exercise that power; and Anglos had generalizable qualities that made such power possible. Young makes a list of such qualities in describing one of Micheaux's "good Negroes," a list that is very much like the one assembled earlier in this study to classify Micheaux's good, middle-class characters. Young says that Micheaux's typical hero "takes the initiative and he works hard. He reads and he can delay gratification. He is frugal and he plans ahead. He is a puritan of sorts; he is conservative; and he possesses the pioneer spirit. He is business-minded, and he is a follower of Booker T. Washington" (p. 141).

Young goes on to say that if Micheaux thought these qualities were enough to insure the success of blacks in America, even on the Western frontier, then he was naive. Young has a good point (confirmed by stories such as Wright's *Black Boy*), but he pushes it too far. Progress for blacks has required both protest (including mass, public violence) and upward class mobility (including adoption of middle-class values). In general, Young would place emphasis on protest, Micheaux on "character" and class mobility; even so, there is plenty of evidence of protest in Micheaux's films (even after white censorship of his protest material), especially the early films, as well as in his novels and correspondence. The specific questions of Micheaux's attitude toward protest and of his attitude toward Booker T. Washington will be taken up later in this chapter.

Micheaux's Ideal Woman

While it is true that Micheaux's ideal woman is extremely intelligent, competent, and enterprising—suggesting a kind of early male feminism in his work—it is admittedly also true, as Young says, that Micheaux's ideal woman always seems to suggest whiteness in her physical manifestation. Young's argument that Micheaux's ideal woman is virtually white is seemingly telling evidence that Micheaux identified deeply with whites. The heroine in *The Case of Mrs. Wingate*, one of Micheaux's late novels, is modeled physically on a famous Austrian-American contralto, as Young points out:

After Wyeth [Micheaux's hero] meets her for the first time, we are given a physical description of her:

As she poised for the question he watched her closely, and again was reminded of her extremely Germanic extraction; and again he thought of the great [contralto] Madame Schumann-Heink. To him as he studied her, she was the strangest colored girl he had ever met. She did not have the usual Negro inclination, accent, composure; she was anything but a colored girl in the way he knew them. And yet, she *was* colored, this was obvious in the brownishness in her otherwise bluish eyes, the wave of her hair, the darker color of her skin, which should have been, according to her mannerisms, real white.

Bertha's ethnicity seems to vacillate between black and white; her "race" is just as unclear as the color of Agnes' eyes in [Micheaux's second novel] *The Homesteader*.[3]

Micheaux must have had a strong attraction for the idealized image of the white woman, the sort of image created by D. W. Griffith and his camera person, Billy Bitzer, with Mary Pickford, Mae Marsh, and Lillian Gish. In real life, Micheaux may also have had a deep desire and perhaps a deep love for the Scottish white woman who was his neighbor in South Dakota. He spent a significant portion of his artistic life dealing with his apparent frustration at not feeling free to consummate this early love affair. Three of his seven novels and several of his films are reprises of that story. In his later film work, the woman with whom he did have a successful long-term marriage in real life, Alice B. Russell, may have been a partial embodiment of his initial love object. Alice Russell's lightness of skin and practical intelligence and competence answered two important requirements of Micheaux's ideal woman. It is significant that Micheaux found a life partner who was competent to be the producer not necessarily of children but definitely of films—his wife, Alice B. Russell, the A. Burton Russell who appears as producer in the credits of his later films. It is also significant, however, that Russell, in her roles as actress for Micheaux's films, tended to play matronly parts, while the dream-girl parts were played by actresses closer (but seldom very close) to the physical ideal of D. W. Griffith's lily-white younger women. This casting may have been a function of the fact that Micheaux and Russell were middle-aged during most of their marriage and their producing career together, but it may also be true that Russell did *not* perfectly match Micheaux's ideal woman iconographically.

Of the films that still exist, the dream girl would seem to be approximated most closely by the Scottish white woman, Agnes, in *The Exile* (played by Nora Newsome) and by black women characters who are passing for white in Micheaux's stories, such as Rena in *Veiled Aristocrats* (played by Lucille Lewis) and Naomi in *God's Stepchildren* (played by Gloria Press). All these actresses are either white or could easily pass for white. These actresses, however, do not play characters that are white-like in any simple sense. Agnes gets far less narrative attention in *The Exile* than does the African-American vamp in Chicago (played by Eunice Brooks), who is less Caucasian in appearance yet who is meant to be attractive; and in *God's Stepchildren,* the super-white, Griffith-like Naomi is considered by Micheaux to be a pariah because of her duplicity and machinations. Naomi, in other words, in spite of being the lightest and most Caucasian woman in the film, is also the worst character, and she is punished by the narrative. And the light-skinned, Pre-Raphaelitic Rena in *Veiled Aristocrats* emphatically rejects whiteness.

Much more typical of Micheaux's casting of leading women are Evelyn Preer (*Within Our Gates*),[4] Ethel Moses (*God's Stepchildren, Underworld, Birthright* [1939]), Edna Mae Harris (*Lying Lips, The Notorious Elinor Lee*), Starr Calloway (*The Girl from Chicago*), and Dorothy Van Engle (*Murder in Harlem, Swing!*). All these women are light-skinned, but none of them could easily pass for white, except perhaps Dorothy Van Engle—she comes the closest to the Caucasian look of Fredi Washington or Lena Horne. That look, however, is itself quite different from the look of Micheaux's lost Scot, Agnes, as constructed in *The Exile.* If

Micheaux's dream girl is to be understood to be based on his white love object and on Griffith's ideal child–woman, then there are very few good examples of this ideal in his extant films, and the ones that exist are not often treated well by his narratives. Two things are clear enough, that all Micheaux's leading women are relatively light-skinned and that all of them, except the incredibly "good" Agnes and the incredibly "bad" Naomi, are identifiably black.[5]

Miscegenation and Racial Loyalty

The pattern of consummating relationships between identifiably black leading men and leading women is consistent with Micheaux's stated desires and his ethical position in his first novel, in which he falls in love with a white woman but will not marry her because she is not black. His given reasons for not marrying his white lover are loyalty to his race and a wish not to violate the norms of his region, which are necessarily set by the white people who make up the vast majority of the population of South Dakota.[6] Young emphasizes only Micheaux's possible conformity with white feelings against misogyny, while Arlene Elder accepts both qualities: "His reason for not pursuing the relationship, which is reciprocal, reveals both his dependence upon white good will and his racial loyalty."[7]

Young's unwillingness to credit Micheaux's racial loyalty, which is clear to Elder and which is emphatically and consistently present throughout Micheaux's novels and films, points to a bias in Young's argument. Micheaux's ideal of the virtually white dream girl is one of the strongest pieces of evidence in Young's thesis that Micheaux is a white-identified racist consumed by self-hatred. Young fails to consider, however, the complexity of Micheaux's ideal. It is not fair of Young to say that Micheaux had a problem when, in fact, virtually *all* American men and women, black or white, have the same problem. They all must deal with the cultural conditioning that favors a certain type of white woman as the model love object and sex object. The image of the romantic girl–woman, developed as an ideal by, among many others, the Pre-Raphaelite and art nouveau painters and sculptors, was a virtually universal emblem of feminine beauty and desirability, founded in whiteness but affecting global aesthetics. Such cosmopolitan hegemony accounts for the confusions of twoness evidenced in Micheaux's Scottish-woman approximation of Pre-Raphaelite models and "New-Caledonian" Klan molls like Elsie Stoneman in *The Birth of a Nation*.

It does not seem correct to use the presence of the ideal of the virtually white love object as a basis for a general identity reversal for a black man. There are too many black men whose identification with their blackness is significant and positive (however complex) who have been enchanted by the American normative ideal of the white woman. The great boxer Jack Johnson, the very exemplum of strong, dark manhood, married a white woman; so did Frederick Douglass and other black men whose racial loyalty was otherwise beyond question. The painful, soul-searching argument of an Eldridge Cleaver and the articulate anger of a Michele Wallace would need to be taken into account before handing

Fig. 19a. Alice B. Russell (*right*) is often paired with the leading women in Micheaux's films. Here, in *Murder in Harlem,* she and her daughter (in the film) admire a book that is being sold door to door by the Micheaux-like leading man. They constitute a bigenerational admiration society; Micheaux returns the favor, since these women are both versions of his ideal woman.

Fig. 19b. That ideal, however, is more complex than it may appear. In this pairing from *God's Stepchildren,* the mother, again Alice Russell, is still valorized, but the "ideally" beautiful daughter is a pariah because she is skin-proud and racially disloyal.

Fig. 19c. In *The Exile,* the hero seems to be paired with an ideal woman, a successful, light-skinned beauty; but the ideal is again complicated by the fact that the woman is involved in illegitimate businesses and sordid affairs, and she is rejected according to the film's value system.

Fig. 19d. The real and successful ideal woman in *The Exile* is Agnes, the light-skinned "Scottish girl." She looks as white as any of Micheaux's idealizations, but the film rejects her as a partner for the leading man until she discovers and proudly reports that she is in fact African-American.

Fig. 19e. Rena in *Veiled Aristo-crats* is another thoroughly white-looking leading woman, but again, she emphatically rejects whiteness and joyfully marries an ambitious and competent dark-skinned man.

down a definitive assessment of Micheaux's ideal woman. It would count against Micheaux that he was both a victim and an artistic perpetrator of this identity problem, but it would count *for* him that he always came down, in literal fact, on the side of racial loyalty (even if his loyalty does little to mitigate the harm done to dark, African-featured women by Micheaux's pattern of casting mostly light-skinned, Caucasian-looking leading women). It would also count for Micheaux's racial loyalty that so many black men who otherwise had racially significant careers have struggled with the same problem and have very often succumbed to it in ways that Micheaux successfully resisted. Many of these men would not see miscegenation as a problem of racial loyalty at all but rather as a *human right* properly extended to all who fall in love, regardless of race or gender. Micheaux, rightly or wrongly, saw miscegenation as racially disloyal, and he refused it, probably at great emotional cost to himself. One cannot, then, say, as Young does from the evidence of Micheaux's ideal woman, that Micheaux identified obsessively with white people, since he also seems to desire black women consistently and to punish passing for white among black women who match the ideal of the white woman. And owing to the *general* nature of the problem of black (and white) men desiring a certain type of woman, the mere fact that Micheaux is implicated in the problem along with most other males is a poor foundation for judging him to be *unusually* or pathologically identified with whites.

Jim Crow

Young claims that Micheaux "treated Jim Crowism as insignificant or almost nonexistent" (p. 1). Young quotes Robert Bone's judgment that black novelists like Micheaux maintained that "there is no barrier to success which diligence and perseverance cannot hurdle. Rather than face the hard facts of caste, these novelists prefer to indulge in crude success-fantasies" (p. 2). Both Young and Bone are unnecessarily one-sided about Micheaux's philosophy toward black progress. On the one hand, it is not true that Micheaux treated Jim Crowism as insignificant. There are places in his novels and films that make his fury and disgust with Jim Crowism apparent enough. Micheaux gives an example of Jim Crowism in *The Forged Note*.[8] His hero, Wyeth, is stopped at the whites-only gate at a train station and sent to the Jim Crow gate, which is closed. In the meantime, his train is pulling out of the station. He is so angry with the white gatekeeper that he expresses the wish to have been able to face him, man to man, in non–Jim Crow South Dakota, implying that there, Micheaux could give the Jim Crower a good thrashing.

Micheaux's choice, in general, however, was not to dwell on the obstructions to progress but rather to dwell on the means and methods of overcoming them. Unlike the protest writers and filmmakers, whenever Micheaux was faced with obstruction, the challenge he gave himself was to *succeed,* not to decry. To understand Micheaux as underrating white oppression is not to give him credit for the positive aspect of his philosophy that focused on overcoming that oppression. He felt, correctly, that white's would not change their prejudice during his lifetime, and, thus, nothing was to be gained from decrying that; certainly, for him, there could be no gain in self-respect from the artistic practice of protest that Young has called for. Again in *The Forged Note,* Micheaux's hero, Wyeth, states that prejudice is not right, but that it still remained.[9] What are we to do then, his hero asks—grieve? If we are to make men of ourselves, he says, neither bemoaning nor boasting is in order. Later in the same novel (p. 442), the hero says that dwelling on white men's prejudice will cause pessimism; who doesn't know about prejudice already? Micheaux's position was that whites might hate blacks forever. Far from being a white racist himself, Micheaux had hardened himself to the white racist attitude toward *him* to the point that he considered that attitude a force of nature, not unlike the wind and cold of the plains. And nature was just nature—sometimes a friend and sometimes an enemy—but it was not to be protested. Perhaps this position was naive, but it was not unheroic, and it was not ridiculous.

There is no good purpose to be served by Young in so vehemently attacking a position such as Micheaux's, one that founds itself on self-respect and hard-headed determination to get results in spite of everything. There is no point in pushing so hard against the tendency of such a determination to learn from other Americans how they succeed in making a better life for themselves, even if they are white and relatively privileged. One can agree with Young that those African Americans who chose to fight back, to protest the erosion of the African aspects of their culture and personalities, were heroic, that they made a crucial and saving contribution to black progress in America. However, separatism and protest can present their own problems and could be criticized, just as vehemently as Young criticizes assimilationism, for being counterproductive. The perspective of history suggests that there are good reasons why both positions, assimilationism and separatism, have been respectable political choices in the face of perennial white racism.

Micheaux, then, did not treat Jim Crowism as insignificant, as Young states, and Micheaux did not ignore the hard facts of caste, as Bone suggests; Micheaux *assumed* those realities. He did not "accept" them in the way Young and Bone imply; he did not feel inferior, nor did he assume that Jim Crow and the caste system were politically correct, so in that sense, he did not accept them. He did "accept" the incorrigible *fact* of Jim Crow and of caste, but that acceptance made Jim Crowism not insignificant but, on the contrary, as significant as nature itself and as primary as the basic narrative of success and failure for blacks as individuals and as a group. The fact that he was not loved by whites and that he was hindered by racism in his ambition was highly significant to him. Micheaux and his heroes and heroines accepted that those painful realities were true. He did not accept, however, that he was unworthy of love, even by whites, and he did not accept being hindered by anyone in his art or in his life. Micheaux fought and manipulated censorship throughout his career, as Charlene Regester's recent work shows in great detail. Young's critique of Micheaux has somehow viewed such admirable strength as personal corruption and political weakness. The truths that accompany Young's critique do not warrant such an unfair characterization of Micheaux's accomplishment. Young has pushed his reading way too far.

The Washington–DuBois Conflict

Young mounts his critique of Micheaux on the framework of the debate between Booker T. Washington and W. E. B. DuBois, stating that Micheaux was personally committed to Washington's philosophy (pp. 1, 24, 33, 35, 121–22) and opposed to that of DuBois (pp. 9, 24, 44, 99, 119, 121, 132). Unfortunately, Young's handling of the Washington–DuBois controversies is similar to his handling of Micheaux. Washington is painted as a has-been Uncle Tom and DuBois as the righteous challenger and spokesman for a racial pride that Washington had denigrated. Each of these characterizations is too simple to begin with (setting aside, for the moment, the question of how Micheaux might have felt about Washington and DuBois). The debate between Washington and DuBois becomes caricatured and flat if separated from its roots. Washington was a former slave, for example, and DuBois was the son of a historically freeborn family in the East. Washington was self-educated and DuBois had a (well-earned) privileged education at Fisk University, Harvard, and the University of Berlin. Each was a representative of, a spokesperson for, and an unswerving *servant* of black uplift, but their backgrounds and points of view could hardly have been more different. Each could point to towering success in terms of his worldly accomplishments and his ideals of racial identity: Washington had been able to rise to the status of world leader and had built an institution to match his status; DuBois rose to similar status and built a cultural legacy and international political network that epitomized black intellectual peerage. Both were ambitious, but both were focused entirely on racial progress; the labels of "conservative" and "radical," when applied to one or the other of them, fail to alter that fact in the least.

In presenting Washington and DuBois (for discussion) as models for behavior, one must consider the workings of the models within their historical points of view. Francis L. Broderick, for example, points out in his book on DuBois that Washington understood and addressed the masses of black people with a softness of speech and an accommodation of manner that also made him welcome at the dinner table of the President of the United States.[10] One can infer from this set of relationships, as Young does, that Washington was a "Tom" who was selling out the masses, but one can, from another point of view, see that Washington was leading the masses up the road from slavery, a road that he had just traveled, and was communicating their progress and needs to people in a position to help them, people who otherwise would not hear, would not understand, and thus would not care. Broderick points out that DuBois's speech, by contrast with Washington's, was nervous and was always directed toward his highly educated, urbane, and witty peers—hardly ever toward the masses. His words were not comforting or accommodating but rather fretful and aggressive. DuBois, then, radical though he may be called, did not speak from the point of view of the recent slaves or descendants of slaves; they might have had no idea where he was coming from. DuBois's challenge of the gods of the cultural pantheon was, of course, crucially in the interest of *all* black people, but for most of them, DuBois's battle was a distant fray. The exception was when DuBois and Washington battled each other over the issues they had each joined with the white establishment; the sounds of that conflict could be witnessed by all readers of the black press. That battle informed black readers that the struggle against white racism had at least two important fronts, two paradigmatic points of view. Black readers might line up individually behind the points of view each could best understand, depending on individual experience, and critics and scholars might align themselves similarly today, as Young has done. To take a position in such a sweeping dialectic, however, requires an alignment paralleling, in important ways, a class alignment. There may be good reasons for making such a choice, but it then becomes extremely important to try to understand the opposing point of view on its own terms in order to avoid fighting the people who one most wants to help or fighting those whom one needs most as allies or identifying with interests one most wants to resist. Myopia in class alignments remains a poorly understood and confusing aspect of racial politics and American culture, as Benjamin DeMott has recently and furiously reiterated.[11]

One could say that DuBois was exemplary in that he chose the radical side, worked for it all his life, and still tried to understand the mass of black people who were not as educated or as radical as he. His best known book, *The Souls of Black Folk,* is an elegant appreciation of the largest class of the black population (a class one might, to tweak DuBois and to irk Young, perversely call "the untalented nine-tenths"). And DuBois's novel *The Quest of the Silver Fleece* can be characterized as a kind of fictionalized revision of *Booker T. Washington's* autobiography, *Up from Slavery.* DuBois's *Silver Fleece* treats characters who are closer to Washington's real-life experience than to DuBois's own experience. In adopting some of Booker T. Washington's values, *Silver Fleece* also adapts them. DuBois shows narratively the wretched members of his race as they triumph not only through manual labor, skill, and delayed gratification but also through educational and organizational labor and intellect.

In fact, DuBois can be understood as taking the baton from (a reluctant) Booker T. Washington and continuing the relay race of uplift. DuBois, early in his public life, warmly supported Washington's values and accomplishments. When the break between them emerged, DuBois saw it as a transition:

> "So far as Mr. Washington preaches Thrift, Patience, and Industrial Training for the masses," DuBois said, "we must hold up his hands and strive with him, rejoicing in his honors and glorying in the strength of this Joshua called of God and of man to lead the headless host. But so far as Mr. Washington apologizes for injustice, North or South, does not rightly value the privilege and duty of voting, belittles the emasculating effects of caste distinction, and opposes the higher training and ambition of our brighter minds,—so far as he, the South, or the nation does this,—we must unceasingly and firmly oppose them."[12]

The fact that Booker T. Washington may not have experienced his conflict with DuBois as a stair-step transition, a movement to higher levels, should not obscure the fact that DuBois did see it that way. In that sense, one cannot simply pit DuBois *against* Washington as in a melodrama, because neither is a "bad guy." In the prime of his career, Washington's program was progressive. As a former slave, he was able to see a way up from the point of view of emancipated southern blacks and recently migrated northern black workers; he was able to formulate a strategy that former slaves could learn from. DuBois's program was also progressive, but his career was beginning as Washington's career was ending. Their programs cannot be compared except on the diachronic time frame of history. DuBois, as a relatively privileged and freeborn man of color, was able to see a progressive strategy of class mobility from the point of view of an elite. Class mobility for blacks was the goal of both Washington and DuBois, but class mobility is relative to class position. Each spoke from and for different starting points and represented different but equally true realities.

Young has founded his views of Booker T. Washington on Addison Gayle's argument about black novelists. Gayle paints a portrait of Washington as a real version of the stereotyped Uncle Tom, using the story of the young Booker sweeping the floor at Hampton Institute as a paradigm of the Washington worldview:

> he was presented with the supreme test, that determined to gauge his determination: "After some hours had passed, the head teacher said to me: 'The adjoining recitation-room needs sweeping. Take the broom and sweep it.'"
>
> Here was the singular event in the life of Washington; upon his success in sweeping clean a recitation room lay the destiny of the race. Because of his performance here, the history of black folk from 1895 to 1972 will be vastly changed, the work of Douglass, Garnet, and Delany undone, the lives of a number of black men, Monroe Trotter, Thomas Fortune, and W. E. B. DuBois, altered considerably. Imagine the future leader, broom in hand, sweeping the floor "three times" and dusting

"it four," he stands revealed as the embodiment of work and progress, the metaphor of the doctrine of perseverance under great odds, which he later exemplifies. As the reader is forced, through identification, to merge himself into the narrative, sweeping and dusting the floor with the author, awaiting the return of the stern schoolmarm, he shares something of Washington's anxiety, is relieved when, after an examination that would have pleased a drill sergeant, the teacher announces with satisfaction: "I guess you will do to enter this institution."

Though full reward for this accomplishment lay many years in the future, this was Washington's finest hour.[13]

Gayle's focus on the slavish limitations inherent in Washington's values and strategies is appropriate, particularly when understood in the light of the historical era of Black Power in which Gayle was writing. Gayle's sarcastic treatment of the floor-sweeping "epiphany" is brilliant. His comparison of Washington to plantation stereotypes is equally telling:

When [Washington] writes of his indecisiveness on the eve of the Atlanta address, the reader knows full well that even as this historical moment approaches, Washington is the second coming of the stereotype, whose advent was foretold in the works of Harris, Page, and Dixon. That he is but the reincarnation of the uncles, aunties, and mammies of yester-year—the purveyor of sweetness and light, the image of the contented darky become flesh and blood. This observation is not due only to what he said at Atlanta. Most of what he said there was repetition: "As we have proved our loyalty to you in the past, in nursing your children, watching by the sick-bed of your mothers and fathers, and often following them with tear-dimmed eyes to their graves, so in the future, in our humble way, we shall stand by you with a devotion no foreigner can approach, ready to lay down our lives, if need be, in defense of yours. . . . In all things that are purely social, we can be as separate as the fingers."[14]

Gayle's portrait places Washington in the tradition of the loyal freedman servant epitomized by D. W. Griffith in *His Trust* and *His Trust Fulfilled* (1911). Gayle's anger at such white-oriented loyalty and servility by a black man is reminiscent of the rage portrayed by Eldridge Cleaver in "The Allegory of the Black Eunuchs," in which a group of 1960s black militants, including Cleaver, harass an older black man who sits near them:

My contemporaries and I, we had a thing going about elderly Negroes like this one sitting opposite from me. There was something in his style, the way he carried himself, that we held in contempt. We had him written down as an Uncle Tom—not that we had ever seen him buck dancing or licking the white man's boots, but we knew that black rebels his age do not walk the streets in America: they were either dead, in prison, or in exile in another country. . . .

Just then, and with no apparent provocation, the young Eunuch on my left said, pounding his fist on the table for emphasis, "Old Lazarus, why come you're not dead?"

"What?" asked the Infidel, startled more by the suddenness of the question and the menacing tone in which it was hurled at him than by the question itself. . . .

"I asked you why aren't you dead?" repeated the Eunuch on my left.

"If you had laid down your life," the Eunuch cut him off, "at least we could respect you. At least we could say you were a man—a great man. At least we could point to your grave as a sign, a standard, with pride—*with reverence!* But no, you cringing cunctator, you dared to cling to your miserable life, to grow old and gray and fat and funky!" The Accuser broke off and started eating his beans with a vengeance, as though each bean were a white man, and he downed them by the spoonful.[15]

The militant's anger is focused on older black men, as is Cleaver's anger in the reporting of it: "It was a cruel thing we were doing and we knew it because we had done it before to others. In one sense we were only playing with him, probing him, examining him, studying him, but on another level we were deadly serious."[16] Cleaver, however, also retrieves a sense of history that makes ultimate understanding possible, pointing out the Oedipal nature of conflicts of leadership and direction and balancing the cruelty inherent in such conflicts with the knowledge of the necessity of conflict and its role in overcoming the inevitable limitations and gradual obsolescence of all fathers, all parents, all leaders. Cleaver implies the historical origins of Oedipal cruelty and places cruelty in a perspective that allowed for a wider understanding *between* generations through the listing of specific conflicts between respected leaders:

(After all, his entire generation was being asked the same question in a million different guises: Charlie Parker asked Lester Young, Dizzy Gillespie asked Louis Armstrong, Mao Tse-tung asked Chiang Kai-shek, Fidel Castro asked Batista, Malcolm X asked Martin Luther King, Robert F. Williams asked Roy Wilkins, Norman Mailer asked the Totalitarian Squares.)[17]

Though Cleaver intends a pattern of radical generational challenge, many of the figures he names are clearly worthy of respect even though they are the challenged, not the radical challengers. The pattern includes a spectrum of Oedipal "rejects," from Chiang Kai-shek, Batista, and the Totalitarians, on the one hand, to Lester Young, Louis Armstrong, and Martin Luther King, on the other. Even if Cleaver is so militant as to publicly repudiate the ameliorating behavior of an Armstrong and a King, he nevertheless cannot seriously be equating them to a Batista. Cleaver's Oedipal cruelty is ambivalent.

Gayle's brilliant critique of Washington needs to be tempered by the understanding of how Booker T. Washington, in *Up from Slavery,* changed the minstrel joke through a process that Houston Baker, Jr., calls "mastery of form."[18] Baker has demonstrated how such works must be read in their historical context so that the progressive aspects of an African American addressing a large, white audience after the demise of Reconstruction can be fully appreciated.

Addison Gayle's attack on Booker T. Washington, though brilliant and purposeful in the context of the early 1970s, looks unnecessarily cruel when compared to Cleaver's more self-conscious critique of "Uncle Toms" and Baker's explication of the modernism of African-American "mastery of form" and "deformation of mastery." Gayle is unwilling to place himself in the historical and personal shoes of a former slave who is trying to lead other former slaves.

While such unwillingness may be understandable, Young's justifiable admiration of Gayle's rhetorical accomplishment has led Young to anachronistic critical excesses in his judgments about Micheaux.

Micheaux and Booker T. Washington

Young has based much of his critique on his finding that Micheaux was personally committed to Booker T. Washington. Young fails to consider, however, the problems of point of view—of region, class, freedman status, generational difference, and historical period—that are involved in understanding Washington's positions and accomplishments. He also fails to consider the possibility that Micheaux could have been a critic as well as a supporter of Washington and that Micheaux could have supported many other thinkers and leaders, each of whom would constitute a complex qualification of Micheaux's attitude toward Washington. Young fails to consider that Micheaux may, while disagreeing with DuBois on some issues, have strongly supported him on other issues, that Micheaux may not have viewed the Washington–DuBois conflict in the Manichean way that some critics paint it. Micheaux was famous for his independent thinking. In fact, Young castigates Micheaux several times for being so outspokenly independent and stubborn in his ideas that he alienated people. Micheaux all his life thought of himself as a gadfly who constantly challenged people's received ideas. He wanted people to think for themselves, and he refused, even under the pressure of criticism in the black press and of censorship, to lead his own life any other way.

Micheaux, for example, argued with the black press all his life about the middle-class proclivity to want to see only "positive images" of blacks portrayed in novels and films. He never succumbed, in his work, to that pressure, contrary to the implications of Joseph Young's critique. Young's opinion, which is stated several times (pp. 51, 68, 70), that Micheaux began including positive images of blacks only because of the pressure of the black press and of censorship, is outrageously inaccurate and unfair. Micheaux included positive images of blacks in every work he ever created, without exception. In fact, part of his complaint about "modern" black works such as Claude McKay's, Langston Hughes's, Zora Neale Hurston's, and Richard Wright's is that they often failed to *center* their character studies on positive images, which Micheaux always did. Micheaux's relationship with the censors is complex, but Young cannot get away with suggesting that Micheaux on the one hand kowtowed to the white establishment and on the other hand constantly and "rightly" had to be chastened by the white establishment's censor boards. The censors, however, were, as one might expect, afraid of a lot more than Micheaux's "unfair representations" of poor black people. The following discussion, by John R. Alley, of the censorship of a Micheaux film in Virginia illuminates the motives of white censors:

> The Virginia Board of Censors was created in 1922 as a part of the politico/religious movement that had earlier been the driving force behind the adoption of pro-

hibition. In the legislation defining the Board one of the central tenets was a concern with blocking material which would tend to incite violence. The Board interpreted this, it seems, solely in terms of the presumed threats posed by the racial themes depicted in motion pictures from black film makers. Ironically, a Board that would almost immediately seem unsympathetic to the expression of ideas by black film makers, met its first and most vigorous opposition from D. W. Griffith and Thomas Dixon. Both men were involved in a nationwide campaign against state censor boards and in support of free filmic expression. Griffith and Dixon appeared before the Virginia General Assembly as a part of that effort which began after the furor over their film *Birth of a Nation.* The Board appeared unconcerned over the racial tension generated by *Birth of a Nation.* It did use the supposed threat of racial violence as a weapon to exercise prior restraint and to cast immediate suspicion on all movies made by black film makers. The immediate target of the Board became Oscar Micheaux.

Sensing the irony Micheaux wrote to the Board in 1925, "I must also add that you are unduly alarmed as to how my race is likely to take even the discussion in the second reel (*The House Behind the Cedars*). There has been but one picture that incited the colored people to riot, and that still does, that picture is the 'BIRTH OF A NATION.'"

John Alley includes a facsimile of one of the other letters that Micheaux addressed to the Virginia Censor Board, which Alley says "illustrates Micheaux's intense and continued struggle with the censors." Because such primary materials concerning Micheaux's work are rare, it is quoted below in full:

Oct. 6, "24 [*sic*]
Virginia State Board of Motion Picture Censors,
Richmond, Va.

Gentlemen:
As several of the Censors complained of the "Race Riot" in our production "A SON OF SATAN," we eliminated the same, but which reduced the picture from 7 to 6 reels. In that form, the same has been approved by the New York and Penna Board as you can see.
We have the revised print here now and can send it on back for another review by you if you feel that is nessecary [*sic*]. Otherwise we will appreciate your sending on the license and seal when you return the inclosed, thereby obliging,
Yours Very truly,
MICHEAUX FILM CORPORATION
by [signed "Oscar
Micheaux"] Pres.

P.S. W. B. Hunter of our Company presented this subject for your examination, but failed to get your approval in July.

This letter shows that four years after having been censored extensively for portraying a lynching in *Within Our Gates,* Micheaux is still including controversial protest material, a "race riot." It also shows that it is not the lack of positive images of African Americans that concerns the censors, it is the presence of inflammatory, "radical" material.

If censor boards were to be congratulated, as Young would have it, for forcing filmmakers such as Micheaux to improve their portrayal of black characters, then why was the Virginia censor board "unconcerned" about *The Birth of a Nation,* which was being mercilessly attacked for its portrayal of blacks by the black press and the NAACP? Why focus on black filmmakers, whose portraits of blacks would generate discussion that would be kept pretty much within the black community and that would be unlikely to generate any more than just that—discussion? The answer is given in Alley's statement:

> Micheaux's letter was prompted by action reported by Board chairman Evan Chesterman who informed him that his film "was rejected in toto, on the ground of presenting the grievances of the negro in very unpleasant terms, and even touching on dangerous ground, inter-marriage between the races." The "dangerous ground" to which the Board referred was viewed, in Chesterman's words, as violating "the spirit of the recently enacted anti-miscegenation law which has put Virginia in the forefront as a pioneer in legislation aimed to preserve the integrity of the white race."

Is this the sort of censorship that Young feels helped Micheaux make more responsible movies? Is Micheaux's strong written response to the censor board indicative of what Young feels is Micheaux's lifelong career of kowtowing to whites?

A better characterization of Micheaux's relationship with censor boards is one of a dynamic tension between resistance and pragmatic compromise. The compromise, which has been widely noted in the scholarship on Micheaux as a pervasive confusing and corrupting influence on his texts (and certainly not as an agency of improvement of those texts), is illustrated in Alley's statement:

> Faced with the white power establishment that could effectively deny him access to all theaters, Micheaux decided to make extensive cuts in order to make *The House Behind the Cedars* acceptable to the Board. The Board "allowed him to use their own cutting room and to cut the film in accordance with their suggestions, taking out practically a whole reel. . . . "
> Therefore, the film shot in Roanoke was free to be distributed in the Commonwealth.

The choice for Micheaux, in his decision to compromise his work by cooperating with censor boards, was a choice between survival or failure as an independent filmmaker. He chose survival. His choice may not be admirable from the point of view of those who celebrate radical integrity, but that choice was balanced by the other side of Micheaux's response to censor boards—his perennial resistance to them, which is illustrated again by Alley:

> Even as the battle of the *Cedars* raged, Micheaux was under attack by the Board for another of his films, *Birthright.* In a related letter from Chesterman to the Mayor of Roanoke the Chairman wrote: " 'Birthright' according to official reports received at this office was released by the Michaux [*sic*] Film Corporation, a con-

cern which produces films showing negro actors and designed for negro amusement houses. The picture passed the Maryland Board of Censors only after undergoing a dozen or more eliminations designed to lessen its offensiveness. We have reason to believe that it bears upon the race question and embodies scenes and subtitles which this Board would find most objectionable."[19]

Micheaux clearly was proceeding unfazed by the censoring of his films. Each time he released a film, he fought the battles of censorship in all his markets, then went out and made another film that he knew would bring another censorship fight. Not only had he followed *Birthright* (1924) with the equally "objectionable" film *Cedars,* in spite of constant trouble with the censors, but he then went on to remake such films during the sound era, continuing his "objectionable" anti–Jim Crow themes. *Cedars* was remade as *Veiled Aristocrats* in 1932, and *Birthright* was remade under the same title in 1939. All of these films deal directly with controversial issues of racial equality and injustice. Micheaux was anything but putty in the hands of the censors.

It is simply not conceivable, given the weight of evidence in these documents and in Micheaux's novels and films, that he would be slavishly supportive of any leader, strategy, or worldview. One might not agree with Micheaux's position at any given point, but it would be a mistake to suggest that any position of Micheaux's was the result of an uncritical commitment to support or to resist any leader or program. He was thoroughly his own person.

Micheaux absorbed cultural experience voraciously, and in that sense, he was more like DuBois than Washington. He enjoyed people and felt driven to talk to them, learn from them, argue and change them, and transform and experiment with them in his fiction and films. He loved to read and to go to plays and musical performances and films. Before he even thought of becoming a writer or a filmmaker, Micheaux, as a young homesteader in the 1910s, helped to build the new Carnegie Library in Dallas, South Dakota, and he suggested to the library that they write to a source Micheaux knew in Newark, New Jersey, for books. To label Micheaux as a follower of Booker T. Washington's philosophy without accounting for the plurality of Micheaux's influences leads to a simplistic reading of his films. Micheaux does include a portrait of Booker T. Washington that is hanging on the living-room wall of the home of the good, middle-class family in his early film, *Body and Soul* (1925); that Micheaux admired Washington, no one doubts. But he also includes beside the Washington portrait in *Body and Soul* an equally prominent portrait of Frederick Douglass and smaller portraits of other heroes of the race. Addison Gayle places Douglass and Washington on opposite sides of a radical-vs.-conservative bipolarity; in Gayle's bitterness about the historical import of Washington's floor-sweeping epiphany, Gayle blames Washington for dismantling the good, radical work of Frederick Douglass and others. Micheaux, however, clearly could encompass both kinds of leader, each in his historical context. Not only that, Micheaux could joke about Booker T.'s floor-sweeping epiphany; in *Symbol of the Uncon-*

quered (1920), Micheaux intercuts a shot of a portrait of Washington, which hangs on a homesteader's cabin wall, with shots of his uplift hero (the usual Micheaux surrogate), who is ineffectually trying to sweep the floor but who is only raising a domestic dust storm that the leading woman laughs at.

Young has based a large part of his conception of Micheaux's racial loyalty on his interpretation of Micheaux's commitment to Washington as an alignment with black conservatism, against black radicalism, following Gayle's scheme of bipolarity. If that is true, how does one explain the equal prominence of Douglass and Washington in Micheaux's pantheon in *Body and Soul*? The answer is that Micheaux tended not, in fact, to be limited by labels such as "radical" and "conservative," even though he did use those terms to set general categories for discussion. When Micheaux generalized, his tendency was to qualify the generalizations. After stating in *The Conquest* that there were "two distinct factions of the negro race, who might be classed as Progressives and Reactionaries" and that the Progressives were "led by Booker T. Washington and with industrial education as the material idea, and with good, active citizens,"[20] Micheaux (two pages later) placed Washington's philosophy in the broader context of DuBois's criticism of the limitations of focusing exclusively on vocational education:

> [DuBois] claimed in his book that the public had become so over-enthused regarding Booker T. and industrial education, that the colored schools for literary training were almost forgotten, and, of course, were severely handicapped by a lack of funds. His was not criticism, but was intended to call attention of the public to the number of colored schools in dire need of funds, which on account of race prejudice in the south, must teach classics. This was true, although industrial education was the first means of lifting the ignorant masses into a state of good citizenship.[21]

Throughout Micheaux's writing and filmmaking career, his admiration for one person's thinking never meant the necessary rejection of another person's thinking, even if the two thinkers were in conflict with each other. Micheaux concurs with DuBois's attempt to correct the limitations of Washington's program, but Micheaux's concurrence does not require his rejection of Washington. Micheaux sets Washington's program in the context of its history ("industrial education was the first means") and its proximity to the condition of slavery ("lifting the ignorant masses into a state of good citizenship"). Micheaux goes on to theorize about the motives of one of the most severe critics of Booker T. Washington:

> The Reverend and I could not in any way agree. He was so bitter against industrial education and the educator's name, that he lost all composure in trying to dodge the issue in our argument, and found himself up against a brick wall in attempting to belittle Mr. Washington's work. Most of the trouble with the elder was, that he was not an intelligent man, never read anything but negro papers, and was interested only in negro questions. He was born in Arkansas, but maintained false ideas about himself. He never admitted to having been born a slave, but he

was nearly sixty years of age, and sixty years ago a negro born in Arkansas would have been born in slavery, unless his parents had purchased themselves. If this had been the case, as vain as he was, I felt sure he would have had much to say about it. He must have been born a slave, but of course had been young when freed. He had lived in Springfield, Missouri, after leaving Arkansas, and later moving to Iowa, where, at the age of twenty-seven years, he was ordained a minister and started to preach, which he had continued for thirty years or more. He never had any theological training.[22]

This typical character study by Micheaux contradicts Young's thesis about Micheaux in several ways. First, in emphasizing the Reverend's lack of intelligence and lack of theological training, Micheaux was implying respect for intellectual talent and higher education, which contradicts Young's opinion that Micheaux is anti-DuBois (pp. 9, 24, 119), anti-"talented tenth" (p. 44), and anti-education (pp. 99, 121, 132). Second, in suggesting that the Reverend is denying his background as a slave, Micheaux was implicitly accepting his own family's background in slavery. He was identifying with black people in a way that was honest to their history and condition and in a way that Young emphatically denies him throughout his study of Micheaux. Micheaux was also emphasizing the proper perspective from which to understand his support of Washington—a practical and historical perspective.

These positions are consistent with Micheaux's attitude throughout his career. Micheaux's feelings about DuBois were strongly positive:

> Immediately following the publication of the volume referred to [*The Souls of Black Folk*, by DuBois], thousands of anti–Booker T.'s proceeded to place the writer as representing their cause and formed all kinds of clubs in his honor, or gave their clubs his name. They pretended to feel and to have everyone else feel, that they had at last found a man who would lead them against Booker T. and industrial education.
>
> They made a lot of noise for a while, which soon died out, however, as the author of the book *was far too broad minded and intelligent in every way,* to be a party to such a theory, much less, to lead a lot of reckless people, who never had and never would do anything for the uplifting of their race [emphasis added].[23]

One has a hard time reconciling this virtual encomium for DuBois with such typical statements by Young as the following: "Although excessively anti-DuBois, Micheaux was influenced by DuBois' literary style" (p. 9). In establishing his case that Micheaux was anti-education, Young uses examples such as the following:

> Ledbetter might have considerable education from an academic standpoint, but he knows nothing about being a successful cashier at a bank. Dorothy's father assumes that bank cashiers must have more than just education to keep their jobs: "'That is one of the great and major failures of our race! We seem to think that all we've got to do to be successful, is just to acquire an education.'" (p. 123)

Micheaux was not denigrating higher education here. He was making a distinction between kinds of education. It is true that he was hard on those with higher

Fig. 20a. In *The Symbol of the Unconquered,* Micheaux makes a respectful joke of the famous dusting and floor-sweeping scene from Booker T. Washington's *Up from Slavery.* While helping the heroine, Evon Mason, open up her grandfather's old homestead, Micheaux's hero, Hugh Van Allen, holds up a candle and discovers . . .

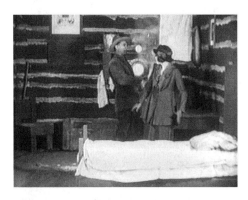

Fig. 20b. . . . a framed picture of Booker T. Washington.

Fig. 20c. As if inspired, Van Allen immediately sets down the candle and starts shaking the dust out of a tablecloth, replicating the first assignment that Booker T. received when applying for entry to the Hampton Institute as a young man. But Van Allen is apparently not as "competent" as Booker T. was, since he raises a minor dust storm that alarms Miss Mason.

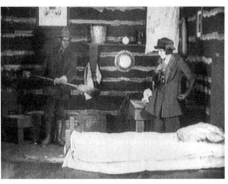

Fig. 20d. Van Allen then grabs a broom . . .

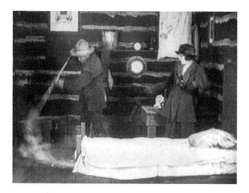

Fig. 20e. . . . continuing the farcical parody of Booker T.'s sweeping epiphany by raising another dust storm . . .

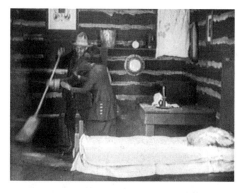

Fig. 20f. . . . and forcing . . .

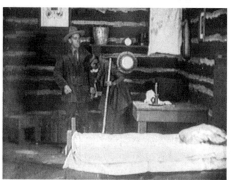

Fig. 20g. . . . the nearly asphyxiated Miss Mason to take over.

education who claimed knowledge in areas in which they had none, who claimed academic knowledge as a substitute for deeper or more practical experience, and who traded on their academic knowledge at the expense of less educated black people. The following statement is characteristic of Micheaux:

"Ridiculous!" cried Dr. Vaughn, with an expression of disgust. "Been to school, graduated from college, teaches school and is supposed to know everything! No man knows everything! And with due respect to the principal of our high school, and what education he does have, which from an academic standpoint I presume to be considerable. But from the standpoint of being a cashier in a bank and lending people's money, he knows absolutely nothing!"[24]

Micheaux placed these words, and the subsequent, quite-reasonable analysis of how a great number of black banks failed, in the mouth of a medical doctor—a highly educated man. If Micheaux comes down hard here on the presumptuousness of certain academic leaders, he is doing it through the agency of one with the highest academic degree offered. Micheaux respected all sorts of knowledge, but he did not respect one sort that claimed the ground of another sort, and he did not respect academic leaders who did not respect the need for business leaders:

> Another successful race man—without money! We are the only group in all America to assume success without money. As a result, and of our seeming ability not to be able to make any, like all the other groups in America, whenever one of us happens to be appointed or placed in a position of trust and responsibility whereby we might help the others, but where it might be more profitable to somebody else that we not be helped, one of these "successful" and *educated leaders* sells us down the river.[25]

Young takes Micheaux to task over this passage, perhaps rightly, for not naming examples of such betraying leaders, and Young implies that Micheaux may have been unjustly implicating DuBois (p. 123). Micheaux could hardly have meant DuBois, however, as one of these educated leaders, given the great respect evidenced in Micheaux's statements (elsewhere) about DuBois's intelligence, integrity, and political judgment. It is easy enough to imagine (though hardly to be considered proven by Micheaux) that there existed educated black leaders in Micheaux's era who might have approximated the countless educated leaders in any era who see education and leadership as an avenue to enrich themselves at the expense of the public interest. Micheaux's analysis above—of the need for blacks to create their own wealth in the interest of their own independence—remains cogent. One can maintain such a position, as Micheaux did, without denying DuBois's importance and without supporting Booker T. Washington's program dogmatically or ahistorically.

As Young and anyone else can see, Micheaux's attachment to Booker T. Washington was genuine, but Micheaux cannot be characterized as a *follower* of Washington. Rather, Micheaux *identified* with Washington as a great leader, as a self-made man, as a conqueror of racial oppression, and as an educator who taught his own people an important method of empowerment. Micheaux did not see himself as having been taught, by Washington's method, to sweep floors or to find and keep a job but rather as having been taught by Washington's *example* to build an empire of his own, like Washington did. After all, the title of Micheaux's first novel is not *Works and Days* or *Travails* or even *Success and Failure;* it is *The Conquest,* and it is dedicated "To the Honorable Booker T. Washington." Even though the title of *The Conquest* is half-ironic (part of the conquest is *of* Devereaux by his father-in-law, a black, Southside Chicago preacher who Devereaux and Micheaux despise), it is clear that Micheaux did not see his "conquering" hero, Devereaux, as one of Washington's disciples but rather as Washington's peer.

Micheaux aligned himself implicitly with Washington's priorities of economics over politics (wealth over votes), though Micheaux, and Washington too, were certainly in favor of African-American franchisement. In defense, on the one hand, of Micheaux's early admiration for Washington (and defense is only needed in the face of some polarizing arguments in the literature that pit Washington's legacy against DuBois's), is the historical fact that Micheaux came of age during the height of Washington's influence. And in support of Washington's priorities is the historical fact of the *explicit* primacy of money over votes that characterized the political system in the era of the Tammany (and other) urban machines. In defense, on the other hand, of DuBois, it is important to recognize that it was necessary to *have* the vote in order to be a player in the ethnic politics of the era. The Tammany machine was specifically ethnic; it could wield the Irish vote as its principal asset. Money and votes were equally necessary for the political machines to work, and if ethnic groups could deliver votes, then ethnicity was an asset to political machines.

Finally, however, money was more powerful politically than the vote. Anyone in America with money could find votes to buy, as Theodore White has made clear in *America in Search of Itself: The Making of the President, Part I.* And money, or capital, was greatly expandable, while the vote was less so. DuBois was right that the vote was necessary to garner goods and services from the local political machines, but Washington was right that money provided access to a wider agenda than did the mere provision of goods and services.[26]

Booker T. Washington was also right. Agricultural and mechanical training was later recognized by whites in the South as a high priority for their own advancement, which caused whites to adjust their own priorities along the line of Booker T. Washington's analysis and to honor his foresight by withdrawing some of their support and enthusiasm for him in order to reserve for whites the jobs that Washington had the foresight to train blacks to step into. The whites who were in control then began relegating Washington's *industrially* trained graduates to *domestic* work instead. DuBois's contribution, and his claim to succession in national leadership after Washington, was his insistence on the importance of access to information, knowledge, and methods of thought and analysis in modern life in all realms, including *both* the economic and political realms. Oscar Micheaux, in his own way, understood both of these leaders.

Vulgar Racial Theory

Young's demonstration of Micheaux's pseudo-scientific racial theories (p. 27), craniological theories (pp. 46, 54, 61, 81, 142), and Micheaux's willingness to generalize as much about other ethnic groups as he did about his own (p. 56) are damaging criticisms, but they are not as damaging as Young suggests. Given the era of Micheaux's coming of age (the age of immigration from Europe and of black migrations to the North), and given the fact that Micheaux was self-educated, it is remarkable that he is as free from prejudice and pseudo-science as he is. Even such respectable scholars as Charles Darwin treated craniology seriously, and Sir George Grove still *assumed* its value when he wrote the entry on Franz Schubert in 1881 for *Grove's Dictionary of Music and Musicians*. And in the third edition of that dictionary, published in 1928, Grove's craniological analysis was still being published:

> [Schubert's] exterior by no means answered to his genius. . . . his nose [was] insignificant. But there were two things that to a great extent redeemed these insignificant traits—his hair, which was black, and remarkably thick and vigorous [footnote by Grove: "All three portraits agree in this. An eminent surgeon of our own day {1881} is accustomed to say, 'Never trust a man with a great head of black hair, he is sure to be an enthusiast.'"], as if rooted in the brain within.[27]

Most telling, in relation to Micheaux's observations about strong chins, is the following line by Grove: "[Schubert] had the broad strong jaw of all great men, and a marked assertive prominence of the lips." These musicological observations were made three years before Micheaux's birth by a man with a privileged European education and a widely recognized scholarly authority; they are being quoted here from a dictionary that was published in 1928—during the height of Micheaux's career—and that was then and remains today the standard general reference work in musicology. Grove's article is thoroughly annotated by its third-edition editor, who did not feel the need to annotate Grove's remarks on Schubert's physiognomy.

Race and ethnicity were the issues of Micheaux's day. There are generations still living today who grew up under a strong influence of popular and extreme racial and ethnic consciousness. One need not celebrate that; one ought, however, to recognize that many of them are moral people caught in an outdated paradigm.

The surprising aspect of Micheaux's accomplishment is that his own forays into these theories are seldom more pernicious than those of the general culture, and they are often emphatically less so. His admiration for strong chins could be compared to the current generation's admiration or disdain for certain types of physical characteristics, such as the size of a woman's breasts or the fullness of her lips and a man's baldness or tallness. Admittedly, it might make sense to discuss Micheaux's interest (obsession would be too strong a term; it is more like a loose theory) in strong chins as a fetish; that would be a point of interest, but not a basis for a sweeping judgment about his racial and political identity.

Aryan Superiority, Nietzsche, and Nazis

Young, however, has attempted to implicate Micheaux in the Nazi anti-Semitism and vulgarizations of Nietzsche because of Micheaux's strong-chin theories and his discussions of race and ethnicity. That attempt is ill-considered. Nietzsche remains far too interesting and controversial a thinker to yield any support to the loose remarks of Young's critique, and Micheaux's clear intention, in the story about the Nazis in his novel *The Case of Mrs. Wingate*, was to reject Nazism, not to support it. Young, in typical fashion, makes too little of Micheaux's hero's absolute and repeated resistance to Nazi appeals. Young says:

> Heinrich [the black Nazi agent] is rather successful at manipulating most of the Blacks he encounters, except for [Micheaux's hero] Wyeth. He cannot persuade Wyeth to make a film designed for a black audience condemning Jewish filmmakers, even when he insists that they are responsible for the failure of his film career. Wyeth is above revenge. He believes that Jews, although incompetent at making black films and thereby destroying the industry, are motivated simply by profit, nothing more. Heinrich's failure to persuade Wyeth forces the Nazis to formulate a new plan to obtain his support. Their new scheme involves advancing him the money to make his own picture so he will feel morally obligated to make theirs afterwards. . . . but again they fail. Heinrich gets the film produced with the assistance of a German filmmaker, and it does cause race riots. (p. 111)

Young has presented this evidence not to praise Micheaux's hero for his resistance to anti-Semitism but to show Micheaux's intention to portray snobbily " 'superior' or Aryan Black[s]" (p. 110). Young's attempts all too often interpret such exemplary and heroic behavior on Micheaux's part as, for some reason, reprehensible. In this case, he does it by linking "superior" to "Aryan." Young has mounted considerable evidence, preceding the above statement, to suggest that Micheaux admired some aspects of the more Aryan, German-born blacks, especially in comparison to the inability of most American blacks to approximate the Germans in their level of urbanity and competence. Young dismisses, however, the main point—that the Aryan aspect of these blacks, though attractive, is, for Micheaux, dangerous. The idea of the "dangerous attraction," as discussed in previous chapters of this book, is inherent in the high production values associated with assimilation. Dangerous attraction is an important characteristic of twoness. In the case presented above, Micheaux's hero deals with twoness, as Micheaux's heroes and heroines always do, by recognizing and rejecting the dangerous aspects of the attraction. Micheaux's hero, from the perspective of racial progress, does the right thing by rejecting the German entreaties.

Anti-Semitism

What is surprising about Micheaux's attitude toward the Jews is not that he had an attitude, which virtually everyone did (and still does—see James Baldwin on black anti-Semitism in *Notes of a Native Son* and, more recently, Henry Louis Gates, Jr.), but that his attitude *resisted* bigotry when bigotry would have helped excuse Micheaux's own recent personal failure in the film industry and when bigotry was being used by many urban blacks as an explanation for black failure during the 1930s and 1940s. Micheaux, in fact, countered such arguments with, for example, the observation that Jews had been key figures in increasing the freedom of blacks.

The following very long quotation from Micheaux's novel about Nazi spies presents a clear picture of Micheaux's approach to anti-Semitism and Nazism:

[Kermit Early, the Nazi spy said,] "After the second generation all other nationalities, except the Chinaman and us [blacks], of course, become more or less molded into one group. White Americans. Only the Jew remains outside the realm, he never changes. He may claim to be an American if he's born here, but—"

"—he is [said (Micheaux's hero) Wyeth]. The same as everybody else who's born here, including us."

"I don't mean it just that way. What I meant to say is that in his dealing, association and otherwise, he remains always a Jew."

"I agree with you in that respect. And for the Jew's own benefit, that is unfortunate, for after all is said and done he *is* a white man, just as white from the standpoint of pigment, as any other white person."

"Now you're getting somewhere," said Kermit [Early]. "I suppose my asking such a question appears a bit odd, far fetched as it were, for currently we have only a passing interest in the Jew. We meet him only when we go into his store to buy something. Beyond a business transaction like the purchase of clothing, or food or otherwise, we have no interest in common with him. But I had a very good reason for asking the question I did as you will, if not presently, ultimately see and understand."

At the moment Wyeth, by his expression, did not understand.

"Now, while you were writing on your book in Chicago, you told me that the Jews were responsible for your being forced to suspend making pictures. I happen to know, personally, that you have gone along in the making of colored pictures very successfully for a number of years. Yet within two years after they combined and became a competitor, you've been forced to suspend, and after you were forced out, they folded up and disappeared as competitors, also. Why?"

"Well, regarding the statement about saying that Jews had forced me to suspend, I didn't mean it literally. I want to explain that I just have a way when I refer to certain people by emphasizing their race. If we talk long, you'll hear me say those Negroes or we Negroes or us Negroes or those Italians or that Greek and so on down. When I speak that way, due to having grown more emphatic than necessary, for I should just say those persons, or something else. Well, to cut a long story or explanation short, I didn't mean anything in particular by it."

"Still you did say the Jews had put you out of business," argued Kermit.

"Any competition in the matter of making motion pictures is Jewish competition, for the show business and the picture business, especially is greatly monopolized by them. Anyway, answering your first question, 'what do I think of the Jews'? I still don't know what you mean. But I have no particular opinion regarding them any more that [*sic*] I have an opinion about any other group," said Wyeth.

Kermit shrugged his shoulders.

"I simply asked how you felt about them."

"You must have had a reason. A man of your training, education and contact, wouldn't just ask such a question without a reason. Out with it?" Kermit looked at him as if he didn't care to go any further at the moment, but suddenly said:

"Then you like the Jews, maybe? Is it possible that you consider him a friend of the Negro; of ours?"

"I don't consider him anything of the kind. He's as good a friend of the Negro as he is of anybody else, but being a friend of anybody's isn't exactly his forte. He's too involved in trade and commerce, cold business and profit. Why should he lose any time or thought being a friend of ours? As I said it isn't worth his time or thought."

"Well, I suppose not. But—" and then he broke off, and didn't finish what he started to say.

Wyeth was curious by now, so he made a gesture and went on:

"Now, Early. Lay your cards on the table. Why have you asked me such a question, anyhow?"

Turning to him more frankly than before, Kermit looked straight at him and replied:

"Because, Wyeth, I'm in a position to do you some good; to possibly help restore you to making pictures. Yes, that's it. To help you."

"That's very fine of you I'm sure. I don't know just how you can help me. Meanwhile, if you *are* in such a position, and you may be [sic]. You're not a man to make such a statement unless you know whereof you speak. Still, there is, perhaps, a string tied to this help you speak of, yes or no?"

"Maybe," replied Kermit with a little shrug of the shoulders.

"Once a man has made pictures, the desire to continue is, I think, forever with him. I made almost fifty full length feature photoplays, and I would make more if I had the money. Before I quit two years ago, I had prepared three very fine stories, broke them down and had two rehearsed and ready to produce—then I was let down by somebody who had every reason to have financed the making of them; somebody who would have profited even more than I."

"Still they let you down."

"They let me down."

"Bet he was a Jew."

Wyeth looked up and smiled.

"I can get you the money, all you need, more than you've ever had to make pictures with before," said Kermit, evenly. "If you're willing to do a little—compromising."[28]

The tendency of both Wyeth and Early (and of Micheaux) to generalize—often badly, sometimes reasonably, but almost always unscientifically—about race and ethnicity reflects the times. Wyeth's explanation of his own tendency to refer to ethnic groups when he should perhaps refer to individuals is, in fact, self-criticism, an admission of a problem and an indication of a constructive attitude toward it. Wyeth's ambiguous smile after Early's "Bet he was a Jew" might be a smile of complicity or it might be a smile of amusement at Early's continuing *idée fixe* on Jews. Or it might be a little of both. It is not, however, a capitulation to Early's campaign against the Jews, since Micheaux continues to reject such ideas and categorically refuses to consider compromising his neutral attitude toward the Jews by making the anti-Semitic film that Early will later propose.[29] If Wyeth's part in this discussion and his negative response to the Nazi line makes him a "superior" Negro, as Young suggests, that superiority is a quality to be wished for, and it is separate from any connection to Aryan supremacism, since the Aryanists are being *rejected* by Wyeth's superiority. Wyeth (and Micheaux) treated Jews as he treated himself and his own ethnic group. He felt that, like African Americans, some Jews were good, some were bad, and those Jews who were competent, honest, and trying to advance themselves (in the movie industry, for example) need not apologize to anyone, including Aryans and blacks, for their success or power.

Things Micheaux Was Not

Young suggests that Micheaux should have been someone else, such as a Marcus Garvey, a military man, a DuBois, or a Harlem Renaissance writer (pp. 144–45). But Micheaux loathed spectacle and respected business competence and thus could not be expected to admire Garvey. Micheaux's two older brothers joined the army during the Spanish–American war; seeing that one chose to return home by freighter at the first opportunity and that the other died of typhoid pneumonia after the service, while still working abroad, may have affected Micheaux's own decision not to enlist. Theodore Roosevelt's later unfair denigration of his black soldiers in Cuba would seem to confirm Micheaux's judgment. In any case, Micheaux was much more ambitious—not to mention independent—than to make a choice for a career in a segregated, racist military service. And there was certainly no unity in the black community about the efficacy of military participation; many of the radical leaders that Young supports would have been the first to reject such an idea. Micheaux did not go to Harvard and the University of Berlin, and thus, he cannot be expected to identify fully with the leaders of the NAACP (who, aside from DuBois and a few others, were mostly white). Micheaux hated much of the literary work of the Harlem Renaissance and found some of it trivial. And he *did* chose to write literature that constantly challenged the status quo, as Young would wish; the status quo he chose to address, however, was as often the one inside the black community as it was that of the white censors outside that community.

Other movements that Micheaux did not join were Pan-Africanism and Negritude. Young has stated that "Micheaux would not or could not understand the Pan African Movement . . . [n]or would he comprehend the importance of Negritude, a significant aspect of which Jean-Paul Sartre suggests is its insistence on being antithetical to everything the white man stands for" (p. 145). It is true that Micheaux might have considered aspects of PanAfricanism and Negritude to be unprogressive. As Young implies, however, we do not really know, because Micheaux made little or no comment on these movements. Micheaux said little about Negritude simply because that movement did not exist in the formative period of Micheaux's career and because Negritude did not reach even the most intellectually elite black American writers until the 1930s; and as the French scholar of African-American culture, Michel Fabre, says, the "[l]iterary and intellectual exchanges went mostly one way—from Harlem to Paris, from the New Negro to negritude, largely through the dissemination of black American works."[30]

Micheaux's Audience

Micheaux's choice sometimes to address unattractive aspects of the black community might have been more acceptable to critics such as Joseph Young if Micheaux were not perceived by Young to be exposing black community problems to white audiences. Young claims throughout his book that Micheaux directed his work toward white audiences and not black audiences (pp. 35, 61, 80, 113, 118). The issue of Micheaux's audience is so important that it deserves a study of its own, which is beyond the scope of this book; nevertheless, it is easy to answer the basic question that Young has raised. There can be little doubt that, at least after the first novel, Micheaux was always writing and making films almost exclusively for a black audience. There may have been a hope in the writing of *The Conquest* that his story would be broadly interesting to whites as well as blacks, owing to the palpable good will, encouragement, and financing he got from his white neighbors in South Dakota. Even that first novel, however, after being delivered to its white subscribers, was sold exclusively to blacks according to a distribution method Micheaux pursued and adapted during the rest of his career. The story of selling that first novel exclusively to blacks is told in detail in his *second* novel, *The Forged Note*. The many other autobiographical portraits of the leading man as black author selling his own books door to door in black communities and at the back doors of white upper-class communities (to black servants and cooks) show exactly who Micheaux's audience was. Some of his movies tell the same story, such as *Murder in Harlem* (1935). The promotional materials on the book jackets and in the introductions and forwards of his books are all aimed at black buyers. All the known business letters for his film companies are in pursuit of distribution arrangements for the black-only and historically black film screening venues. The black press is virtually the only place one can find reviews of and advertisements for Micheaux's books and films.

Conclusion

Joseph Young's entirely negative assessment of Micheaux's work extends to many other major and minor points about Micheaux's novels and includes a chapter on his films. Young's chapter on Micheaux's filmmaking can be dismissed as derivative; it consists of mostly outdated and inaccurate secondary scholarship. Young does not, in fact, claim originality for that chapter. Most of the other critically negative points in Young's book about Micheaux can be answered as the above points have been, and many of the answers adumbrate Micheaux's personality in relation to black culture. For example, Young's charge (p. 3) that Micheaux was afraid to use his real name in *The Conquest* for fear of being despised by his own people because of his association with controversial ideas makes no sense, since Micheaux thrived on controversy all his life and since he proudly put his name on all further work, the more controversial the better. There is no compelling reason to reject Micheaux's own explanation for leaving his name off *The Conquest*. That explanation can be found in *The Forged Note* and again in the film *Murder in Harlem*; Micheaux felt that people would find it easy to despise someone who was *selling his own work* and would take pleasure in pulling the author down "to their level." Micheaux pointed to a tendency of struggling members of the black community to find fault with the progress of those who were successful, a not uncommon observation in black culture and in Anglo-Saxon culture as well (see Harold Bloom's *Anxiety of Influence*). Micheaux, interestingly enough, compared the Jews favorably with other ethnic groups with regard to the perceived prevalence of jealousy within the group.

Occasionally Young does make a point about Micheaux that is hard for an admirer of Micheaux's work to explain. Most of these are small points, and they are few. One example of such a difficulty is Young's use of Micheaux's remark—that picking cotton is "fun"—to support the idea that Micheaux celebrates the plantation tradition. Though one frowns uncomfortably at Micheaux's strange remark, one also realizes that, contra Young, it does not fit into any pattern of support for plantation traditions. One is left with the aggravation of Young's small point, but the force of Micheaux's worldview remains undisturbed. There are other places in Micheaux's corpus of novels and films where personal weaknesses, even meannesses, occur, but they are very few.

Young's misreading of obvious and important points in Micheaux's life and work, such as the ethnicity of his intended audience, structurally invalidates much of his reading of other issues. Young's thesis, however, remains the only extended consideration of Micheaux to date, and Young's position on the issues is still largely unanswered in the literature; some of Young's criticisms are still widely held by critics, scholars, and film programmers, both black and white. Many interested critics still feel, after viewing a few films by Micheaux, that he is confused about his identity to such an extent that he should be rejected instead of held up as an example of African-American cinema. Young's extended case has provided an opportunity to present an overdue response to that argument and at the same time to indulge in details of Micheaux's famous controversiality, which he himself savored. After all, even in his first novel, he perversely relished the characterization of him as a child (by the elders of his church) as "worldly, a free thinker, and a dangerous associate for young Christian folks."[31]

14 Micheaux and Cinema Today

> Modernism is being succeeded not by a totalizing Western postmodernism
> but by a hybrid new aesthetic in which the new corporate forms of communi-
> cations and display will be constantly confronted by new vernacular forms of
> invention and expression. Creativity always comes from beneath, it always
> finds an unexpected and indirect path forward and it always makes use of
> what it can scavenge by night.
>
> —Peter Wollen, *Raiding the Icebox,* pp. 209–10

The "straight lick" that characterizes the campaign of uplift in a racist regime
often had to be delivered with a "crooked stick." Micheaux's vision of uplift is
embodied in the content and style of his films, in their concern for moderation and the middle path. But his straight-lick vision is also embodied in an
institutional model. His film companies were an early example of an independent cinema that both anticipated and resisted a monopolized, image-mediated
society (what Clyde Taylor, after Ralph Ellison, calls Monopolated Light and
Power and what Noel Burch calls the Institutional Mode of Representation).

Revising the American Dream: Institutionalizing Middle-Class Cinema

Micheaux's cinema of self help, educated inquiry, lawful interrogation,
cultural autonomy, and social justice among middle-class citizens continued
through the work of other independent filmmakers, despite continuing unjust
political conditions and structurally unbalanced economic resources. These filmmakers included African Americans such as Kathleen Collins, Bill Gunn, and
Marlon Riggs, and today include William Greaves, St. Clair Bourne, Michelle
Parkerson, Julie Dash, Zeinabu Davis, Charles Burnett, Haile Gerima, Louis
Massiah, Marco Williams, and many others. Their smaller, less totalizing, more
circumspect cinemas and production companies are more consistent with pluralistic citizenship and heteroglot aesthetics, with the "new vernacular forms of
invention and expression" called for by Peter Wollen, above. Perhaps their time,
and Micheaux's time, could be said to have come. The perennial success of
Hollywood's blockbuster strategy, however, suggests that the same material imbalance Micheaux faced—which Martha Rosler has called "factors of ten"—
continues today. The predicament that Ella Shohat and Robert Stam identify for
Third World filmmakers remains true for most of the world's actual and potential filmmakers: "in that the Hollywood system favors big-budget blockbusters,

it is not only classist but also Eurocentric, in effect if not in explicit intention; to be a player in this game one needs to have economic power. Third World filmmakers are asked, in practice, to worship an unreachable standard of cinematic 'civility.'"[1]

Ed Guerrero's and Jesse Rhines's recent studies corroborate the relevance of Micheaux's concerns. Like Mark Reid's important earlier book, *Redefining Black Film,* Guerrero (in *Framing Blackness)* has reviewed the whole history of the black film image in America. Guerrero has spent less time than Reid in analyzing the early period of black film production, which is epitomized by the careers of Oscar Micheaux and Spencer Williams. Guerrero has preferred instead to set up a dialectic between the original defining attitude of Hollywood toward African Americans and the efforts of the post–civil rights movement to create a black cinema. Guerrero's focus on recent cinema, in a context that includes early black cinema, provides an opportunity to relate Micheaux's concerns to current cinema.[2]

Both Guerrero and Rhines argue that the profit motive in Hollywood relegates black cinema, with other minority-audience cinemas, to marginal status. When the cost of producing cinema rose around the time of *The Birth of a Nation,* it was structurally necessary to appeal not only to middle-class values but also to strict racial codes (Guerrero, p. 17), which at that time were openly white supremacist; Guerrero has shown that racism was economically beneficial for Hollywood. When production values rose to the level of sheer opulence, as epitomized by *Gone with the Wind* (1939), the racism that was often part of the message was made palatable by the magnitude and charm of the antebellum plantation (or other wealthy) vision (p. 22). The most opulent films also seemed to erase all but the upper and the servant classes of society. Film after film showed no evidence of a middle class, an extraordinary fact, given the middle-class makeup of the audience. When blacks were included in such films as *Jezebel* (1938), they were represented as happier than comparable working-class whites, to whom the blacks pointedly referred as "po' white trash" (p. 24). This erasure of the social arrangement of captured labor—in which indentured blacks who are part of an opulent vision are happier than free, but poor, whites who are left out of that vision—Guerrero has related to fascism. When fascism actually did arise in Europe in the 1930s, Hollywood's vision of plantation fascism began to look ugly (p. 27).

Guerrero treats glossy images, high production values, and seamless styles as a particular problem for black cinema. Such standards have caused the budgetary "glass ceiling" that relegates minority-related productions to a lower budget than those associated with mainstream films, whose budgets soar above that glass ceiling to produce the most expensive styles possible. Both black and white producers have sometimes approached the problem of the glass ceiling by going for a crossover audience, a move that tends to eradicate the black point of view (pp. 128–31). And the greatest recent crossover star, Eddie Murphy, often challenges racism, but he does not challenge classism (p. 132). Classism in the form of Hollywood megabudgets has proved structurally racist (as well as sexist and heterosexist) in America, since expensive cinema tends to reinforce prevailing power imbalances.

Guerrero has suggested that because of the relationship between profits and grandeur and between grandeur and legitimation, African Americans and society in general should be wary of an uplift strategy that would produce a grand, Hollywood-like cinema that tends to serve the purposes of entrenched power. Guerrero has verged on suggesting that the inflated grandeur that legitimates particular classes of society inheres not just in the content of the mansions within the fictional/historical world of the stories but also in the *production values* that construct those stories:

> About half the film [*Jezebel*] takes place in the grand interior of "Halcyon" mansion, where every narrative kernel is played out in its own room *and correspondingly grand mise-en-scène*. With the use of *extensive tracking shots that were not technically possible* during the production of *Birth*, the camera follows the actors as they glide up and down monumental staircases and through a maze of huge doorways, halls and gigantic rooms.[3] [Emphasis added]

Though Guerrero is more concerned here with the grandeur of constructed content, e.g., mansions, he later makes it clear that something perhaps inherently conservative, inherently oppressive—to minority and marginal cultures—lies in grand production values themselves:

> Sometime in the late 1970s, after a fifteen-year period of experimentation and creative auteurship, . . . the film industry returned to producing big-budget films that reestablished with a vengeance a thematically and formally conservative, linear, illusionist style called "the cinema of recuperation." This return was intensified by the production of films with a politically conservative ideology and the glossy, color-saturated slickness of an ever-improving and imposing technology. Contributing to Hollywood's political shift to the right, by the beginning of the 1980s the major studios were no longer independent, self-contained industries. . . . The days when the mainstream industry tolerated a wide margin of experimentation, countercultural expression, and creative dissonance as a way of invigorating the market with new ideas, images, and product were over.[4]

Jessie Rhines's engaging study has expanded on those ideas. The cycle of grandeur, profits, and conservatism that Guerrero and Rhines have documented could be characterized as a feedback spiral. Such feedback in the film industry produces an inflated reflection of the audience and all its traits, both good (sentiment, humor, sympathy, hope) and bad (cruelty, racism, sexism, homophobia, and paranoia). It also creates a class of producers who, like Harry Cohn's derriere, are hypersensitive reflections of the desires and fears of often hegemonized or "colonized" consumers. Such feedback systems within unregulated markets magnify the differences between majority and minority constituencies, amplifying their otherness in ways that increase ignorance and fear. Paradoxically, mass culture reduces the possibility of community.

After sketching a history of the development of a grand and expensive cinema for the American middle class, Guerrero says: "Perhaps only an 'other' or independent cinema is capable of producing the kind of alternative or 'emer-gent' . . . content that is not, for the most part, determined by the absolute need to turn a short-term profit at the box office" (p. 35). Guerrero does not actually prescribe a social program to promote an " 'other' or independent cinema . . . capable of producing the kind of alternative or 'emergent' . . . content" that he favors. And he is able to rationalize Spike Lee's film *Malcolm X,* even though Lee's film transgresses Guerrero's admirable criteria for "other" cinema through Lee's artificially elevated production values. Guerrero nevertheless supplies the analytical terms that suggest the importance of Micheaux's early work. Micheaux in fact did, half a century ago, both propose and execute such a pro-gram for an 'other' cinema.

Independent Film

Guerrero does argue that black independent film is necessary. As the title of Guerrero's book, *Framing Blackness,* suggests, the blackness framed by Hollywood requires reframing outside Hollywood (pp. 35, 137).

Guerrero has refused, however, to polarize "independent" and "mainstream" cinemas. Not only has he found them tangled together in reality but he has found that both must face hard realities, such as the paradox that black audi-ences (1) need to have their often harsh reality portrayed in the public sphere and (2) also often want to avoid that reality when it *is* portrayed, preferring films of escape instead (p. 168). That paradox means that independent films like Charles Burnett's *To Sleep with Anger* and Julie Dash's *Daughters of the Dust* have trouble finding audiences. A related paradox is (1) the desire, on one hand, of some black filmmakers to achieve mastery of the film craft and (2) the need, on the other hand, to deform that mastery (in terms suggested by Houston Baker). If the mastery of Hollywood's craft by black filmmakers means learning Hollywood linguistic conventions, if mastery means addressing already colo-nized desires of black audiences and extending the crossover avenues farther into white audiences with their white problems, then black filmmakers also need to produce avant-garde languages, socially more urgent messages, and insiders' depictions of the non-crossed-over black world (pp. 180–81).

Spike Lee

Guerrero's thesis concludes on a positive, but wary, note. After leveling respectful but honest criticism at the best of Spike Lee's films, including a cri-tique of their slick production values, Guerrero decides that the epic scale and budget of *Malcolm X* are, nonetheless, justified by the global scale and social import of Malcolm X's thinking (p. 203). Also, Guerrero notes that if Lee had not been able to film on expensive locations abroad, some of the reality and grandeur of Malcolm X's actual accomplishment would have been falsified. Guerrero feels that Lee has captured each register of Malcolm X's life, including the early down-and-out period, and that Malcolm's ideas have been made available more broadly than ever before.

These last two points, however, remain problematic according to Guerrero's own arguments. They are open to the questions of (1) whether it is truly possible to reflect a down-and-out reality in a filthy-rich style, (2) what the political implications would be of supporting such a success if it were possible, and (3) whether a message that reached so many colonized minds can have much of Malcolm X's original import in it. Part of the message of Malcolm X's exemplary life was his avoidance of the temptations of money, class, and privilege (foundations of racism); none of those temptations are avoided by the high style of Lee's film. Thus, by supporting the special need for an expensive style in the portrayal of Malcolm X's accomplishment, Guerrero may be supporting a material misrepresentation of that accomplishment. The salient question is, where was mainstream cinema when Malcolm X was fighting his global-scale fight that had so much social import? And, failing to find an answer to that, where was the black community's cinematic version of Malcolm X's mission? It was in the low-budget independent cinema of, for example, Melvin Van Peebles's *Sweet Sweetback's Baadasssss Song* (1971).

The Black-Cinema Boom

Guerrero's conclusion states that black film has taken a great leap but that such leaps can be expected to be affected by the force of gravity. With the black-cinema boom on the upswing, Guerrero says, it is a good time not to be thinking conservatively, which is the temptation; rather, it is time to be thinking of new variables, perspectives, and methods. For example, African Americans need to move sharply into the businesses of distribution and exhibition, which are monopolized by whites; Oscar Micheaux and others called for this in the 1920s. Then, and now, virtually no black theater owners existed to demand the kind of film material that might be special to black communities. African Americans can use video stores as they use bookstores (the National Black Programming Consortium founded such a store in Columbus, Ohio). But Guerrero has also pointed out that attention to the video market should not mean withdrawal from the big screen, which also requires attention. The big screen ought to see the works by great black authors, it needs the female leads that would be required to treat the works of those black authors, many of whom are women, and it would be enriched by the dramatic realism of those works.

Friends in Court

Guerrero finally calls for more African-American influence over dominant cinema as well as for more non-co-opted, liberated perspectives from cinemas outside the mainstream. Such a balanced position is hard to argue with. If nothing else, simply in the interest of survival in the juggernaut of today's feudalistic capitalism, the Spike Lees and the Hudlins do need to seize their chance to move African Americans into the main centers of production. The burden of proof, however, of the efficacy of those expensive visions is on the proposers and practitioners of that strategy. What, in fact, are the expensive mainstream films that have been or might be truly progressive? So far, the argument for the adequacy of Lee's *Malcolm X* is not convincing.

Dominant Cinema, the Dangerous Attraction

There is, certainly, a need for disfranchised groups to inflect dominant cinema, and the attraction of producers and audiences to such realms of dominance is also admittedly great. One of the fundamental themes of Micheaux's films recognizes the attraction but treats it as a dangerous one. The thrust of Micheaux's career is to resist and critique that attraction of stardom and of glamour by choosing instead moderation in production values and commitment to a broad uplift toward the middle class. In that, Micheaux anticipates the recent call by bell hooks for a definition of uplift that does not take class privilege and excessive wealth as its model and measure of success. Those progressive filmmakers who have acquired the means of dominant cinema, such as Spike Lee and the Hudlin brothers, are undoubtedly showing the way to power and using that power to open the realm of uplift to some of the disfranchised. They are, however, inevitably also legitimating and strengthening a system that is committed to a radical imbalance of economic means as a structural principle. So are white filmmakers such as Martin Scorsese, Francis Coppola, Godfrey Reggio, Robert Longo, David Salles, Julian Schnabel, Cindy Sherman, and anyone else—no matter how adversarial—who works in the industry. To the extent that any such filmmakers try to address in their films the fundamental issues of class (and many of them do), their efforts are in a state of contradiction and, thus, they lose their integrity.

Celebrating outsiders and moderates such as Oscar Micheaux—as this study does—may appear quietistic. After all, if white people got where they are by doing things individualistically, even selfishly, on a grand scale, why should black people not do the same? One answer is that more and more black people probably should and probably will seek positions of dominance, as Spike Lee has. At least they can, from there, resist racism. That is a prodigious accomplishment, one worth celebrating, but it will not solve the more fundamental problem of structural politico-economic disadvantage, or class. If Guerrero is right that racism in dominant cinema has been, in large part, a matter of profits, then introducing African Americans into dominant American cinema will mean that some other "ism" will take the place of racism in the pecking order of American class. It might be heterosexism, anti-alienism, Christian supremacism, anti-Islamicism, or anti-welfarism. The particular objects of prejudicial discrimination are epiphenomenal; the underlying phenomenon is class. In film production, class is the structural imbalance of power that lends efficacy to prejudice and that feeds prejudice in order to feed off of it. Such feedback systems are materially self-amplifying and antithetical to educated inquiry and democratic citizenship.

Conclusion

Micheaux's filmmaking both represented and embodied uplift. Not only are Micheaux's visions of an educated citizenry pluralistic and heteroglot, but they are also immanently materialist, representing a praxis in which visions of uplift (i.e., theory) arose along with an institutional matrix (i.e., practice) that appropriately realized those visions. His film companies matched his vision, and, thus, they had a rare integrity. They were an early example of a viable alternative mode of production, an independent, middle-class cinema. Micheaux's career was not just anti-racist; it also anticipated and resisted a monopolized, hyper-mediated society of the image.

Micheaux's lifelong example of the "straight lick" is a contribution to the story of human emancipation. Micheaux's accomplishment demonstrates that great art can and does emerge in tight circumstances and that such art can sketch and narrate paths toward cultural autonomy. Micheaux's critical reception shows, however, that such art necessarily discovers its own territory and forges its own terms.

Racism was Micheaux's specific context of oppression. Racism has been one of the most debilitating ideologies of class dominance. The focus on class in this study is not meant to suggest that racism was not the most negative and destructive experience of Oscar Micheaux's life. Rather, the point is to emphasize that Micheaux chose to focus on the "discrimination" in "racial discrimination," which is the painful and destructive aspect of that double term. Race itself (if it can be said to exist at all outside racist ideology) is not painful and is thus not the prime issue for Micheaux. Hostile discrimination is painful, and discrimination is the active ingredient in class.

Seldom have the (economic) class implications of racism been more clearly stated than in the following statement by Senator James Haddon of South Carolina (in 1858): "In all social systems there must be a *class* to do the menial duties . . . or you would not have that other class which leads to progress, civilization and refinement. It constitutes the very mud-sill of society and political government. . . . Fortunately for the South, she found a *race* adapted to that purpose" [emphasis added].[5] "Race" is a major criterion for sorting out classes; it was treated so throughout Micheaux's career and still is by many of today's independent filmmakers. Class, however, remains the paradigm within which racial discrimination has meaning and consequences.

Micheaux's forty-three-film, seven-novel assault on class-based cruelty and underdevelopment and class-based resistance and development remains compelling because the specific circumstances that he treated remain dire. D. W. Griffith founded his vision of a middle-class cinema in the early twentieth century on Senator Hadden's philosophy of race and class, and the fundamental economics of Hadden's and Griffith's vision have yet to be revised in the 1990s (though they are being internationalized). African Americans have gained initial entry to the American dream, but the class foundation of that (now global) dream is still intact.

Thus, the problem that Micheaux addressed in his long career is still very much the point of any critical cinematic practice. The challenge remains—in the face of today's titanic $300 million visions *for* the middle classes—to build an institutionalized cinema *of* the middle classes, a cinema worthy of Micheaux's prodigious pioneering accomplishment.

Appendix 1
On Class and the Classical

"Class" is such a problematic term that the 1968 edition of the *International Encyclopedia of the Social Sciences* did not include a separate entry, though the 1930 edition had included a large entry of several pages as well as closely related separate entries on class consciousness and class struggle. The entries of 1930 are complex and interesting. The leading definition of class reads thus: "The concept of class is concerned with the social differentiation of groups. In ancient times social differentiation was one not of class but of status or rank."[1] The definition proceeds to posit that class should be understood as social stratification rather than just as any conceivable social grouping and that class should be understood to differ from the earlier idea of status in that stratifications of status were relatively impermeable, whereas modern stratifications of class allow for individual movement in and out of the class. Various methods of identifying stratification are discussed in the entry of 1930, and these methods are organized under two opposing kinds of factors—objective ones and subjective ones. Among the objective factors are those of Marx (founded on the relations of ownership and non-ownership of the means of production) and those of Weber (founded on access to, as well as ownership of, means; on standard of living; and on cultural expectations and possibilities). The entry of 1930 tries to explain the plethora of different attributes of class by following the passage of the idea of class through different historical periods, with their varying conditions. Before reviewing the history of the idea, however, the entry of 1930 attempts another general definition:

> In tracing this historical evolution it will be necessary to premise a concept of class of the most general sort, to include all those situations where graduations of rank and relations of dependence occur, associated with differences of social position and variations in both outer and inner conditions of life so marked that we may speak of the group as having a common economic position.[2]

It is unclear from this definition whether class is to be regarded as social position or economic position, whether class position is a gradation of rank or a relation of material dependence, and whether the defining conditions of class are outer or inner, or either, or both. One begins to understand the temptation of social science to abandon such a difficult term. Even though the main point of that portmanteau definition is encyclopedic and intends to collect the various versions of an idea of class that have accumulated over time, and even though the rest of the entry on class that follows that definition is instructive and specific, readers nevertheless have some cause to wonder if an idea of class has integrity under the pressure of such fundamental fragmentation and historical change.

The 1968 edition of the social science encyclopedia did in fact eliminate "class" as a main entry, but class continued to crop up in the middle of its other entries. Under the subheading "social class groups" in a discussion of ethnic groups in stratified societies, the following definition appears: "Sociologists generally consider a class to be an aggregate of people occupying roughly the same status, which is different from that of people in other classes and which, unlike status in a caste or estate system, allows movement from one stratum to another." This definition simplifies the idea, making it dependent on the idea of status. Also, the definition continues with qualifications that refer to some of the confusing elements of the previous definitions, but it relegates those elements to a subordinate position: "It is never easy to decide to what degree a social class is an institutionalized group or exactly how it is related to economic and political status and prestige." Again, status is the key idea, but the related realms of economics and politics are added to the realm of the social, specifically to recognize their tendency to confuse the issue. The immediate continuation of the definition adds the element of ethnicity, which might be important to relating class more specifically to Micheaux's concerns:

> When some of the qualifications for membership are also those for belonging to
> an ethnic category or group, the difficulties of analysis may become very great
> indeed. An aggregate of people is not a social class just because they think of themselves as one; it is a social class because some activities are obligatory to all or most
> members and act as a sign that the people form a group and are eligible for access
> (appropriately graded according to their class) to resources that are valued by the
> society. When these activities are also qualifications for membership of ethnic or
> cultural groups, then ethnic and class groups coincide.[3]

One way of describing the predicament of the black middle class is to say that if whiteness is a qualification for membership in the American middle class, then the black middle class in some sense is not of the American middle class; and since African Americans are American, the term "American middle class" breaks down around ethnicity and race. Said "the other way around," if blackness itself is a sign not only of ethnicity but of class, then the black middle class would be stuck in the lower classes—again a double contradiction, since middle class and lower class should not be equatable and since class position itself has been defined by both the 1930 and the 1968 entries as permeable. That is, if blackness is taken to mean skin color and other racial characteristics rather than cultural ethnicity, and if black Americans cannot move out of the American lower classes because they cannot change their "race," then an idea of caste (the color line) would need to be considered in relation to a class system. Shelby Steele's story of his college debate coach, who placed Steele in a double bind by expecting Steele to "understand" why African Americans "did not make good neighbors," shows how confusions of caste and class begin to display themselves when the fabric of the veil of caste starts to wear thin.[4]

The preceding definition of class depends on an idea of status. The entry under "status, social" in the "classless" 1968 encyclopedia of the social sciences divides social status into two basic ideas—first, it can be a synonym for "any position within a social system"; or second, it can be scaler, indicating a position on a social hierarchy of superiority and inferiority. Both these ideas might apply to the study of Micheaux's relation to the middle class. The first idea, that status is any position within a social system, is quite general. Specificity is provided by examples of statuses and by the distinguishing of status from "role"; the examples and distinctions are suggestive:

> The term *status* is often not clearly distinguished from the term *role,* and some
> use the two terms almost interchangeably. But one can make the distinction easily
> enough if one keeps in mind that status defines *who* a person is (e.g., he is a child,
> or a Negro, or a doctor), while role defines *what* such a person is expected to do

(e.g., he is too young to work; he should not want to push himself ahead; he should care about patients).

The idea of "who a person is" is clarified further by the stipulation given previously (in the above entry) that status is determined not by "intrinsic characteristics of men [*sic*], but [by] social organization." A related example points to the North American idea of the "Negro" as a designation of a single status that is based on any traceable degree of dark color, as contrasted with the idea of the Brazilians, who "see eight distinct degrees of color, with each corresponding to a distinct status." Such an idea of status, then, is useful in expressing in an abstract way the fact that all African Americans comprise a single group from the point of view of certain social organizations that are derived from ideologies of white supremacism. If the additional facts are considered—that "[e]very-one has more than one status" and that "[n]o status, in any social situation, encompasses the person"[5]—the idea of status provides an abstract way of expressing a fundamental contradiction within the idea of the black middle class, whereby a given person can seem to possess the characteristics of two status positions that may be in contradiction with each other or to possess a single status position that may be seen as middle-class from the African-American point of view and as lower-class from the white-supremacist point of view. The idea of a contradictory double status is related to the discussions of DuBois's idea of "twoness."

The second idea given in the encyclopedia entry, that status is scaler and refers to the relative inferiority and superiority of people, provides an abstract way of expressing the social organization of relative personal worth. The encyclopedia entry states that "formerly superiority of status could mean any sort of hierarchical ordering—of power, wealth, or honor—to many it now refers only to esteem, prestige, honor, respect, that is, to various forms of evaluation." Such an idea of status aids any discussion about the class position of Micheaux's work, since Micheaux's middle path always implies a *vertical* hazard, and since among the principle qualities at stake in Micheaux's films are social esteem and personal dignity. The attainment of social esteem and personal dignity—in a word, status—is a principal reason that Micheaux anchors many of his values in a middle class.

Though social esteem and personal dignity need not depend on each other directly and could, in fact, even be inversely related, they are interdependent in many cases. Indeed, if Karl Marx's idea in the economic and philosophical manuscripts of 1844 is accepted, that individual-man is always species-man and social-man—an idea that has been developed in several directions by Foucault, Althusser, Lacan, and others in the era of post-structuralism—then the idea of personal dignity as separate from social esteem can only be an abstraction and an illusion. In the philosophy of the Frankfurt School and in postmodernism as defined by Fredric Jameson, the personal and the social have become indivisible to a fault, making the individual subject, per se, difficult to find or discuss.

Class and the Classical

The narrowing of the meaning of the idea of status in the scaler sense to the realm of honor—the elimination of the realms of power and wealth—simplifies the terminology but introduces the problem of a terminology for the realms of power and wealth. What terms are to be used for general political or economic groups, on the one hand, or for the scaler hierarchies of power and wealth, on the other? And how is the relationship of power and wealth to status and honor to be understood?

One modern and one ancient semantic connection between the two terms "class" and "classic" each illustrate a fundamental and continuing connection between social status and economics. Amiri Baraka has said that part of Bessie Smith's popularity was her ability to make money (though this observation was not intended to denigrate her talent); Smith and the other classic blues singers did not sing "*strictly* to make money, but their immense popularity was the result of their *ability* to make money."[6] Classic blues, which was introduced primarily by the famous women blues singers, of whom Bessie Smith has been the most celebrated example, was the first significantly professional manifestation of the blues:

> Socially, classic blues and the instrumental styles that went with it represented the Negro's entrance into the world of professional entertainment and the assumption of the psychological imperatives that must accompany such a phenomenon. . . . [T]he wandering country blues singers of earlier times had from time to time casual audiences who would sometimes respond with gifts of food, clothes, or even money. But again it was assumed that *anybody* could sing the blues. . . . [Then] the artisan, the professional blues singer, appeared; blues-singing no longer had to be merely a passionately felt avocation, it could now become a way of making a living.[7]

The term "classic" is generally used today to denote work "of recognized value" that serves "as a standard of excellence" or that is "historically memorable"[8] for the society as a whole. In other words, it is a term of honor in the realm of social status. Socially, classic blues was a more esteemed blues than were primitive or folk blues. Baraka, however, has made it clear that the social esteem of classic blues has been associated partially—but inseparably—with the economic realm: "Classic blues suffered irreparably [in integrity] because to a certain extent its popularity was based on an *economic* principle."[9]

Equally instructive is the fact that the status implications of the *ancient* use of the term "classic" derive directly from the same linguistic roots as the idea of "class," and those roots also grow firmly in a culture of politics and economics. When the Latin grammarian Aulus Gellius wrote in the second century A.D. "*classicus . . . scriptor, non proletarius*" ["classical, not proletarian, writer"], he was making a distinction between different politico-economic levels of Roman citizenship, levels or *classes* formally established for the purposes of taxation by the Roman king Servius Tullius in the sixth century B.C. The term "classical" for Gellius referred to citizens with property and political rights, while "proletarian" referred to the lowest rank, whose only supposed contribution to society was to reproduce itself as a labor force. Gellius's classical writers had class, whereas his proletarian writers had no class, so to speak. In the second century, the implications of relative literary value were linked directly, by the term "classical," to politics (as in citizenship rights, according to Tullius, eight centuries before Gellius) and economics (private property and taxation, again Tullius). As Baraka has implied, the same analogy holds for the classic and folk blues in America twenty-four centuries after Tullius and eighteen centuries after Gellius; classic blues is linked by the term "class" to money and to what Baraka calls citizenship. Baraka has claimed that citizenship and money were granted by white America to Duke Ellington, for example, for his classical jazz, but not to the artists of the so-called primitive blues.[10]

Noting the three widely separated historical examples (Tullius, Gellius, and Baraka) of a deep relation between cultural values and political economic values, and recognizing the continuing triumph of capitalism since the Enlightenment, it is appropriate, when looking for a model of class structure, to turn to the writer whose discussions of the logic of capital were seminal: Karl Marx. The idea of class was, of course, central to most of Marx's work, though he put off formulating that central idea for a lifetime. The final chapter of *Capital,* entitled "The Classes," was to be Marx's summary statement on class, but he only wrote a page or so before he died. Ralf Dahrendorf has performed the intrepid scholarly task of finishing that chapter for Marx. Near the beginning of his study of class conflict in industrial society, Dahrendorf has inserted a ten-page essay called " 'The Classes': The unwritten 52nd chapter of Volume III of Marx's *Capital,*"[11] a construction using as much of Marx's own language as possible, as drawn from Marx's related writings. The ten pages are useful to establish a concept of class, but a summary will suffice here.

The Last Chapter of *Capital*

Marx stated that the problem was to reveal the laws of development of modern society and that fundamental to those laws was the motivating fact of class struggle based on antagonism between accumulated and direct labor. This antagonism had resulted in three large groupings of people, based on ownership of three large classes of elements necessary to production: labor, capital, and land. These divisions, as well as their derivative criteria (such as sources and relative amounts of income and division of labor), still did not constitute a model of class, since they were themselves a result of a structure of economic conditions that was still undescribed. Central to that structure was the idea of property as a changing but always specific relation of domination and subjection. The identification of the propertied and the propertyless and their mutual opposition was less important than was the identification of the specific way in which property was formed (mode of production). The bourgeois class, then, was formed by the use of wage labor for the creation and augmentation of capital as the private property of individuals. Classes were formed as a result of common material conditions based on relative position in the structure of production. Common material conditions alone, however, were not in themselves adequate to constitute classes—there must be community, national association, or political organization. That criterion was not necessarily easily met in the case of the wage laborers, since the class that owned the means of production tended to dominate not only the organization of the economy but also the administration of the political state and the whole superstructure of sentimental and intellectual life.

For Marx—since he was interested in understanding development rather than only status quo—class formation depended on conflict. A class was formed only in opposition to another class. The class interest that gave rise to class formation could exist before class formation; thus, one could say that a bourgeois class could stand opposed in class interest to a proletarian class, and vice versa, even before the bourgeois class organized politically and before the proletarian class defined itself. Since Marx considered conflicting interests to have been the driving force of social change, he was able to derive two large competing classes, the bourgeoisie and the proletariat. The competition between landowners and capitalists he was able to resolve by showing that more and more, in the industrial society of the mid-1800s, it had been the type of production rather than the type of property (land or capital) that had determined rank and influence. And of all the classes opposed to the bourgeoisie, only the proletariat had been potentially revolutionary; therefore, they had been the class that could most effect change, and other existing classes could be left out of account. Thus, Marx achieved his binary, dialectical model of class formation.

Opposing classes derived experience by fighting to maintain their interests in the economic sphere (wages and conditions). When fully mature, they became organized political actors attempting to effect legislation and, eventually, political parties. For Marx, class struggle was emphatically political. Only if (or when, as Marx believed) the proletariat overthrew the bourgeoisie would there be an end to political class conflict, since the proletariat could have been expected to establish a society in its own interest—that is, a society politically constituted from the point of view of non-owners of property.

Conclusion

Marx's analysis remains the most cogent basis for any critique of capitalism, and capitalism is arguably the dominant factor of modern life. Several ideas from Dahrendorf's description of Marx's idea of class comprise themes in this examination of Micheaux's films, including the distinction between accumulated (dead) labor and direct (living) labor; the idea of property (in the form of production values) as a relation of domination and subjection; the idea of class as a common material condition among individuals; and the perception of a connection between the owners of the means of production and the operations of the state and the cultural institutions that produce sentiment and intellectuality.

Appendix 2
Filmography

This short filmography is based on extensive, but not definitive, primary documentational research conducted by the author; his assistant, Carlos E. Gutiérrez; and by the collaborators on the more detailed filmography for the forthcoming book *Oscar Micheaux and His Circle*. At the time of this writing, those collaborators included Corey K. Creekmur, Charles Musser, Pearl Bowser, Charlene Regester, and J. Ronald Green. When that collaborative filmography appears, it will undoubtedly be the most complete and reliable to date; all previous filmographies are now seriously out of date.

Key to Annotations

1. Square brackets, [], contain information about each film's accessibility.
2. Arched brackets, {}, contain information about early documentary sources that were used to determine title, date, and other information about each film.
3. For ready reference, extant films are indicated by an asterisk before the film's date.

Dates, Titles, Annotations
Note: Titles are listed in chronological order.

Silent Films

1919 *The Homesteader* [not extant] {plot summary, Chicago *Defender,* 22 Feb. 1919, p. 14}.

*1920 *Within Our Gates* [Library of Congress, 35 mm; VHS, Smithsonian] {plot summary, Chicago *Defender,* 10 Jan. 1920}.

1920 *The Brute* [not extant] {advertisement, Chicago *Defender,* 14 Aug. 1920, p. 5; review, New York *Age,* 18 Sept. 1920, p. 6}.

*1920 *The Symbol of the Unconquered* [Museum of Modern Art] {advertisement, Chicago *Defender,* 2 Nov. 1920, p. 6; Micheaux letters in the George P. Johnson Collection show that this project had a working title of *The Wilderness Trail*}.

1921 *The Gunsaulus Mystery* [not extant] {review, New York *Age,* 16 Apr. 1921, p. 6; plot summary, New York *Amsterdam News,* 21 Oct. 1925, p. 7}.

1922 *The Dungeon* [not extant] {plot summary and review, Chicago *Defender,* 8 July 1922}.

1922 *The Virgin of Seminole* [not extant] {review and advertisement, Chicago *Defender,* 2 Dec. 1922}.

1922 *The Hypocrite* [not extant] {*Billboard,* 27 Jan. 1923; possibly unreleased and later incorporated as a film within the film *Deceit* (1923); see note for *Deceit*}.

1923 *Jasper Landry's Will* [not extant] {"Race Screen Star Becomes Popular New York Favorite," New York *Age*, 31 Mar. 1923; alternate titles mentioned in the literature are *Uncle Jasper's Will*, *Jaspar Landry's Will*, and *Joseph Lander's Will*}.

1923 *The Ghost of Tolston's Manor* [not extant] {*Billboard*, 5 May 1923, p. 50}.

1923 *A Fool's Errand* [not extant] {no definitive evidence of production; mention of its "being shot now at Roanoke and Norfolk, Va." in "Race Screen Star Becomes Popular New York Favorite," New York *Age*, 31 Mar. 1923; and mention of it being "ready" in *Billboard*, 5 May 1923}.

1923 *Deceit* [not extant] {Chicago *Defender*, 1 Dec. 1923; no evidence of actual release in 1923; probably released in 1927 as evidenced by an advertisement in the *Defender*, 18 June 1927, p. 9A; and an article on Evelyn Preer in the Pittsburgh *Courier*, 16 Apr. 1927 mentions it as "released this year." Some secondary sources state that the earlier film *The Hypocrite* was incorporated into *Deceit* as a film within the film.}.

1924 *Birthright* [not extant] {advertisement, New York *Age*, 12 Jan. 1924; review, *Billboard*, 19 Jan. 1924, p. 54; plot summary, Chicago *Defender*, 15 Mar. 1924, p. 6A}.

1924 *A Son of Satan* [not extant] {Norfolk *Journal and Guide*; review, Chicago *Defender*, 31 Jan. 1925}.

1924 *The House Behind the Cedars* [not extant] {review, Philadelphia *Tribune*, 13 Dec. 1924, pp. 1, 3}.

1925 *The Devil's Disciple* [not extant] {advertisement, Chicago *Defender*, 10 Oct. 1925, p. 8A; short review, New York *Amsterdam News*, 14 Oct. 1925, p. 7}.

*1925 *Body and Soul* [George Eastman House; Museum of Modern Art; VHS] {announcement of screening, New York *Age*, 11 Nov. 1925, pp. 5, 9}.

1926 *The Conjure Woman* [not extant] {publicity still, New York *Amsterdam News*, 14 July 1926}.

1926 *The Spider's Web* [not extant] {advertisement and plot summary, New York *Amsterdam News*, 5 Jan. 1927. This film was remade in the sound era as *The Girl from Chicago*, 1932.}

1927 *The Millionaire* [not extant] {still, advertisement, and plot summary, Chicago *Defender*, 19 Nov. 1927, pp. 9A, 10A}.

1928 *Thirty Years Later* [not extant] {advertisement, New York *Amsterdam News*, 14 Mar. 1928, p. 8; mention of an aberrant title, *Thirty Years After*, as "Micheaux's latest photoplay" in Pittsburgh *Courier*, 14 Apr. 1928}.

1928 *The Broken Violin* [not extant] {announcement that Micheaux is "about to release," Pittsburgh *Courier*, 25 Aug. 1928; notice of film having run at the Renaissance Theatre in New York "the entire week of September 16," Chicago *Bee*, ? Oct. 1928}.

1928 *Marcus Garland* [not extant] {announcement that Micheaux is "now photographing," Pittsburgh *Courier*, 25 Aug. 1928}.

1929 *Wages of Sin* [not extant] {no available primary document; date, cast, plot summary in Sampson, *Blacks in Black and White*, p. 133; Sampson, p. 12, mentions the film was halted by the Chicago censor board in 1929}.

1929 *When Men Betray* [not extant] {New York *Age*, 28 Sept. 1929, p. 6 (AFI Catalog); advertisement, Baltimore *Afro-American*, 3 Aug. 1929. This is possibly the retitled rerelease of the censored *Wages of Sin*}.

1930 *Easy Street* [not extant] {Pittsburgh *Courier*, 11 Oct. 1930, Pt. II, p. 8}.

Sound Films

1930 *A Daughter of the Congo* [not extant] {New York *Age*, 5 Apr. 1930; announcement of "Micheaux's latest," Pittsburgh *Courier*, 12 Apr. 1930}.

*1931 *The Exile* [16 mm, plus 35 mm fragments, Library of Congress; VHS] {article on financial reorganization of Micheaux's company and intent to shoot *The Exile*, Pittsburgh *Courier*, 10 Jan. 1931; reviews of New York premier, New York *Age*, p. 6, and Pittsburgh *Courier*, 23 May 1931}.

*1931 *The Darktown Revue* [35 mm, Library of Congress] {article mentions intent to shoot short subjects, Pittsburgh *Courier*, 10 Jan. 1931}.

*1932 *Veiled Aristocrats* [George Eastman House, 16 mm; fragment, Library of Congress, 35 mm; VHS] {*Film Daily*, 8 Jan. 1932, p. 2 (American Film Institute Catalog)}.

*1932 *Ten Minutes to Live* [Library of Congress, 35 mm, 16 mm; VHS] {Chicago *Defender*, 18 June 1932}.

*1932 *The Girl from Chicago* [Library of Congress, 16 mm; VHS] {credits on film print give 1932 date; could have been released in 1933}.

1933 *The Phantom of Kenwood* [not extant] {mentioned as "your last production" by Ralph Matthews in "An Open Letter to Mr. Oscar Micheaux," Baltimore *Afro-American*, 20 May 1933}.

1934 *Harlem After Midnight* [not extant] {Atlanta *Daily World*, 9 Sept. 1934; New York *Age*, 22 Dec. 1934; listed by numerous secondary sources, including amateur Micheaux archivist George P. Johnson}.

*1935 *Murder in Harlem*, or *Lem Hawkins' Confession* [extant as *Murder in Harlem*, Southwest Film/Video Archives at SMU, 35 mm; Phoenix Films, 16 mm and VHS] {short review of *Lem Hawkins' Confession*, Lou Layne, "Moon Over Harlem," New York *Age*, 25 May 1935, p. 4}.

1936 *Temptation* [not extant; fragment, trailers for a feature extant at Library of Congress] {Houston *Informer*, 27 Nov. 1937 [Sampson]}.

*1937 *Underworld* [Library of Congress, 16 mm] {Baltimore *Afro-American*, 29 May 1937 [Regester]}.

*1938 *God's Stepchildren* [Southwest Film/Video Archive; VHS] {Kansas City *Call*, 28 May 1928 [Sampson]}.

*1938 *Swing!* [Library of Congress, 16 mm; VHS] {Klotman and Sampson list the title without the exclamation point, which does appear in the title sequence of the film print itself}.

*1939 *Birthright* [first two reels missing, 35 mm, ¾″ Video, Library of Congress] {New York *Amsterdam News*, 6 Nov. 1937}.

*1939 *Lying Lips* [Library of Congress, 16 mm; VHS] {Sampson's and Library of Congress date; no primary documentation}.

*1940 *The Notorious Elinor Lee* [Library of Congress, 16 mm] {*Time,* 29 Jan. 1940 [AFI]}.

1948 *The Betrayal* [not extant] {New York *Amsterdam News,* 19 June 1948; review, New York *Times,* 26 June 1948}.

Appendix 3
Selections from the Black Press

This section is listed in chronological order. These annotated entries are selected from items that are relevant to Oscar Micheaux that were found in the African-American press by student research assistant Carlos Gutiérrez. This section is representative of press coverage; it is not definitive.

April 29, 1911. Chicago *Defender*. "Oscar Micheaux in City." This is the most exciting of all the entries found in the black press that bear on Micheaux's biography. It substantially confirms the "thinly veiled" events of the autobiographical novels, especially *The Conquest, The Homesteader,* and *The Wind from Nowhere*. The subheadings of this article read thus: "Seemed to Be in Family Mix-Up, Yet Would Not Speak; Seen With Dr. Daily at Father-in-Law's Door, But Neither He Nor the Doctor Were Admitted; Dr. Bryant (White) is Their Family Physician, Is Thought Is the Cause of the Lockout."

February 22, 1919. Chicago *Defender*. "'The Homesteader': Oscar Micheaux's Famous Story Makes Great Picture." A review of Micheaux's first film, the lead story of the "Drama and Movie" section of the paper. Describes production conditions and plot, as well as the "educational value" of the film. Much of the copy was probably supplied by Micheaux.

On the same page is a large advertisement for the film, with much descriptive information (for example, "A photo-play lasting almost three hours") and six photographs of the stars and of Micheaux.

March 1, 1919. Chicago *Defender*. "'The Homesteader': Oscar Micheaux's Great Production Booked at Vendome Theater." A review of the second run of the film, including information about censorship problems, the interventions on the film's behalf by leading African Americans such as Ida B. Wells Barnett, and a spirited description of the plot.

January 10, 1920. Chicago *Defender*. "'Within Our Gates.'" This review of Micheaux's second film discusses censorship problems and the plot of the film; it includes a long quotation from the film, which is of interest because the original titles have been lost. The titles in the print reconstructed by the Library of Congress and the Smithsonian Institution were adapted from a Spanish translation with the aid of historical evidence.

There is also a large advertisement for the film on the same page; it discusses the cost of the film and its thematic concerns of racial prejudice and African-American indignation.

Also on the same page is a review of a play called "The Brute," presented (by the Lafayette Players?) at the Avenue Theater. This information is significant because it documents the probable source of the property and the actors for Micheaux's next film, "The Brute."

March 6, 1920. New York *Age,* p. 6. "Colored Motion Pictures Are In Great Demand," by Lester A. Walton. Micheaux is mentioned in a generally optimistic context.

August 14, 1920. Chicago *Defender,* p. 5. Advertisement for Micheaux's third film, *The Brute.*

August [14?], 1920. Detroit *Plain Dealer?*. Advertisement for *The Brute.*

September 4, 1920. Chicago *Defender.* "The Brute." A review of Micheaux's third film, which was "creating a sensation and breaking attendance records at every place it is being shown," in this case, at the Atlas theater.

September 18, 1920. New York *Age.* "Sam Langford's Wallop Makes 'The Brute' A Screen Success," by Lester A. Walton. This long review may be one of the earliest hints of the kind of criticism Micheaux was to receive for his "negative" portrayals of African-American life. After stating his preference for positive subject matter, the reviewer praises several aspects of the film.

December 21, 1920. Baltimore *Afro-American.* Large advertisement for Micheaux's fourth film, *The Symbol of the Unconquered.*

?, 1921. *Competitor,* p. 61 (photocopy of this page with handwritten source information found in the "Oscar Micheaux" file at the Black Film Center/Archive at Indiana University). A review of *Symbol of the Unconquered* and a report on a speech given by Micheaux to the Associated Negro Press. The review emphasizes the film's stand against "passing for white" and "the Ku-Klux Klaners." It also reports the distribution of Micheaux's films in England, France, Italy, Spain, and in Africa and the "leading South American republics."

January 21, 1921. Philadelphia *Tribune.* "Synopsis 'The Symbol of the Unconquered.'" This plot description, probably written by Micheaux, mentions "a Negro . . . masquerading as white"; "a Negro[-]hating Squawman"; a leading woman who rides to the rescue and who, though mistaken for white, is later discovered to be black; and her black hero, who "becomes a millionaire."

Just above this synopsis is a small advertisement for the same film.

July 8, 1922. Chicago *Defender.* Under "Motion Picture News," a long review by D. Ireland Thomas of Micheaux's ninth film, *The Dungeon.* Thomas notes that the "advertising matter for this production has nothing to indicate that the feature is Colored, as the characters are very bright; in fact, almost white. 'The All-Star Colored Cast' that is so noticeable with nearly every Race production, is omitted on the cards and lithographs." Thomas then summarizes the plot.

1923. *Simms' Blue Book and Directory,* p. 80. An entry for the Micheaux Film Corporation under the state of Illinois lists the company's Chicago address, the locations of branch offices, the officers of the company, and the films released and forthcoming. It also includes a production still.

March 31, 1923. New York *Age,* p. 6. "Race Screen Star Becomes Popular New York Favorite." An article about Micheaux's discovery of Shingzie Howard on a stock-selling trip to Steelton, Pennsylvania. Several of Micheaux's films are mentioned.

January 25, 1924. Baltimore *Afro-American.* "'Birthright,'" by J. A. Jackson. One of the most detailed and best argued reviews to deal sympathetically with Micheaux's "negative" subject matter. Jackson states that Micheaux's (eleventh) film, *Birthright,* "was apparently not intended for colored audiences," since "the brutal frankness hurts, and some of the titles put a sting into the evening's entertainment." In spite of the sting, Jackson adds that "just because it has been so well done, everyone of us should see it." Jackson feels the main weight of the film is a critique of Jim Crow: "When anyone decries the migration, or asks why it is, tell them to see 'Birthright.' It will answer the question better than you possibly can."

February 9, 1924. Philadelphia *Tribune*, p. 14. "'Birthright,'" by J. A. Jackson. A reprint of the above review of January 25, 1924, in the Baltimore *Afro-American*.

November 22, 1924. Philadelphia *Tribune*. "'Birthright' at Royal Theatre Draws Praise[:] Picture Presents Possibilities In Cinema Field If Properly Nourished." A very positive review of the film, with praise for the owners of the theater for showing it. The reviewer (Micheaux may have supplied this copy, judging from the "puffed" writing style) feels that this film and screening bode well for black cinema.

November 29, 1924. Philadelphia *Tribune*, p. 3. "The Royal Theatre. Film 'Birthright' Causes Much Comment," by Walley Peele. The reviewer reports that among some positive comments on the film, there were many that were negative, "the main exception [to the film] being taken to several sub-titles and the broad use of the word 'nigger.'" The reviewer takes the position that the film is educational and that, though sometimes painful, it tells the truth and needs to be seen so that the viewers can contribute to making conditions better. The last line of the review is a plea for concern and cooperation among African Americans, using poor whites as an analogous case of class struggle: "Wherever you find a low white, they are born companions [. . .] and cannot get along without each other even in the land where race prejudice is the predominating influence."

December 13, 1924. Philadelphia *Tribune*, pp. 1, 3. "'The House Behind the Cedars' Shown at Royal Sunday: Producer, On Hand, Makes Statement Explaining His Aims; Invited Guests Impressed." This report—on a special presentation, by Micheaux, of his twelfth film—is complimentary.

This article also includes a fairly long, important formal statement, drafted by Micheaux, explaining the difficult conditions of African-American film production, the importance of facing difficult truths, and the need for constructive but fair and informed criticism. That statement appeared over Micheaux's signature in several black newspapers; it is often quoted and is reprinted in full in Henry Sampson's book *Blacks in Black and White* (pp. 53–55). One significant typographical error occurs in Sampson's reprint—on page 54: "He is united in his themes" should read "He is limited in his themes" (cf. *Tribune*, also *Courier* entry immediately below).

December 13, 1924. Pittsburgh *Courier*. "Oscar Micheaux Writes on Growth of Race in Movie Field: Producer Can Succeed Only With Our Aid: Tells of Struggles and Hurtful Criticism of Biased Writers Concerning 'Birthright.'" This is the *Courier*'s printing of the same statement by Micheaux, which is discussed immediately above.

December 27, 1924. Chicago *Defender*, Billy Booster. Discusses the problems of black film production, recommending the creation of a star system and using Micheaux's film, *The Brute*, as a positive example. This article was probably inspired by the wide circulation of Micheaux's statement of December 13, discussed above.

February 7, 1925. Chicago *Defender*. "Motion Picture News," by D. Ireland Thomas. Reports that Seaborn Griggs, operating from the Strand theater in Roanoke, had become the exchange manager for Micheaux's films.

February 14, 1925. Chicago *Defender.* "Motion Picture News," by D. Ireland Thomas. Advises where one can write to various black film companies, including Micheaux's in Roanoke. Also responds to a letter of inquiry from a juggler who proposes to make extra money on his travels through the use of race movies. Thomas suggests it would be difficult, since "[g]ood new 'Race' features are very hard to get—almost impossible."

February 14, 1925. Pittsburgh *Courier.* "Paul Robeson, Miss Russell Star In Micheaux's Latest Movie Film, 'Body and Soul.'" Reports Micheaux's private screening, in Washington, D.C., of *The House Behind the Cedars* and Micheaux's recent completion of *Body and Soul.* Also notes that Micheaux "is going abroad in April . . . to visit London and all of the larger cities on the continent, probably Cairo, and several Russian cities . . . to obtain world distribution of Micheaux films."

December 19, 1925. Pittsburgh *Courier,* p. 9. "In the Theatrical World: Musical and Dramatic Review, Radios, Records, Vaudeville and Movies," by Sylvester Russell. One section of this collection of items is a discussion of Micheaux's "race antagonisms," and it reports that Micheaux has changed his policy since his early days and after his long stay in the South. Russell approves of Micheaux's omission of "objectionable race features" and celebrates the popularity of Micheaux's new film, *The Devil's Disciple.* Russell states that Micheaux has acquired "all the features of artifice in scenario and scenic calculations to which the white man has resorted." He also reports that *The House Behind the Cedars* has been readvertised because of the newsworthiness of the Rhinelander interracial marriage. He reports that Swan Micheaux is about to leave Chicago to open a Micheaux film exchange in New York.

January 30, 1926. Pittsburgh *Courier.* "White Picture Films Barred Abroad and Fail In The South." Notes that white films using "colored actors showing old race tradition[s]" were failing in the South, while "Micheaux pictures are going big." Notes also that (white) American films had been barred in Poland.

February 27, 1926. Pittsburgh *Courier.* "At Louisville Theatres." Notice of a screening of *Body and Soul* at the Palace.

July 31, 1926. Baltimore *Afro-American,* p. 5. "The Spotlight: Photo-Plays: Colored Movies." Complains that the worst enemy of the race movie is its fan, who accepts white standards. Advises fans that to "bear with such men as Oscar Micheaux and other pioneers today means bigger and better race pictures tomorrow."

October 2, 1926. Pittsburgh *Courier.* "Theatre Building Activity Gaining," by Geo. Perry. Perry analyzes the problem black film producers such as Micheaux have in raising production capital. "White producers are able to acquire advance production capital upon the strength of signed contracts with first run theatres." Perry notes that deals are progressing in several cities for black ownership of theaters.

January 29, 1927. Baltimore *Afro-American,* p. 7. "Along The White Way," by Maybelle Robinson Chew. Micheaux's film *The Spider's Web* is reviewed and found "modern and thrilling." Plot and actors are discussed.

January 29, 1927. Baltimore *Afro-American,* p. 7. "Royal: 'Spider's Web.'" This review of *The Spider's Web* appears immediately below the review discussed above. It welcomes the appearance of Evelyn Preer, but says the real star is Grace Smyth, whose dancing and vigor are "the pictures' [*sic*] one bright spot." The reviewer complains of Preer's perpetual frown and forced smiles. This mixed review concludes that the film's ballroom scene "is the most elaborate thing ever done by a producer of colored pictures, yet the picture is not without its faults."

January 29, 1927. Baltimore *Afro-American*, p. 7. "Local Folks In Micheaux Film." This story appears beside the two reviews discussed above and reports on Micheaux's solicitation, screen testing, and employment of two Baltimore citizens in *The Spider's Web*. This article is evidence of one of Micheaux's practices of involving local people in his productions; no doubt, he counted on articles such as this one to help increase local interest in the films when they were screened.

April 16, 1927. Pittsburgh *Courier*, sec. 2, p. 1. "Evelyn Preer Ranks First As Stage and Movie Star," by Floyd J. Calvin. Preer is called "a pioneer in the cinema world for colored women," primarily because of her work with Micheaux. It is reported that Preer considers Micheaux's *The Devil's Disciple* to be her best work. She also predicts (unrealistically and unaccountably) that the best chances for black women will come with white directors, "who realize we have talent and will employ us just as they will other talent."

June 11, 1927. Pittsburgh *Courier*, sec. 2, p. 1. "Evelyn Preer Nearly Drowned In Realistic Movie Scene," by Evelyn Preer. This is the first of a three- or four-part autobiographical series by Preer. She describes the production of the first film she was in, Micheaux's *The Homesteader*, which she says was filmed in Chicago and Iowa (actually, probably South Dakota). Her account of the shooting of *Birthright* in Roanoke includes her "near drowning," which she does not blame on Micheaux, who wanted to use a dummy for the scene. Stories like this are in the same genre as those told by Lillian Gish about the filming of the scenes on the ice floes in Griffith's *Way Down East* (1924).

June 18, 1927. Pittsburgh *Courier*. "My Thrills in the Movies," by Evelyn Preer. Anecdotes about Micheaux's films, *Within Our Gates* and *The Brute*.

June 25, 1927. Pittsburgh *Courier*. "My Thrills in the Movies," by Eveyln Preer. Anecdotes about Micheaux's film *Deceit*.

April 14, 1928. Pittsburgh *Courier*. "In Movies." A small notice of Mable Kelly's casting by Micheaux in "Thirty Years After" (*Thirty Years Later*, 1928).

August 25, 1928. Pittsburgh *Courier*. "New Movie To Be Out Soon." Notice of the release of Micheaux's *The Broken Violin* and of the shooting of *Marcus Garland*.

April 12, 1930. Pittsburgh *Courier*, p. 7. "Micheaux Produces Another," by Geraldyn Dismond. A long notice on the production and release of *A Daughter of the Congo*.

January 10, 1931. Pittsburgh *Courier*. "Micheaux Film Corporation Is Re-Organized: All-Talking Pictures Will Be Produced On More Expensive Scale: 'The Exile,' First of His Pictures, Will Be Started At Metropolitan Studios January 15—Noted Stage Stars Engaged." This is an important article regarding the financing by white businessmen of Micheaux's sound films. It mentions that there will be no stock offerings and that the officers are Micheaux, president; Frank Schiffman, vice president and secretary; and Leo Bracher, treasurer. The article criticizes the white talkies *Hearts in Dixie* and *Hallelujah* for portraying blacks as southern in their "native state" even after four million blacks had migrated. It reports that Micheaux will do short subjects as fillers for Broadway openings and possible road shows of his feature films (*The Darktown Revue* was produced in 1931, the only short subject in Micheaux's corpus).

January 10, 1931. New York *Age*, p. 6. "Lafayette Theatre Heads Buy Majority Stock In Oscar Micheaux Film Co." Same basic information as the January 10 *Courier* story above.

May 23, 1931. New York *Age*. "'The Exile' At Lafayette Theatre," by W. E. Clark. Reports on the opening to capacity crowds of this first Micheaux talking film. Clark's review is critical of its many "obvious faults," but considers it to be Micheaux's best picture. Mentions that the exterior view of "the Charles M. Schwab mansion on Riverside drive" is used to represent "a notorious house in the Windy City." Clark judges that "it is doubtful if the cabaret scenes by Leonard Harper will get pa[st] the censors of the other states."

May 20, 1933. Baltimore *Afro-American*. "An Open Letter to Mr. Oscar Micheaux," by Ralph Matthews. A long critique, both general and detailed, of Micheaux's career with numerous, mostly negative, suggestions. Matthews admires Micheaux's sincerity and tenacity but abhors his "jumbly-fumbly" technique and his choice of actors. Finds actors too studied and unspontaneous, too jaundiced: "the night club life writes too plainly its lines upon the faces of most of your stars. Their freshness is gone, and the cruel camera exposes all of their blemishes to the naked eye." Castigates Micheaux's casting of Marie-Dressler types as lovers, saying Hollywood is "too smart" to do that. Advises Micheaux to avoid stories about low life and about millionaires. Suggests using "unsophisticated girls for [his] juveniles." Recommends approaching "real" black writers such as Hurston, Richardson, and Lawson, as well as stories from newspapers about real life, and avoiding sermonizers and social justice crusaders—"There are more themes than the ever-present struggle between the races." Finally, he invites Micheaux to use newspapermen like himself: "Let us in on your stars. We help you ram them down the public's throat. We'll help you make them Garbos and Gables, Bennetts and Barrymores. Movie stars at best are just lucky nit-wits coated with hooey. Why shouldn't we lift a few brown-skinned damsels from the dish pans and scrub buckets and cover them with tinsel?"

May 25, 1935. New York *Age*, p. 4, "Moon Over Harlem," by Lou Layne. Layne complains of the insistent use of the "n" word in Micheaux's film *Lem Hawkins' Confession* (also known as *Murder in Harlem*): "Alex Lovejoy is pictured writing a note being dictated by his employer, who uses the term 'Negro.' Four times Lovejoy made it 'nigger,' in the last instance actually spelling the word so that there might be no mistake." This is not an accurate description of the scene that survives in *Murder in Harlem*, a scene analyzed in detail in chapter 10 above. It does, however, represent the spirit of that scene in that the Lovejoy character is taking his employer's use of "Negro" as a euphemism for the derogatory "n" word that racist whites generally use. Layne states angrily that Micheaux is indulging in cheap humor at the expense of the race: "Not only has he shown poor judgment in his attempt at humor, but a conference with his lawyer will show him that he's left himself open to a suit for libel. Any citizen held up to ridicule on the printed page—(of which the movie screen is but a subsidiary)—is justified in filing such a suit, and if the race is not so justified, there is no justice." This is a fair sample of the criticism Micheaux faced for his "negative images." The analysis in chapter 10 above shows that liberating rather than ridiculing the race was Micheaux's intention; this scene actually should be read as a protest rather than an exploitation of racist epithet.

July 25, 1936. Baltimore *Afro-American*, "'Green Pastures' in the Movies Is Called Insult to 'De Lawd': AFRO Critic Says Oscar Micheaux, Harlem's Shoestring Producer, Could Have Turned out a Better Job; Race's Supposed 'Simplicity' Given as Excuse for Making Cheap, Shoddy Production," by Ralph Matthews. The subtitles of this article convey the gist of it.

November 6, 1937. New York *Amsterdam News*. "Onlookers See Actor Pinched On Movie Plot." Several paragraphs of description of Micheaux's shooting—on Union Hall Street between 109th and 110th avenues [*sic*] in Harlem—of some scenes from *The Birthright*, including Micheaux's handling of some missed lines and resultant retakes.

September 30, 1939. New York *Amsterdam News*. "All-Colored Movie Field Has Weak Foundations; Producers Hit Each other; Additional Ills Told: History of Negro Films Described/What Fans Want Again Stressed," by Dan Burley. An analysis of the problems of black cinema, which is characterized as being in its "second infancy." To the much discussed failings of "subject matter and talent" is added "a weak foundation," meaning the lack of an African-American business infrastructure to support the "independent producers, agents, magnates and impresarios, each hoeing his own row and taking pot shots at the . . . other fellows." Micheaux figures heavily and positively in the description of the history of race movies (though the early film *Pride of His Race* is misattributed to him) and also in the discussion of the qualities needed in cinema contemporary to this article:

> "Lying Lips" and other recent Oscar Mischaux [*sic*] pictures are being nixed by Harlem theatres in favor of pictures made by white concerns. . . . [E]very theatre-goer and performer should squawk to the high heavens to nip in the bud a situation that may have ugly developments. . . .
> Mischaux [*sic*]-made pictures are said to have a wider appeal than those made by the white concerns. Mischaux, it has been pointed out, puts what Negroes want to see in his pictures, while his rivals shy away from Mischaux subjects and suffer losses. Colored audiences want sex and glamor in their talkies. . . .
> . . . while the Paul Robeson pictures made in England have been technically tops . . . , their appeal to colored audiences have [*sic*] suffered because colored audiences don't want to see the stevedore and roustabout roles Robeson portrays. The Negro knows he's identified with stevedores, roustabouts, ne'er-do-wells and vagabonds and consequently doesn't like it when he's called on to pay his cash to see it.

Though Burley is calling for "sex and glamor," he is also implying that Micheaux's focus on middle-class main characters is more attractive than the focus on working-class characters in Robeson's technically superior films. These comments highlight the dilemma of financial independence (black ownership and authorship) vs. technical quality (production values), and they suggest the minefield of race and class issues that Micheaux had to cross in the marketing of his films. This review is positive, supporting Micheaux's independence and attractive subject matter; other reviews are negative, lambasting his technical compromises and negative images.

June 26, 1948. New York *Times*. "First All-Negro Film at Mansfield," by T. M. P. This review of Micheaux's last film, though not from the black press, is quoted in full here, minus film credits:

> Just for the record, and that alone, "The Betrayal," first all-Negro motion picture to have Broadway première, now is being shown twice daily on a reserved-seat basis at the Mansfield Theatre. As the author, director and producer, Oscar Micheaux set his sights high, tackling a purposeful and multifarious theme which requires slightly more than three hours to expound. The story develops in painful detail the marital woes of an enterprising young Negro who develops an agricultural empire in South Dakota. The film also contemplates at some considerable

length the relationship between Negroes and whites as members of the community as well as partners in marriage.

Mr. Micheaux, unfortunately, does not present his ideas clearly and the picture is often confusing. Some of the most dramatic lines and sequences are so gauche as to provoke embarrassed laughter. "The Betrayal" is further handicapped by sporadically poor photography and consistently amateurish performances and direction.

Mar ?, 1951. Pittsburgh *Courier*. "Movie Pioneer Dies Suddenly: Oscar Micheaux, Producer-Author." This notice of Micheaux's death is quoted in full here:

> Charlotte, N.C.—Death last Sunday claimed well-known Negro movie producer pioneer Oscar Micheaux, who died in a Charlotte hospital following a short illness.
>
> Mr. Micheaux was recognized as the first Negro motion picture director and producer to make a movie over three reels long with an all-Negro cast.
>
> MADE 44 MOVIES
>
> His initial picture was the "Homesteader," which was first shown in 1918. Since that time, Mr. Micheaux was credited with having produced forty-four of the eighty-two Negro pictures made.
>
> He was author of "The Wind From Nowhere," "The Case of Mrs. Wingate" and "The Story of Dorothy Stanfield."
>
> The noted movie producer became ill in Charlotte while here selling books as a part of a proposed tour of the South.
>
> BODY TO KANSAS
>
> Mr. Micheaux's body was shipped Tuesday night to his home in Great Bend, Kan. He is survived by his widow, Mrs. Alice Micheaux, 48 Morningside Drive, New York City, where the couple resided.

Notes

Introduction

1. For detailed reviews of the critical literature on Micheaux over the past quarter of a century, see Charlene Regester, "The Misreading and Rereading of African American Filmmaker Oscar Micheaux," *Film History*, Vol. 7, No. 4, 1995, and J. Ronald Green, "The Reemergence of Oscar Micheaux," in *Oscar Micheaux and His Circle*, ed. Pearl Bowser, Jane Gaines, and Charles Musser, forthcoming.

2. *Visions of Uplift: The Films of Oscar Micheaux* (J. Ronald Green, forthcoming from Indiana University Press) will contain a more detailed version of the biographical sketch below. For biography, see also Betti Carol VanEpps-Taylor, *Oscar Micheaux . . . Dakota Homesteader, Author, Pioneer Film Maker: A Biography* (Rapid City, S.D.: Dakota West Books, 1999).

3. Oscar Micheaux, *The Conquest: A Story of a Negro Pioneer* (1913; reprint, Lincoln: University of Nebraska Press, 1994).

4. When homesteaders failed to "prove up," to make good on their land according to the government requirements, which called for certain improvements and for minimum physical residency on the land, the homesteads could be sold as "relinquishments" to other would-be homesteaders. That is how Micheaux got his first land.

5. According to historian Lee Arlie Barry of Gregory, South Dakota, Micheaux would walk fifty miles to these several homesteads, often barefoot by preference.

6. See chapter 1.

7. The George P. Johnson collection is available on microfilm at other research libraries.

8. Kevin K. Gaines, *Uplifting the Race: Black Leadership, Politics, and Culture in the Twentieth Century* (Chapel Hill: University of North Carolina Press, 1996), p. 15.

9. Gaines, *Uplifting the Race,* p. 17.

10. The terms "lower class" and "upper class" are used throughout this study to denote categories that are distinguishable from "middle class," a vexed term defined at the beginning of chapter 6. These categories are notoriously complex (see the definitional essay on class in appendix 1), but in this study they are defined primarily by economic condition and life expectations and are not inherently derogatory or complimentary.

11. Wexman, "The Family on the Land: Race and Nationhood in Silent Westerns," in *The Birth of Whiteness: Race and the Emergence of U.S. Cinema*, ed. Daniel Bernardi (New Brunswick, N.J.: Rutgers University Press, 1996), p. 151.

12.   Clyde R. Taylor, *The Mask of Art: Breaking the Aesthetic Contract—Film and Literature* (Bloomington: Indiana University Press, 1998), pp. 184–85.

1. Micheaux vs. Griffith

1.   *The Romance of Happy Valley* was released January 26, 1919; *Within Our Gates* was begun soon after the Chicago race riots of July 27–30, 1919, was finished before November, and then faced two months of censorship negotiations before its release in January 1920 ("'Within Our Gates,'" Chicago *Defender,* January 10, 1920). The article on the film in the *Defender* emphasized its "silent indignation," saying that the film "tells it all" in its attack on "prejudice, lynching, and 'concubinage.'" There can be little doubt that the film was made in anger, and given Micheaux's voracious viewing and reading habits and given the explicit vendetta within the black community against D. W. Griffith, there can be little doubt that the title of *Within Our Gates* was "signifying" on Griffith's epigraph for *The Romance of Happy Valley.*

2.   Prints (in excellent condition) of both *Within Our Gates* and *Symbol of the Unconquered* have been rediscovered in the past decade.

3.   Quoted in John R. Alley, "The Virginia State Board of Motion Picture Censors vs. Micheaux Film Corporation: An Interpretive Summary," a commentary drawn from Alley's research in progress on film censorship in Virginia, an excerpt of which was distributed at the Virginia Festival of American Film in 1991.

4.   "Jull Jones" is undoubtedly a misprint of Juli Jones, a professional alias and pen name for the path-breaking black filmmaker, film critic, agent, and actor William Foster.

5.   Chicago *Defender,* May 22, 1915.

6.   See Thomas Cripps, *Slow Fade to Black: The Negro in American Film, 1900–1942* (New York: Oxford University Press, 1977, 1993), chapter 3, and index entries under *Birth of a Nation* and *Birth of a Race.*

7.   He was also forced to do so more and more over the course of his career because of the pressures of censorship. This important observation, that Micheaux's films are progressively less overt and more covert in their references to white injustices to blacks (more "signifying," in the sense of Henry Louis Gates's study *The Signifying Monkey*), was formulated and brought to my attention by Cinda Becker in a student paper.

8.   Ed Guerrero, *Framing Blackness: The African American Image in Film* (Philadelphia: Temple University Press, 1993).

9.   Other forms of inclusiveness might be extrapolated from this principled approach, such as sexual preference and other forms of ethnic prejudice. Micheaux seldom touched on issues of sexual preference, however, and his remarks on other, less Eurocentric ethnic groups are confusing. He makes disparaging remarks about the lack of social and economic contributions by American Indians in comparison with African Americans (see his novel *The Conquest*), but he steadfastly defends the right of Jewish immigrants to control Hollywood and to drive him and other African Americans out of busi-

ness if they are capable of it (see his novel *The Story of Dorothy Stanfield*)—in other words, he refused the easy choice of anti-Semitism as a handy excuse for his own eventual business failure. Also, in mitigation of the disparaging remarks about Indians, Lee Barry, a local historian of Micheaux and of the Rosebud territory of South Dakota, reported at the Micheaux Film Festival in 1998 that Micheaux was friendly with and sympathetic to the local Indians.

10. The unusual choice of a "feminized" last name, Vivian, for the hero of this film was pointed out by Joseph Wlodarz in a student paper.

11. See Michael Rogin's discussion of Griffith's replacement of the vivacious, dark, and modern Blanche Sweet with the fragile, white, and old-fashioned Lillian Gish as a way of masking his own fears: Rogin, "'The Sword Became a Flashing Vision': D. W. Griffith's *The Birth of a Nation*," *Representations*, No. 9, Winter 1985, pp. 158–65.

12. The terms "bourgeois" and "aristocratic" are used throughout this essay somewhat loosely owing to (1) the confusion of the postbellum southern economy, in which a virtually feudal system was being forced into capitalism, and (2) the confusion of Griffith's attempt to import an aristocratic, feudal, rural ideal into a capitalist, industrial, urban art form. Griffith's propagation of that ideal worked for a while, because his audience was making the same transition he was. This study cannot do justice to the problems presented by those terms.

13. Not only did Micheaux begin his artistic career by writing novels, but throughout his life, writing served as a sideline and as a source of stories for his films.

14. Oscar Micheaux, *The Conquest*, p. 154.

15. Oscar Micheaux, *The Homesteader* (1917; reprint, Lincoln: University of Nebraska Press, 1994). Though *The Homesteader* was Micheaux's third novel, it was the second of several novels on the subject of the Scotch girl; Micheaux made a film of the same title from *The Homesteader*, the first of several films on the same subject. The later films included a sound version of *The Homesteader*, titled *The Exile*, which was made in 1931; this film is extant and is discussed elsewhere in this study.

16. Oscar Micheaux, *The Forged Note* (Lincoln, Neb.: Western Book Supply Co., 1915), pp. 24–25.

17. William Rothman, *The "I" of the Camera: Essays in Film Criticism, History, and Aesthetics* (New York: Cambridge University Press, 1988), pp. 16–17.

18. Theodore Dreiser, *Sister Carrie* (1900; reprint, New York: New American Library, 1962), p. 90.

19. Miriam Hansen, *Babel and Babylon: Spectatorship in American Silent Film* (Cambridge, Mass.: Harvard University Press, 1991), p. 228.

20. Hansen, *Babel and Babylon*, pp. 225–26.

21. Page numbers for *The Forged Note* will be included in the body of the text in this chapter.

22. *The Forged Note*, pp. 441–43.

23. It is true, however, that Micheaux's independent approach to business fits a

pattern described in an early work of African-American sociology, a pattern in which "Negroes form few partnerships and . . . those formed are rarely of more than two persons." The effect of the reluctance or inability to form "[c]ooperative or corporate business enterprises" had "its most telling effect in preventing accumulation of capital for large undertakings" that could compete with the large corporate entities of white America. (DuBois's novel *The Quest of the Silver Fleece* is in large part a muckraking novel about a white-supremacist syndicate that corners the market in cotton and cheats the small African-American entrepreneurs, including the protagonists of the novel, making them virtual slaves.) The black sociologist suggested that small businesses should be able to combine and build wealth and power for African Americans: "For example, the group of 50 barber shops or of 36 grocers would each support a jobber if they pooled their patronage" (George E. Haynes, *The Negro at Work in New York City: A Study in Economic Progress* [New York: Columbia University Press, 1912], in Herbert Aptheker, *A Documentary History of the Negro People in the United States, 1910–1932: From the Emergence of the N.A.A.C.P. to the Beginning of the New Deal* [Secaucus, N.J.: Citadel, 1973], pp. 44–45).

24. Miriam Hansen's analysis of Griffith's version of the rescue fantasy is pertinent here as an extreme form of the male rescue of the working woman. Hansen's "working woman" performs the quintessential "women's work," prostitution: "By invoking the Magdalen tradition, Griffith might have hoped to legitimize the film's interest in prostitution and prostitutes, both Babylonian and Modern. . . . Yet more important, the figure of the penitent Magdalen provides an interpretive parallel for the fate of the Friendless One [Miriam Cooper in *Intolerance*] and thus elucidates the rescue scenario of the Modern narrative" (Hansen, *Babel and Babylon*, p. 225).

    This form of the rescue fantasy, which fits Griffith's material so well, in straight and inverted forms, is almost certainly irrelevant to Micheaux's rescues.

25. Harold Bloom, *The Anxiety of Influence: A Theory of Poetry* (New York: Oxford University Press, 1973), chapter 1. Eric Hobsbawm and Terence Ranger, *The Invention of Tradition* (Cambridge, UK: Cambridge University Press, 1983), chapter 1.

26. Misprision as resistance—readings "against the grain" of hegemony and perverse readings of classical and mainstream texts—is often advocated in the field of cultural studies as a way of making a place for marginalized worldviews, such as African-American, feminist, and queer worldviews.

27. DuBois, *Silver Fleece*, pp. 433–34; emphasis in original.

28. J. Milton Waldron, J. Anderson Taylor, and W. J. Howard, "'Doomed to Destruction,'" August 13, 1910, in Aptheker, *Documentary History*, p. 16.

29. There is a narrative flaw in the film in that Sylvia seemed to have no qualms about her engagement to Conrad Delbert, the thoroughly upright middle-class fiancé from whom she becomes estranged at the beginning of the film. Joseph Wlodarz has pointed out in classroom discussion, however, that the *nature* of that estrangement—a mistakenly perceived sexual transgression by her with a white man—resonates perfectly with her later problem with Dr.

Vivian. It also rhymes with the plots of the DuBois and Micheaux novels discussed above.

30. See especially *Underworld*, but also *The Exile*. An important unpublished student paper by Joseph Wlodarz identifies and discusses the feminization of Micheaux's heroes and the masculinization of his heroines. As noted earlier, Wlodarz mentions, among more substantive points, that "Vivian" is an unusually feminized name for an American hero.

31. Such "lateness" is still visible in the high incidence of light-skinned African Americans in America, a condition emblematized in *Within Our Gates* by Dr. Vivian himself (among others).

32. Kevin Gaines's discussions of the role of nativist and anti-immigrant ideas in African-American uplift is informative; see "Immigration" and "Nativism" in the index of *Uplifting the Race*.

33. Unofficial translation of the Spanish of *La Negra*. The print of *Within Our Gates*, distributed on video by the Smithsonian Institution, reads: "And you, Sylvia, have been thinking deeply about this, I know—but unfortunately your thoughts have been warped."

   "In spite of your misfortunes, you will always be a patriot—and a tender wife. I love you."

   "And a little while later we see that Sylvia understood that perhaps Dr. Vivian was right after all."

2. Micheaux's Class Position

1. Shelby Steele, *The Content of Our Character: A New Vision of Race in America* (New York: St. Martin's Press, 1990), pp. 95, 98.

2. Steele, *Content*, pp. 98–99.

3. Melvin Van Peebles, *Sweet Sweetback's Baadasssss Song* (New York: Lancer Books, 1971).

4. "The Violence of Public Art: *Do the Right Thing*," in W. J. T. Mitchell, *Picture Theory: Essays on Verbal and Visual Representation* (Chicago: University of Chicago Press, 1994), p. 392.

5. Paula J. Masood, "Cities in Black: Cinematic Representations of the African American Urbanscape," forthcoming.

6. Mark Reid, "Commodification, Reception and Indigestion: Simulacra in *Do the Right Thing*," unpublished paper read at the Screen Studies Conference, Glasgow, Scotland, 1991.

7. William Julius Wilson, *The Declining Significance of Race: Blacks and Changing American Institutions* (Chicago: University of Chicago Press, 1978), p. ix. Wilson includes the following as a footnote to the above quotation: "This conception of 'class' is a modified version of Max Weber's explication of the concept. See *From Max Weber: Essays in Sociology*, edited, with an introduction, by Hans Gerth and C. Wright Mills (New York: Oxford University Press, 1946), pp. 181–82."

8. Gaines, "Fire and Desire: Race, Melodrama, and Oscar Micheaux," in *Black American Cinema*, ed. Manthia Diawara (New York: Routledge, 1993), p. 65.

9. Amiri Baraka, *Blues People: Negro Music in White America* (New York: William Morrow and Co., 1963), p. 123.

10. Martha Rosler, "Video: Shedding the Utopian Moment," in *Illuminating Video: An Essential Guide to Video Art* (New York: Aperture and Bay Area Video Coalition, 1990), p. 50.

11. Guerrero, *Framing Blackness*, p. 203.

12. See discussion of Spike Lee's *Malcolm X* in Guerrero, *Framing Blackness*, and in J. Ronald Green's review of Guerrero in *Film Quarterly*, Summer 1995, and in chapter 14 of this volume.

13. Green, "Twoness," in Diawara, *Black American Cinema*, p. 34.

14. When Gaines states that motion picture economics have historically thrust filmmakers, no matter what their class origins, into the bourgeois class, she cites Paul Willemen's 1987 essay on Third Cinema ("The Third Cinema Question: Notes and Reflections," in *Questions of Third Cinema*, ed. Paul Willemen and Jim Pines [London: BFI Publishing, 1989]). Willemen's essay and other essays on Third Cinema are useful for demonstrating the difficulties of drawing the bourgeois-class line. Willemen's book also can be suggestive of the closeness and relevance of Micheaux's concerns and accomplishments to the reality of progressive artists today.

There is no need to concede, however, as Willemen has done (and as many criticisms of Micheaux have implied) that the work of Third Cinema is "not particularly exemplary in the sense of displaying stylistically innovative devices," except in the sense in which Willemen finishes that idea—"devices to be imitated by others who wish to avoid appearing outdated." The possible trivial (e.g., outdatedness) and non-trivial (e.g., class or ethnic provenance) significance of stylistic innovation can be separated and the non-trivial aspects explored and assessed.

3. Twoness and Micheaux's Style

1. W. E. B. DuBois, *The Souls of Black Folk*, in *Three Negro Classics* (New York: Avon, 1965), pp. 214–15.

2. Thomas Cripps, *Slow Fade to Black* (London: Oxford University Press, 1977).

3. Donald Bogle, *Toms, Coons, Mulattoes, Mammies, and Bucks* (New York: Viking, 1973); Daniel J. Leab, *From Sambo to Superspade: The Black Experience in Motion Pictures* (Boston: Houghton Mifflin, 1975).

4. Cripps, *Slow Fade*, p. 3.

5. Cripps, *Slow Fade*, p. 7.

6. Cripps, "Oscar Micheaux: The Story Continues," in Diawara, *Black American Cinema*, pp. 74–75; Jesse Algernon Rhines, *Black Film/White Money* (New Brunswick, N.J.: 1996), pp. 83, 86, and passim.

7. Nelson George, *The Death of Rhythm and Blues* (New York: Pantheon, 1988), pp. 57, 58.

8. As this manuscript was nearing completion, Robert L. Johnson, the chairman and founder of Black Entertainment Television, announced a plan "to start a venture to make low-budget films with black stars, financed and produced by African-Americans and aimed largely at the black urban market" (see Geraldine Fabrikant, "BET to Establish a Film Unit Aimed at Black Urban Market," *New York Times,* July 10, 1998).

9. bell hooks, "Representations of Whiteness in the Black Imagination," in hooks, *Black Looks: Race and Representation* (Boston: South End, 1992); Carol J. Clover, *Men, Women, and Chain Saws: Gender in the Modern Horror Film* (Princeton, N.J.: Princeton University Press, 1992).

10. Robert Stam, "Bakhtin, Polyphony, and Ethnic/Racial Representation," in *Unspeakable Images: Ethnicity and the American Cinema,* ed. Lester D. Friedman (Urbana: University of Illinois Press, 1991), pp. 259–60.

11. Clover, *Chain Saws;* Robin Wood, *Hollywood from Vietnam to Reagan* (New York: Columbia University Press, 1986).

12. This argument addresses *Slow Fade.* Cripps revised his assessment of independent film in his next book, *Black Film as Genre,* which recognizes special values in some of those "failed" underground black films. Cripps, however, substantially returns to the argument of *Slow Fade* in his most recent book, *Making Movies Black.* See Green, "Reemergence," for further discussion of *Black Film as Genre.*

13. The term "rhetoric" refers to the tendency of dominant discourses (such as Hollywood's) or oppositional discourses (such as race movies in relation to Hollywood) to construct arguments, either directly or indirectly. For example, if the "good guys" in Hollywood movies are virtually always white and the "bad guys" include whites but also people of color, then the rhetoric of the discourse of Hollywood movies can be seen as "pro-white." In distinguishing rhetoric from "natural fact" or "reality," it is assumed that in reality, not all people of color are "bad" and some people of color are "good," so the choice not to include those aspects of reality in a discourse becomes rhetorical, whether intentionally so or not. If, in Hollywood cinema, the traits of "rightness" or "competence" are reserved overwhelmingly for male characters, while the traits of being wrong or incompetent (or merely supportive) are reserved for women, then the rhetoric of the discourse of Hollywood movies can be deemed "patriarchal."

The term "aesthetic" refers to the standards of beauty or sensual pleasure displayed or implied by the discourse, as evidenced by its style in relation to its rhetoric. For example, if the "good guys" are virtually always white and tall and are photographed from below so that they look even taller and more dominant, and if they are also associated with "beautiful" photography, then the association of these choices of style with the rhetoric of "goodness" of the good guys implies a standard of beauty that is associated positively not only with tallness (and dominance) but also with whiteness itself. "Beauty" and whiteness, by always appearing together, imply each other. Stylistic choices in the production of films are made, consciously or unconsciously, in the context of such mutually inflecting rhetorical and aesthetic fields; those fields may be complex or simple, but they are always operative.

14. Harold Bloom, *The Anxiety of Influence* (New York: Oxford University Press, 1973).

15. Cripps, *Slow Fade,* p. 172.

16. Cripps, *Slow Fade,* pp. 260–61.

17. Ronald Hayman, *Fassbinder: Film Maker* (New York: Simon and Schuster, 1984), p. 138.

18. Roy Armes, *Third World Film Making and the West* (Berkeley: University of California Press, 1987).

19. Cripps, *Slow Fade,* p. 6.

20. bell hooks, "Micheaux: Celebrating Blackness," *Black American Literature Forum,* Vol. 25, No. 2, Summer 1991, pp. 351–60.

21. Neal Gabler, *An Empire of Their Own: How the Jews Invented Hollywood* (New York: Crown Publishers, 1988), p. 5.

22. In Roland Barthes, *Image-Music-Text,* trans. and ed. Stephen Heath (New York: Hill and Wang, 1977).

23. Richard Taruskin, "Facing Up, Finally, to Bach's Dark Vision," *New York Times,* January 27, 1991, pp. H25, H28.

24. See Museum of American Folk Art, *Self-Taught Artists of the 20th Century: An American Anthology* (San Francisco: Chronicle Books, 1998).

25. John Russell Taylor, in *Cinema: A Critical Dictionary,* ed. Richard Roud (New York: Viking, 1980), Vol. 2, p. 817.

26. DuBois, *Souls,* p. 215.

4. Negative Images

1. Grupenhoff, "The Rediscovery of Oscar Micheaux," *Journal of Film and Video,* Vol. 40, No. 1, Fall 1988, p. 46. See also the excellent discussion of Micheaux in Richard Grupenhoff, *The Black Valentino: The Stage and Screen Career of Lorenzo Tucker* (Metuchen, N.J.: Scarecrow Press, 1988).

2. See J. Ronald Green and Horace Neal, Jr., "Oscar Micheaux and Racial Slur: A Response to 'The Rediscovery of Oscar Micheaux,'" *Journal of Film and Video,* Vol. 40, No. 4, Fall 1988, for an expanded version of this chapter, including examples of the negative critical responses to Micheaux's work.

3. Transcribed from the copy of the film at the Library of Congress.

4. Bogle, *Toms,* p. 31.

5. Bogle, *Toms,* p. 33.

6. J. Hoberman, "A Forgotten Black Cinema Resurfaces," *The Village Voice,* November 17, 1975, p. 88.

7. See Green, "Two Micheaux Family Members," *The Newsletter of the Oscar Micheaux Society,* Vol. 5, Summer 1996.

8. Grupenhoff, *The Black Valentino: The Stage and Screen Career of Lorenzo Tucker* (Metuchen, N.J.: Scarecrow, 1988), pp. 66–74.

5. The Middle Path

1.   The term "bourgeois" implies in this study a direct or identificatory relationship with the owners of the means of production, in the sense that Marx defined the term. "Middle class" implies a middle position within the more Weberian definition of "class" as an economically and culturally inflected expectancy of one's "chances in life," as reformulated recently by William Julius Wilson and as discussed elsewhere in this study.

2.   Baraka, *Blues People,* p. 225.

3.   Baraka, *Blues People,* p. 225.

4.   Baraka, *Blues People,* p. 226.

5.   Aptheker, *Documentary History,* p. 15 and passim; W. E. B. DuBois, *Selections from "The Crisis": Volume 1, 1911–1925,* ed. Herbert Aptheker (Millwood, N.Y.: Kraus-Thomson, 1983), pp. 2, 30, 94 and passim. "Peonage" is indexed in Aptheker, and though "tenant farming" and "sharecropping" are not, they are often discussed on the same pages indexed under "peonage." DuBois, *Selections,* is not indexed, but references to peonage and tenantry are not difficult to locate throughout the text.

6.   Erskine Caldwell and Margaret Bourke-White, *You Have Seen Their Faces* (New York: Viking Press, 1937); James Agee and Walker Evans, *Let Us Now Praise Famous Men* (Boston: Houghton Mifflin, 1941).

7.   See Gaines, *Uplifting the Race,* and Masood, "Cities in Black."

8.   Houston A. Baker, Jr., *Modernism and the Harlem Renaissance* (Chicago: University of Chicago Press, 1987), p. 29.

9.   Charles Johnson, *Middle Passage* (New York: Atheneum, 1990).

10. William Uricchio and Roberta E. Pearson, "Dante's Inferno and Caesar's Ghost: Intertextuality and Conditions of Reception in Early American Cinema," in *Silent Film,* ed. Richard Abel (New Brunswick, N.J.: Rutgers University Press, 1996), p. 224.

11. Cf. Julio García Espinosa, "For an Imperfect Cinema," in *Twenty-five Years of the New Latin American Cinema,* ed. Michael Chanan (London: British Film Institute, 1984), pp. 28–33.

12. Taylor, *Mask of Art,* footnote 15, pp. 331–32.

13. David Bordwell, Janet Staiger, and Kristin Thompson, *The Classical Hollywood Cinema* (New York: Columbia University Press, 1985), p. 101.

14. Lafcadio Hearn, *Kwaidan: Stories and Studies of Strange Things* (1932; reprint, New York: Dover, 1968), p. 26.

15. Interestingly enough, Theodor Adorno used the L'Arlésienne suites as a significant example of findings about audience reception of music in the studies he conducted with Paul Lazersfeld at Princeton University just eight years after Micheaux's film was made: "People from more modest income groups—who do, however, pride themselves on their bourgeois status and incline to what they consider culture—would respond to elevated entertainment, rather, to nineteenth-century operas and standard favorites such as the Arlésienne

suites" (*Introduction to the Sociology of Music,* trans. E. B. Ashton [New York: Seabury Press, 1976], p. 59).

16.   See Joyce E. Jesionowski, *Thinking in Pictures: Dramatic Structure in D. W. Griffith's Biograph Films* (Berkeley: University of California Press, 1987), p. 57 and passim.

17.   Micheaux, *The Conquest,* pp. 24–26.

6. Middle-Class Cinema

1.   Gaines, *Uplifting the Race,* pp. 13, 15.

2.   A similar view of Griffith has been expressed by Clyde Taylor in "The Re-Birth of the Aesthetic in Cinema," *Wide Angle,* Vol. 13, Nos. 3 and 4, July–August 1991, pp. 12–30, which appears in revised form in Taylor's *Mask of Art.*

3.   See Wilson Record, *The Negro and the Communist Party* (1951; reprint, New York: Atheneum, 1971); Harold Cruse, *The Crisis of the Negro Intellectual* (New York: William Morrow and Co., 1967); and *The Negro and the American Labor Movement,* ed. Julius Jacobson (Garden City, N.Y.: Anchor, 1968). See also appendix 1 of this volume.

4.   Max Weber, *The Protestant Ethic and the Spirit of Capitalism,* trans. Talcott Parsons (New York: Scribners, 1958, 1976), p. 17.

5.   Micheaux, *The Conquest,* pp. 70–71.

6.   Weber, *Protestant Ethic,* p. 17.

7.   "John Ford's *Young Mr. Lincoln,*" a collective text by the editors of *Cahiers du cinéma* first printed in *Cahiers,* No. 223 (1970), reprinted in Bill Nichols, *Movies and Methods: An Anthology* (Berkeley: University of California Press, 1976), pp. 493–529.

8.   Robert Johnson, *The Complete Recordings,* Columbia Records C2T 46222.

9.   Gunther Schuller, *Early Jazz: Its Roots and Musical Development* (New York: Oxford, 1968), pp. 229–33.

10.   David Levering Lewis, *When Harlem Was in Vogue* (New York: Alfred A. Knopf, 1981), pp. 22, 24.

11.   Lewis, *When Harlem Was in Vogue,* p. 32.

12.   Frank C. Taylor, *Alberta Hunter: A Celebration in Blues* (New York: McGraw-Hill, 1987), p. 32.

13.   See the next chapter for a longer discussion of Bessie Smith and Ethel Waters.

14.   James R. Grossman, *Land of Hope: Chicago, Black Southerners, and the Great Migration* (Chicago: University of Chicago Press, 1989).

15.   Quoted in Lewis, *When Harlem Was in Vogue,* p. 32.

16.   From Karl Marx, *Theories of Surplus Capital,* quoted in Nancy Condee and Vladimir Padunov, "'Makulakul'tura': Reprocessing Culture," *October,* No. 57, Summer 1991, p. 79.

17.   Guerrero, *Framing Blackness,* pp. 21–26.

18.   Bogle, *Toms,* pp. 82–94.

19. Louis Althusser, *For Marx* (New York: Vintage, 1970), p. 111.

20. For discussion of Micheaux's critique of and campaigns against racist obstruction, see Jane Gaines, "Fire and Desire: Race, Melodrama, and Oscar Micheaux," in *Black American Cinema,* ed. Manthia Diawara (New York: Routledge, 1993); Pearl Bowser and Louise Spence, "Identity and Betrayal: *The Symbol of the Unconquered* and Oscar Micheaux's 'Biographical Legend,'" in *The Birth of Whiteness: Race and the Emergence of U.S. Cinema,* ed. Daniel Bernardi (New Brunswick, N.J.: Rutgers University Press, 1996); Charlene Regester, "Black Films, White Censors: Oscar Micheaux Confronts Censorship in New York, Virginia, and Chicago," in *Movie Censorship and American Culture,* ed. Francis G. Couvares (Washington, D.C.: Smithsonian, 1996); and J. Ronald Green, "Oscar Micheaux's Interrogation of Caricature as Entertainment," *Film Quarterly,* Vol. 51, No. 3, Spring 1998.

7. White Financing

1. Elaine Feinstein, *Bessie Smith* (New York: Viking Penguin, 1985), pp. 14–15.

2. Feinstein, *Bessie Smith,* p. 40.

3. Feinstein, *Bessie Smith,* p. 47.

4. Feinstein, *Bessie Smith,* p. 46.

5. Feinstein, *Bessie Smith,* p. 48.

6. Feinstein, *Bessie Smith,* p. 57.

7. Feinstein, *Bessie Smith,* pp. 24–25.

8. James Weldon Johnson, *Black Manhattan* (New York: Alfred A. Knopf, 1930), p. 95. See also Allen Woll, *Black Musical Theatre: From "Coontown" to "Dreamgirls"* (1989; reprint, New York: Da Capo, 1991), p. 4.

9. Henry T. Sampson, *Blacks in Blackface: A Source Book on Early Black Musical Shows* (Metuchen, N.J.: Scarecrow, 1980), pp. 61–66.

10. Micheaux's complex negotiation of racial caricature and stereotype in entertainment is discussed in succeeding chapters.

11. In *Black Manhattan,* see chapters 9, 10, 11, 15, 16, and 17; the intervening chapters provide good contextual discussions of the same period, treating social class, the church, the Washington–DuBois conflict, Garveyism, and other issues.

12. Woll, *Black Musical Theatre,* p. 6.

13. DuBois, *Souls,* p. 215.

14. James Weldon Johnson, *Along This Way: The Autobiography of James Weldon Johnson* (New York: Viking, 1933; reprint, 1968), pp. 172–73.

15. Houston A. Baker, Jr., *Blues, Ideology, and Afro-American Literature: A Vernacular Theory* (Chicago: University of Chicago Press, 1984), p. 3.

16. Baraka, *Blues People,* p. 17.

17. Cf. Gaines, "The Racial Content of Class," in *Uplifting the Race,* pp. 13–17; see also appendix 1 of this volume.

18. The sections in Michael Omi and Howard Winant, *Racial Formation in the*

United States: From the 1960s to the 1980s (New York: Routledge and Kegan Paul, 1986), on race and ethnicity in relation to immigrants are particularly useful summaries of this issue; e.g., pp. 21–24.

19. Heywood Broun, New York World, October 30, 1924, in Woll, Black Musical Theatre, p. 109.

20. Woll, Black Musical Theatre, p. 76.

21. Woll, Black Musical Theatre, p. 93.

22. Woll, Black Musical Theatre, p. 94.

23. Whiteness may be even more evident as a prevailing issue within a rhetoric of the films' more or less covert "signifying" to black audiences. An extended analysis of Micheaux's specifically African-American signifying is badly needed.

24. Grossman, Land of Hope; Nicholas Lemann, The Promised Land: The Great Black Migration and How It Changed America (New York: Alfred A. Knopf, 1991).

25. Chris Albertson, Bessie (New York: Stein and Day, 1972), pp. 36–37.

26. Feinstein, Bessie Smith, pp. 22–24.

27. Baraka, Blues People, p. 162. Baraka's quotation is from Vic Bellerby.

28. Baraka, Blues People, p. 162.

29. Baraka, Blues People, p. 148.

30. Baraka, Blues People, pp. 147–48.

31. Baraka, Blues People, pp. 86–87.

32. Ethel Waters, His Eye Is on the Sparrow (Garden City, N.Y.: Doubleday, 1951), p. 137.

33. Waters, His Eye, pp. 138–39.

34. Cripps, Slow Fade, p. 323.

35. Mark A. Reid, "The Achievement of Oscar Micheaux," Black Film Review, Vol. 4, No. 2, Spring 1988, p. 7.

36. David Levering Lewis, "Harlem Is My Home," in Harlem Renaissance: Art of Black America (1984; reprint, New York: Harry N. Abrams, 1994), p. 79.

37. Donald Bogle (Toms, passim) and Nathan Huggins (Harlem Renaissance, pp. 258–60) discuss the phenomenon of black entertainers signaling to their black audiences their true feelings about their roles—Huggins's is the less sanguine of the two analyses, but Huggins was discussing an earlier period than was Bogle.

38. See Gates, Signifying Monkey, pp. 66, 68; and Roger D. Abrahams in Gates, p. 54.

39. Baraka, Blues People, pp. 167–68.

8. Stereotype and Caricature

1. Roi Ottley, "New World A-Coming": Inside Black America (Boston: Houghton Mifflin, 1943), pp. 106–107.

2. Huggins, Renaissance, p. 26.

3. Huggins, *Renaissance*, pp. 25–26.

4. Charles Musser, *Before the Nickelodeon: Edwin S. Porter and the Edison Manufacturing Company* (Berkeley: University of California Press, 1991), p. 20.

5. Musser, *Nickelodeon*, pp. 20–21.

6. Musser, *Nickelodeon*, pp. 302–303.

7. Henry T. Sampson, *The Ghost Walks: A Chronological History of Blacks in Show Business, 1865–1910* (Metuchen, N.J.: Scarecrow, 1988).

8. Alain Locke, *The Negro and His Music* (1936; reprint, New York: Arno, 1969), p. 11.

9. Huggins, *Renaissance*, pp. 13, 14.

10. Sampson, *The Ghost Walks*, p. 433.

11. Huggins, *Renaissance*, p. 258–59.

12. bell hooks, *Killing Rage: Ending Racism* (New York: Henry Holt, 1995), p. 6.

13. Bogle, *Toms*, p. 41.

14. Bogle, *Toms*, p. 43.

15. Huggins, *Renaissance*, p. 259.

16. Harold Bloom, *The Anxiety of Influence: A Theory of Poetry* (London: Oxford, 1973), p. 14. Bloom defines "misprision" from Lucretius as a "swerve," as of atoms, to allow the possibility of change in the universe and, thus, in literature, as a "poetic misreading" or "corrective movement" in the adaptation of a previous literary work.

17. Huggins, *Renaissance*, p. 260.

9. Revising Caricature

1. Huggins, *Renaissance*, pp. 64–65.

2. G. D. Pike, *The Jubilee Singers, and Their Campaign for Twenty Thousand Dollars* (Boston: Lee and Shepard, 1873), p. 107.

3. Pike, *Jubilee*, p. 107.

4. Pike, *Jubilee*, pp. 76–77.

5. Pike, *Jubilee*, p. 75.

6. Pike, *Jubilee*, p. 82.

7. Pike, *Jubilee*, pp. 90, 91.

8. Rawn Spearman, "Vocal Concert Music in the Harlem Renaissance," and Georgia A. Ryder, "Harlem Renaissance Ideals in the Music of Robert Nathaniel Dett," both in Samuel A. Floyd, Jr., ed., *Black Music in the Harlem Renaissance: A Collection of Essays* (New York: Greenwood Press, 1990).

9. That association is described in more detail in, among other places, an article by Michel Roudevitch that relates the importance of 1920s and 1930s jazz to early cartoons: "Blackcartoon: Mickey est-il nègre?" [Mickey, Is he Black?], *CinémAction*, No. 46, 1988, pp. 79–81.

10. Huggins, *Renaissance*, p. 269.

11. Thomas Kochman, *Black and White Styles in Conflict* (Chicago: University of Chicago Press, 1981). As this note was being written, a television news story reported a virtually identical exchange between a leader in the U.S. Senate committee hearings on the confirmation of Clarence Thomas—President Bush's nominee to replace Thurgood Marshall on the Supreme Court—and the leader of a group of African-American clerics who were testifying against the nomination. The Senate committee member accused the black clerics of presenting their material overdramatically for the effect of spectacle; the black clerics expressed dismay at his inability to understand the appropriateness of their sense of urgency. They expected their earnestness to be taken in good faith, just as Trotter had expected his earnestness to be understood at Wilson's committee hearings in 1914.

12. Grossman, *Land of Hope*, pp. 16–17.

13. Grossman, *Land of Hope*, pp. 18–19.

14. Grossman, *Land of Hope*, p. 34.

15. Huggins, *Renaissance*, pp. 260–61.

16. Huggins, *Renaissance*, p. 263. Huggins's invocation of *legerdemain* and incantation suggests the subtle appropriateness of the title of Langston Hughes and Milton Meltzer's book *Black Magic: A Pictorial History of the Negro in American Entertainment* (Englewood Cliffs, N.J.: Prentice-Hall, 1967), from which Huggins has drawn several of his illustrations, including the one of Kersands. For Huggins's more extended discussion of the psychological damage of extreme caricature, see pages 259–63.

17. Micheaux, *The Conquest*, p. 145.

18. Gabler, *An Empire of Their Own*.

19. Steele, *Content*, pp. 98–99.

20. In Cripps, *Slow Fade*, pp. 260–61.

10. Interrogating Caricature as Entertainment

1. Albertson, *Bessie*, p. 122.

2. Albertson, *Bessie*, p. 122.

3. See, for example, the discussion of racial self-respect by George Edmund Haynes's *The Trend of the Races* (1922; reprint, Miami: Mnemosyne, 1969), in Aptheker, *A Documentary History*, pp. 363–64. For instance, "Enemies and some friends complain that Negroes show a lack of belief in their own race; that apparently their highest ambition is to be white. These criticisms apparently have basis in fact. They overlook, however, three cardinal conditions which Negroes confront. First, Negroes are surrounded by white people, ten to one, whose idea of physical beauty is a white skin, sharp features, and straight hair. By a well known principle of group psychology the individuals in the minority tend to conform to the ideas and habits of the majority. . . .

"In the second place, whoever has observed and reflected upon facts open to everyday inspection knows that, on the one hand, to have white skin or to be known as a white man or woman is to have an open door to whatever

ability and effort can achieve. . . . Negroes have had many of their attempts to set up their own standards blown to the winds by derision. The wonder is not that a few of them want to be white, but rather, that the race has so persistently clung to racial ideas and excellencies through so many generations.

"Finally, much of the white man's notion of what the Negro aspires to be is either an imaginative white man's construction of what he conjectures he would strive for, were he a Negro, or it is what some Negro has let the white gather in response to leading questions. . . . The Negro is a master in responding to the white man according to the latter's wishes."

4. See again chapter 6 of Huggins's *Harlem Renaissance* concerning the psychological and social damage of entertainment caricature and the inhabiting of minstrel roles as a protective cover in daily life.

5. Jane Feuer, *The Hollywood Musical* (Bloomington: Indiana University Press, 1982), pp. 13–15.

6. Jessie Fauset, "Some Notes on Color," *The World Tomorrow* (New York), March 1922, pp. 76–77, in Aptheker, *A Documentary History,* p. 354.

7. Micheaux, *The Conquest,* p. 145.

8. Micheaux, Philadelphia *Afro-American,* January 24, 1925.

9. All transcriptions from the film, such as this one, have been made from a film print purchased from Phoenix in New York. Their source is the film print of *Murder in Harlem* discovered in Tyler, Texas, by G. William Jones of the Southwest Film/Video Archives in Dallas.

10. bell hooks, "Micheaux," *Black American Literature Forum,* Vol. 25, No. 2, Summer 1991, p. 360.

11. Interrogating False Uplift

1. E.g., J. Hoberman, *Village Voice,* November 17, 1975, p. 88, and Joseph A. Young, *Black Novelist as White Racist: The Myth of Black Inferiority in the Novels of Oscar Micheaux* (New York: Greenwood, 1989).

2. Conservative middle-class African-American intellectuals today continue to express the need for not just black group identity but also individualistic effort: "It was the emphasis on mass action in the sixties that made the victim-focused black identity a necessity. But in the nineties and beyond, when racial advancement will come only through *a multitude of individual advancements,* this form of identity inadvertently adds itself to the forces that hold us back. Hard work, education, *individual initiative,* stable family life, property ownership—these have always been the means by which ethnic groups have moved ahead in America. Regardless of past or present victimization, these 'laws' of advancement apply absolutely to black Americans also" (Steele, *Content,* p. 108; emphasis added).

3. Willard B. Gatewood, *Aristocrats of Color: The Black Elite, 1880–1920* (Bloomington: Indiana University Press, 1990), pp. 24–25.

4. Gatewood, *Aristocrats,* p. 25.

5. E. Franklin Frazier, *Black Bourgeoisie* (New York: Free Press, 1957).

6. Gatewood, *Aristocrats*, p. 25.

7. hooks, *Killing Rage*, p. 177.

12. Passing and Film Style

1. Cf. Michael Rogin, *Blackface, White Noise: Jewish Immigrants in the Hollywood Melting Pot* (Berkeley: University of California Press, 1996), pp. 94–95.

2. The terms "higher" and "lower" are relative, since Hitler would have claimed his monistic, fascistic style for the "lower" classes, the "folk." He would have blamed degenerate styles on the "higher" classes of intellectuals and cultured Jews.

3. Again, for reviews of past literature on Micheaux, see Regester, "Misreading and Rereading," and Green, "Reemergence."

4. Transcription from video copy of the film available from Grapevine Video in Phoenix.

5. Bogle, *Toms*, pp. 59–60.

6. Baker, *Blues, Ideology*, p. 13 and passim.

7. James Weldon Johnson, *The Autobiography of an Ex-Colored Man* (1927; reprint, New York: Avon, 1965), pp. 478–79.

8. Johnson, *Autobiography*, p. 499.

9. Johnson, *Autobiography*, pp. 510–11.

10. Johnson, *Autobiography*, p. 511.

11. Eileen Southern, *The Music of Black Americans: A History* (New York: W. W. Norton, 1971), p. 302.

13. Racial Loyalty

1. Young, *Black Novelist*.

2. Page numbers from Young's *Black Novelist* will appear in the body of the text in this chapter.

3. Young, *Black Novelist*, pp. 106–107.

4. Only the extant films are listed. Preer also appeared in many of Micheaux's silent films that are not known to have survived.

5. This analysis could be extended to the leading women of Micheaux's non-extant films by examining well-documented credits or visual evidence from production stills or publicity paper. An informal survey of such materials suggests that the pattern of light-skinned, identifiably black leading women extended throughout Micheaux's film career.

6. Betti VanEpps-Taylor emphasizes the presence of significant small groups of African-American pioneers in South Dakota that she feels Micheaux would have known about (*Oscar Micheaux*, pp. 53–55). This interesting fact would not change the overwhelmingly white character of the society surrounding the homesteading Micheaux.

7. Arlene Elder, "Oscar Micheaux: The Melting Pot on the Plains," *The Old Northwest: A Journal of Regional Life and Letters,* Vol. 2, No. 3, September 1976, p. 305.

8. Micheaux, *The Forged Note,* pp. 426–27.

9. Micheaux, *The Forged Note,* p. 372.

10. Francis L. Broderick, *W. E. B. DuBois: Negro Leader in a Time of Crisis* (Stanford, Calif.: Stanford University Press, 1959).

11. Benjamin DeMott, *The Imperial Middle: Why Americans Can't Think Straight about Class* (New York: William Morrow and Co., 1990).

12. Broderick, *DuBois,* p. 69.

13. Addison Gayle, Jr., *The Way of the New World: The Black Novel in America* (Garden City, N.Y.: Anchor/Doubleday, 1975), pp. 33–34.

14. Gayle, *New World,* p. 35.

15. Eldridge Cleaver, *Soul on Ice* (New York: Dell, 1968), pp. 155–56.

16. Cleaver, *Soul,* p. 157.

17. Cleaver, *Soul,* p. 156.

18. Baker, *Modernism and the Harlem Renaissance,* pp. 25–36.

19. Alley concludes: "These comments and notations are part of a book in preparation concerning the life and times of motion picture censorship in the Commonwealth of Virginia." John Alley's statement, which is cited above almost in toto, is titled "The Virginia State Board of Motion Picture Censors vs. Micheaux Film Corporation: An Interpretive Summary" and was published as a handout by the Virginia Festival of American Film during their 1991 festival in Charlottesville.

20. Micheaux, *The Conquest,* p. 251.

21. Micheaux, *The Conquest,* p. 253.

22. Micheaux, *The Conquest,* pp. 253–54.

23. Micheaux, *The Conquest,* p. 253.

24. Oscar Micheaux, *The Story of Dorothy Stanfield* (New York: Book Supply Co., 1946), p. 214.

25. Micheaux, *Dorothy Stanfield,* p. 215.

26. Malcolm X formulated the choice differently in his speech in April of 1964, "The Ballot or the Bullet." Like Booker T. Washington, Malcolm X considered economics to be crucial, and (also like Washington) he placed the solution in the hands of African Americans, calling for blacks to control their own economic realm by keeping their spending within the black community. Malcolm X, however, considered the vote to be just as crucial. Even in the act of calling for violent self-defense, Malcolm X said, much as DuBois did, that "the Negro in this country holds the balance of power, and if the Negro in this country were given what the Constitution says he is supposed to have, the added power of the Negro in this country would sweep all of the racists and the segregationists out of office. It would change the entire political structure of the

country. It would wipe out the Southern segregationism that now controls America's foreign policy, as well as America's domestic policy" (*Malcolm X Speaks,* ed. George Breitman [New York: Grove, 1965], p. 57). The explicit point is that for African Americans, the ballot would mean the avoidance of violent revolution; the implicit point is that the ballot would allow African Americans to go about the building of their own economic future without basic political hindrances.

27. *Grove's Dictionary of Music and Musicians,* 3rd ed., ed. H. C. Colles (London: Macmillan, 1928), Vol. 4, p. 624.

28. Micheaux, *The Case of Mrs. Wingate* (New York: Book Supply Co., 1945), pp. 93–96.

29. Micheaux includes this scene, with the same emphatic rejection of a $100,000 bribe to make an anti-Semitic film, in an unpublished three-act play script also titled "The Case of Mrs. Wingate."

30. Michel Fabre, *From Harlem to Paris: Black American Writers in France, 1840–1980* (Urbana: University of Illinois Press, 1991), p. 152.

31. Micheaux, *The Conquest,* p. 17.

14. Micheaux and Cinema Today

1. Ella Shohat and Robert Stam, *Unthinking Eurocentrism: Multiculturalism and the Media* (London: Routledge, 1994), pp. 184–85.

2. Some of the following discussion is adapted from my review of Guerrero's book in *Film Quarterly,* Summer 1995, pp. 47–49.

3. Guerrero, *Framing Blackness,* p. 23.

4. Guerrero, *Framing Blackness,* p. 115.

5. Quoted in Steven Gregory, "Race and Racism: A Symposium," *Social Text,* No. 42, Spring 1995, p. 16.

Appendix 1. On Class and the Classical

1. Paul Mombert, "Class," in *Encyclopaedia of the Social Sciences* (New York: Macmillan, 1930), Vol. 3, p. 531.

2. Mombert, "Class," p. 532.

3. H. S. Morris, "Ethnic Groups," in David L. Sills, ed., *International Encyclopedia of the Social Sciences,* Vol. 5 (New York: Macmillan and Free Press, 1968), pp. 169–70.

4. Steele, *Content,* pp. 103–104.

5. Morris Zelditch, Jr., "Status, Social," in David L. Sills, ed., *International Encyclopedia of the Social Sciences,* Vol. 15, p. 251.

6. Baraka, *Blues People,* p. 119.

7. Baraka, *Blues People,* pp. 81–82.

8. *Webster's Seventh New Collegiate Dictionary* (Springfield, Mass.: Merriam, 1965).

9.   Baraka, *Blues People,* p. 119.

10. Baraka, *Blues People,* pp. 127, 130, 141.

11. Ralf Dahrendorf, *Class and Class Conflict in Industrial Society* (Stanford, Calif.: Stanford University Press, 1959; a revised and expanded translation, by the author, of *Soziale Klassen und Klassenkonflikt in der industriellen Gesellshaft,* 1957), pp. 9–18.

Bibliography

Primary Materials

Lewis, Mildred Micheaux. I have had numerous conversations, in person and by telephone, with Mrs. Lewis, whose grandfather was Oscar's uncle.

Micheaux, Alfreda. I have had several conversations by telephone with Ms. Micheaux, a cousin of Oscar's.

Micheaux, Oscar.
1. The self-published race novels, on which Micheaux based many of his films, in chronological order, are as follows:
The Conquest. Lincoln, Neb.: Woodruff Bank Note Co., 1913. Reprint McGrath Publishing Co., 1969. Reprint, with introduction by Learthen Dorsey, Lincoln: University of Nebraska Press, 1994.
The Forged Note. Lincoln, Neb.: Western Book Supply Co., 1915.
The Homesteader. Sioux City, Iowa: Western Book Supply Co., 1917. Reprint, McGrath Publishing Co., 1969. Reprint, with introduction by Learthen Dorsey, Lincoln: University of Nebraska Press, 1994.
The Wind from Nowhere. New York: Book Supply Co., 1941.
The Case of Mrs. Wingate. New York: Book Supply Co., 1945.
The Story of Dorothy Stanfield. New York: Book Supply Co., 1946.
The Masquerade. New York: Book Supply Co., 1947.
2. "The Case of Mrs. Wingate." A typescript of "A Play in Three Acts/based on the Best-selling Novel of the name/To be Produced and Directed by Oscar Micheaux," New York: The Case of Mrs. Wingate Co., Inc., 1946. The original typescript is in the possession of Alfreda L. Micheaux, Wichita, Kansas. My photocopy of that typescript will be donated to the Museum of Modern Art. This play is modeled on, but is significantly different from, Micheaux's novel of the same title.
3. The George P. Johnson Collection at the Library of the University of California at Los Angeles. The business letters received from Oscar (and Swan) Micheaux by George P. Johnson are too numerous to mention, but they are footnoted, where appropriate, in the body of this book. The Johnson collection is readily available on microfiche in many research libraries. I have photocopies of those items that relate to Micheaux.
4. "*Micheaux Family* of Barton and Stafford Cos., Kansas," though not authored by Micheaux, is the history of the family as compiled professionally by the Barton County Genealogical Society in Great Bend, Kansas. It includes reports of records and documents such as newspaper articles, census records, court records, real-estate records, and obituaries, all of which are carefully referenced. Most of the sources are contemporary, dating from the early twentieth century; information about the family extends well back into the nineteenth century.
  The dossier includes photocopies of the license issued by Cook County, Illinois, for Micheaux's first disastrous marriage to Orlean E. McCracken; the license is dated April

20, 191[0?; copy unclear]. The dossier includes a copy of Micheaux's death certificate, issued by the North Carolina State Board of Health, which lists the date of death as March 25, 1951; the place of death as Good Samaritan Hospital in Charlotte, North Carolina; and the cause of death as hypertension heart disease with decompensation [due to] arteriosclerosis.

This dossier is the property of individual family members. My photocopy will be deposited with the Museum of Modern Art if permission is granted by the family.

5. Micheaux's open letter of late 1924, which was printed in several African-American newspapers: for example, the Philadelphia *Tribune,* December 13, 1924, pp. 1, 3.

Robinson, Harley W., Jr. I have had several conversations with Mr. Robinson, Oscar's nephew, at the Oscar Micheaux Annual Film Festival in Gregory, South Dakota, and by telephone.

Secondary Materials

Abrahams, Roger D. *Talking Black.* Rowley, Mass.: Newbury House, 1976.
Adorno, Theodor. *Introduction to the Sociology of Music.* Trans. E. B. Ashton. New York: Seabury Press, 1976.
Agee, James, and Walker Evans. *Let Us Now Praise Famous Men.* Boston: Houghton Mifflin, 1941.
Albertson, Chris. *Bessie.* New York: Stein and Day, 1972.
Allen, Fredrick Lewis. *Only Yesterday and Since Yesterday: A Popular History '20s and '30s: Two Volumes in One.* 1931. Reprint, New York: Bonanza, 1986.
Alley, John R. "The Virginia State Board of Motion Picture Censors vs. Micheaux Film Corporation: An Interpretive Summary." A handout at the Virginia Festival of American Film. Charlottesville, 1991.
The American Film Institute Catalog of Motion Pictures Produced in the United States. Kenneth W. Munden, exec. ed. New York: R. R. Bowker, 1971–.
Aptheker, Herbert, ed. *A Documentary History of the Negro People in the United States, 1910–1930.* Secaucus, N.J.: Citadel, 1973.
Baker, Houston A., Jr. *Black Literature in America.* New York: McGraw-Hill, 1971.
———. *Blues, Ideology, and Afro-American Literature: A Vernacular Theory.* Chicago: University of Chicago Press, 1984.
———. *Modernism and the Harlem Renaissance.* Chicago: University of Chicago Press, 1987.
Baker, Ray Stannard. *Following the Color Line: American Negro Citizenship in the Progressive Era.* 1908. Reprint, New York: Harper and Row, 1964.
Bakhtin, M. M. *The Dialogic Imagination.* Trans. Michael Holquist; ed. Caryl Emerson and Michael Holquist. Austin: University of Texas Press, 1981.
Baldwin, James. *The Devil Finds Work.* New York: Dial, 1976.
———. *Nobody Knows My Name.* New York: Dell, 1963.
———. *Notes of a Native Son.* Boston: Beacon Press, 1955.
Baraka, Amiri (LeRoi Jones). *Black Music.* New York: William Morrow and Co., 1967.
———. *Blues People: Negro Music in White America.* New York: William Morrow and Co., 1963.
———. *Home: Social Essays.* New York: William Morrow and Co., 1966.
Barthes, Roland. *Image-Music-Text.* Ed. and trans. Stephen Heath. New York: Hill and Wang, 1977.

Baudry, Jean-Louis. "The Apparatus: Metapsychological Approaches to the Impression of Reality in Cinema." *Communications*, No. 23, 1975. Trans. John Andrews and Bertrand Augst, *Camera Obscura*, No. 1, Fall 1976.

Bennett, Lerone, Jr. *Before the Mayflower: A History of the Negro in America, 1619–1964.* Chicago: Johnson, 1962.

———. *The Negro Mood and Other Essays.* Chicago: Johnson, 1964.

Bernardi, Daniel, ed. *The Birth of Whiteness: Race and the Emergence of U.S. Cinema.* New Brunswick, N.J.: Rutgers University Press, 1996.

Bhabha, Homi. "A New Black Intellectual: Black and White and Read All Over." *Artforum*, October 1995.

Black Filmmakers Hall of Fame. "Oscar Micheaux: Some Recollections" [author unnoted; handwritten note date of 1978; document in Black Film Center/Archive at Indiana University].

Bloom, Harold. *The Anxiety of Influence.* New York: Oxford University Press, 1973.

Bogle, Donald. *Blacks in American Films and Television: An Encyclopedia.* New York: Simon and Schuster, 1988.

———. *Toms, Coons, Mulattoes, Mammies, and Bucks: An Interpretive History of Blacks in American Films.* New York: Viking, 1973.

Boime, Albert. *The Art of Exclusion: Representing Blacks in the Nineteenth Century.* Washington, D.C.: Smithsonian, 1990.

Bone, Robert A. *Down Home.* New York: Putnam, 1975.

———. *The Negro Novel in America.* New Haven, Conn.: Yale University Press, 1965.

Bordwell, David, Janet Staiger, and Kristin Thompson. *The Classical Hollywood Cinema.* New York: Columbia University Press, 1985.

Bourdieu, Pierre. *Distinction: A Social Critique of the Judgement of Taste.* Trans. Richard Nice. Cambridge, Mass.: Harvard University Press, 1984.

Bowser, Pearl. "Interview: The Micheaux Legacy" (interview with Toni Cade Bambara and Louis Massiah). *Black Film Review,* Vol. 7, No. 4, 1993, pp. 10–14.

———. Program Notes. *New American Filmmakers Series,* No. 17, Whitney Museum of American Art, May 22–June 10, 1984.

———. "Sexual Imagery and the Black Woman in American Cinema." In *Black Cinema Aesthetics,* ed. Gladstone Yearwood. Athens, Ohio: Afro-American Studies at Ohio University, 1982.

Bowser, Pearl, and Jane Gaines. "Black Gold: New Finds/Old Films." *Black Film Review,* Vol. 7, No. 4, 1993, pp. 2–5.

———, eds. Special issue on the history of black film. *Black Film Review,* Vol. 7, No. 4, 1993.

Bowser, Pearl, and Louise Spence. "Identity and Betrayal: *The Symbol of the Unconquered* and Oscar Micheaux's 'Biographical Legend.'" In *The Birth of Whiteness: Race and the Emergence of U.S. Cinema,* ed. Daniel Bernardi. New Brunswick, N.J.: Rutgers University Press, 1996.

Boyd, Todd. *Am I Black Enough for You? Popular Culture from the 'Hood and Beyond.* Bloomington: Indiana University Press, 1997.

———. "The Meaning of the Blues." *Wide Angle,* Vol. 13, Nos. 3 and 4, July–October 1991.

Boyers, Robert, et al. "Race and Racism: American Dilemmas Revisited." *Salmagundi,* Nos. 104–105, Fall 1994–Winter 1995.

Bragdon, Henry Wilkinson. *Woodrow Wilson: The Academic Years.* Cambridge, Mass.: Harvard University Press, 1967.

Broderick, Francis L. *W. E. B. DuBois: Negro Leader in a Time of Crisis.* Stanford, Calif.: Stanford University Press, 1959.

Brown, Sterling. *The Negro in American Fiction and Negro Poetry and Drama.* 1937. Reprint, New York: Arno, 1969.

Burch, Noël. *Life to Those Shadows.* Berkeley: University of California Press, 1990.

Cade, Toni (Toni Cade Bambara), ed. *The Black Woman: An Anthology.* New York: New American Library, 1970.

Caldwell, Erskine, and Margaret Bourke-White. *You Have Seen Their Faces.* New York: Viking Press, 1937.

Calloway, Earl. "Oscar Micheaux's Headstone Ceremony Announced." Chicago *Defender,* August 6, 1988, p. 35.

Campbell, Mary Schmidt. Introduction for the Studio Museum in Harlem. *Harlem Renaissance Art of Black America.* New York: Harry N. Abrams, 1994.

Cham, Mbye B., and Claire Andrade-Watkins, eds. *Blackframes: Critical Perspectives on Black Independent Cinema.* Cambridge, Mass.: MIT Press, 1988.

Chesnutt, Charles W. *The House Behind the Cedars.* Boston: Houghton Mifflin, 1900.

———. *The Marrow of Tradition.* 1901. Reprint, Ann Arbor: University of Michigan Press, 1969.

Cleaver, Eldridge. *Soul on Ice.* New York: Dell, 1968.

Clover, Carol J. *Men, Women, and Chain Saws: Gender in the Modern Horror Film.* Princeton, N.J.: Princeton University Press, 1992.

Colles, H. C., ed. *Grove's Dictionary of Music and Musicians.* 3rd ed. London: Macmillan, 1928.

Comolli, Jean-Luc, and Jean Narboni. "Preface to 'Young Mr. Lincoln.'" *Screen,* Vol. 13, No. 3, 1972. In *Film Theory and Criticism: Introductory Readings,* ed. Leo Braudy and Marshall Cohen. New York: Oxford University Press, 1999.

Cox, Clinton. "'We Were Stars in Those Days.'" New York *Sunday News* [Magazine], March 9, 1975, pp. 15–16, 18, 26–27.

Cripps, Thomas. *Black Film as Genre.* Bloomington: Indiana University Press, 1979.

———. *Making Movies Black: The Hollywood Message Movie from World War II to the Civil Rights Era.* New York: Oxford, 1993.

———. "Movies in the Ghetto (B.P.): (Before Poitier)." *Negro Digest,* February 1969.

———. "Oscar Micheaux: The Story Continues." In *Black American Cinema,* ed. Manthia Diawara. New York: Routledge, 1993.

———. "Paul Robeson and Black Identity in American Movies." *The Massachusetts Review,* Summer 1970, pp. 468–85.

———. *Slow Fade to Black: The Negro in American Film, 1900–1942.* New York: Oxford University Press, 1977, 1993.

Crouch, Stanley. *Notes of a Hanging Judge: Essays and Reviews, 1979–1989.* New York: Oxford, 1990.

Cruse, Harold. *The Crisis of the Negro Intellectual.* New York: William Morrow and Co., 1967.

Dahrendorf, Ralf. *Class and Class Conflict in Industrial Society.* 1957. Reprint, Stanford, Calif.: Stanford University Press, 1959.

Dayan, Daniel. "The Tutor-Code of Classical Cinema." *Film Quarterly,* Vol. 28, No. 1, Fall 1974.

Delany, Martin Robison. *The Condition, Elevation, Emigration, and Destiny of the Colored People of the United States.* 1852 (self-published). Reprint, New York: Arno, 1968.

Deleuze, Gilles, and Félix Guattari. *What Is Philosophy?* Trans. Hugh Tomlinson and Graham Burchell. New York: Columbia University Press, 1994. (Originally published in 1991, as *Qu'est-ce que la philosophie?*)

DeMott, Benjamin. *The Imperial Middle: Why Americans Can't Think Straight about Class.* New York: William Morrow and Co., 1990.

Diakité, Madubuko. *Film, Culture, and the Black Filmmaker: A Study of Functional Relationships and Parallel Developments.* New York: Arno, 1980.

Diawara, Manthia, ed. *Black American Cinema.* New York: Routledge, 1993.

——. "Cinema Studies, the Strong Thought and Black Film." *Wide Angle,* Vol. 13, Nos. 3 and 4, July–October, 1991.

Dixon, R. M. W., and J. Godrich. *Recording the Blues.* New York: Stein and Day, 1970.

Donaldson, Melvin Burke. *The Representation of AfroAmerican Women in the Hollywood Feature Film, 1915–1949.* Ann Arbor, Mich.: University Microfilms, 1984.

Douglass, Frederick. *Narrative of the Life of Frederick Douglass, an American Slave: Written by Himself.* Edited by Houston A. Baker, Jr. New York: Penguin, 1982.

DuBois, W. E. B. *An ABC of Color.* Berlin: Seven Seas, 1963.

——. *Dusk of Dawn: An Essay toward an Autobiography of a Race Concept.* New York: Harcourt, Brace and World, 1940.

——. *The Quest of the Silver Fleece.* Chicago: A. C. McClurg, 1911.

——. *The Souls of Black Folk.* 1903. Reprint, New York: Avon, 1965.

——. *Writings in Periodicals Edited by W. E. B. Du Bois: Selections from The Crisis, Volume 1 1911–1925,* ed. Herbert Aptheker. Millwood, N.Y.: Kraus-Thomson, 1983.

Dyer, Richard. *Heavenly Bodies: Film Stars and Society.* New York: St. Martin's Press, 1986.

——. "Into the Light: The Whiteness of the South in *The Birth of a Nation.*" In *Dixie Debates: Perspectives on Southern Cultures,* ed. Richard H. King and Helen Taylor. New York: New York University Press, 1996.

Elder, Arlene. "Oscar Micheaux: The Melting Pot on the Plains." *The Old Northwest: A Journal of Regional Life and Letters,* Vol. 2, No. 3, September 1976.

Ellison, Ralph. *Shadow and Act.* New York: Random House, 1964.

Fabre, Michel. *From Harlem to Paris: Black American Writers in France, 1840–1980.* Urbana: University of Illinois Press, 1991.

Fabrikant, Geraldine. "BET to Establish a Film Unit Aimed at Black Urban Market." *New York Times,* July 10, 1998.

Fauset, Jesse. "Some Notes on Color." *The World Tomorrow* (New York), March, 1922. Reprinted in Herbert Aptheker, ed., *A Documentary History of the Negro People in the United States, 1910–1930.* Secaucus, N.J.: Citadel, 1973.

Feinstein, Elaine. *Bessie Smith.* New York: Viking, 1985.

Feuer, Jane. *The Hollywood Musical.* Bloomington: Indiana University Press, 1982.

Floyd, Samuel A., Jr. *Black Music in the Harlem Renaissance: A Collection of Essays.* New York: Greenwood, 1990.

Fontenot, Chester J., Jr. "Oscar Micheaux, Black Novelist and Film Maker." In *Vision and Refuge: Essays on the Literature of the Great Plains,* ed. Virginia Faulkner. Lincoln: University of Nebraska Press, 1982.

Frazier, E. Franklin. *Black Bourgeoisie.* New York: Free Press, 1957.

Frazier, Thomas R., ed. *Afro-American History: Primary Sources.* 1970. Reprint, Chicago: Dorsey, 1988.

Gabler, Neal. *An Empire of Their Own: How the Jews Invented Hollywood.* New York: Crown Publishers, 1988.

Gaines, Jane. "*The Birth of a Nation* and *Within Our Gates:* Two Tales of the American

South." In *Dixie Debates: Perspectives on Southern Cultures,* ed. Richard H. King and Helen Taylor. New York: New York University Press, 1996.

———. *Classical Hollywood Narrative: The Paradigm Wars.* Durham, N.C.: Duke University Press, 1992.

———. "Fire and Desire: Race, Melodrama, and Oscar Micheaux." In *Black American Cinema,* ed. Manthia Diawara. New York: Routledge, 1993.

Gaines, Kevin K. *Uplifting the Race: Black Leadership, Politics, and Culture in the Twentieth Century.* Chapel Hill: University of North Carolina Press, 1996.

Gates, Henry Louis, Jr. "Black Demagogues and Pseudo-Scholars." *New York Times,* July 20, 1992, p. A11.

———. *Figures in Black: Words, Signs, and the "Racial" Self.* New York: Oxford University Press, 1987.

———. *The Signifying Monkey: A Theory of African-American Literary Criticism.* New York: Oxford, 1988.

———. "The Trope of the New Negro and the Reconstruction of the Image of the Black." *Representations,* No. 24, Fall 1988.

Gatewood, Willard B. *Aristocrats of Color: The Black Elite, 1880–1920.* Bloomington: Indiana University Press, 1990.

Gayle, Addison, Jr. *The Way of the New World: The Black Novel in America.* Garden City, N.Y.: Anchor/Doubleday, 1975.

Gayle, Addison, Jr., ed. *The Black Aesthetic.* Garden City, N.Y.: Doubleday, 1971.

Geertz, Clifford. *Local Knowledge.* New York: Basic Books, 1983.

Gehr, Richard. "One-Man Show." *American Film,* May 1991.

———. "Saving Mr. Micheaux." *American Film,* May 1991.

George, Nelson. *The Death of Rhythm and Blues.* New York: Pantheon, 1988.

Gilliatt, Penelope. "Black Film." *The New Yorker,* April 18, 1970, pp. 34–35.

———. [Untitled review]. *The New Yorker,* April 12, 1976.

Gloster, Hugh M. *Negro Voices in American Fiction.* 1948. Reprint, New York: Russell and Russell, 1965.

Gomery, Douglas. *Shared Pleasures: A History of Movie Presentation in the United States.* Madison: University of Wisconsin Press, 1992.

Green, J. Ronald. "America in bianco e nero." *Diario della settimana* (the weekly magazine of the Italian daily *L'Unità*), October 14, 1997, pp. 56–58.

———. "Micheaux Film Festival." *Film Quarterly,* Spring 1998, p. 28.

———. "The Micheaux Style." *Black Film Review,* Vol. 7, No. 4, 1993.

———. "Micheaux v. Griffith." *Griffithiana,* October 1997, Vols. 60/61, pp. 32–49.

———. "Oscar Micheaux's *Darktown Revue:* Caricature and Class Conflict." In *In Touch with the Spirit: Black Religious and Musical Expression in American Cinema,* ed. Phyllis R. Klotman and Gloria J. Gibson-Hudson. Bloomington: Indiana University Black Film Center/Archive and Department of Afro-American Studies, 1994.

———. "Oscar Micheaux's Interrogation of Caricature as Entertainment." *Film Quarterly,* Spring 1998, pp. 16–31.

———. "The Reemergence of Oscar Micheaux." In *Oscar Micheaux and His Circle,* ed. Pearl Bowser, Jane Gaines, and Charles Musser, forthcoming.

———. Review of *Framing Blackness: The African American Image in Film* by Ed Guerrero. *Film Quarterly,* Summer 1995, pp. 47–49.

———. "Toward a Definitive Listing of Oscar Micheaux's Films." *The Newsletter of the Oscar Micheaux Society,* Vol. 3, Summer 1994.

——. "Two Micheaux Family Members." *The Newsletter of the Oscar Micheaux Society,* Vol. 5, Summer 1996.

——. "'Twoness' in the Style of Oscar Micheaux." In *Black American Cinema,* ed. Manthia Diawara. New York: Routledge, 1993.

Green, J. Ronald, and Horace Neal, Jr. "Oscar Micheaux and Racial Slur: A Response to 'The Rediscovery of Oscar Micheaux.'" *Journal of Film and Video,* Vol. 40, No. 4, Fall 1988.

Gregory, Steven. "Race and Racism: A Symposium." In Social Text, No. 42, Spring 1995.

Griggs, Sutton E. *The Hindered Hand.* 1905. Reprint, New York: AMS, 1969.

——. *Imperium in Imperio.* 1899. Reprint, New York: Arno, 1969.

——. *Overshadowed.* 1901. Reprint, Freeport, N.Y.: Books for Libraries Press, 1971.

——. *Pointing the Way.* Nashville, Tenn.: Orion, 1908.

Grossman, James R. *Land of Hope: Chicago, Black Southerners, and the Great Migration.* Chicago: University of Chicago Press, 1989.

Grupenhoff, Richard. *The Black Valentino.* Metuchen, N.J.: Scarecrow, 1988.

——. "The Rediscovery of Oscar Micheaux." *Journal of Film and Video,* Vol. 40, No. 1, Winter 1988.

Guerrero, Ed. *Framing Blackness: The African American Image in Film.* Philadelphia: Temple University Press, 1993.

Ham, Debra Newman. *The African-American Mosaic: A Library of Congress Resource Guide for the Study of Black History and Culture.* Washington, D.C.: Library of Congress, 1993.

Harlem Renaissance: Art of Black America. New York: Studio Museum in Harlem; Harry Abrams, 1987.

Harris, William J. *The Poetry and Poetics of Amiri Baraka: The Jazz Aesthetic.* Columbia: University of Missouri Press, 1985.

Hatfield, Edwin F. *Freedom's Lyre; or, Psalms, Hymns, and Sacred Songs, for the Slave and His Friends.* New York: S. W. Benedict, 1840.

Hayman, Ronald. *Fassbinder: Film Maker.* New York: Simon and Schuster, 1984.

Hearn, Lafcadio. *Kwaidan: Stories and Studies of Strange Things.* 1932. Reprint, New York: Dover, 1968.

Heath, Stephen. *Questions of Cinema.* Bloomington: University of Indiana Press, 1981.

Hebert, Janis. "Oscar Micheaux: A Black Pioneer." *South Dakota Review,* Winter 1973–74, pp. 62–69.

Heller, Scott. "A Pioneering Black Filmmaker: Scholars Have Rediscovered Oscar Micheaux and Established Him as a Key Figure." *Chronicle of Higher Education,* March 3, 1995, pp. A6–A7, A12–A13.

Hennebelle, Guy, ed. *Le cinéma noir américain,* a special issue of *CinémAction.* Paris: Cerf, 1988.

Henri, Florette. *Black Migration: Movement North, 1900–1920.* Garden City, N.Y.: Doubleday, 1975.

Hill, Errol. *The Theater of Black Americans,* Vol. 1: *Roots and Rituals: The Search for Identity/The Image Makers—Plays and Playwrights: A Collection of Critical Essays.* Englewood Cliffs, N.J.: Prentice-Hall, 1980.

——. *The Theater of Black Americans,* Vol. 2: *The Presenters: Companies of Players/The Participators—Audiences and Critics: A Collection of Critical Essays.* Englewood Cliffs, N.J.: Prentice-Hall, 1980.

Hill, Herbert, ed. *Anger, and Beyond: The Negro Writer in the United States.* New York: Harper and Row, 1966.

Hoberman, J. "Blankety-Blank." *Village Voice,* May 29, 1984, p. 58.

——. "A Forgotten Black Cinema Resurfaces." *The Village Voice,* November 17, 1975, back page, pp. 85–86, 88.

——. *Vulgar Modernism: Writing on Movies and Other Media.* Philadelphia: Temple University Press, 1991.

Hoggart, Richard. *The Uses of Literacy: Aspects of Working-Class Life with Special References to Publications and Entertainments.* London: Chatto and Windus, 1957.

hooks, bell. *Black Looks: Race and Representation.* Boston: South End, 1992.

——. *Killing Rage: Ending Racism.* New York: Henry Holt, 1995.

——. "Micheaux: Celebrating Blackness." *Black American Literature Forum,* Vol. 25, No. 2, Summer 1991, pp. 351–60. Reprinted in hooks, *Black Looks.*

——. *Yearning: Race, Gender, and Cultural Politics.* Boston: South End Press, 1990.

Huggins, Nathan Irvin. *Harlem Renaissance.* New York: Oxford, 1971.

Hughes, Carl Milton (pseud.). *The Negro Novelist.* Freeport, N.Y.: Books for Libraries Press, 1967.

Hughes, Langston. *The Ways of White Folks.* New York: Alfred A. Knopf, 1934.

Hughes, Langston, and Milton Meltzer. *Black Magic: A Pictorial History of the Negro in American Entertainment.* Englewood Cliffs, N.J.: Prentice-Hall, 1967.

Hurston, Zora Neale. *Jonah's Gourd Vine.* Philadelphia: Lippincott, 1934.

——. *Tell My Horse.* 1938. Reprint, Berkeley, Calif.: Turtle Island, 1981.

Hyatt, Marshall. *The Afro-American Cinematic Experience: An Annotated Bibliography and Filmography.* Wilmington, Del.: Scholarly Resources, 1983.

Jacobson, Julius, ed. *The Negro and the American Labor Movement.* Garden City, N.Y.: Anchor, 1968.

Jafa, Arthur. Article on Micheaux's film style. *Black Film Bulletin,* Autumn/Winter 1993/94.

James, C. L. R. *Beyond a Boundary.* 1963. Reprint, New York: Pantheon, 1983.

Jerome, V. J. *The Negro in Hollywood Films.* New York: Masses and Mainstream, 1950.

Jesionowski, Joyce E. *Thinking in Pictures: Dramatic Structure in D. W. Griffith's Biograph Films.* Berkeley: University of California Press, 1987.

Johnson, Abby Arthur, and Ronald Maberry Johnson. *Propaganda and Aesthetics: The Literary Politics of Afro-American Magazines in the Twentieth Century.* Amherst: University of Massachusetts Press, 1979.

Johnson, Charles. *Middle Passage.* New York: Atheneum, 1990.

Johnson, J. Rosamond. *Rolling Along in Song: A Chronological Survey of American Negro Music.* New York: Viking, 1937.

Johnson, James Weldon. *Along This Way: The Autobiography of James Weldon Johnson.* 1933. Reprint, New York: Viking, 1968.

——. *The Autobiography of an Ex-Colored Man.* 1927. Reprint, New York: Avon, 1965.

——. *Black Manhattan.* New York: Alfred A. Knopf, 1930.

Johnson, James Weldon, and J. Rosamond Johnson. *The Books of American Negro Spirituals Including The Book of American Negro Spirituals and The Second Book of Negro Spirituals.* 1925, 1926. Reprint, New York: Viking, 1953.

Jones, G. William. *Black Cinema Treasures: Lost and Found.* Denton: University of North Texas Press, 1991.

Jones, LeRoi. See Baraka, Amiri.

Kent, George E. Kent. *Blackness and the Adventure of Western Culture.* Chicago: Third World, 1972.

King, Richard H., and Helen Taylor, eds. *Dixie Debates: Perspectives on Southern Cultures.* New York: New York University Press, 1996.

Kisch, John, and Edward Mapp. *A Separate Cinema: Fifty Years of Black-Cast Posters.* New York: Farrar, Straus and Giroux, 1992.

Klapp, Orrin E. *Heroes, Villains and Fools: Reflections of the American Character.* Englewood Cliffs, N.J.: Prentice-Hall, 1962.

Klotman, Phyllis Rauch. *Frame by Frame: A Black Filmography.* 1979. Reprint, Bloomington: Indiana University Press, 1997.

Klotman, Phyllis Rauch, and Gloria J. Gibson-Hudson, eds. *In Touch with the Spirit: Black Religious and Musical Expression in American Cinema.* Bloomington: Indiana University Black Film Center/Archive and Department of Afro-American Studies, 1994.

Kochman, Thomas. *Black and White Styles in Conflict.* Chicago: University of Chicago Press, 1981.

———, ed. *Rappin' and Stylin' Out: Communication in Urban Black America.* Urbana: University of Illinois Press, 1972.

Krehbiel, Henry Edward. *Afro-American Folksongs: A Study in Racial and National Music.* 1913. Reprint, New York: Frederick Ungar, 1962.

Larsen, Nella. *Passing.* New York: Alfred A. Knopf, 1929.

———. *Quicksand.* New York: Alfred A. Knopf, 1928.

Lawson, Thomas W. *Frenzied Finance,* Vol. 1: *The Crime of Amalgamated.* New York: Ridgway-Thayer, 1905.

Leab, Daniel J. *From Sambo to Superspade: The Black Experience in Motion Pictures.* Boston: Houghton Mifflin, 1975.

Lemann, Nicholas. *The Promised Land: The Great Black Migration and How It Changed America.* New York: Alfred A. Knopf, 1991.

Levine, Lawrence W. *Black Culture and Black Consciousness: Afro-American Folk Thought from Slavery to Freedom.* New York: Oxford, 1977.

Lewis, David Levering. "Harlem Is My Home." In *Harlem Renaissance: Art of Black America.* 1987. Reprint, New York: Harry N. Abrams, 1994.

———. *W. E. B. DuBois: Biography of a Race, 1868–1919.* New York: H. Holt, 1993.

———. *When Harlem Was in Vogue.* New York: Alfred A. Knopf, 1981.

Locke, Alain. *The Negro and His Music.* 1936. Reprint, New York: Arno, 1969.

London, Jack. *Martin Eden.* New York: Macmillan, 1909.

Lott, Eric. "Cornel West in the Hour of Chaos: Culture and Politics in *Race Matters.*" *Social Text,* No. 40, Fall 1994.

———. *Love and Theft: Blackface Minstrelsy and the American Working Class.* New York: Oxford University Press, 1993.

Lounsbury, Myron Osborn. *The Origins of American Film Criticism, 1909–1939.* New York: Arno, 1973.

Malcolm X. *Malcolm X Speaks.* Edited by George Breitman. New York: Grove, 1965.

Mapp, Edward. *Directory of Blacks in the Performing Arts.* Metuchen, N.J.: Scarecrow, 1978.

Marsh, J. B. T. *The Story of the Jubilee Singers; with Their Songs.* New York: Riverside Press, 1880.

Martin, Michael T., ed. *Cinemas of the Black Diaspora: Diversity, Dependence, and Oppositionality.* Detroit: Wayne State University Press, 1995.

Masilela, Ntongela. "Interconnections: The African and Afro-American Cinemas." *The Independent,* January/February 1988.

Masood, Paula J. "Cities in Black: Cinematic Representations of African American Urban-scape." Unpublished book manuscript.

Maynard, Richard A. *The Black Man on Film: Racial Stereotyping.* Rochelle Park, N.J.: Hayden Book Co., 1974.

Mayne, Judith. *Cinema and Spectatorship.* London: Routledge, 1993.

McKay, Claude. *Harlem: Negro Metropolis.* 1940. Reprint, New York: Harcourt Brace Jovanovich, 1968.

———. *Home to Harlem.* New York: Harper and Bros., 1928.

Meier, August, and Elliott Rudwick, eds. *The Making of Black America,* Vol. 1: *The Origins of Black Americans.* New York: Atheneum, 1974.

Metz, Christian. *The Imaginary Signifier: Psychoanalysis and the Cinema.* Trans. Celia Britton, Annwyl Williams, Ben Brewster, and Alfred Guzzetti. Bloomington: Indiana University Press, 1982.

Mezzrow, Mezz, and Bernard Wolfe. *Really the Blues.* Garden City, N.Y.: Doubleday, 1972.

Mombert, Paul. "Class." In *Encyclopaedia of the Social Sciences,* Vol. 3, p. 531. New York: Macmillan, 1930.

Morris, H. S. "Ethnic Groups." In *International Encyclopedia of the Social Sciences,* ed. David L. Sills, Vol. 5 (New York: Macmillan and Free Press, 1968), pp. 169–70.

Moses, Wilson Jeremiah. *The Golden Age of Black Nationalism, 1850–1925.* Hamden, Conn.: Archon, 1978.

Münsterberg, Hugo. *American Problems: From the Point of View of a Psychologist.* New York: Moffat, Yard, 1912.

Murray, Albert. *Stomping the Blues.* New York: McGraw-Hill, 1976.

Murray, James P. *To Find an Image: Black Films from Uncle Tom to Super Fly.* Indianapolis: Bobbs-Merrill, 1973.

Museum of American Folk Art. *Self-Taught Artists of the Twentieth Century: An American Anthology.* San Francisco: Chronicle Books, 1998.

Musser, Charles. *Before the Nickelodeon: Edwin S. Porter and the Edison Manufacturing Company.* Berkeley: University of California Press, 1991.

Nesteby, James R. *Black Images in American Films, 1896–1954: The Interplay between Civil Rights and Film Culture.* Lanham, Md.: University Press of America, 1982.

Noble, Peter. *The Negro in Films.* 1948. Reprint, New York: Arno, 1970.

Null, Gary. *Black Hollywood: The Negro in Motion Pictures.* Secaucus, N.J.: Citadel, 1975.

Ogle, Patrick, ed. *Facets African-American Video Guide.* Chicago: Facets Multimedia/ Academy Chicago, 1994.

Omi, Michael, and Howard Winant. *Racial Formation in the United States: From the 1960s to the 1980s.* New York: Routledge and Kegan Paul, 1986.

Ottley, Roi. *"New World A-Coming": Inside Black America.* Boston: Houghton Mifflin, 1943.

Patterson, Lindsay, ed. *Black Films and Film-makers: A Comprehensive Anthology from Stereotype to Superhero.* New York: Dodd, Mead, 1975.

Peterson, Bernard L., Jr. "The Films of Oscar Micheaux: America's First Fabulous Black Filmmaker." *Crisis,* April 1979. Revised and republished as "A Filmography of Oscar Micheaux: America's Legendary Black Filmmaker," in *Celluloid Power: Social Film Criticism from "The Birth of a Nation" to "Judgment at Nuremberg,"* ed. David Platt. Metuchen, N.J.: Scarecrow, 1992.

Pike, G. D. *The Jubilee Singers, and Their Campaign for Twenty Thousand Dollars.* Boston: Lee and Shepard, 1873.

Pines, Jim. *Blacks in Films: A Survey of Racial Themes and Images in the American Film*. London: Studio Vista, 1975.

Pines, Jim, and Paul Willemen, eds. *Questions of Third Cinema*. London: British Film Institute, 1989.

Ray, Robert B. *A Certain Tendency of the Hollywood Cinema, 1930–1980*. Princeton, N.J.: Princeton University Press, 1985.

Record, Wilson. *The Negro and the Communist Party*. New York: Atheneum, 1971.

Regester, Charlene. "Black Films, White Censors: Oscar Micheaux Confronts Censorship in New York, Virginia, and Chicago." In *Movie Censorship and American Culture*, ed. Francis G. Couvares. Washington, D.C.: Smithsonian, 1996.

———. "Lynched, Assaulted, Intimidated: Oscar Micheaux's Most Controversial Films." *Popular Culture Review*, Vol. 5, No. 1, February 1994.

———. "The Misreading and Rereading of African American Filmmaker Oscar Micheaux." *Film History: An International Journal*, Vol. 7, No. 4, 1995, pp. 426–49.

———. "Oscar Micheaux's *Body and Soul*: A Film of Conflicting Themes." In *In Touch with the Spirit: Black Religious and Musical Expression in American Cinema*, ed. Phyllis R. Klotman and Gloria J. Gibson-Hudson. Bloomington: Indiana University Black Film Center/Archive and Department of Afro-American Studies, 1994.

———. "Oscar Micheaux the Entrepreneur: Financing *The House Behind the Cedars*." *Journal of Film and Video*, Vol. 49, No. 1–2, Spring/Summer 1997, pp. 17–27.

———. "'The Symbol of the Unconquered': Restored by Turner Classic Movies." *The Newsletter of the Oscar Micheaux Society*, Vol. 7, Summer 1998.

Reid, Mark A. "The Achievement of Oscar Micheaux." *Black Film Review*, Vol. 4, No. 2, Spring 1988, p. 7.

———. "Commodification, Reception and Indigestion: Simulacra in *Do the Right Thing*." Unpublished paper read at the Screen Studies Conference, Glasgow, Scotland, 1991.

———. *Redefining Black Film*. Berkeley: University of California Press, 1993.

Rhines, Jesse Algeron. *Black Film/White Money*. New Brunswick, N.J.: Rutgers University Press, 1996.

Rogin, Michael. *Blackface, White Noise: Jewish Immigrants in the Hollywood Melting Pot*. Berkeley: University of California Press, 1996.

Roudevitch, Michel. "Blackcartoon: Mickey est-il nègre?" [Mickey, Is He Black?]. *Ciném-Action*, No. 46, 1988, pp. 79–81.

Ryder, Georgia A. "Harlem Renaissance Ideals in the Music of Robert Nathaniel Dett." In *Black Music in the Harlem Renaissance: A Collection of Essays*, ed. Samuel A. Floyd. New York: Greenwood Press, 1990.

Salley, Columbus. *The Black 100: A Ranking of the Most Influential African-Americans, Past and Present*. New York: Citadel Press, 1993.

Salt, Barry. *Film Style and Technology: History and Analysis*. London: Starword, 1983.

Sampson, Henry T. *Blacks in Black and White: A Source Book on Black Films*. Metuchen, N.J.: Scarecrow, 1977.

———. *Blacks in Blackface: A Source Book on Early Black Musical Shows*. Metuchen, N.J.: Scarecrow, 1980.

———. *The Ghost Walks: A Chronological History of Blacks in Show Business, 1865–1910*. Metuchen, N.J.: Scarecrow, 1988.

Schiffman, Jack. *Harlem Heyday: A Pictorial History of Modern Black Show Business and the Apollo Theatre*. Buffalo, N.Y.: Prometheus Books, 1984.

Schuller, Gunther. *Early Jazz: Its Roots and Musical Development*. New York: Oxford, 1968.

Sennett, Richard, and Johnathan Cobb. *The Hidden Injuries of Class*. New York: Random House, 1973.

Sharp, Saundra. "At Long Last: Director's Guild Honors Oscar Micheaux." *Black Film Review,* Summer 1986, pp. 33–34.

———. "Collectors' Dreams: Tracking Down Lost Frames and Lobby Cards." *Black Film Review,* Fall 1986, pp. 16–20.

Shohat, Ella, and Robert Stam. *Unthinking Eurocentrism: Multiculturalism and the Media*. London: Routledge, 1994.

Snead, James. *White Screens/Black Images*. New York: Routledge, 1994.

Soitos, Stephen F. "Oscar Micheaux." In *The Oxford Companion to African American Literature,* ed. William L. Andrews et al. New York: Oxford, 1997.

Southern, Eileen. *The Music of Black Americans: A History*. New York: W. W. Norton, 1971.

———. *Readings in Black American Music*. New York: W. W. Norton, 1971.

Spearman, Rawn. "Vocal Concert Music in the Harlem Renaissance." In *Black Music in the Harlem Renaissance: A Collection of Essays,* ed. Samuel A. Floyd. New York: Greenwood Press, 1990.

Spencer, Jon Michael. *Protest and Praise: Sacred Music of Black Religion*. Minneapolis: Augsburg Fortress, 1990.

Stam, Robert. "Bakhtin, Polyphony, and Ethnic/Racial Representation." In *Unspeakable Images: Ethnicity and the American Cinema,* ed. Lester D. Friedman. Urbana: University of Illinois Press, 1991.

Steele, Shelby. *The Content of Our Character: A New Vision of Race in America*. New York: St. Martin's Press, 1990.

Stribling, T. S. *Birthright*. 1922. Reprint, Delmar, N.Y.: Scholars' Facsimiles and Reprints, 1987.

Taruskin, Richard. "Facing Up, Finally, to Bach's Dark Vision." *New York Times,* January 27, 1991, pp. H25, H28.

Taylor, Clyde R. "Crossed Over and Can't Get Black: The Crisis of 1937–1939." *Black Film Review,* Vol. 7, No. 4, 1993, pp. 22–27.

———. *The Mask of Art: Breaking the Aesthetic Contract—Film and Literature*. Bloomington: Indiana University Press, 1998.

———. "The Re-Birth of the Aesthetic in Cinema." *Wide Angle,* Vol. 13, Nos. 3 and 4, July–August 1991, pp. 12–30.

Taylor, Frank C. *Alberta Hunter: A Celebration in Blues*. New York: McGraw-Hill, 1987.

Taylor, John Russell. "Satyajit Ray." In *Cinema: A Critical Dictionary,* ed. Richard Roud, Vol. 2. New York: Viking, 1980.

Taylor, Quintard. *In Search of the Racial Frontier: African Americans in the American West, 1528–1990*. New York: W. W. Norton, 1998.

Travis, Dempsey J. *An Autobiography of Black Chicago*. Chicago: Urban Research Institute, 1981.

Uricchio, William, and Roberta E. Pearson. "Dante's Inferno and Caesar's Ghost: Intertextuality and Conditions of Reception in Early American Cinema." In *Silent Film,* ed. Richard Abel. New Brunswick, N.J.: Rutgers University Press, 1996.

VanEpps-Taylor, Betti Carol. *Oscar Micheaux . . . Dakota Homesteader, Author, Pioneer Film Maker: A Biography*. Rapid City, S.D.: Dakota West Books, 1999.

Van Peebles, Melvin. *Sweet Sweetback's Baadasssss Song*. New York: Lancer, 1971.

Wallace, Michele. *Invisibility Blues: From Pop to Theory.* London: Verso, 1990.

Washington, Booker T. *Up from Slavery.* 1901. Reprint, New York: Avon, 1965.

Wasko, Janet. *Movies and Money: Financing the American Film Industry.* Norwood, N.J.: Ablex, 1982.

Waters, Ethel, with Charles Samuels. *His Eye Is on the Sparrow.* Garden City, N.Y.: Doubleday, 1951.

Weber, Max. *Economy and Society: An Outline of Interpretive Sociology.* Berkeley: University of California Press, 1978. (Based on *Wirtschaft und Gesellschaft,* 4th German ed., 1956.)

West, Cornel. *Race Matters.* New York: Vintage, 1994.

Wexman, Virginia Wright. *Creating the Couple: Love Marriage, and Hollywood Performance.* Princeton, N.J.: Princeton University Press, 1993.

White, Theodore H. *America in Search of Itself: The Making of the President, 1956–1980.* New York: Harper and Row, 1982.

Wilson, William Julius. *The Declining Significance of Race: Blacks and Changing American Institutions.* Chicago: University of Chicago Press, 1978.

———. *The Truly Disadvantaged: The Inner City, the Underclass, and Public Policy.* Chicago: University of Chicago Press, 1987.

Woll, Allen. *Black Musical Theatre: From "Coontown" to "Dreamgirls."* 1989. Reprint, New York: Da Capo, 1991.

Wollen, Peter. *Raiding the Icebox: Reflections on Twentieth-Century Culture.* Bloomington: Indiana University Press, 1993.

Wood, Robin. *Hollywood from Vietnam to Reagan.* New York: Columbia University Press, 1986.

Woodland, J. Randal. "Oscar Micheaux." In the *Dictionary of Literary Biography,* Vol. 50, pp. 218–25. Detroit: Gale Research Company, 1986.

Wright, Richard. *Black Boy.* New York: Harper and Bros., 1945.

———. *Native Son.* London: Harper and Bros., 1940.

Yearwood, Gladstone L. *Black Cinema Aesthetics: Issues in Independent Black Filmmaking.* Athens, Ohio: Ohio University Center for Afro-American Studies, 1982.

Young, Joseph A. *Black Novelist as White Racist: The Myth of Black Inferiority in the Novels of Oscar Micheaux.* New York: Greenwood, 1989.

Zelditch, Morris, Jr. "Status, Social." In *International Encyclopedia of the Social Sciences,* ed. David L. Sills, Vol. 15 (New York: Macmillan and Free Press, 1968), pp. 250–57.

Index

passing for white, 32, 108, 176–77, 183–92, 186. *See also* skin tone

Passing (Larsen), 188, 189

pathos, 50–51

patriarchy, xv, 6, 12, 29, 175

Pearson, Roberta, 75

peasants, 37

peonage, 71, 72, 74, 80, 83, 259n5

Peterson, Sidney, 69

Phenomenology of Mind, The (Hegel), 21

photography, 52

Pickford, Mary, 198

Pierce, Elijah, 46, 53

Pike, G. D., 139, 141, 142, 166

Pollock, Jackson, 114

Porter, Edwin S., 55, 129–30, 139, 151

positive images, 57, 131, 146, 147, 208

postmodernism, 78, 88, 225

poverty, xiv, xv, 86, 136

Pre-Raphaelite ideal woman, 60, 198, 199

Preer, Evelyn, 8, *28*, 198

Preminger, Otto, 164

Presley, Elvis, 164

production, relations of, 98–99

production values, 38, 39–40, 53, 76; ethics of, 101–102; exaggerated, 97–98; in *The Exile*, 123–24, *125–26*, 127–28; high and low, 49, 70, 76, 86, 89; high production values as dangerous attraction, 83–84; Hollywood, 47, 49, 50; logic of, 89–91; middle-class goals and, 68–70; music and, 55; as property, 238; racial uplift philosophy and, 102; signifiers and, 76–78; stardom and, 119; style and, 70–71

Progressives, 212

Prohibition, 123, 127

proletariat, 37

Promised Land, The (Lemann), 112

propaganda, 139–40

prostitution, 19, 21, 56, 100, 127, 254n24

Protestant (Calvinist) work ethic, 92, 110, 118

Protestant Ethic and the Spirit of Capitalism, The (Weber), 90

purity: class, 21; racial, 7, 8, 12, 21; sexual, 6, 12, 13–15, 21, 23, 25, 29

Quest of the Silver Fleece, The (DuBois), 18, 23–24, 25, 204, 254n23

race, xiii, 57, 67, 110; class and, 32–35; pseudo-science and, 217–18, 221; self-hatred and, 32–33

race movies, xiv, 34, 47; assimilation and, 44–45; blackness and, 116; capitalization and, 39; cinematic canon and, 44; directors of, 105–106; early studies of, 41; imitation of Hollywood, 46; jazz and, 36, 40; low-budget production of, 120; Micheaux's place in history of, 249; music in, 52–53, 55; relations of production in, 89; skin tone in, 66; stardom in, 119, 175; transition to sound, 119; white financing of, 91

race music, 79, 88, 153

race riots, 145, 209

racial uplift philosophy, xiv–xv, 19, 123, 181; bourgeois values and, 37; caricature and, 137; citizenship and, 27; class and, 31, 230; coupling and, 20–21; false uplift, 174–75, 179–81; material success and, 84; middle class and, 86; negative images and, 57–61, *62–66*, 65–67; style and, 54; whiteness and, 121

racism, xv, 6, 17, 175; African-American manhood and, 27; caricature and, 152; class and, 231; classism and, 226–27; as enemy of racial uplift, 41; foundations of, 229; humanism and, 194; incompetence in labor market and, 130; Micheaux's view of, 202; middle class and, 86; in the military, 222; in musical theater, 110; racial slurs, 57–61, 193; skin tone and, 34, 61; stereotypes and, 67, 168; struggle against, 204; triumph of, 8; of white upper classes, 72

ragtime, 132, 143

Rainer, Yvonne, 78, 88

Rainey, Ma, 40, 107

rap, 113

rape, 4, 12, 49, 111, 169; migrations and, 148; white-on-black, 25, 26, 29, 33; white supremacism and, 25

Ray, Satyajit, 54, 55

Reagan, Ronald, 78

realism, 51, 145–47

reception, 78–79

Reconstruction, 16, 37, 74, 149; collapse of, 133, 144–45, 207

Redefining Black Film (Reid), 226

Regester, Charlene, 203

Reggio, Godfrey, 230

Reid, Mark, 35, 47, 119, 122, 226

religion, 19

rescue fantasy/theme, 5, 6, 12, 15–17; in *Birth of a Nation*, 8, *9*, 14; editing and, 78; in Micheaux's work, 17, 20, 21–23; as redemption, 21–23

respectability, 32

restitution, 24–25, 26

Rhines, Jessie, 43, 47, 226, 227

RON GREEN is Associate Professor of Film Studies in the Department of History of Art at the Ohio State University. His writings on Micheaux and on other topics have appeared in journals such as *Film Quarterly, Griffithiana, Black Film Review, Quarterly Review of Film and Video, Journal of Film and Video, Cinema Journal, Afterimage,* and *Aperture,* as well as in Manthia Diawara's *Black American Cinema* and in Pearl Bowser, Jane Gaines, and Charles Musser's *Oscar Micheaux and His Circle* (forthcoming). He has served as president of the National Alliance of Media Arts Centers, as trustee of the American Film Institute, and as assistant director of the Public Media Program of the National Endowment for the Arts.

AEA- 0101

WITHDRAWN

Gramley Library
Salem College
Winston-Salem, NC 27108